Geocriticism and Spatial Literary Studies

Series Editor
Robert T. Tally Jr.
Texas State University
San Marcos, TX, USA

Geocriticism and Spatial Literary Studies is a new book series focusing on the dynamic relations among space, place, and literature. The spatial turn in the humanities and social sciences has occasioned an explosion of innovative, multidisciplinary scholarship in recent years, and geocriticism, broadly conceived, has been among the more promising developments in spatially oriented literary studies. Whether focused on literary geography, cartography, geopoetics, or the spatial humanities more generally, geocritical approaches enable readers to reflect upon the representation of space and place, both in imaginary universes and in those zones where fiction meets reality. Titles in the series include both monographs and collections of essays devoted to literary criticism, theory, and history, often in association with other arts and sciences. Drawing on diverse critical and theoretical traditions, books in the Geocriticism and Spatial Literary Studies series disclose, analyze, and explore the significance of space, place, and mapping in literature and in the world.

More information about this series at
http://www.palgrave.com/gp/series/15002

Monika Szuba · Julian Wolfreys
Editors

The Poetics of Space
and Place in Scottish
Literature

Editors
Monika Szuba
University of Gdańsk
Gdańsk, Poland

Julian Wolfreys
Independent Scholar
London, UK

Geocriticism and Spatial Literary Studies
ISBN 978-3-030-12644-5   ISBN 978-3-030-12645-2   (eBook)
https://doi.org/10.1007/978-3-030-12645-2

Library of Congress Control Number: 2019931014

Cover design by Laura de Grasse
Cover image by Monika Szuba

This Palgrave Macmillan imprint is published by the registered company Springer Nature Switzerland AG
The registered company address is: Gewerbestrasse 11, 6330 Cham, Switzerland

SERIES EDITOR'S PREFACE

The spatial turn in the humanities and social sciences has occasioned an explosion of innovative, multidisciplinary scholarship. Spatially oriented literary studies, whether operating under the banner of literary geography, literary cartography, geophilosophy, geopoetics, geocriticism, or the spatial humanities more generally, have helped to reframe or to transform contemporary criticism by focusing attention, in various ways, on the dynamic relations among space, place, and literature. Reflecting upon the representation of space and place, whether in the real world, in imaginary universes, or in those hybrid zones where fiction meets reality, scholars and critics working in spatial literary studies are helping to reorient literary criticism, history, and theory. *Geocriticism and Spatial Literary Studies* is a book series presenting new research in this burgeoning field of inquiry.

In exploring such matters as the representation of place in literary works, the relations between literature and geography, the historical transformation of literary and cartographic practices, and the role of space in critical theory, among many others, geocriticism and spatial literary studies have also developed interdisciplinary or transdisciplinary methods and practices, frequently making productive connections to architecture, art history, geography, history, philosophy, politics, social theory, and urban studies, to name but a few. Spatial criticism is not limited to the spaces of the so-called real world, and it sometimes calls into question any too facile distinction between real and imaginary places, as it frequently investigates what Edward Soja has referred to as the 'real-and-imagined' places we experience in literature as in life. Indeed, although a great deal of important research has been devoted to the literary representation of certain identifiable and well-known places (e.g. Dickens's London, Baudelaire's Paris, or Joyce's Dublin), spatial critics have also explored the otherworldly spaces of literature, such as those to be found in myth, fantasy, science fiction, video games, and cyberspace. Similarly, such criticism is interested in the relationship between spatiality and such different media or genres as film or television, music, comics, computer programs, and other forms that may supplement, compete with, and potentially problematise literary representation. Titles in the *Geocriticism and Spatial Literary Studies* series include both monographs and collections of essays devoted to literary criticism, theory, and history, often in association with other arts and sciences. Drawing on diverse critical and theoretical traditions, books in the series reveal, analyse, and explore the significance of space, place, and mapping in literature and in the world.

The concepts, practices, or theories implied by the title of this series are to be understood expansively. Although geocriticism and spatial literary studies represent a relatively new area of critical and scholarly investigation, the historical roots of spatial criticism extend well beyond the recent past, informing present and future work. Thanks to a growing critical awareness of spatiality, innovative research into the literary geography of real and imaginary places has helped to shape historical and cultural studies in ancient, medieval, early modern, and modernist literature, while a discourse of spatiality undergirds much of what is still understood as the postmodern condition. The suppression of distance by modern technology, transportation, and telecommunications has only enhanced the sense of place, and of displacement, in the age of globalisation. Spatial criticism examines literary representations not only of places themselves, but of the experience of place and of displacement, while exploring the interrelations between lived experience and a more abstract or unrepresentable spatial network that subtly or directly shapes it. In sum, the work being done in geocriticism and spatial literary studies, broadly conceived, is diverse and far reaching. Each volume in this series takes seriously the mutually impressive effects of space or place and artistic representation, particularly as these effects manifest themselves in works of literature. By bringing the spatial and geographical concerns to bear on their scholarship, books in the *Geocriticism and Spatial Literary*

Studies series seek to make possible different ways of seeing literary and cultural texts, to pose novel questions for criticism and theory, and to offer alternative approaches to literary and cultural studies. In short, the series aims to open up new spaces for critical inquiry.

San Marcos, USA   Robert T. Tally Jr.

ACKNOWLEDGEMENTS

The editors would like to thank individually and collectively the contributors to the present volume, those who started down this road, sometimes wondering doubtless if they would ever get anywhere, given that at times it seemed as if we had torn up the map and thrown away the compass. But then, in the words of a certain Scottish author, it's better to travel hopefully than to arrive... We can only hope everyone concerned feels that the destination has been worth the long road to the north. We would also like to thank the latecomers to the project who readily, and cheerily agreed to join the trek: in order of appearance, Alan Riach, Tom Ue, John Brannigan, and Mary Ann Caws. To quote Miss Bates, 'it is such a happiness when good people get together—and they always do'. Our thanks are also due to David Malcolm and Agnieszka Sienkiewicz-Charlish, co-organisers of the 'Place and Space in Scottish Literature and Culture' conference at the University of Gdańsk, which took place on 8–10 October 2015 in Sopot, where the first versions of some of the chapters were presented.

The editors would like to thank Magda Salvesen, Curator, of the Jon Schueler Estate, and the Jon Schueler Estate (all images © Jon Schueler Estate) for permission to reproduce the paintings that appear in the Chapter "Jon Schueler (1916–1992): Intensity and Identity", by Mary Ann Caws.

CONTENTS

NOTES ON CONTRIBUTORS

Jessica Aliaga Lavrijsen is Senior Lecturer at the Centro Universitario de la Defensa Zaragoza (Spain). She was a founder member of the publishing house Jekyll and Jill until 2016, where she edited, revised, and also translated a few books, such as *El otro McCoy*, by Brian McCabe (Jekyll and Jill 2012). After finishing her Doctoral Thesis on contemporary Scottish fiction, she published several articles, book chapters, and books on Scottish literature, such as *The Fiction of Brian McCabe* (Peter Lang 2014), as well as on trauma, such as *Is This a Culture of Trauma?* (Interdisciplinary Press 2013), as she was a member of the project 'Trauma and Beyond: The Rhetoric and Politics of Suffering in Contemporary Narrative in English' until 2015. She is currently working on the Transmodern, as part of a Project titled 'Palimpsestic Knowledge: A Transmodern Literary Paradigm', and she continues reading and writing on contemporary Scottish fiction, with some new incursions into the genre of science fiction.

Paul Barnaby graduated in French and Italian from the University of Edinburgh (1986) and stayed on for doctoral studies in nineteenth-century Italian Literature, focusing on the Sicilian novelist Luigi Capuana and the reception of the French Naturalist novel. While completing his Ph.D., he worked on a number of projects at the National Library of Scotland, including editing the Bibliography of Scottish Literature in Translation (BOSLIT). He went on to work as a Research Fellow on the Reception of British and Irish Authors in Europe project at the School of Advanced Study, University of London. Returning to Scotland, he became Project Officer and Editor of the Walter Scott Digital Archive at Edinburgh University Library, a comprehensive information site on Scott and an online base for Scott studies. Assuming wider responsibilities as Scottish Literary Collections Curator, he has gone on to develop web pages designed to enhance access to the University of Edinburgh Library's collections of Scottish literary manuscripts. Between 2014 and 2018, he combined library work with a post translating and sub-editing contributions to the Leverhulme-funded project 'Sidonius Apollinaris: A Comprehensive Commentary for the Twenty First Century' in Edinburgh University's School of History, Classics and Archaeology. He has published essays and delivered conference papers on the translation and reception of Scottish literature (particularly Scott), on the Italian reception of French Naturalism, and on Edinburgh University's collections of literary archives.

John Brannigan teaches English in University College Dublin. He is the author of *Archipelagic Modernism: Literature in the Irish and British Isles, 1890–1970* (Edinburgh UP, 2015), and former editor of the *Irish University Review*.

Alexandra Campbell is Early Career Fellow in English Literature at the University of Edinburgh. Her research emerges at the intersection of several critical discourses including critical ocean studies, the environmental humanities, and world literature perspectives. She is particularly interested in ecologies and poetries of the sea and is currently working on her first monograph, provisionally titled 'Hydropoetics: Atlantic Modernity, World Ecology and the Techno-Ocean', which examines the cultural and historical parameters of oceanic resource exploitation in contemporary North Atlantic writing, focusing on discourses of extraction, disposal, and transmission at sea. She has published or forthcoming articles in *The Journal of Postcolonial Writing, Humanities, Études Écossaises* and *Anglistik* and has a book chapter in the forthcoming Bloomsbury title, *John Burnside: Contemporary Critical Perspectives.*

Mary Ann Caws is Distinguished Professor Emerita of Comparative Literature, English, and French and Resident Professor at the Graduate School of the City University of New York. Professor Caws was co-Director of the Henri Peyre French Institute from 1980 to 2002 and a former Trustee of the Alliance Française (Washington, DC). She is an

Officer of the Palmes Académiques (awarded by the French Minister of Education), a Chevalier dans l'ordre des Arts et des Lettres (awarded by the French Government), recipient of Guggenheim, Rockefeller, and Getty fellowships, and a fellow of the American Academy of Arts and Science. Professor Caws is the author of *The Eye in the Text*; *Reading Frames in Modern Fiction*; *The Inner Theatre of Recent French Poetry*; *The Modern Art Cookbook*, among others, and of critical biographies of Virginia Woolf, Henry James, Marcel Proust, Salvador Dali, Pablo Picasso, *Blaise Pascal: Miracles and Reason*, and *The Life and Work of Dora Maar*. She is the editor of *The Harper Collins World Reader*; *Textual Analysis*; *The Yale Anthology of Twentieth-Century French Poetry*, *Surrealism*; *The Surrealist Painters and Poets*; and *Surrealist Love Poetry*. She has translated Tristan Tzara's *Approximate Man and Other Writings*; André Breton's *Mad Love*; Jacques Derrida and Paule Thévenin's *The Secret Art of Antonin Artaud*; and *Ostinato* by *Louis-René des Forêts*. She is the co-translator and editor of *Selected Poems and Prose of Stéphane Mallarmé, Mallarmé in Prose, The Essential Poems and Texts of Robert Desnos, Poems of André Breton, Paul Eluard, Capital of Pain, René Char: Furor and Mystery and Other Texts, Pierre Reverdy*. Forthcoming: *Creative Gatherings: Meeting Places of Modernism*, and 'Losing Nothing: Arakawa and Madeline Gins', *Gagosian Quarterly*, September 2018.

Ewa Chodnikiewicz is a Ph.D. candidate at the University of Gdańsk. Her interests and area of research are connected with nature writing and ecocriticism in modern British and Scottish literature. Her recent papers include the following: 'A Forgotten Place that Remembers'—the relations of cultural memory with nature in *Gossip from the Forest* by Sara Maitland, 'A Woman Living on The Edge: The Sense of Motherhood, Landscape and Loss' in *The Call of the Undertow* by Linda Cracknell, and 'Between Silence and Noise: the Analysis of Sylvia Plath's Poem "Tulips"'.

Aniela Korzeniowska is Professor in Translation Studies as well as Head of the Department of Applied Linguistics and of the Scottish Studies Research Group at the Institute of English Studies, University of Warsaw. Over the last years, she has been combining her interest in translation with issues concerning Scotland's languages and literature, with emphasis on identity. Besides numerous articles published within both Translation and Scottish Studies, her publications include *Successful Polish-English Translation. Tricks of the Trade* (co-authored by

Piotr Kuhiwczak, 1994, 3rd ed. 2005), *Explorations in Polish-English Mistranslation Problems* (1998), *Translating Scotland. Nation and Identity* (2008). She has co-edited (with Izabela Szymańska) four volumes within the Scotland in Europe/Europe in Scotland series (2013 [2], 2015 and 2017) and is the co-organiser of a series of international conferences entitled 'Scotland in Europe', the fourth planned to take place in September 2018.

Robin MacKenzie taught in the School of European Languages at Swansea University from 1990 to 2004 and is now Honorary Lecturer in the School of Modern Languages at the University of St Andrews. He started academic life as a specialist in modern (post–1850) French fiction, publishing a monograph and a number of articles on the work of Marcel Proust, as well as essays on Mérimée, Fromentin, and the modern French novelist Julien Gracq. His current research interests lie primarily in comparative literature: recent publications include articles on Proust as reader of Stevenson, ecological themes in novels by Lawrence Norfolk and Christoph Ransmayr, and the fiction of contemporary Scottish writer Christopher Whyte. He is currently one of the General Editors of *Forum for Modern Language Studies* and a member of the Executive Committee of the British Comparative Literature Association.

Petra Johana Poncarová is a Ph.D. candidate at the Department of Anglophone Literatures and Cultures, Charles University, Prague. She started her studies by a B.A. degree cum laude in English and Scandinavian studies. Early on, she became interested in Scottish Gaelic, but as the language is not taught anywhere in the Czech Republic, she attended several summer courses at Sabhal Mòr Ostaig, University of Highlands and Islands. In May 2014, she completed an intensive two-term course in Gaelic for fluent and native speakers at the same institution. Her M.A. thesis, focused on poetry of place in the works of Sorley MacLean and Derick Thomson, is the first monograph on Scottish Gaelic literature ever written in the Czech Republic and also one of few extended works of criticism which study MacLean and Thomson together. She specialises in modern Scottish literature, mainly modern Scottish Gaelic poetry and fiction. In her Ph.D. dissertation, she discusses political issues in Derick Thomson's writing. In cooperation with the University of Glasgow, she founded the Derick Thomson website (https://ruaraidh-macthomais.wordpress.com/). Her other research interests include the works of Tormod Caimbeul and Christopher Whyte, and the Ossian controversy. She has presented the results of her research at conferences in the Czech Republic, Scotland, Poland, France, and Germany. She translates from English and Gaelic into Czech and generally strives to promote Scottish Gaelic in the Czech Republic, also by teaching the language privately. She contributes to the Gaelic-only quarterly magazine Steall.

Alan Riach Professor of Scottish Literature at Glasgow University, born in Airdrie, Lanarkshire, in 1957, took his first degree from Cambridge in 1979, completed a Ph.D. in Scottish Literature at the University of Glasgow in 1986, and worked in New Zealand at the University of Waikato from 1986 to 2000. He is the author of numerous books and articles, general editor of Hugh MacDiarmid's collected works and co-editor of *The Edinburgh Companion to Twentieth-Century Scottish Literature* (2009) and *Scotlands: Poets and the Nation* (2004). His books of poems include *This Folding Map* (1990), *First & Last Songs* (1995), *Clearances* (2001), *Homecoming* (2009) and *The Winter Book* (2017). He is the editor of *The International Companion to Edwin Morgan* (2015) and has published highly praised English-language versions of the great Gaelic poems of the eighteenth century, Duncan Ban MacIntyre's *Praise of Ben Dorain* (2014) and Alasdair Mac Mhaighster Alasdair's *The Birlinn of Clanranald* (2015).

Monika Szuba is Lecturer in English Literature at the University of Gdańsk, Poland. Her research covers twentieth-century and twenty-first-century Scottish and English poetry and prose, with a particular interest in ecocriticism informed by phenomenology. She has edited a collection of essays *Boundless Scotland: Space in Scottish Fiction* (University of Gdańsk Press, 2015). Her study *Contemporary Scottish Poetry and the Natural World: Burnside, Jamie, Robertson and White* will be published by Edinburgh University Press in 2020.

Tom Ue is Assistant Professor of English at Dalhousie University and Honorary Research Associate at University College London. He is the author of *Gissing, Shakespeare, and the Life of Writing* (Edinburgh University Press) and *George Gissing* (Northcote House Publishers/British Council) and the editor of *George Gissing, The Private Papers of Henry Ryecroft* (Edinburgh University Press). Ue has held a Frederick Banting Postdoctoral Fellowship at the University of Toronto Scarborough.

Bartosz Wójcik translator, literary critic, and cultural manager, defended his doctoral dissertation in 2013, attended academic conferences in Poland and abroad (Barbados, Czech Republic, England, Jamaica, Germany, Romania, and Scotland), published scholarly papers on the works of, among others, Patience Agbabi, Jean Binta Breeze, Linton Kwesi Johnson, Kei Miller, Mutabaruka, Michael Smith, and Derek Walcott, author of *Afro-Caribbean Poetry in English: Cultural Traditions* (Peter Lang, 2015); most recently published '"Your journey, even when bumpy,/will be sweet": Jamaica in Kei Miller's *A Light Song of Light*' (*Journal of West Indian Literature* Vol. 23: 1&2, April–Nov 2015, pp. 73–88) and 'Jamaican Soundscapes in Selected Poems by Kei Miller: A Prelude in Seven Notes' (*Sound Is/As Sense. Essays on Modern British and Irish Poetry.* Vol. 6. Ed. Wolfgang Görtschacher and David Malcolm. ISBN: 978-83-7865-443-8. Gdańsk: University of Gdańsk Press, 2016, pp. 217–235); and works at the Centre for the Meeting of Cultures in Lublin, Poland (spotkaniakultur.com).

Julian Wolfreys is author and editor of more than forty books and has, most recently, completed a monograph, *Haunted Selves, Haunting Landscapes in English Literature and Culture 1880–Present* (Palgrave), considering the relationship between selfhood, identity, and being, and landscape, ranging from Thomas Hardy to Alice Oswald. The author also of a novel, *Silent Music* (Triarchy Press) and three volumes of poetry, he is also currently working on a monograph on Virginia Woolf, another on Jacques Derrida and is co-editing, with Monika Szuba, a collection of essays in honour of J. Hillis Miller.

LIST OF FIGURES

Introduction:
The Proximity of Scotland

Monika Szuba and Julian Wolfreys

MAKING A SPACE FOR PLACE

Place is making something of a comeback. In fact, the idea of place and the material specificity of places have been increasingly focused on in philosophically inflected literary studies for the last two decades roughly, and at least since the publication of Edward Casey's ground-breaking study (no pun intended) *The Fate of Place: A Philosophical History*, in 1997.[1] Casey changed many thinkers' understanding of the history of the distinctions between space and place, and his influence may be said to be much broader than in the discipline of philosophy. Indeed, much contemporary literary criticism, whether in the fields of affect theory, ecocriticism, or the latter's younger but more urgently considered interdisciplinary sibling, studies in the Anthropocene. Though not an explicitly philosophical collection, the present volume reflects a number of concerns of ecocritical, anthropocenic, and certain phenomenological strains in critical discourse today, addressing both

M. Szuba (✉)
University of Gdańsk, Gdańsk, Poland

J. Wolfreys
London, UK

© The Author(s) 2019   1
M. Szuba and J. Wolfreys (eds.), *The Poetics of Space and Place in Scottish Literature*, Geocriticism and Spatial Literary Studies,
https://doi.org/10.1007/978-3-030-12645-2_1

questions of space and place, with an emphasis on the latter. With its focus firmly drawn on the particularities of places, topographies, and constructions of different Scottish locations, this volume considers both the urban and the rural landscapes of Scotland, placing the various narrative and poetic subjects covered in this collection squarely in their Caledonian worlds.

If, as John Stilgoe remarks, in his *What Is Landscape*, there are 'keys' that 'unlock essential landscape',[2] the authors of the essays that make up this volume take up those keys, opening for their readers the emplacement of place in the Scottish texts being considered, through the literary-critical equivalents of 'looking around, walking and noticing and thinking, putting words to things, especially simple things'.[3] Of course, this collective act on the part of the volume's authors is already a response to each of the authors being commented on—for those authors have in effect and in practice pursued similar practices, in order to explore so as to produce 'localisms...and glimmering portals'[4] onto various, often quite different Scottish worlds, producing in the process, in the case of each and every literary example, a perception of subjects, 'people intimate with a local place'.[5] In the process, what is revealed beyond—or perhaps before—the blandness of generic landscape definition, one comes to realise that writing about the human subject in the world, whether built environment, nonhuman place or a combination, a hybrid of both, is a writing that *sees* and so *realises*, in a double sense of this latter world. For, on the one hand, to realise is to come to understand: I realise that I am here and nowhere else. On the other hand, realisation is an act of making visible, of perceiving so as to visualise more powerfully. One realises the idea in the image, such a realisation being both an expression of understanding as interpretation, having to do with the singularity of a given location or site, and so, realisation as a reflection of who one is, how one is determined by place. Before attempting to address the nearly impossible question of what is Scottish about Scottish places, this introduction will offer a brief overview of Edward Casey's fundamental argument concerning the historical refocussing from space to place. Though Casey is not immediately central to the essays in this volume, his presentation of the significance of place provides the reader with a necessary understanding of the equally necessary distinction between space and place, as the place, epistemologically speaking, from which to depart.

EDWARD CASEY AND THE PHILOSOPHICAL GROUNDING OF PLACE

Casey begins his magisterial redrawing of the frame for discussion with the remark that '[w]hatever is true for space and time, this much is true of place: we are immersed in it and could not do without it. To be at all—to exist in any way—is to be somewhere' (ix). This fundamental comprehension of the nature of one's Being—a *being-there* as Heidegger was to call it—seems to have escaped the more obviously political studies of literature, the materialism of which, though keen on the contexts of history, of fact and event, nonetheless in their concerted efforts at representing the past as though the past remained present as such, nevertheless have seemed, whether in historical or literary study, to have lost sight or forgotten about the Being of beings and their lived, experienced, and witnessed being-there. For such studies, place is merely setting, however detailed its representation may be. As such, it loses the singularity and effect it has on individuals in the reading of those historical and narrated lives and through such empirical reduction becomes an 'unclarified notion', to cite Casey once more, in which historians, sociologists, and other bad readers of literature combine what is best described as 'magnitude of promise with dearth of realization' (*FP* xii). As Edward Casey noted towards the end of the last century, 'investigations of ethics and politics continue to be universalist in aspiration—to the detriment of place, considered merely parochial in scope', entire discourses having become 'place-blind, as if speaking and thinking were wholly unaffected by the locality in which they occur' (*FP* xii). Until Casey's study at least, place remained 'veiled' (to employ a Heideggerian term) by space to a great degree.

Modern thought—and by modern thought we are also acknowledging early modern thought in passing—privileged the thinking of space in all its openness and empty conceptuality. Space was understood 'in its entirety' to be 'continuous and infinite, homogeneous and isotropic… [a] pure extensionality' (*FP* 200). At the same time, and to its cost, place became and remained the lesser of the pair, marginalised, decentred as a focus, understood merely as 'distance' or the 'identity of position' (*FP* 200). The 'triumph of space' in modern thought, says Casey, 'over place is the triumph of space in its endless extensiveness'; a triumph, we might add, that finds its analogical twin in the modern thinking of presence, of logocentrism, first detailed in all its veiling effects by Jacques Derrida in *De la grammatologie*, *L'écriture et la différence*, *Marges de la philosophie*, *La voix et le phénomène*, and *La dissémination* approximately fifty years ago.[6]

Space, returning to Casey's argument, ends in what he calls its 'modernist conception' by failing to locate things or events in any sense other than that of 'pinpointing positions on a planiform geometric or cartographic grid' (*FP* 201). Space we might say does not place the map *before* the territory, so much as it proposes the map is sufficient, is all there is, nothing else—certainly not being's experience and witnessing of, and reaction to place—matters. The territory is an inconvenient irrelevance in the face of the hegemonic majesty of space's endlessness. However, 'the most effective way to appreciate the importance of place', cautions Casey, is not to treat it, that is to say to think it in the manner that space has been thought, relegating place to the nonthought or unthought. For such a 'totalizing treatment would lead to nothing but vacant generalities' (*FP* 202). We require a sense of place 'rediscovered by means of the body' and the 'most propitious clues…, like loose threads' are 'easily accessible'; 'such a thread is provided by the body in the case of place' (*FP* 203). As readers, we can only return place to a proper understanding by pursuing readings that implicitly or explicitly overcome the 'mentalist' subsumption of 'all discrete phenomena' to mere representations of the mind (*FP* 203).

To understand and so read place and its relation to the human experience, we must turn to a rhetoric of place that goes beyond mere representation or characterisation and strives to capture or give to the reader the analogical apperception of that which is 'actually experienced in qualitative terms' (*FP* 204). It is the matter of qualitative experience that connects for us Casey's thinking with Stilgoe's construction of how one comes to realise 'landscape', and so makes a place for Scotland to take place, if you will, in various ways in the literary texts in question. The literary text, rather than the historical or philosophical, is the place—every text gives rhetorical place to the taking-place we call experience through its presentation of the body in relation to the world—where we may come to understand the significance of place to one's experience of *being-there*. And this is so, to cite Casey citing Kant—which philosopher for Casey inaugurates the re-installation of place to its proper location in thought, leading to the thinking of Whitehead, Husserl, and Merleau-Ponty—because literature or perhaps *the literary* (to risk a highly provisional definition of a scandalously nebulous and evasive quasi-concept) is that place, that series of places, each in their own singularity, where we might experience *as if we were other* how '*Whatever is, is somewhere and somewhen*' (*FP* 204).[7] For Kant, because we know relational and directional terms such as back, forward, front, up, down, left, and right, we 'perceive sensible objects as placed and oriented in regions' (*FP* 205). It is the corporeal a priori of the body that gives to mind a sense of its emplacedness; the literary text seeks out a language that can figuratively trace and so embody this experience of being placed—and not merely abstractly but always in relation to and with the experience of the specificity of place at given moments. This is, inescapably, a condition of our perceptual worlds. Thus, for Kant, we 'cannot know things that are at once sensible and external to us except "in so far as they stand *in relation to ourselves*"' (*FP* 208).

The problem that arises from Kantian thinking concerning place though is that it runs the risk of being merely the identification of what Casey calls 'simple location' (*FP* 211). The place in which we sit, as we write or read, in which we stand, is unremarkably *this* place or *that* place. Both are identifiable as locations in space. However, our bodies do not only know this or that place; our corporeal prehensions of place learn through the iterable variations of experience, allowing for and making possible the thinking of comparison, analogy, difference, and so forth— as a result of which we are capable of extracting from the specificities our corporeal and phenomenal encounters with the 'environing world' (*FP* 214): 'place', argues Casey, speaking of Alfred Whitehead's conception of the body–world relation, comes to have an intermediary role that consolidates the 'here' of my experience and the 'there' of the place that I experience, through 'our access to [place] through and by—that is to say, *with*—our own animate and intimate body' (*FP* 215). The human experience as it is perceived or apperceived *through* the body is what gives access to what Edmund Husserl calls 'the surrounding world of life', resulting for the phenomenologist in the understanding of the *Lebenswelt*, the 'life-world'.[8]

But if Husserl privileged the 'positioned' body, determining and determined by place, thereby apprehending itself as 'the bearer of I'[9] experiencing the phenomenality and materiality of the here, he also realised in the *Logical Investigations* how 'expression supposes an intention of meaning', as Derrida translates *Bedeutungs-intention*. Its 'essential condition is therefore the pure act of animating intention, and not the body to which...intention unites itself and gives life'.[10] Expression—language, writing—is the extension of sense, tracing the place and giving form to the experience and memory of place. Thus, the literary representation of place provides a formal means, irreducible to a single discourse, that which is the encounter between self and world. Language, all language, but we would argue, especially through the singular richness of literary expressions, translates from sense to meaning in the production of what Derrida describes as a 'verbal fabric',[11] in exploring and revealing the relationship between sense and meaning for the self being presented, and presenting itself in place in all its specificities. It is the dynamic of this verbal fabric with which this volume involves itself.

SCOTTISH SINGULARITIES

But what of Scotland? Is there a Scotland or is there more than one Scotland? Scotland names a nation, a geopolitical entity, as if it were a unity, as if it were a national community, and with that a history and cultural topography are also invoked. As one eminent contributor to this volume remarks

> ...we might begin with a recognisable image of Scotland as a place of natural beauty and symbolic authority, but we must deepen our understanding with a sense of the historical complexity of Scotland's national identity before we can begin to fully encounter the richness of Scottish literature.
>
> 'Scotland' is a word that names a particular nation, defined by geographical borders. However, in the early twenty-first century, since the union of the crowns of Scotland and England in 1603 and the union of the parliaments of Edinburgh and London in 1707, this nation exists within the political state of Great Britain and Northern Ireland, with its global legacy of British imperialism. Therefore *it must be imagined in two different dimensions*: as part of a political state called the United Kingdom, and as a single nation of separate cultural distinction, along with other nations in the world.
>
> For people who live within the borders of this nation, certain things will be conferred by languages, geology, climate and weather, architectural design, terrain, current cultural habits and a history of cultural production, that might be different from such things elsewhere. The languages in which most Scottish literature is written – Gaelic, Scots and English – confer their own rhythms, sounds, musical dynamics, and relations between them confer their own character upon the priorities of expression in speech

and writing. Geography creates another range of characteristics. Growing up in different cities (few are as different as Glasgow and Edinburgh) or growing up near the coast in a tidal landscape, with the sea returning the way it does, is different from growing up in a rainforest or a desert.[12]

And growing up in Edinburgh as opposed to Glasgow, or in a small town or village on the north-east coast, is different each time, for all that might be shared across these and any other place in Scotland. One of the editors of the present volume was told with a smiling pride by a Dundonian that people from Glasgow, and by extension the west coast, were far more cheerful than people from the east. There is always already though a doubleness in the name 'Scotland', as Alan Riach observes. The name 'Scotland', in naming an undifferentiated entity, fails to grasp, precisely because it obscures (as do all such 'national' names) the many and varying differentiations understood as distinct places, regions, areas, cities, geographical, and other locales, which, though associated with the mastery of the proper name, resist any such easy gathering. What is to be read in its many different iterations across the essays gathered here is what one of the contributors, in one of his many wonderfully insightful and original publications, *Archipelagic Modernism: Literature in the Irish and British Isles, 1890–1970*, describes with a use of typically effective litotes 'a sense of rootedness' that appears in each representation, each narrative or poem as a 'timelessness' but also as being marked by 'social change'.[13]

Scotlands abide because Scotlands are always changing, always more than one, and irreducible to any but the most generic misreadings of place. Perhaps the name 'Scotland' (allowing the singular form to be also the key to a singular-plural, to borrow a phrase of Jean-Luc Nancy's) abides with such force in literary manifestations and with a particular pull irreducible to any facile romanticism, precisely because as Hugh MacDiarmid remarked of the Shetland Islands in *The Islands of Scotland* that 'all that is still greatest in literature and art and philosophy was created…in places as lonely and bare as these islands are'.[14] Scotland is not, of course, an island, even though it is gathered collectively as part of the 'British Isles' and, equally obviously, has its own islands, those on which MacDiarmid comments being not the least. The island question aside though, what we take to be key in MacDiarmid's remark is that double phenomenological sense of loneliness and bareness. Without essence, the idea of 'Scotland' is essentially accessed in perceptions of the lonely and the bare. Another way to imagine this is to suggest that one dwells more closely, more intimately in one's own Scotland, be that the north-east coast, the islands, or Glasgow as a result of existing within, and so feeling most intensely, a bare life, life as it is most forcefully felt, whether this might be in the barely existent subject's utterances who is hidden within the atmosphere and climate of place in the poetry of Robin Robertson (see the chapter on Robertson, below), or in a very different manner in the deserted pathways, the emptiness of the river, and the realisation that humans are animal and, moreover, it is the 'structure of language itself which is treacherous', as Alexander Trocchi has it.[15]

Whether one situates oneself in the MacDiarmid or the Trocchi camp, each writer understands that there is, in being Scottish a sense of the specificity of Being, of there being an 'each time of Being... [a] being-with of each time with every [other] time'[16]—hence John Brannigan's sensitive registration of rootedness as being at once 'timelessness' and caught up in ineluctable change. This perception of Being is always enfolded in the world, in each moment of the world, from which there can occur at each moment that sense of one's being part of a specific world. Scottish literature can and often does express just this each time, this being-with, retaining through the perception of self-and', self-with', and self-in-world both the singularity of the experience and the shared, apperceived plurality of other moments of recognition and apperception. While one might argue this for any literature, it is the contention of the editors that for innumerable cultural and epistemological reasons, the '"with" is [felt in particular Scottish texts as] the fullest measure of (the) incommensurable meaning (of Being)'.[17] Thus, in reading Scottish novelists, poets, essayists, one has the acute sense as one so rarely does with English writers how, through the subject's consciousness the world 'springs forth everywhere and in each instant, simultaneously'.[18] Through particular Scottish writers, one gains access to a materialist 'ontology of being-with'[19]: of the self finding its being with the world in which it places itself and in which it is emplaced by the realisation of that world in all its material and phenomenological detail. It is that detail, and so through this that sense of finding oneself and of feeling as if ones being were with the world of the various Scotlands constructed through the readings of this volume.

ABOUT THIS VOLUME

The authors and texts considered in this volume are as diverse as Scotland itself, with apologies for veering dangerously near cliché. Among those writers and texts discussed are George Mackay Brown's *Time in a Red Coat*, the archipelagic texts of Kathleen Jamie, Kevin MacNeil, and Angus Peter Campbell, and also, in another essay, the northern archipelagos of the Scottish imagination in the fictions of, once more, George Mackay Brown, Margaret Elphinstone, and Sarah Moss; Jamie's non-fiction prose is given the serious attention it deserves, while the Glasgow novel across the twentieth century, specifically in the works of A. McArthur, H. Kingsley Long, Archie Hind, Alasdair Gray, and James Kelman, is brought into focus, as is the Glasgow of Tom Leonard and the Dundee of Mark Thomson. Greenock and the River Tay are variously addressed, in Ken MacLeod's science fiction novel *Descent*, and in the poetry of Douglas Dunn, Robert Crawford, and again, Kathleen Jamie. Gaelic language writing, in the example of Derick Thomson's *An Rathad Cian* (*The Far Road*), is introduced to a wider audience, while John Burnside's embodied sense of place is explored through the lens of Maurice Merleau-Ponty, to great and telling effect and Robin Robertson's poetry is given a phenomenological reading for its shifting atmospherics influenced by the climate and materiality of the north-east coast of Scotland. Lastly, Kei Miller's 'Under the Saltire Flag' is presented through a close reading that negotiates the problematics of local and foreign, cultural transference and identity transition.

As the range of texts addressed, with canonical and less familiar authors presented cheek by jowl, attests, arguably, no 'regional' or 'national' literature in the British Isles is more vital than that coming out of Scotland. With regard to the often fraught and contested questions of space, place, environment, and the relationship of the individual to culture, language, memory, and history, Scottish writing—fiction, non-fiction prose, poetry—is exploratory, engaged, diverse, and having about it a sense of ambiguous, not to say ambivalent 'embeddedness' in the world from which it comes, and which it in turn mediates. While this volume does not focus directly on the question of Scottishness as a national cultural identity (as distinct from English or 'British' identities), and while the volume is not promoting a political discussion through the reading of literature (devolved Scotland, Brexit, or other fashionable sociocultural topics), the present volume aims to explore and introduce the critical reader to the diversity of Scottish literature in its concern with place, environment, and locus, covering the lowlands, the highlands, the islands, and Scotland's urban spaces. In doing so, it will open up unexpected views of Scottishness, of subjectivity, culture, and the densely woven imbrication of self-hood, language, and locus. Despite the seemingly wide-ranging concerns (and the volume does aim to be broadly inclusive rather than risk being exclusive through a narrower focus), the present volume demonstrates a powerful sense of belonging and cultural affinity lasting over 200 years. The volume's cohesiveness lies in recognising, and so attempting to present and represent the manner in which Scottish writing, of different periods and different regions, in its very *difference* from itself, is unavailable to broad, unifying cultural definitions or determinations; with this understanding comes the important recognition that no ontological or epistemological model can define 'Scottish Literature' as such, but the difference must be respected and recognised, issues that will be addressed in the introduction. What offers connection and cohesiveness in the volume is the abiding interest on the part of Scottish writers from different backgrounds, periods, interests, and working in different genres in landscape, in the intimate connection between self and world, subject and place. Scottish literature celebrates this intimacy and the regional diversity of a culture that is many-faceted and heterogeneous. It is, as the volume attempts to show, this heterogeneity that defines Scottishness, and that Scottishness in turn is only to be understood through a critical appreciation of the Scots writer's enduring fascination with and attachment to place and space.

   Though this collection of essays speaks predominantly to writing of the twentieth and twenty-first centuries, it also seeks, if not to contextualise, then frame at least the focus through three other essays, by Alan Riach, Tom Ue, and Mary Ann Caws. Alan Riach discusses a poem probably written in the mid-eighteenth century: Alasdair mac Mhaighstir Alasdair's 'The Birlinn of Clanranald', a Gaelic language text. Providing his own translations, Riach argues that the 'place' of the poem in history and its geographical trajectory seem to be clearly identifiable. Yet for all its literal detail and verisimilitude, the poem insists that we consider its meaning in metaphorical terms, and that the 'space' it occupies can-not be defined by its history of publication, its readership, or its lan-guage, but in its intimation of human potential in the face of inimical forces, natural and human. 'Space' and 'place' in this work are fiercely contested. Tom Ue brings us forward to the nineteenth century and the work of Robert Louis Stevenson in a study concerned with the contesta-tion of space and place, albeit in very different ways. Both essays 'preface' as it were the modern understanding of space and place in Scottish liter-ature. Indeed, their inclusion as exemplary discussions of space and place in pre-twentieth century Scottish literature argues for a reconsideration, in the context of Scottish literature and the literature of place, of what is meant by modernity, regionality, and subjectivity. Mary Ann Caws, noted literary critic, provides the volume with a summation and departure; while the book is for the most part about writing, Caws offers a read-ing of the paintings of Scottish locations by Jon Schueler (1916–1992). Why in a collection of essays on literature, a lone essay about painting. In the case of all the essays on poems, novels, non-fiction prose, an essen-tial and reiterated focus is on the question and the problems of rep-resentation, of how one sees, what one sees, and how one is made to feel through one's sensory immersion in the world, in place, thereby finding one's being-with the moment, the event of encountering place. Much of Scottish literature in situating place addresses the representation of place through a representation of climate, of atmosphere, of phenome-nological registration, thereby taking up the quest to make the reader see, to feel, to hear, to realise. There is, as Caws demonstrates through her sensitive readings of Schueler's paintings of Mallaig, an intimacy, an intensity in the realisation for the subject (the painter, the writer, the reader, the viewer) of place. Thus, we as readers move through spaces that are transformed by the 'imaginings and sightings', in this case of Jon Schueler, but too in each of the texts herein discussed. And it has to be said that a painting, made as it is of what Caws calls, quite correctly, 'marks', that it too is a text, there to be read, if we just allow ourselves to find ourselves, in, *with*, the moment of the world as it discloses itself to us and so takes us in. This perhaps is the most significant aspect of the Scottish text of place. It involves us, informs us, opens itself to us, and so opens us to consider the world as each time a moment of origin, and with that, we open ourselves to an apprehension of our being-there, our being-in-the-world.

NOTES

1. Edward S. Casey, *The Fate of Place: A Philosophical History* (Berkeley: University of California Press, 1997). All further references will be given parenthetically, as *FP*.
2. John R. Stilgoe, *What Is Landscape?* (Cambridge: MIT Press, 2015), xiii.
3. Ibid., xiii.
4. Ibid., xiii.
5. Ibid., xiii.
6. Jacques Derrida, *De la grammatologie* (Paris: Minuit, 1967); *L'écriture et la différance* (Paris: Seuil, 1967); *La voix et le phénomène* (Paris: Quadrige, 1967); *La dissémination* (Paris: Seuil, 1972); *Marges de la philosophie* (Paris: Minuit, 1972).
7. Casey takes this from the translation of Kant's 'On the Form and Principles of the Sensible and Intelligible World' (1770), published in *Kant: Theoretical Philosophy, 1755–1770*, trans. and ed. David Walford, in collaboration with Ralf Meerbote (Cambridge: Cambridge University Press, 1992), 361–416, 409.
8. Edmund Husserl, *The Crisis of European Sciences and Transcendental Phenomenology*, trans. and intro, David Carr (Evanston: Northwest University Press, 1970), 108–109.
9. Edmund Husserl, *Ding und Raum. Husserliana 16*, ed. Ulrich Claesges (The Hague: Nijhof, 1964), 162.
10. Jacques Derrida, 'Form and Meaning: A Note on the Phenomenology of Language', in *Margins of Philosophy*, trans. Alan Bass (Chicago: University of Chicago Press, 1982), 155–73, 161.
11. Derrida, 'Form and Meaning', 172.
12. Alan Riach, *What Is Scottish Literature?* (Glasgow: Association for Scottish Literary Studies, 2009), 3–4; emphasis added.
13. John Brannigan, *Archipelagic Modernism: Literature in the Irish and British Isles, 1890–1970* (Edinburgh: Edinburgh University Press, 2015), 147.
14. Hugh MacDiarmid, *The Islands of Scotland* (London: Batsford, 1939), x–xi.
15. Alexander Trocchi, *Young Adam* (Edinburgh: Rebel, 1996), 4. Perhaps Trocchi is, in many ways, representative or emblematic of certain modern Scottish writers, down to today, including Robin Robertson and John Burnside. A student of English and Philosophy at Glasgow University, by all accounts brilliant, and studying continental philosophy, looked on largely as anathema south of the border, Trocchi was at the time something of a 'cultural outsider', as John Pringle puts it in his introduction to the novel (vi). Such 'outsiderness isn't exile, for only by

being outside Scotland could he see it clearly, like the philosophical vision that the narrator [of *Young Adam*] brings to the turgid and stultifying Scotland' (vi), and represented for Trocchi in the 'absolutist and parochial' (vii) figure of Hugh MacDiarmid (who apparently decried Trocchi as 'cosmopolitan scum!').
16. Jean-Luc Nancy, *Being Singular Plural*, trans. Robert D. Richardson and Anne E. O'Byrne (Stanford: Stanford University Press, 2000), 83.
17. Ibid., 83.
18. Ibid.
19. Ibid.

Works Cited

Brannigan, John. *Archipelagic Modernism: Literature in the Irish and British Isles, 1890–1970.* Edinburgh: Edinburgh University Press, 2015.
Casey, S. Edward. *The Fate of Place: A Philosophical History.* Berkeley: University of California Press, 1997.
Derrida, Jacques. *De la grammatologie.* Paris: Minuit, 1967.
———. *L'écriture et la différance.* Paris: Seuil, 1967.
———. *La voix et le phénomène.* Paris: Quadrige, 1967.
———. *La dissémination.* Paris: Seuil, 1972.
———. *Marges de la philosophie.* Paris: Minuit, 1972.
———. 'Form and Meaning: A Note on the Phenomenology of Language'. *Margins of Philosophy.* Trans. Alan Bass. Chicago: University of Chicago Press, 1982. 155–73.
Husserl, Edmund. *Ding und Raum. Husserliana* 16. Ed. Ulrich Claesges. The Hague: Nijhof, 1964.
———. *The Crisis of European Sciences and Transcendental Phenomenology.* Trans. and Intro. David Carr. Evanston: Northwest University Press, 1970.
Kant, Immanuel. 'On the Form and Principles of the Sensible and Intelligible World' (1770). *Kant: Theoretical Philosophy, 1755–1770.* Trans. and Ed. David Walford, in collaboration with Ralf Meerbote. Cambridge: Cambridge University Press, 1992. 361–416.
MacDiarmid, Hugh. *The Islands of Scotland.* London: Batsford, 1939.
Nancy, Jean-Luc. *Being Singular Plural.* Trans. Robert D. Richardson and Anne E. O'Byrne. Stanford: Stanford University Press, 2000.
Riach, Alan. *What Is Scottish Literature?* Glasgow: Association for Scottish Literary Studies, 2009.
Stilgoe, John R. *What Is Landscape?* Cambridge: MIT Press, 2015.
Trocchi, Alexander. *Young Adam.* Edinburgh: Rebel, 1996.

Contested Beginnings

Location and Destination in Alasdair mac Mhaighstir Alasdair's 'The Birlinn of Clanranald'

Alan Riach

'THE BIRLINN OF CLANRANALD' is a poem which describes a working ship, a birlinn or galley, its component parts, mast, sail, tiller, rudder, oars and the cabes (or oar-clasps, wooden pommels secured to the gunwale) they rest in, the ropes that connect sail to cleats or belaying pins and so on, and the sixteen crewmen, each with their appointed role and place, and it describes their mutual working together, rowing, and then sailing out to sea, from the Hebrides in the west of Scotland, from South Uist to the Sound of Islay, then over to Carrickfergus in Ireland. The last third of the poem is an astonishing, terrifying, exhilarating description of the men and the ship in a terrible storm that blows up, threatening to destroy them, and which they pass through, only just making it to safe harbour, mooring and shelter. It was written in Gaelic sometime around 1751–1755 and first published posthumously in 1776, in an edition compiled by the poet's son. The most carefully edited modern Gaelic text is in *Selected Poems*, edited by Derick S. Thomson (Edinburgh: The Scottish Gaelic Texts Society, 1996).

A. Riach (✉)
University of Glasgow, Glasgow, Scotland, UK

© The Author(s) 2019
M. Szuba and J. Wolfreys (eds.), *The Poetics of Space and Place in Scottish Literature*, Geocriticism and Spatial Literary Studies,
https://doi.org/10.1007/978-3-030-12645-2_2

Its author, Alasdair mac Mhaighstir Alasdair, also known as Alexander MacDonald (c.1693/98–c.1770) was a teacher and soldier, a Jacobite officer during the rising of 1745 and Gaelic tutor to Prince Charles Edward Stuart. His father was an Episcopalian Church of Scotland minister, who taught the boy and introduced him to classical literature. He knew about sea voyages, literally, but he also had read about them in the poems of Homer and Virgil. In the poem, there is clear evidence that the author knew and had experienced the sea, but there is also a supremely literary sensibility at work, especially when we come to the storm, where a wealth of poetic resources of hyperbole and imagery are drawn upon. The modernity of this passage is startling, and it could almost be described as psychedelic or surrealist.

Alasdair attended the University of Glasgow and grew quickly familiar with the literature and culture of his era. Not only contemporary and recent poetry in Scots and English, but the European context of all cultural production came into his knowledge. He has been called 'The Bard of the Gaelic Enlightenment' but if at times his poetry is indeed 'bardic' in a traditional oral sense, he is more accurately described as a highly literate and knowledgeable literary poet, an Enlightenment figure indeed, and a pre-Romantic Scottish nationalist, whose primary language was Gaelic.

In 1729, he became a schoolteacher, an English teacher, working in various parts of Moidart and the west of Scotland. In 1738, he was teaching at Kilchoan, Ardnamurchan. One of his most famous songs of this period was the lyrical, 'Allt an t-Siucar'/'Sugar Burn'. In 1741, Alasdair's *A Galick and English Vocabulary*, effectively the first Gaelic–English dictionary (of around 200 pages), was published, commissioned by the anti-Catholic, anti-Gaelic, Society in Scotland for the Propagation of Christian Knowledge (SSPCK), to help spread the English language and extirpate Gaelic. Alasdair had worked on it in the belief that it would help take Gaelic forward, but he soon came to oppose everything to which the SSPCK was committed. Making this book, if anything, confirmed his own commitment to his language and culture. His poems took on increasingly sharp edges.

Called to account for satiric and inappropriate writing, it is said that he abandoned his teaching to help in the Jacobite rising and that he was among the first at Glenfinnan when the flag was raised on 19 August 1745. Many of his poems and songs openly extol the virtues of the Jacobite cause and satirise the Hanoverians and their Scottish supporters, the Campbells. He was a captain in the Clan Ranald regiment, in charge of fifty recruits, and taught Gaelic to the Prince himself. He converted to Catholicism, perhaps at this time, but perhaps much earlier. After Culloden, he and his family were fugitives. His house was ransacked by Hanoverian troops.

He and his family settled on the island of Canna in 1749 and stayed there till 1751, when he travelled to Edinburgh to publish a book of his poems, *Ais-Eiridh na Sean Chánoin Albannaich/The Reawakening of the Old Scottish Language*, replete with satires on the Hanoverian succession. In the poem, 'An Airce'/'The Ark', he promises that the Campbells will be plagued and scourged for their treason to Scotland, while he himself will build a ship of refuge for those Campbells true to the Jacobite cause, and all moderates who, after swallowing an effective purgative of salt sea water, would be willing to reject allegiance to the British crown. The authorities were outraged.

Aware of the threat of prosecution, he moved to Glen Uig but then moved again to Knoydart, then to Morar and finally to Sandaig, in Arisaig. He often visited South Uist, where his friend Iain MacFhearchair (John MacCodrum) was bard to Sir James MacDonald of Sleat. The MacDonalds and Clan Ranald were his people, and their family connections extended throughout the west of Scotland and to Ireland, to Carrickfergus.

On his deathbed, his last words were addressed to friends watching over him, who were reciting some poems of their own. Alasdair awoke, corrected their metres and versification, showed them how to do it with some verses of his own, then quietly lay back and drifted away. He is buried in Kilmorie cemetery, Arisaig.

The biography of the poet offers us some secure coordinate points and a trajectory through a tumultuous period not only in Scottish but in British history, across the 1707 union of parliaments through the Jacobite risings of the first half of the century, to their aftermath in the second half. Place, in this sense, is secure, even while the spaces we might identify as Gaelic, Scottish and British, are contested. However, when we come to 'The Birlinn of Clanranald' as a poem, the questions become more complex. We might conclude from the biographical and historical context that 'The Birlinn of Clanranald' was not widely known in its author's lifetime, and that its historical moment is of some consequence. There is more to it, of course.

The original Gaelic poem is both traditional and radical. The versification is rhythmic, rhymed, with regular patterns. This would make it
as familiar and accessible in its own time and language as free verse is to
us. Equally, though, a poem in the forms of its era requires a necessary
quickening, whether in address or approach or assumption. Rhyming
poems in the twenty-first century are not easily read fresh. Often
enough, free verse or open-form poems can also feel tired. And there is
more. The poem is not a fragmented narrative but coherent, and yet its
coherence is blasted by opposing forces. The balance in the poem, in its
form as well as in its narrative, is delicate but strong, resistant to, but at
the mercy of, forces that oppose and cut across it.

Structurally, there are sixteen parts, and there seem to be clearly
eight sub-sections in the last part, the storm. This last part takes up
about a third of the whole poem. This is a literary work, carefully put
down on paper. It is not a composition made to a musical structure and
held in the memory until transcribed, as was the case with the other
great Gaelic poem of this era, Duncan Ban MacIntyre's 'Praise of Ben
Dorain'. Alasdair mac Mhaighstir Alasdair intended that 'The Birlinn of
Clanranald' should be read, as well as heard.

Ambiguities abound. Specific references to the structure and operation of the birlinn, its parts and their purposes, what the crew do, actually, are given in intricate detail. And yet there are contradictions. A
birlinn is usually understood as having one sail and one mast. This is
what seems to be the case in the poem. Yet in various places, especially at
the beginning and end of the Gaelic text, plural terms for these items are
used. Today, of course, nobody knows what birlinns were actually like.
As far as we know, none survive. In 1493, the Lordship of the Isles was
given over to King James IV. It was ordered that every birlinn should
be destroyed, as the power of the fleet and the authority of the seafaring clans was a threat. The ships were burned. Reconstructions have
been made, and courageously sailed. But questions remain. Perhaps
too much importance is given to the word, 'birlinn': it seems to have
appeared in the title of the poem in the late Victorian era and is used in
the poem sparingly, while 'long' ('luinge') is used three times, 'bairc/
caol-bhairc' three times and 'iubhrach' once. As Michel Byrne has
informed me, 'In spite of the destruction of his Lordship's navy, island
chiefs obviously continued to sail with their retinue (and to be praised
as great sailors in panegyric song), so is there much in the poem to make
us think MacDonald had anything other than an eighteenth-century ship

in mind?' This remains one of a number of questions about authenticity and reference that take the poem beyond the literal world of historical fact and the rigours of material reconstitution. It lives in more than history. It moves through time as well as over seas.

As such, it is worth quoting an author whose experience of ships, sailing and seamanship authorises his judgements of the experience of sea travel. Adam Nicolson, in *Seamanship* (London: HarperCollins, 2004), says this of one of the boats on which he voyaged through Atlantic waters, including those around the Hebrides: 'Of course a boat is not a natural thing. She is the most cultural of things, the way she works dependent on a line of thought that goes back to the Bronze Age: the form of the hull and the weighted keel; the lift and drive given by a sail; [...] the ingenuity of blocks and tackles, strops, sheets, halyards and warps, the sheer cleverness of knots. The knowledge that is gathered in a boat is a great human inheritance, especially valuable because it is not material but intangible, a legacy made only of understanding' (32).

The elemental realities Nicolson describes here cross time and locations with the most fundamental coordinate points that remain essential from the Bronze Age to the twentieth century. They are also human, experienced, remembered and applied in the company of other sailors. They are, on the one hand, indifferent to human feeling and aspiration, and on the other, humanly vulnerable, tough and resilient. This might appear to be an axiomatic dichotomy, yet specific space and place in this light are not irrelevant: currents, climate, seasonal weathers, geographical landfalls, depths and distances are all particular to any voyage and complex beyond any sense of simplicity. Yet the general truths Nicolson is describing are perennial and in literary or cultural terms evoke most strongly tropes of symbolism with which we have become increasingly familiar in the century or so since mass media encroached Western society to the point of visual saturation. Of course, the commercial priority of that saturation is different from that of the sea voyage.

Nicolson continues: 'You can see the boat, in other words, as our great symbol, the embodiment of what we might be. In her fineness, strength and robustness, in the many intricate, interlocking details of her overall scheme; even in the bowing to nature of her wing-like sails and the auk- or seal-like curves of her body; in all this, she is a great act of civility. The sea is an "it", the boat is a "she", and the courage of that confrontation is why people love the boats they know. Boats are us against it, what we can do despite the world. Each sailing hull is a precious thought, buoyant, purposeful, moving on, afloat in the sea that cares nothing for it. From the deck of a boat, out of sight of land, as Auden wrote in "The Sea and the Mirror", his great poem on art and consciousness, "All we are not stares back at what we are"' (33).

There is a specific geographical location for 'The Birlinn of Clanranald' and it is perfectly possible to chart the route the birlinn takes on her voyage. In terms of place and geography, it would seem, we are secure. The poem tells us that the birlinn emerges from the mouth of Loch Eynort in South Uist, voyages south-south-east to the Sound of Islay then heads south-west, crossing to Carrickfergus in Ireland. But ambiguities remain. No explanation for this voyage is given. Why are these men travelling thus? Why take that route? There are more questions unanswered than resolved by these navigational assurances.

As Murray Pittock says, 'The Birlinn's journey, from South Uist to Carrickfergus in Ireland on St. Brigid's Day, the eve of Candlemas, unites the sea-divided Gael of Clan Donald, the last Scottish family to fight in an Irish rebel army, just as it formed such an important part of the last Scottish army of 1746. The invocation of tradition (the bow) and Spanish weapons can be held to represent the ancient unified world of the Gael, and the calls of Irish Gaelic poetry for Spanish military help'. Pittock emphasises this indication of the significance of the date given in the poem for the voyage: 'The date of the voyage is surely important: Brigid, the Mary of the Gael, was also associated with a Gaelic pagan inheritance. Her day – traditionally thought a good day for a sea voyage – was linked to the return of fertility and the coming of spring, a token and hope of the renewing year. In this it was clearly linked to the Christian Candlemas'. Pittock concludes: 'This was a world with which, as a Catholic convert, Alasdair would have been familiar'. So, place and date, the space crossed and the time occupied in the evocation of the voyage at its most literal already have specific reference and meaning that spans particular religious denomination and pagan or non-orthodox belief systems and mythic structures of spiritual reality. At the heart of all, these terms are balanced between what is certain and what is unknown.

And if we note that balance of certainties and the unknown, at the heart of creating a new version of the poem is the question: How to translate it?

I undertook an English-language version of the poem after many years of study. It was a poem which had haunted my imagination since childhood. But without a fluent knowledge of Gaelic, my acquaintance with it was principally through other, older translations. But there were other specific problems. In terms of the imagery, as noted, the birlinn, the parts of the ship, the crew and their expertise are all given in detail. Yet there are questions. For example, when the crew come to the place where the sailing begins, and Big Malcolm the Stalwart, son of Old Ranald the Ocean, stands up by the leading oar, before the crew, to call for a rowing song, where exactly is he standing? The leading oar is not at the prow of the ship, as you might imagine, but is marking a rhythm for others to follow, and the oarsmen themselves would be facing the other way, with their backs to the prow, facing towards the stern of the ship, so Big Malcolm would be in front of them, at the stern.

There are questions of vocabulary. What do the oars rest in? Some translations have 'oar-ports', which are circular holes with a gash to one side, so the blade of the oar slips through the gash and the shaft rest in the hole; but some have 'thole-pins' which are literally pins, or thick shafts, stuck into holes in the gunwale and chained or tied to the side. But the oars would surely be knocked out of these in rough seas. The appropriate term, I discovered, is most likely 'cabe', which is like a wooden fist rising out of the gunwale, shaped like the pommel of a saddle, with a strap of leather or rope running from it down to the gunwale, so that each oar has some flexibility as well as security. These matters of details occupied me for a long time while I made my English version.

It is perhaps worth comparing a few examples of different English versions. Here is the opening of the last section, the voyage, first in Hugh MacDiarmid's version from 1935, made with the help of Sorley Maclean:

The sun bursting golden-yellow
Out of his husk,
The sky grew wild and hot-breathing,
Unsheathing a fell tusk,
Then turned wave-blue, thick, dun-bellied,
Fierce and forbidding,
Every hue that would be in a plaid
In it kneading;
A 'dog's-tooth' in the Western quarter
Snorters prophesied;
The swift clouds under a shower-breeze
Multiplied.

Derick Thomson's 1974 version runs like this:

Sun bursting goldenly
from its meshing;
the sky became scorched and gloomy,
awe-inspiring.

The waves grew dark, thick, dun-bellied,
angry and sallow;
the sky had every single hue
you find in tartan.

A dog's-tooth appeared in the west,
a storm threatened;
swift-moving clouds by wind shredded,
equally showers too.

Iain Crichton Smith, in 1977, has this:

Sun unhusking to gold-yellow
    from its shell,
the sky growing seared and lurid,
amber bell.

Thick and gloomy and dun-bellied,
surly curtain,
vibrating with every colour
in a tartan.

Rainbow in the west appearing
tempest-born,
speeding clouds by growing breezes
chewed and torn.

Ronald Black's 2001 translation of this passage runs thus:

As the sun burst yellow-golden
    Out of her husk,
The sky grew overcast and singed,
Truly ugly.

It grew wave-blue, thick, dun-bellied,
Sallow, surly,
With every colour in a tartan plaid
Spread on the sky,

And a bit of rainbow over in the west,
It looked like a storm –
Scudding clouds being torn apart by wind
And showery squalls.

And my own version is this:

Furnace-gold, hot-yellow, yolk-yellow, brass-brazen sun, burning
through fish-nets of clouds, trellises meshed, burning them open,
emerges, and the clouds burn back, close in once again,
cover all things, changing, sky becomes ash, blackening, and a blue

splash there, and then, thickening, bulging, effulging,
turning sick, pale, brown, beige, tawny, impending, bellying
down, and the fretwork rematches itself, closes in, hue
thick as tartan, dark weaves, anger flashes, and there high in the west,
a broken shaft, a dog-tooth of rainbow, colour stripes swelling,
a fang of sharp colour, clouds moving faster to cover it over, and the
winds
pick up speed, toss the clouds as if showers of boulders,
grey fragments of stone, chips of earth, avalanching in sky.

It is not necessary to attempt justifications here but I would observe a
few important differences between my version and all the others. I abandoned any attempt to emulate the rhythmic structure of the original's
versification. This seemed crucial, for to follow that would have resulted
in a musical mimicry and I could not hope to match that with the close
accuracy of meaning provided by the Gaelic-speaking translators above.
My hope was to match the meaning of the original with a more exfo-
liated, elaborated, yet surprising and hopefully still quickening version,
almost an interpretation, expanded in what might be called a paraphras-
ing of the original. Literalism, here, in some crucial way, was not going
to work. Yet this is not to abandon the original but to attempt to come
at it, or rather bring it towards us, in a different way.

There is what seems an arbitrary space between 'blue' and 'splash' in my version of this passage. Why should there be a space here? Let me describe what I was thinking of: there is a moment when, on shipboard, the rise and fall of the water might lift you to a point of seeming equilibrium, then drop you vertiginously, quickly, into a trough. In this passage, the reader and the witness on board are looking up and out at the sky, noting the gathering storm. The sight of something 'blue' might catch the eye with hope, a momentary sense of possibility, escape, before the transient notion of 'splash' brings us back to water and onward flow. It's a moment for holding your breath. The other lines run on, with thickening density and increasing velocity but a break between lines like this gives pause and gathers tension. At least, that's what I was hoping for.

Then there is the question of who is speaking and to whom? Parts of the poem read like commands to the crew, parts as if an omniscient narrator is describing events, but at the same time, all of it gives you the sense that you are on board the ship itself, moving through the waters. The questions here can be answered partially. We are invited to imagine voices and actions in relations of power, commanding and observing. The responses given are a result of agreed loyalty and respect, and the enactment of trusted and proven expertise. But the poem speaks with a voice of its own, not defined entirely by any single character or figure, whether a member of the crew, a captain, a clan chief, or the voice of the ocean itself, though all these have their forms of address, at different moments.

Then there is the voyage and how to convey movement. The whole poem is moving, is in movement, at different speeds, in different places, fluently, easefully, then under pressure and straining, then in terrible action, erratic, yet determined.

Every line of the poem takes place in the evocation of movement upon water. When we think of Wordsworth's poetry, most often we are carried by the pace of a person walking. The same is true of our progress through Dante's *Inferno*. In Robert Burns's 'Tam o' Shanter', we begin by arriving in a market town towards the end of the day, become quickly settled in a tavern, then proceed on horseback, in an unsteady, rather inebriated ride, and then in the last part of the poem, we move fast, on horseback at full gallop. 'The Birlinn of Clanranald' by contrast to all of these, is moving across water, first by rowing, and with the accompaniment of a rowing song, then under sail, as the seas become bigger and the waves higher, and then through a terrible storm, where the unpredictable weights and vertiginous rising and descending of the ship is represented in the verse itself.

This is inherent in the rhythms of the language used. As Robert Lowell says, in the 'Introduction' to Imitations (1971), 'the excellence of a poet depends on the unique opportunities of his native language' (xiii). So how to convey what is Gaelic in English? I have no formula or recipe, only to try as I did, bearing in mind, somehow, both structure and music, the presence of the poem and its history, and the presence and the history of both Gaelic and English.

And there is the matter of the poem's religious context. It was written after Alasdair's conversion to Catholicism and opens with a prayer for a blessing to be given by the Holy Trinity, Father, Son and Holy Ghost. I might have let that stand. All other translators have done so. Yet I wanted to say something here that might comprise a blessing even atheists could acknowledge. I started well enough, I thought, with 'the great lord god of movement'—that sets a promise for the whole poem—and 'the great lord god of nature' is surely as present in what we encounter, as movement. But that does not give a trinity. After a while, I hit upon 'the great lord god of permanence'—whatever that might be, something we hope and believe might stay present, giving coordinate points to rely on, forever, whatever makes us human in the circumstances, from well before Homer to now. These three gods are, so to speak, coordinating points for every part of the poem and make of it a greater comprehensive human entity, a composition that has coherence, an identity, even in translation, that might be conveyed. The translation, then, has got to be, not only from Gaelic to English, but from the late eighteenth to the early twenty-first century.

So then, keeping in mind when it was written, we might ask, when is it set?

In terms of its political context, the poem was written post-Apocalypse, post-Armageddon, in more than one sense, after Culloden. Shelter is required. A journey must be made. What tone could be voiced to convey that?

Readers of poems know how this works. Reality and metaphor are never opposed. Literalism is often the enemy. Meticulous detail of fact can be good, verisimilitude has a real purpose. But the poem does not and could not convey literally what was contemporary with its author. It refers to a world long, long pre-Culloden, not the eighteenth but the fifteenth century, and earlier. Not pre-Union of Parliaments, but even pre-Union of Crowns. Remember: all the original birlinns were destroyed. The poem has immediacy, certainly, but it is an act of reclamation and an assertion of faith. It is, in its way, a resurrection.

That might prompt reflection on the possible meaning of the poem. What answer could we give if we were to ask, simply: What does it mean?

The poem is so visceral and grainy in its depiction of realities, it almost seems hostile to metaphoric interpretation, but there is an interpretation of the poem that the historical context in which it was written suggests, without straining the purpose of metaphoric implication too far.

As noted, it was composed in the aftermath of the Jacobite rising of 1745 and the massacre at Culloden in 1746, and its author was an officer in the Jacobite army. The poem, perhaps, reflects upon this social and human disaster in ways that go further than its literal meaning. It presents a clan and a crew of men working in extreme coordination, disciplined and intuitive, in conditions of knowledge drawn from experience, but they and their vessel are subjected to a storm of unprecedented violence, a natural imposition that calls up inimical forces from well beyond anything that might have been predicted. The courage and skills of the crew and the strength of the ship carry them through, but at a cost, and without any sense of inevitability. The safe harbour they come to is in Ireland, and the connection between the Celtic west of Scotland and the Irish coast their voyage makes, is, also, a signal of an ancient kinship, across differences, of the Celtic peoples and the human needs of all people, as opposed to inimical forces in nature and anti-human forces in the political world that intervene to wreak havoc and destruction on us all.

As Silke Strohe writes in *Uneasy Subjects: Postcolonialism and Scottish Gaelic Poetry*, 'retrospection is often a necessary stage in the development of a culture confronted with marginalisation. It may help the marginalised to gain or maintain a belief in the validity and potential of their own communities and cultures, thus laying foundations for later and more direct forms of cultural resistance with a more contemporary focus' (77). By placing the voyage in an unspecified past, by evoking the birlinn, a ship from a previous dispensation, long before the Hanoverian succession, Alasdair gives us a sense of historical depth reaching into mythic reality, whose strengths can be conveyed through the verisimilitude of the details, and thus whose meaning can be brought back not only to his own contemporary but quite deliberately a future reality.

The struggle in his own life may have been specific to the Jacobite and Hanoverian conflict but the forces aligned against human potential are perennial. These inimical forces are always there, ready to break into the worlds we might make for ourselves, family, friends and companions. Human greed and vanity deregulate or restructure the world and our best responses to it. This is as true today as ever. But in poems and music, paintings and sculptures, the structures of ships and the design of our dwelling-places, art of all kinds, there are ways to oppose and resist those natural and unnatural impositions. The appetite for self-extension is humanly healthy, so long as it does not reach to the point of bloated self-regard.

The poem is based on the premise of the accepted limits of necessity and the noble work of pushing against them all. Through the living creatures it depicts and the motion it enacts on its voyage, the poem moves not *towards* but *within* a poetics of the environment.

It is an enactment of virtues: different skills, coordination, weathering, strength, suppleness and subtlety, loyalty, determination, hope. It is a play, a drama, a weathering of storm.

It occupies space through time. Its place may be geographically charted yet its moment comes again in every articulation, every reading, silent or voiced, alone or in company. Its historical context, place and space, may be described in such detail as I have given but like any work of great literature its intimation is of human potential. The significance of that does not end. It comes to rest, though, in the prospect of the future.

WORKS CITED AND FURTHER READING

Black, Ronald. 'Alasdair mac Mhaighstir Alasdair and the New Gaelic Poetry'. *The Edinburgh History of Scottish Literature Volume Two: Enlightenment, Britain and Empire (1707–1918)*. Ed. Ian Brown, Thomas Owen Clancy, Murray Pittock, and Susan Manning (Period ed.). Edinburgh: Edinburgh University Press, 2007. 110–24.

———. *The Campbells of the Ark: Men of Argyll in 1745 Volume One: The Inner Circle*. Edinburgh: John Donald, 2017; *The Campbells of the Ark: Men of Argyll in 1745 Volume Two: The Outer Circle*. Edinburgh: John Donald, 2017.

Dressler, Camille, and D. W. Stiubhart, eds. *Alexander MacDonald: Bard of the Gaelic Enlightenment/Alasdair Mac Mhaighstir Alasdair, Bard an t-Soilleara-chaidh Ghaidhealaich*. South Lochs, The Isle of Lewis: The Islands Book Trust,

2012. See especially Murray Pittock 'Jacobite Society and Culture in the Age of Alasdair mac Mhaighstir Alasdair' (56–62), Meg Bateman, 'The Bard and the Birlinn' (74–84), and Gavin Parsons, 'The Birlinn and the Bard' (85–89).

Lowell, Robert. *Imitations*. London: Faber and Faber, 1971.

MacLachlan, Christopher, ed. *Crossing the Highland Line: Cross-Currents in Eighteenth-Century Scottish Writing*. Glasgow: Association for Scottish Literary Studies, 2009. See especially Ronald Black, 'Sharing the Honour: Mac Mhgr Alastair and the Lowlands' (45–56), and Christopher MacLachlan, 'Literary Edinburgh in the Time of Alexander MacDonald' (57–66).

Nicolson, Adam. *Seamanship: The Story of the Sea, a Man and a Ship*. London: HarperCollins, 2004.

Strohe, Silke. *Uneasy Subjects: Postcolonialism and Scottish Gaelic Poetry*. Amsterdam, New York: Rodopi, 2011.

ENGLISH-LANGUAGE VERSIONS OF 'THE BIRLINN OF CLANRANALD'

Barr, Gordon. Full Text, available online at www.moidart.org.uk/…/gbarram-cma/gordon%20ama%20part%202.pdf. Accessed 26 February 2015.

Black, Ronald. (b.1946). Extracts, in *An Lasair: Anthology of 18th Century Scottish Gaelic Verse*. Edinburgh: Birlinn, 2001.

Blackie, J. S. (1809–1895). Extracts, in *The Language and Literature of the Scottish Highlands*. Edinburgh: Edmonston and Douglas, 1876.

Crichton Smith, Iain. (1928–1998). Extract, 'The Storm' (1977), from *New Collected Poems*. Manchester: Carcanet, 2011.

MacDiarmid, Hugh. (1892–1978). Full Text, Made with the help of Sorley MacLean, *The Birlinn of Clanranald*. St Andrews: The Abbey Bookshop, 1935; reprinted in *The Golden Treasury of Scottish Poetry*. London: Macmillan, 1941.

MacDonald, A., Minister of Killearnan, and Rev. A. MacDonald, Minister of Kiltarlity: Full Text, in *The Poems of Alexander MacDonald (Mac Mhaighstir Alasdair)*. Ed. with trans., Glossary and Notes (Inverness: Northern Counties Newspaper and Printing and Publishing Company, 1924).

Nicolson, Alexander. (1827–1893). Full Text, in *Echoes of the Sea: Scotland & the Sea—An Anthology*. Ed. Brian D. Osborne and Ronald Armstrong. Edinburgh: Canongate, 1998.

Pattison, Thomas. (1828–1865). Full Text, in *The Gaelic Bards*. Glasgow: Archibald Sinclair, 1890.

Riach, Alan. (b.1957). *The Birlinn of Clanranald: The Original Gaelic Poem by Alasdair Mac Mhaighstir Alasdair (Alexander MacDonald) with a New English Version*. Newtyle, Angus: Kettillonia, 2015.

Thomson, Derick (1921–2012). Extracts, in *An Introduction to Gaelic Poetry* London: Victor Gollancz, 1974.

Troubled Inheritances in R. L. Stevenson's *Kidnapped* and Conan Doyle's "The Adventure of the Priory School"

Tom Ue

Inheritance and narrative are inextricably intertwined. As Allan Hepburn has argued, "Inheritance implies transmission of property and thus creates the expectation of narrative sequence when possessions move from hand to hand. Stories about inheritance therefore concern the meaning of ownership and genealogy, both of which can be disturbed by the disinherited or those who refuse their inheritances" (3). Hepburn reads Conan Doyle's "The Five Orange Pips" (1891) as a Holmesian example whereby "legacies bear a taint that cannot be expiated; it can only be passed along in a genealogy of fatalities, as if property itself mortally afflicts its possessor" (5). He thus suggests a mismatch between the promise and the outcome of legacies in fiction, and for the mutual dependence of property and stories:

> All legacies are troubled, in the sense that they promise happiness in material or financial form and regularly deliver, in fiction at least, complication and unhappiness. By evolving incidents out of the primary matter of

T. Ue (✉)
Dalhousie University, Halifax, NS, Canada

© The Author(s) 2019
M. Szuba and J. Wolfreys (eds.), *The Poetics of Space and Place in Scottish Literature*, Geocriticism and Spatial Literary Studies,
https://doi.org/10.1007/978-3-030-12645-2_3

inheritance—a death, a will, a fortune, a usurper, a conflict, another will, a second death, a new heir, a fresh dilemma—property perpetuates itself. The sequence of events varies, but narratives of inheritance are de facto bracketed by death. Property requires its stories as much as stories require property. (5)

Examples of inheritance are especially prominent in Victorian writing. As John R. Reed notes, "the subject of inheritance is so familiar as to be almost offensive" (268). This plot device typically bears minimal spiritual significance, contributing only narrative interest, yet "[t]he many moral complications and resolutions growing out of the inheritance convention included some interesting variations" (270, 272). Entangled with issues of identity, the inheritance plot operates, unsurprisingly, as a kind of "moral barometer" at a time when notions of the earthly and the spiritual, and of wealth and faith, are increasingly brought together (275–276). "In Victorian literature", Reed finds, "the poor, by virtue and high-mindedness could prove themselves worthy of the highest award that nineteenth-century England could think to bestow—land, and wealth, and married bliss. In a similar way, the wealthy, by proving that, despite their wealth, they had the moral fiber and the practical ability to live fruitful lives, merited the same award of land and wealth that was their ordinary privilege" (278).

With the dawning of modernity, the promise that one will be rewarded for his or her virtue and fidelity is displaced by "a more realistic assessment of an existence in which any inheritance was doubtful and only the inextinguishable heritage of the individual will and imagination could confirm its possession" (288). Stevenson's and Conan Doyle's fiction routinely reflects on, and comments upon, such dynamics. When Jim and his mother try (unsuccessfully) to recruit volunteers from the neighbouring hamlet to help defend the Admiral Benbow in *Treasure Island* (1883), for example, the latter claims a portion of the late Billy Bones' legacy as money owed to Jim's father and, consequently, a part of Jim's rightful inheritance: "She would not, she declared, lose money that belonged to her fatherless boy" (21). Once the chest is opened, she insists: "I'll show these rogues that I'm an honest woman ... I'll have my dues, and not a farthing over" (23). Meanwhile, inheritance becomes a means by which Conan Doyle explores historical, familial, and colonial legacies in *The Sign of Four* (1890) and *The Hound of the Baskervilles* (1902).[1] This chapter takes, as a point of departure, Conan Doyle's observations about the structural logic of the masculine novel and, by extension, the masculine story to analyse his conversation with Stevenson regarding inheritance. It attends to Stevenson's *Kidnapped* (1886) and Conan Doyle's "The Adventure of the Priory School" (1904), in both of which inheritance plots are obstructed by abduction ones. My central claims are that the abduction plots allow these writers to ruminate on the (mis)managements of, and the (in)equalities caused by, inheritance and, in so doing, call its conventions into question. If, as Reed argues, the typical inheritance story involves "sudden acquisitions of wealth that enable lost heirs to cease their wanderings and settle down to happy and useful lives with the mates of their choice" (281), then this chapter contributes to its theorisation by recovering the central role that abduction plays and by revealing more extensive cross-pollination between Stevenson's and Conan Doyle's projects.

STEVENSON AND CONAN DOYLE

On 20 November 1888, in the run-up to *Micah Clarke*'s (1889) publication, Conan Doyle wrote to his mother Mary Doyle:

> You must not say that Cloomber [1889] is as good as the Pavilion [1880], for you should never let your kind maternal feelings cloud your critical judgment. The Pavilion is far the better: 1) Because the characters of Northmour Cassilis, Clara &c all stand out very clear, which none of mine do 2) Because it is strong without preternatural help, which I think is always more to an author's credit 3) Because it is more compact and the interest never flags for a moment. I think however that if you said Micah was better than either Kidnapped [1886] or The Black Arrow [1888] you might not be wrong. (256)[2]

Conan Doyle compares Stevenson's "The Pavilion on the Links" favourably to his novel *The Mystery of Cloomber*, which was serialised in *The Pall Mall Gazette* between 10 and 29 September 1888; still, he had considerable faith in *Micah*, confident that it is stronger than two of his contemporary's greatest hits. He comments more extensively in "Mr. Stevenson's Methods in Fiction", an essay for *The National Review* on January 1890 that reviews *The Master of Ballantrae* (1889) and that surveys Stevenson's career to date. Conan Doyle declares Stevenson's latest offering a masterpiece: "If a strong story, strongly told, full of human interest, and absolutely original in its situations, makes a masterpiece, then this may lay claim to the title" (646). While he acknowledges the imprecision "by which genius can be measured and tested" (646) and the need for the lapse of at least a generation for the public to make such decisions, Conan Doyle argues that Stevenson has already distinguished himself with two earlier outings.[3] Regarding "Pavilion", he remarks, "Mr. Stevenson's style is always most pure, and his imagination is usually vivid, but in this one tale the very happiest use of words is wedded to the most thrilling, most concentrated interest" (647). The characters "stand out so strongly and so clearly—the more Titanic for the lurid background against which they move" (647). Accordingly, the *Strange Case of Dr Jekyll and Mr Hyde* (1886) will continue to resonate with new readers: "The allegory within it would lengthen its days, even should new methods and changes of taste take the charm from the story. As long as man remains a dual being, as long as he is in danger of being conquered by his worse self, and, with every defeat, finds it the more difficult to make a stand, so long *Dr. Jekyl* [sic] will have a personal and most vital meaning to every poor, struggling human being" (647). Conan Doyle is disappointed with many of the short stories in the *New Arabian Nights* (1882), *More New Arabian Nights: The Dynamiter* (1885), and *The Merry Men and Other Tables and Fables* (1887) and with novels like *The Black Arrow* (1888) and *The Wrong Box* (1889). Yet, even in the story that "misses its mark, there will always remain some strange, telling phrase, some new vivid conception, so apt or so striking, that it is not to be dismissed from the memory" (648).

Stevenson is a master of both the short story and the novel, particularly the former: "Poe, Nathaniel Hawthorne, Stevenson: those are the three, put them in what order you will, who are the greatest exponents of the short story in our language" (649). He grows out of the influence of George Meredith, moving "from the subtle, dainty lines of *Prince Otto* [1885] to the direct, matter-of-fact, eminently practical and Defoe-like narratives of *Treasure Island* [1883] and that of *Kidnapped*" (650). Regarding these two latter adventure stories:

> Both are admirable pieces of English, well conceived, well told, striking the reader at every turn with some novel situation, some new combination of words which just fits the sense as a cap fits a nipple. *Treasure Island* is

perhaps the better story, while *Kidnapped* may have the longer lease of life as being an excellent and graphic sketch of the state of the Highlands after the last Jacobite insurrection. Each contains one novel and admirable character, Alan Breck in the one, and Long John in the other. (650–651)

If the strength of characters, such as Long John, derives from Stevenson's prose style, which frequently operates "by comparison, innuendo, or indirect reference", then the novels' limitations rest upon their lack of "female interest": "We feel that it is an apotheosis of the boy's story—the penny number of our youth *in excelsis*" (651). Conan Doyle attributes this aspect to the "modern masculine novel", which he sees as the novel's attempt to meditate on matters beyond marriage: "In the career of the average man his marriage is an incident, and a momentous incident; but it is only one of several. He is swayed by many strong emotions; his business, his ambitions, his friendships, his struggles with the recurrent dangers and difficulties which tax a man's wisdom and his courage" (652). Nonetheless, Conan Doyle is entirely satisfied with *Ballantrae*, finding it "broader in its scope, and freer in its handling than either of its predecessors [*Treasure Island* and *Kidnapped*]" (653). He reflects on Stevenson's "gift of silence", his preoccupation with story over ruminations about life and the universe (654), and praises "his curious instinct for saying in the briefest space just those few words which stamp the impression upon the reader's mind" (656). Finally, Conan Doyle credits Stevenson for making the mutilated villain his own, "he handles it so artistically that it never fails to produce its effect" (656).

Stevenson, in turn, was enthusiastic about Conan Doyle's fiction, and notably the Holmes stories. In correspondence with Edward L. Burlingame, on c. 2 January 1893 and on c. 5 December 1893, he asks for *The Adventures of Sherlock Holmes* (1892) and *The Sign of Four* respectively (4, 192), and with Charles Scribner, on 17 July 1893, for *The Refugees* (1893) (134). On 5 April 1893, Stevenson commends the detective's creator for the pleasures proffered by his stories:

> Dear Sir, You have taken many occasions to make yourself agreeable to me, for which I might in decency have thanked you earlier. It is now my turn; and I hope you will allow me to offer you my compliments on your very ingenious and very interesting adventures of Sherlock Holmes. That is the class of literature that I like when I have the toothache. As a matter of fact,

it was a pleurisy I was enjoying when I took the volume up; and it will interest you as a medical man to know that the cure was for the moment effectual. Only the one thing troubles me: can this be my old friend Joe Bell? (49–50)[4]

Later that year, Stevenson will report to his friend, in a letter dated 23 August, how he related "The Adventure of the Engineer's Thumb" (1892), a story from the *Adventures*, to his native overseer Simelē. Although he had to explain the story's cultural references, his audience's response was overwhelmingly positive: "[I]f you could have seen the drawn, anxious features and the bright, feverish eyes of Simelē, you would have (for the moment at least) tasted glory. You might perhaps think that, were you to come to Samoa, you might be introduced as the Author of 'The Engineer's Thumb'. Disabuse yourself. They do not know what it is to make up a story. 'The Engineer's Thumb' (God forgive me) was narrated as a piece of actual and factual history" (155). On 18 May 1894, Stevenson asks Baxter for "The second Sherlock Holmes book by Conan Doyle" (292). He writes, again, to Conan Doyle on 9 September 1894 to praise his article in the "My First Book" series in the *Idler*, one to which Stevenson had also contributed: "If you found anything to entertain you in my *Treasure Island* article, it may amuse you to know that you owe it entirely to yourself. *Your* 'First Book' was by some accident read aloud one night in my Baronial 'All. I was consumedly amused by it, so was the whole family, and we proceeded to hunt up back *Idlers* and read the whole series" (360).

ABDUCTION AND INHERITANCE

"To read Stevenson", Adrian Poole observes, "is to be absorbed in reading male faces and bodies, the signs by which men, boys, and beasts distinguish themselves from each other" (260). Both *Kidnapped* and "The Priory School" are populated by embedded narratives; both exemplify the modern masculine story that Conan Doyle describes; and both explore the applications of socially constructed power. Ian Duncan writes, in his introduction to the former, "Most readers find the inner story, a rough idyll of outlaw friendship and cross-country flight, more compelling than the story of the kidnapped heir that brackets it" (ix). In what follows, I focus on the narrative frame to suggest that it sustains a metaphor regarding estate and man, one that assumes significance for reading David's dealings with the house of Shaws' landlord. This allegory is established early on, when Mr. Campbell, the minister, asks David if he is sorry to leave the village. David replies:

> Why, sir, ... if I knew where I was going, or what was likely to become of me, I would tell you candidly. Essendean is a good place indeed, and I have been very happy there; but then I have never been anywhere else. My father and mother, since they are both dead, I shall be no nearer to in Essendean than in the Kingdom of Hungary; and to speak truth, if I thought I had a chance to better myself where I was going I would go with a good will. (7)

Places, as we see here, are defined by, and imbricated with, the people that we associate with them. David's first impressions of the house of Shaws, in the form of gossip, are underwhelming. When he asks for directions, he discovers that the house's name "seemed to surprise those of whom I sought my way" (11), and repeated experiences make him think "there was something strange about the Shaws itself" (11). More extended conversation with a carter brings forth an explicit warning: "Well, mannie, ... it's nane of my affairs; but ye seem a decent-spoken lad; and if ye'll take a word from me, ye'll keep clear of the Shaws" (12). A barber cryptically tells David that Mr. Balfour is "nae kind of a man, nae kind of a man at all" (12), and Jennet Clouston directs him to his destination—"a great bulk of building standing very bare upon a green in the bottom of the next valley" and "a kind of ruin; no road led up to it; no smoke arose from any of the chimneys; nor was there any semblance of a garden" (12–13)—and goes so far as to curse the lord and his house. Stevenson holds in contrast the house and its environs: "The more I looked, the pleasanter that country-side appeared; being all set with hawthorn bushes full of flowers; the fields dotted with sheep; a fine flight of rooks in the sky; and every sign of a kind soil and climate; and yet the barrack in the midst of it went against my fancy" (13).

The incongruity between the house and its setting economically invokes the estate's unrealised potentials. Under better management, we infer, it would have looked inhabited and welcoming; and it would have appeared less obtrusive in relation to its immediate surroundings. Closer inspection does not make the house more inviting: "Presently it [a little faint track] brought me to stone uprights, with an unroofed lodge beside them, and coats of arms upon the top. A main entrance it was plainly meant to be, but never finished; instead of gates of wrought iron, a pair of hurdles were tied across with a straw rope; and as there were no park walls, nor any sign of avenue, the track that I was following passed on the right hand of the pillars, and went wandering on toward the house" (13). One of the house's wings is, in fact, unfinished. Ebenezer, in his tall nightcap and with his loaded blunderbuss, is every bit as decrepit as his house, his attire registering his lack of care:

> He was a mean, stooping, narrow-shouldered, clay-faced creature; and his age might have been anything between fifty and seventy. His nightcap was of flannel, and so was the nightgown that he wore, instead of coat and waistcoat, over his ragged shirt. He was long unshaved; but what most distressed and even daunted me, he would neither take his eyes away from me nor look me fairly in the face. (16)

Just as the house had seen better days—Ebenezer explains how his father had begun to enlarge the house, an operation that he had aborted because he thought it wasteful—David's uncle was not always as he is. An innkeeper recalls: "He's a wicked auld man, and there's many would like to see him girning in a tow: Jennet Clouston and mony mair that he was harried out of house and hame. And yet he was ance a fine young fellow, too. But that was before the sough gaed abroad about Mr Alexander; that was like the death of him" (36–37). Mr. Rankeillor, the consequential lawyer, will corroborate this account much later in the novel: "But your uncle, Mr David, was not always old, ... and what may perhaps surprise you more, not always ugly. He had a fine, gallant air; people stood in their doors to look after him, as he went by upon a mettle horse. I have seen it with these eyes, and I ingenuously confess, not altogether without envy ..." (180).

Kidnapped may be read in terms of David's negotiation between the economies of coin and letter, that is, in terms of "Davie 'grow[ing] up' as he leaves behind the linguistic and monetary economies of a separate 'undeveloped,' preliterate society" (Sorensen 285). Stevenson appears to interlay temporal and spatial coordinates and to locate separate states of social development in the Highlands and the Lowlands through their representational exchange systems (279). Nevertheless, as Janet Sorensen persuasively argues, Stevenson "asserts an intricate and wide-ranging vision of linguistic, cultural, and material exchange that challenges both fixed divisions between 'developed' and 'undeveloped' economic spaces and the false analogy that would make the symbolic economies of language and money the same" (279). This is apparent in the novel's understanding of the inheritance plot. Mr. Rankeillor tells David that his father had married his mother, while Ebenezer took the estate. According to the lawyer, this arrangement is lamentable for all of the stakeholders. What is striking is the effect of Ebenezer's narrative on David. David comes to emphasise, if not sympathise, with his uncle, as he wonders: "And yet that is certainly the strangest part of all ... that a man's nature should thus change" (181). The abduction plot halts and defamiliarises the inheritance story by revealing that it is neither as fair nor as natural as it may seem. David's experiences inform his scheme to repossess his estate. The chapter titled "I Come into My Kingdom" sees Ebenezer tested and his character realised more fully: he would not have David killed even if it means paying more (though, we might think, he had sent David up a broken-off staircase but chapters before); and he confesses to having hired Captain Hoseason to kidnap and sell David. Ebenezer and Mr. Rankeillor agree on terms that confer to the former a home and some financial security: "By the terms of this, my uncle bound himself to satisfy Rankeillor as to his intromissions, and to pay me two clear thirds of the yearly income of Shaws" (191). Ebenezer may have lost in love early in life, but he does not go without a roof in his old age *only* as a result of this new arrangement. As Poole puts it, "the novel ends with the wicked kinsman still in possession .... David can see the peak of his uncle's nightcap in one of the top windows 'bobbing up and down and back and forward, like the head of a rabbit from a burrow'" (263). That the chapter concludes with David "lay[ing] till dawn, looking at the fire on the roof and planning the future" (191) gestures towards the possibility that, under his management, the house of Shaws' potentials would be realised, but that is well into the future. Poole writes of David, in the present, "He is still adrift, at sea one might say, or yearning to be back there and out there, not settled safely inside" (263).

Conan Doyle's "The Priory School", subsequently collected in *The Return of Sherlock Holmes* (1905), similarly foregrounds an inheritance story. Recent work by Douglas Kerr has opened up new ways for thinking about law and order in relation to Conan Doyle's life and fiction. Conan Doyle neglects the fates of criminals who are sent to prison and omits information in the Holmes stories relating to prisons, court, police station and procedure, and even the crimes with which police regularly deal: "In fact there is a relatively narrow suite of crimes and disturbances in Conan Doyle's fiction, and a perfunctory account of punishments. Indeed ... on the evidence of his stories crime and punishment seems to be the one [cultural domain] that he knew and cared least about" (136–137). Through close readings of the first four stories in *Adventures*, and particularly "The Red-Headed League" (1891), Kerr attributes such gaps to Conan Doyle's implicit faith in the legal system: "This insouciance about the machinery of justice suggests some complacency: the police may be flatfooted and need to be corrected by Holmes, but then the institutions of law and order can be confidently left to get on with their business" (142). Holmes can depend upon the apparatus of the law—"its operations did not need to be shown, they could just be assumed" (154)—but Conan Doyle himself will experience its shortcomings at close hand when he becomes involved with George Edalji's case in 1906, "in England, or at least in Staffordshire, in 1907, the institutions supposed to guarantee that ambience of law and order—the courts and judges and juries, the police and their commanders and their procedure, the law itself, the penal system, the government bureaucracy under the oversight of Parliament—could not be relied on" (154–155). My reading of "The Priory School" incorporates, and expands, Kerr's by attending to some ways in which Conan Doyle interlays moral and legal crimes. For Conan Doyle, as for Stevenson, family stories are especially hospitable for such social explorations. As Andrew Glazzard observes, "The plots of the Holmes stories, like those of the Victorian novels with which Doyle was deeply familiar, turn again and again on a suppressed family history. The Holmes saga is insistently concerned with the discovery of what goes on under the domestic roof ..." (92). Where Stevenson reconciles David with his uncle, Conan Doyle makes explicit moral judgment through Holmes, while offering implicit criticism of the forces that indulge the Duke.

Joseph A. Kestner discerns a pattern in *Return*. Following "The Empty House" (1903), which sees Holmes' return from Reichenbach Falls, six stories involve "the defections of men from male codes and the male script", and six "the threat women present to males in the culture" (84). "The Priory School" is the fifth story in *Return*, and it fits squarely in the first cluster. The titular school's founder and principal Thorneycroft Huxtable seeks Holmes' services regarding the abduction of his pupil Arthur, the Duke of Holdernesse's son and heir. The former Cabinet Minister is one of the greatest and perhaps the wealthiest subjects of the Crown and he had recently separated from his Duchess, who now takes up residence in the South of France. Ten-year-old Arthur had disappeared from the school in the middle of the night, along with Heidegger, a German master, and Holmes is recruited to locate Arthur and to identify the culprit(s). Holmes discovers that James Wilder, the Duke's secretary, had orchestrated the abduction. Arthur was taken away by Reuben Hayes, the Duke's disgruntled former tenant and head coachman. Pursued by Heidegger, Hayes struck and killed the German master with a stick, and he confined Arthur in his public house, where he remains. Holmes successfully cracks the case—he arranges for Hayes' apprehension and determines the Duke to be responsible—though he is surprised, in turn, by his employer's revelations. Huxtable introduces Arthur as the Duke's "only son" (74), and Holmes' encyclopaedia confirms Arthur to be his "[h]eir and only child" (74). James is, despite these insistences, the Duke's firstborn and Arthur's older half-brother. "When I was a very young man", the Duke relates, "I loved with such a love as comes only once in a lifetime. I offered the lady marriage, but she refused it on the grounds that such a match might mar my career" (93). As in *Kidnapped*, the abduction plot opens up the inheritance story to increased scrutiny. By birth, James is dispossessed of his claims to both his father and his estate. The Duke confesses to Holmes and Watson that he could not acknowledge James' paternity, even if he provided for him materially: "He surprised my secret, and has presumed ever since upon the claim which he has upon me, and upon his power of provoking a scandal which would be abhorrent to me" (93). The Duke protects James out of love for his mother and for his own reputation. Through James, he may well be imagining a different permutation of himself and

the life he is leading. As Andrew Miller has insightfully argued in relation to realist fiction and counterfactual narratives, children can be read
as both an extension of, and a departure from, oneself:

> [W]hen I am in the presence of children who have bodies like mine, my
> desire to inhabit another life is not obstructed but rather encouraged as
> I see my physical likeness (or something close enough if the desire is des-
> perate enough) out there in little. Children can present us—with whatever
> truth—the hope that our futures might be different from our pasts, that
> indeed we might become new people, reborn, living beyond our deaths: a
> Paul Dombey to survive Paul Dombey. (124)[5]

The story's tension is centred less on the Duke's motivations for helping his elder son than on the larger debates concerning moral and legal
crimes, particularly the Duke's treatment of his social inferiors (i.e. the
other characters). When Holmes demands his fee after disclosing Arthur's
whereabouts and identifying the culprit, the Duke replies: "I shall be as
good as my word, Mr. Holmes. I am about to write your check, however
unwelcome the information which you have gained may be to me. When
the offer was first made, I little thought the turn which events might
take. But you and your friend are men of discretion, Mr. Holmes?" (92).
The Duke doubles the reward that he had originally promised in hopes
to purchase Holmes' and Watson's silence: "I must put it plainly, Mr.
Holmes. If only you two know of this incident, there is no reason why
it should go any farther. I think twelve thousand pounds is the sum that
I owe you, is it not?" (92). As Holmes protests, the Duke has neglected
the unfortunate Heidegger, who was killed half-dressed in his chase. The
Duke blames Hayes, argues that James is morally but not legally guilty,
and finally makes a plea to the detective: "A man cannot be condemned
for a murder at which he was not present, and which he loathes and
abhors as much as you do. The instant that he heard of it he made a complete confession to me, so filled was he with horror and remorse" (92).
As Kestner and Glazzard argue, the Duke's defence "is one of Doyle's
most blistering accounts of the transgressive behaviour of the aristocracy"
(Kestner 90). Conan Doyle implies, through his behaviour, that access to
social and material advantage ought to be earned as much as inherited:

> [T]he duke assumes that his social inferior will accept the bribe and acqui-
> esce to the aristocratic demand. Not only that, but the duke proceeds to
> ascribe guilt and blame. ... That Wilder has confessed to the duke and

expressed remorse is, in this world of privilege, sufficient to atone for murder, kidnapping, and deception. (Glazzard 97)

Holmes reprimands the Duke on both moral and legal grounds: "In the first place, your Grace, I am bound to tell you that you have placed yourself in a most serious position in the eyes of the law. You have condoned a felony, and you have aided the escape of a murderer, for I cannot doubt that any money which was taken by James Wilder to aid his accomplice in his flight came from your purse" (94–95).[6] The detective criticises the Duke's treatment of Arthur; orders a servant to bring him home; and promises the Duke that he will not make public why Hayes, who is certainly headed for the gallows, had kidnapped Arthur. Holmes tries to orchestrate long-term reparation by seeing that James leaves the Duke's household—James will head to Australia—and that the Duke and Duchess will be reunited.

Elsewhere, I have argued that marriage in George Gissing's *Veranilda* (1904) neither obviates nor mitigates the larger, social problems that the novel poses (108–110). The same argument might, with dexterity, be applied to this story. The Duke failed Hayes, whose complaint of wrongful termination is inserted as an aside: "I've less reason to wish the Dook well than most men … for I was his head coachman once, and cruel bad he treated me. It was him that sacked me without a character on the word of a lying corn-chandler" (87). Indeed, Huxtable introduces the Duke as being "never very friendly with anyone", "He is completely immersed in large public questions, and is rather inaccessible to all ordinary emotions" (77). More germane to the argument that I am making, the Duke's failure to integrate James more fully into his household encourages his criminal ambitions and plans:

> I answer that there was a great deal which was unreasoning and fanatical in the hatred which he bore my heir. In his view he should himself have been heir of all my estates, and he deeply resented those social laws which made it impossible. At the same time, he had a definite motive also. He was eager that I should break the entail, and he was of opinion that it lay in my power to do so. He intended to make a bargain with me—to restore Arthur if I break the entail, and so make it possible for the estate to be left to him by will. (94)

According to the *Fines and Recoveries Act 1833*, any provision "by which lands are or shall be entailed, or agreed or directed to be entailed, shall be deemed a settlement", and once an entail becomes a settlement, it can be broken by a Deed of Disentailment.[7] The Duke may opt for the term "bargain" instead of "blackmail", but his account exposes James' inability to picture a fairer system wherein inheritance and opportunity are more evenly distributed. This social question remains unanswered though the crime is solved, and James continues to be Arthur's less fortunate counterpart.[8] Strikingly, the story ends not with this case but with the discovery that Hayes was using horseshoes dug from the moat of Holdernesse Hall to counterfeit cows' tracks, shoes that the marauding Barons of Holdernesse had apparently used in the Middle Ages to misdirect pursuers. As Glazzard asserts, this material artefact links the Duke's inheritance to "violence, deceit and force", providing a plausible reason, perhaps, for James' propensity for cruelty (98). The estate may owe its wealth, at least partially, to criminal activity, but what is more, this context situates the case in a larger genealogy of injustices. In *The Hound of the Baskervilles* (1902), Conan Doyle suggests, through Sir Charles and Sir Henry, the potential for improving Baskerville Hall and the larger Devon community; in "The Priory School", he similarly invites us to look forward to what is to come. The charming and once happy Arthur, like Stevenson's David, carries some potential to bring about rectification.

Acknowledgements I am enormously grateful to Noel Brown, John James, Monika Szuba, and Julian Wolfreys for their incisive reading and productive interlocution, and to my students at Dalhousie University and the University of Toronto Scarborough, with whom I have discussed a number of Conan Doyle's works. I thank Christine Bolus-Reichert, Ian Duncan, Daniel Stashower, and Simon Stern for their help and encouragement and, for their assistance, Lindsay McNiff, Frank Tong, and the staff of Dalhousie University Libraries and the University of Toronto Libraries. This paper was written with the support of Dalhousie University, the Social Sciences and Humanities Research Council of Canada, and the University of Toronto Scarborough.

NOTES

1. See my discussion of Conan Doyle and his writing in *The Companion to Victorian Popular Culture*.
2. I am grateful to Daniel Stashower for directing me to this letter.
3. See, for comparison, George Gissing's *The Private Papers of Henry Ryecroft* (1903). Notwithstanding the differences between Conan Doyle's and

Gissing's projects, they make similar arguments regarding the need for subsequent generations of readers to determine a work's value.

4. For Conan Doyle's response, and an account of their exchange, see notes 1–2 on page 50 of the *Letters*.

5. Kestner makes a similar suggestion when he links James' criminality to his father's and the aristocracy's atavistic behaviour (91). Glazzard, meanwhile, proposes incest and paedophilia as possible reasons for the Duke's determination to protect James (94–96).

6. For an illuminating discussion of the place of trials in the realist novel, see Hilary M. Schor's "Show-Trials: Character, Conviction and the Law in Victorian Fiction". Schor examines Walter Scott's *The Heart of Midlothian* (1818), Elizabeth Gaskell's *Mary Barton* (1848), and George Eliot's *Adam Bede* (1859) and *Felix Holt, the Radical* (1866) to argue that they "imagine the sense of a trial not only as 'mere show' but as a show genuinely 'exemplary' in a variety of ways"; that these trials show "not the power of law but the 'heart' of the heroine who through her testimony oppose her credibility to the false legalism of the trial"; and that "the 'trials' within the novel serve as well to indict the novel's version of truth" (182).

7. I thank Simon Stern for this information.

8. See Nils Clausson's *Arthur Conan Doyle's Art of Fiction: A Revaluation*, particularly chapter 1, for an insightful discussion of this formal feature in Conan Doyle's writing.

Works Cited

Clausson, Nils. *Arthur Conan Doyle's Art of Fiction: A Revaluation*. Newcastle upon Tyne: Cambridge Scholars Publishing, 2018. Print.

Conan Doyle, Arthur. *Arthur Conan Doyle: A Life in Letters*. Ed. Jon Lellenberg, Daniel Stashower, and Charles Foley. London: Harper Perennial, 2008. Print.

———. *The Complete Sherlock Holmes*, 2 Vols. Intro. and Notes by Kyle Freeman. New York: Barnes & Noble Books, 2003. Print.

———. 'Mr. Stevenson's Methods in Fiction'. *The National Review* 14:83 (January 1890): 646–57. Web. 14 October 2018.

Duncan, Ian. 'Introduction'. *Kidnapped*. Ed. Robert Louis Stevenson. Oxford: Oxford University Press, 2014. ix–xxvi. Print.

Fines and Recoveries Act 1833. UK Legislation. The National Archives. Web. 14 October 2018.

Gissing, George. *George Gissing, the Private Papers of Henry Ryecroft*. Ed. Tom Ue. Edinburgh: Edinburgh University Press, forthcoming. Print.

Glazzard, Andrew. *The Case of Sherlock Holmes: Secrets and Lies in Conan Doyle's Detective Fiction.* Edinburgh: Edinburgh University Press, 2018. Print.

Hepburn, Allan. 'Introduction: Inheritance and Disinheritance in the Novel'. *Troubled Legacies: Narrative and Inheritance.* Toronto: University of Toronto Press, 2007. 3–25. Print.

Kerr, Douglas. *Conan Doyle: Writing, Profession, and Practice.* Oxford: Oxford University Press, 2013. Print.

Kestner, Joseph A. *The Edwardian Detective, 1901–1915.* London: Routledge-Taylor & Francis Group, 2018. Web. 14 October 2018. Routledge Revivals.

Miller, Andrew. 'Lives Unled in Realist Fiction'. *Representations* 98:1 (Spring 2007): 118–34. Web. 14 October 2018. JSTOR.

Poole, Adrian. 'Robert Louis Stevenson'. *The Cambridge Companion to English Novelists.* Ed. Adrian Poole. Cambridge: Cambridge University Press, 2009. 258–71. Print.

Reed, John R. *Victorian Conventions.* Athens: Ohio University Press, 1975. Print.

Schor, Hilary M. 'Show-Trials: Character, Conviction and the Law in Victorian Fiction'. *Law and Literature* 11:2 (1999): 179–95. Web. 14 October 2018.

Sorensen, Janet. '"Belts of Gold" and "Twenty-Pounders": Robert Louis Stevenson's Textualized Economies'. *Criticism* 42:3 (Summer 2000): 279–97. Web. 14 October 2018. JSTOR.

Stevenson, Robert Louis. *Kidnapped.* Ed. Ian Duncan. Oxford: Oxford University Press, 2014. Print.

———. *The Letters of Robert Louis Stevenson,* Vol. 8, January 1893–December 1894. Ed. Bradford A. Booth and Ernest Mehew. New Haven: Yale University Press, 1995. Print.

———. *Treasure Island.* Ed. John Seelye. London: Penguin Group, 1999. Print.

Ue, Tom. '*The Adventures of Sherlock Holmes.*' *The Companion to Victorian Popular Culture.* Ed. Kevin A. Morrison. Jefferson: McFarland, 2018. 3–5. Print.

———. '*Arthur Conan Doyle.*' *The Companion to Victorian Popular Culture.* Ed. Kevin A. Morrison. Jefferson: McFarland, 2018. 55–56. Print.

———. 'Indecision, Inaction, and Public Politics in Gissing's *Veranilda.*' *Self and World.* Ed. Monika Szuba and Julian Wolfreys. Special Issue of *Victoriographies* 8:1 (March 2018): 100–19. Print.

———. '*The Sign of Four.*' *The Companion to Victorian Popular Culture.* Ed. Kevin A. Morrison. Jefferson: McFarland, 2018. 223–25. Print.

———. '*A Study in Scarlet.*' *The Companion to Victorian Popular Culture.* Ed. Kevin A. Morrison. Jefferson: McFarland, 2018. 241–43. Print.

PART II

Essaying Place: Fiction and Non-fiction Prose Representations

From Dramatic Space to Narrative Place: George Mackay Brown's *Time in a Red Coat*

Paul Barnaby

INTRODUCTION

George Mackay Brown's 1984 novel *Time in a Red Coat* traverses hundreds of years of history and a succession of both geographical and allegorical spaces,[1] as its heroine voyages from East Asia to Orkney in a quest to 'slay the dragon of war, or at least to reconcile the dragon with the peaceable creatures of the earth' (197). The extensive collection of Brown manuscripts at Edinburgh University Library (GB 237 Coll-50) reveals that the novel itself marks the terminus of a lengthy journey from drama to fiction, evolving from a play of the same name on which Brown worked from 1979 to 1982.[2] This essay will chart its passage from dramatic to narrative time and space, analysing a growing tension between the use of archetypal locations and situations and the increasing deployment of specific geographical and historical indicators.

Edinburgh University Library holds the following manuscripts (all handwritten):

P. Barnaby (✉)
Edinburgh University Library, Edinburgh, UK

© The Author(s) 2019   49
M. Szuba and J. Wolfreys (eds.), *The Poetics of Space and Place in Scottish Literature*, Geocriticism and Spatial Literary Studies,
https://doi.org/10.1007/978-3-030-12645-2_4

Gen. 2134/3/3: Consists of early drafts of the play (some bearing the working titles 'The Vagrant's Tale', 'So I'll Take my Pilgrimage', 'Thus I'll Take my Pilgrimage' or, simply, 'Pilgrimage'). Like many of Brown's working papers, these are written on an astonishing variety of media, including royalty statements, out-of-date calendars, magazine covers, order forms, and backs of envelopes. The drafts include embryonic versions of all scenes that appear in the final version of the play, except Scenes II, VII, and XIII. There are particularly numerous and varied drafts of the first and last scenes (six and nine versions, respectively). Only two draft scenes are dated in Brown's hand, '23 February 1979' and 'March 1979', respectively, but printed dates on Brown's impromptu writing materials suggest that 1979 is the most likely year of composition for all these materials.

MS 2841.1.1: Titled 'Time in a Red Coat: A Play' and marked 'Working draft 3-3-82', this is a fair copy, extensively corrected in places, of a complete fifteen-scene drama. It appears to represent the final state of the play before its transformation into a novel. A note at the end (f. 84) states that Brown worked on it between 1980 and 1982.

MS 2841.1.2: Consists of ten rejected versions of the play's concluding scene, some only fragmentary. Only two of these are dated in Brown's hand: MS 2841.1.2.6 (1 August 1979) and MS 2841.1.2.10 (4 November 1981). One page of MS 2841.1.2.3 is written on the back of an envelope with a postage date of 4 February 1980. MS 2841.1.2.4 is written on the backs of six envelopes with postage dates ranging from 10 to 18 December 1979. The other six versions give no indication of date of composition.

MS 2841.1.3: Consists of early drafts of 'The Magus', Chapter XIV of the published novel. There is no exact equivalent to this episode in any version of the play though it grows out of Scene XIII of MS 2841.1.1. One page of MS 2841.1.3.1 is dated 8 February 1982 in Brown's hand. Otherwise, there are no indications of date of composition.

MS 2841.2-3: A complete draft of the novel dated 'Spring/Autumn 1982'. This is a fair copy with instructions for typing and with very few corrections. With only minor alterations, it is essentially the novel as published. Logically, there must be at least one intervening draft stage missing from the Edinburgh University collection,[3] but it is clear that Brown wrote the novel very quickly (in under six months).

The table below clearly shows just how directly the final version of the play was transformed into the novel:

Play (MS 2841.1.1)		Novel (MS 2841.2-3)	
Scene		*Chapter*	
I	Far Away, Long Ago	I	The Masque
II	She Sets out on a Journey	II	Farewell, Mistress Poppyseed
III	She Comes to a Well of Clear Water	III	The Well
IV	She Is Ferried across a River	IV	River
V	She Comes to an Inn in the Snow	V	The Inn
VI	She Comes to a Nest of Dangerous Men [Nest of Vipers] in the Forest	VI	Forest
VII	She Comes to a Smithy between Forest and City	VII	The Smithy
VIII	She Comes to a Town without Townspeople, a Town all Broken Stone, a Town of Timbers Blackened and Smoking, a Towns of Rats below and Ravens above	VIII	The Taken Town
IX	She Comes to a Stony Acre at the Foothills of a Mountain	IX	A New Field
X	She Stands between Two Armies	X	The Mountain Village
		XI	The Battle
XI	The Longest Journey	XII	The Longest Journey
XII	The Tryst	XIII	The Tryst
XIII	She Watches [Lingers]: The Pageant Goes Past her [Loom of War Unfolds], Scene after Scene	XIV	The Magus
XIV	She Comes to a Village of Otters, Seabirds, and Shells	XV	Ottervoe
XV	She Completes the Circle	XVI	Old and Grey and Full of Sleep

As the scene and chapter titles suggest, the heroine Maurya follows an identical itinerary in play and novel,[4] though, as we shall see, precise geographical and temporal indicators are more frequent and consistent in the novel, and in both texts are more prevalent towards the beginning and end of her journey.

Maurya is born a princess in a palace during the Barbarian invasion of an East Asian Empire. Symbolic Black and White Guardians preside

over her birth and gift her a bag of coins and a flute, respectively (Scene
I/Chapter I). On her wedding day, she escapes from the home of the
nurse who has hidden her from the Barbarians, and embarks on a journey to kill or tame the dragon of war (Scene II/Chapter II). She comes
to a well that has been poisoned to repel invaders. Suspected of being a
spy, she flees towards a river (Scene III/Chapter III). Ferried across the
river, she encounters a floating corpse (Scene IV/Chapter IV). She takes
shelter in an inn, and when it is set alight by marauding troops, helps
extinguish the flames (Scene V/Chapter V). Threatened by a band of
deserters in a forest, she is magically transformed into a tree (Scene VI/
Chapter VI). She encounters a blacksmith who has abandoned his peace-
time work to forge cannonballs (Scene VII, Chapter VII). She enters an
occupied city and witnesses the execution of hostages in reprisal for acts
of resistance (Scene VIII, Chapter XVIII). She comes to a field being
dug by a refugee couple brought together by war despite their lack of a
common language (Scene IX/Chapter IX). In a mountain village during the French Revolutionary Wars, soldiers from both sides meet ami-
cably in an inn on the eve of battle (first half of Scene X/Chapter X).
The battle itself brings victory to Napoleon (second half of Scene X/
Chapter XI). After the battle, Simon, a wounded Orcadian soldier struggles between life and death (Scene XI/Chapter XII). Simon is nursed by
Maurya who promises to join him in Orkney (Scene XII/Chapter XIII).
Maurya observes scenes of nineteenth-century and twentieth-century
wars on a screen (Scene XIII)/Maurya visits a Museum of War curated
by a fellow time-traveller in Victorian England (Chapter XIV). Maurya
and Simon meet in late nineteenth-century or early twentieth-century
Orkney (Scene XIV/Chapter XV). In a near future, Maurya looks back
over her existence. Her bitter monologue is given a final optimistic note
by the apparent arrival of her granddaughter (Scene XV/Chapter XVI).

    It is a moot question whether Brown, at any stage, considered the
theatrical version of 'Time in a Red Coat' to be complete, or whether,
as Maggie Fergusson argues, that after 'working on it for some time,
he decided that the play should in fact be a novel' (247). It is equally
uncertain whether the handwritten corrections to MS 2841.1.1 represent
the last touches to the play or the beginning of its transformation into a
novel. When I refer to the 'final version' or 'final state' of the play, then I
do not imply that it is 'finished', merely that MS 2841.1.1 (with corrections) is the latest existing text in dramatic form.

What is clear, nonetheless, is that the theatrical version of *Time in a Red Coat* was conceived as a work in its own right, and that the manuscripts in Gen. 2134/3/3, MS 2841.1.1, and MS 2841.1.2 should not be approached uniquely as early sketches of the novel. To date, Brown's work as a dramatist has attracted surprisingly little critical attention.[5] Although only five of his plays were published in his lifetime,[6] and fewer than half performed, he is known to have written over fifty theatrical works. Edinburgh University alone holds manuscripts of no fewer than thirty-four plays written between 1949 and 1990. Brown, himself, was curiously reticent about his work as a dramatist, persistently presenting himself in his autobiography *For the Islands I Sing* as a poet and narrator alone. Yet he provides hints elsewhere as to the nature and extent of his theatrical ambitions. In an unpublished interview from 1970, quoted by Rowena and Brian Murray (230), Brown talks of the urgent need for new dramatic forms, based on chronicle rather than conflict and resolution. Alan Bold, in a 1978 monograph based on extensive interviews with Brown, states that he is 'becoming increasingly interested in the possibilities of plays combining conversational naturalism with the fabulous framework' (85), and looks forward to seeing Brown blossom as a dramatist. The following decade did, in fact, see a prolific burst of playwriting, with no fewer than ten of Brown's dramas performed at Orkney's St Magnus Festival between 1981 and 1992 (see Beasant 245–94).[7] Yet critics have preferred to represent the 1980s as a fallow period for Brown as poet and narrator, without noting that much of his creative focus lay elsewhere. The dramatic version of *Time in a Red Coat* should, in fact, be approached as part of a larger theatrical project, in which Brown blends naturalistic dialogue with nonlinear or cyclical structures based on fable or chronicle.

EARLY DRAMATIC DRAFTS

We shall first chart the evolution of the play from the early drafts in Gen. 2134/3/3 and MS 2841.1.2 to the final state of the drama in MS 2841.1.1, before going on to examine the transformation of this manuscript into the published novel.

There are four principal drafts of the opening scene in Gen. 2134/3/3.[8] In the earliest and briefest, the heroine ('the Woman') simply passes through a door, opened by a figure in a white mask.

As she steps onto a sunlit road, he hands her a bag of coins and a map and bids her to complete her journey without looking back. In the second (titled 'She Stands at a Door, Ready for a Journey'), the masked figure is replaced by 'the Guardian' who prefigures the role of the Black Guardian in the final version of the play (and in the novel) by warning the eager heroine ('the Girl') of the dangers of the world and the inevitability of death. In the end, though, he reluctantly lets her pass and begin her journey to 'the house at the end of the road (the House of Legends)'. In a third version, before reaching the door, the heroine (an unspecified 'She') crosses through a series of rooms hung with pictures of the scenes of her future life. Here an inner dialogue between voices alternatively singing the praises and lamenting the dangers of life foreshadows the ritual dialogue of Black and White Guardian in the final version of the play and the novel. The fourth and latest draft finally replaces these symbolic birth-scenes with an actual birth rooted in a geographical setting pre-empting that in the final version of the play and in the novel. The princess is born in a palace with a view of 'a great wall' straddling mountains, 'with towers here and there'. A ritual 'masque of peace' performed by a 'Player' is interrupted by a boy bringing news of a Barbarian invasion. A no-nonsense midwife supervises the heroine's birth, while a 'Black Ward' and 'White Ward' alternately celebrate and lament the mortal lot.[9]

Nonetheless, traces of the earlier, more allegorical drafts of the opening scene persist not only in draft versions of the following scenes but also in their final form in MS 2841.1.1 and in the published novel. In all versions of the 'Well' and 'River' episodes (Scenes/Chapters III–IV), we are required to believe that Maurya has never previously seen water ('What's that beautiful stuff?',[10] MS 2841.1.1, f. 14/*Time in a Red Coat*, 25) or encountered the concepts of river or sea. This is plausible in the early drafts in Gen. 2134/3/3 where these episodes immediately follow her symbolical birth. In the later versions, however, they follow Maurya's wedding-day escape from Mistress Poppyseed's house (Scene/Chapter II), meaning that she has already reached adolescence, and travelled from China to Russia. However secluded her upbringing ('hidden away like a butterfly in a box', *Time in a Red Coat*, 39), this creates an uncomfortable tension between allegory and realism.[11]

There are also traces of the original motivation for the heroine's journey in the final dramatic and novelistic versions. In all four draft openings, Maurya is gifted a bag of coins and a route map which she simply follows to its terminus in Orkney. Unsurprisingly, Brown abandoned this dramatically lifeless mechanism, replacing a preordained itinerary with a hunt to tame or vanquish the dragon of war. However, a puzzling aspect of the novel is that Maurya, particularly in the mountain and forest settings of Chapters V–VI, sometimes appears to be fleeing rather than seeking out conflict.[12] This is actually the case in the early drafts of the play, where she is only gradually exposed to violence and where the map, in fact, 'tells [her] to keep away from soldiers'. Indeed, she originally undergoes a dramatic transformation from an innocence incapable of recognizing a corpse in the river or ill-intentioned soldiers in the forest ('You must be happy folk living in such a beautiful place') through to bloodied experience. In the finished play and novel, she has foreknowledge of war, and is determined to root it out, yet her trajectory still reflects the path mapped for her naïve precursor.[13]

In these early drafts, there is little sense that Maurya's journey traverses continents and centuries, and Brown seldom attempts to superimpose a real-life historical setting onto a fundamentally allegorical landscape. We have seen that the latest version of Scene I in Gen. 2134/3/3 strongly suggests a Chinese setting, but all drafts of Scenes III–IV are devoid of geographical or historical indicators. Characters ('Woman', 'Child', 'Village Elder', 'Ferryman') are unnamed, and locations ('Well', 'River') are archetypal. The first hint that Maurya has travelled across time and space to post-medieval Central Europe occurs in the last of four drafts of Scene V. Here the names of the innkeeper ('Hans') and marauding soldiers ('Stein', 'Witte') are mostly Germanic, while military terms like 'Hussar', 'Major', and 'Colonel' indicate at the earliest a sixteenth-century conflict. With the drafts of Scene VI, we return to nameless types ('Soldiers', 'Boy') in an allegorical space (a forest or wild wood). All three drafts of Scene VIII, however, imply an early modern European setting with their references to muskets, siege guns, and a post-Gutenberg printer's shop. Although character names abound, they do not indicate a precise location. In one version, the names appear Germanic ('Karl', 'Lisa') but in the others (the soldiers 'Macdonald' and 'Duchamp' in one draft, the children 'Tomas', 'Phyllis', 'Rachel', 'Robert' in the other), Brown appears to be consciously blurring geographical indicators in order to evoke a universal, or at least pan-European, conflagration. The drafts of Scenes IX–X offer little more geographical or temporal precision. The soldiers are 'Italian-accented' in one version of Scene X and their weaponry, including 'big guns' and 'artillery', is certainly redolent of a later period than Scene VIII. There are not, however, the clear indications of a Napoleonic campaign present in the final state of the play and in the published novel.

Even at this early stage, however, Maurya's final destination is clearly Orkney. When she nurses the wounded fisherman-soldier in the early drafts of Scene XII ('The Tryst'), they already arrange to meet in the village of 'Ottervoe', a place name that remains constant from first draft to finished novel, with the 'voe' ending unequivocally signalling an Orcadian or Shetlandic setting.[14] The soldier's name varies between Simon Adamson, Simon Thorfin[n]son, and Sven Anders at this stage but each form points to a Norse heritage. The precise historical moment of Maurya's arrival in Ottervoe (Scene XIII) is less certain in the early drafts of Scene XIII, other than being a period where laird and factor prevail, and rent is paid in guineas. Even in the published novel, however, this sequence could be set anywhere from the late nineteenth- to the mid-twentieth-centuries.

The final episode, however, in which the elderly Maurya looks back over her life (Scene XV, Chapter XVI), goes through numerous versions preserved in Gen. 2134/3/3 and MS 2841.1.2. The common thread is Maurya's role as the last defender of the traditional ways of Orkney, after the islanders have abandoned nets and ploughs to work in a mine digging for a mysterious chemical ('Omega 756 Square. Plus 3') reminiscent of the radioactive 'Black Star' in Brown's 1972 novel *Greenvoe*. In all these early versions, the scene ends with nuclear apocalypse, triggered by war or by an accident at the mine. There are clear traces of this in the final chapter of the published novel (which is almost identical to Scene XV of MS 2841.1.1) where Maurya speaks of the good money earned 'up at the mine' (245) and talks of 'the skulls of the little boys, black with fire, all over the hill and the shore' (246). In the novel, though, Maurya may be describing a premonitory future vision rather than lived experience, and the bleak prognosis is offset by the arrival of her granddaughter crying 'Grandma, the boats are in! Sea Quest has the biggest catch again!' (249).

Amongst the early drafts, there is even an epilogue ('The Flute in the Garden', MS 2841.1.2.6), where a nuclear holocaust has reduced the islanders to a tribe of blind cave-dwelling mutants, dubbed 'dragon-men', whom a reincarnation of Maurya leads to a pure source. The finished version of the play and the novel, then, are markedly less pessimistic than the earlier drafts, though Brown may also have feared repeating himself by re-staging the conclusion to *Greenvoe* where the island is contaminated by a radiation leak. The early drafts of the play are much more evidently a response to the 'Second Cold War' of the late 1970s and the first years of the Reagan presidency.[15] Nonetheless, there is surely enough evidence of nuclear anxiety in Chapters XIV ('The Magus') and XVI to belie those critics who detect a flight from history into timelessness in Brown's later work.

FINAL DRAMATIC VERSION

In the later drafts of Maurya's final monologue in MS 2841.1.2, she retrospectively frames her life as a mission to kill or tame the dragon of war. This image does not occur in the early drafts of any of the preceding scenes (in Gen. 2134/3/3). Turning now to the final version of the play (MS 2841.1.1), we find that the dragon also makes a surprisingly late appearance there. In the original fair copy of the manuscript, the heroine is still gifted a map and follows the route that it dictates. In a first series of corrections, however, the map is consistently replaced with an ivory flute. The flute, of course, survives into the novel as 'a symbol, perhaps, of the healing power of the imagination' (Brown, 'Et in Orcadia Ego'). However, it plays a much greater role in the play, where, Maurya explains, 'the flute tells me where to go' (MS 2841.1.1, f. 19). In other words, it replaces the map as a narrative motor, and Maurya initially retains it to the play's conclusion. In a second set of corrections, however, the flute motif is directly incorporated into the hunt for the dragon of war. It is both Maurya's means of locating the dragon and the instrument by which it might be tamed. Finally, however, in a correction to Scene X (the manuscript's most extensively corrected scene); she despairs of the flute's ability to charm the dragon and gifts it to the fisherman-soldier Simon (f. 65). In the novel, Brown removes all hints that Maurya is following the flute, but at the cost of rendering it a rather inert symbol.

If the allegorical nature of Maurya's journey remains in constant evolution in MS 2841.1.2, then it is more coherently and consistently situated in historical time and space. As in the final draft in Gen. 2134/3/3, references to a 'great wall' (f. 1) clearly set Scene I in China. In the entirely new Scene II, Maurya's nouveau riche bridegroom is a 'Mr Khan' (f. 10), suggesting that the Barbarian incursion portrayed in Scene I is the thirteenth-century Mongol invasion of China. In Scene III, a village elder is addressed as 'Ilyich' and a correction identifies the approaching enemy army as 'Tartar soldiers' (f. 15), evoking a Russia at the mercy of the Mongol-Tatar Golden Horde (again thirteenth century). There are no real-life spatio-temporal indicators in Scene IV, but Scene V clearly places us in Central or East-Central Europe, with character names like 'Mitzi' (f. 22) and 'Luntzen' (f. 26) and references to Hungarian 'Bullsblood' wine and 'sturgeon'. The use of military titles like 'Major' implies a post-medieval setting, positing a leap of at least two centuries since the opening scenes. Scene VI offers no clues as to its setting, but in Scene VII the reference to 'florins' and the forging of a 'gun'—or 'cannon balls' in a correction—suggests Renaissance-period Western Europe. Like the drafts in Gen. 2134/3/3, Scene VIII has a generically early modern European setting with the use of bayonets (introduced in the seventeenth century) (f. 39) clearly indicating a further temporal leap. In Scene IX, the identification of the local landowner as 'the lord Pedro' brings us to Spain or Portugal, though the young couple digging a new field are refugees from distant parts of Europe (the young man hailing, according to a correction [f. 47] from 'Leipzig'). Here Brown portrays the demographic upheaval provoked by a non-specific continental conflict where 'the whole of Europe's a battlefield', full of 'folk trudging from place to place, with chairs and clocks and cages' (f. 47). References to 'big guns' or 'gun carriages' (f. 49) being dragged up a mountainside indicate that we are approaching the modern era. The most specific historical references occur in Scenes X–XII, where allusions to the 'Emperor' and the 'Corsican' situate the mountain battle in the Napoleonic Wars. The geographical location is less precise, though the Iberian setting of the preceding Scene IX might point to the Pyrenees. In Scene XIII, Maurya steps out of diegetic space—though, oddly, not out of diegetic time—to watch projected 'scenes of war from later times' from 'the side of the stage' (f. 68). The earliest of these future conflicts is the US Civil War. As in the early drafts, the concluding Scenes XII and XIII are set in Orkney. The reference to 'young ones having to go to Canada and Australia to make a living' (f. 72) places the former in the late nineteenth or early twentieth centuries, while Scene XIII is again set in an apocalyptic near future. Both geographically and temporally, the trajectory established in the final version of the play is, with slight variations, carried over into the novel.

The most extensively revisited and corrected scenes of MS 2841.1.1 may provide hints as to why Brown ultimately chose to develop the play into a novel. Scene X, in particular, where a spectacular mountain battle is followed by the torching of a village, would stretch the resources of any theatrical company. Daunting stage directions are not rare in Brown's published drama: one thinks of the summer bonfire and witch-burning in *A Spell for Green Corn* (Scenes 2 and 5), or the sea battle in *The Loom of Light* (Scene 3).[16] It may be that Brown foresaw the dramatic version of *Time in a Red Coat* being read, recited, or adapted for radio (like *A Spell for Green Corn*[17]) rather than performed on stage. However, the sheer number of multi-layered corrections in Scene X, which renders the manuscript all but illegible in places, must encourage the suspicion that it never achieved definitive dramatic form in Brown's mind.

Brown might likewise have been concerned that the battle in Scene X is followed shortly afterwards by an unequally untheatrical episode in Scene XIII (the relatively brief Scenes XI–XII being set in the immediate aftermath of the battle[18]). In this scene, Maurya is 'compelled'—by whom or what is unclear—to witness scenes from the US Civil War, Boer War, First World War, Spanish Civil War, Second World War, and, finally, Vietnam, which appear as 'immense shadows' that 'flicker as on a cinema screen'. The shadows finally flicker out, and Maurya, raising her fists to her temples, cries: 'O God, stop it! Make them stop it! Please. Is there no end to this?' (f. 70). The stage direction 'as on a cinema screen' seems a little disingenuous. It is difficult to see how it might be followed, other than by projecting filmed material. Besides the fundamentally didactic and undramatic nature of this device, Brown may have worried that the two climactic sequences of the play, the mountain battle and the vision of future wars, were dependent on visual effect rather than dialogue, and that the means of achieving that visual effect were barely adumbrated. Certainly, these are the two episodes that are most fully expanded in the novel: the lengthy and convoluted stage directions of Scene X evolving into a vivid narrative sequence in Chapter XI ('The Battle') and the picture-show pageant of Scene XIII giving way to the war-museum maintained by the time-travelling 'Magus' (Chapter XIV).

The Novel

The published novel contains almost every line of dialogue from the final version of the play, but individual episodes are expanded to create a more vivid sense of both real and allegorical spaces. In particular, the provision of fuller geographical and historical detail permits a closer plotting of Maurya's itinerary. Thus, in Chapters I–II, the 'Barbarians' who breach the 'Great Wall' that rings the 'Empire' are now explicitly dubbed 'ignorant murdering Mongols' (17).[19] Chapter III is more clearly set in Russia, as indicated by the names Ilyich (22) and Vassily (23), the identification of a 'holy man' as a 'starets' (23), the reference to the Urals (24), and the presence of 'ikons' in a church (22). The repeated mentions of 'Tartar soldiers' (28–29) identify the invading army as the Golden Horde. As we have seen, there are no geographical or temporal indicators in Scene IV of the play. Those inserted in Chapter IV of the novel remain somewhat generic, but the references to 'country folk' reserving 'the baron's and the king's shares' (32) of their produce, and to ruinous wars fought between baron and king with 'arrows' and 'swords', place us firmly within the feudal period. As to geography, 'icons in the church' (36),[20] and perhaps 'sturgeon', are suggestive of Orthodox Eastern Europe. Where Scene V of the play has a generically Central European setting, the innkeeper's recollection of 'Cracow Fair' (44) clearly situates Chapter V of the novel in Poland.[21] The emergence of 'merchant' and 'banking house' as the new masters (53), along with references to printed books (50) and 'rifle butts', suggests a post-medieval, possibly Renaissance, time frame. Chapter VI, conversely, is barely more rooted in time and place than its dramatic equivalent. Only the deserters' 'redcoat' uniform (61) again indicates a post-medieval setting. Chapter VII, with its burnt-out church (77) and war between 'fat Luther and the fat Pope' (83), is clearly set during the Reformation. Character names ('Heinz', 82) and allusions to local traditions ('mountain dwarves', 83) point to German-speaking Europe. The besieged city of Chapter VIII, with its allegorical statue of Pax, its 'municipal garden' (86) or 'public park' (97), its 'conservatoire' (88), and its 'ormolu clocks', evokes neo-classical France. Though the nature of the conflict is unspecified, the conquering army is now a bureaucratic machine, the realities of slaughter concealed beneath an impersonal 'Order 12B' (93). The young refugee couple that Maurya encounters in Chapter IX think that they are 'in Spain' but are not 'quite sure' (107), a hypothesis supported by references to the landlord 'Don Pedro' (107) and to Goya (109). Thus far, in purely geographical terms, Maurya's itinerary is a good deal more linear than some critics (e.g. Burns 72–73; Spear 90) have allowed. In Chapters X–XIII, though, she doubles back to a mountainous border region of France, where Napoleon (now explicitly named) is ensconced in 'the château of the absent seigneur'. The *Grande*

Armée is pitched against a force 'of mixed Prussians and Poles and English', amongst whom Maurya encounters the press-ganged Orcadian fisherman Simon Thorfinnson. Chapter XIV is perhaps the novel's most precisely located sequence with clear references to Dover (186), London (187), Oxford (191), and the heroine's 'Channel passage' (189). Maurya arrives in England in 'the seventh decade of the nineteenth century', the mid-Victorian setting further confirmed by references to the 'late Crimean campaign' (1853–1856), the recent Siege of Lucknow (1857) (191), and the laureateship of Tennyson (1850–1892) (198). The Orkney setting of the concluding Chapters XV–XVI is made explicit by a reference to the capital Kirkwall on 234. Temporal indicators are less exact. In Chapter XV, the factor's attire of 'a grey worsted jacket belted at the waist, and [..] grey worsted knickerbockers, grey stockings, and brown well-polished brogue shoes' (229) suggests late nineteenth or early twentieth centuries. The 'tapes' and 'discs' (246) of Chapter XVI imply, as in the dramatic version, an apocalyptic near future.

Particularly in the later chapters, however, the evocation of historical time and place is blurred by Brown's choice of character names. The local populace in the ostensibly French-set Chapters VIII (Anna, Tomas, Phyllis, Rachel, Robert, Liza) and X–XIII (Andrew, Louis, Abel, Erik, Samuel, Simon, Jeanne, Trod, Paul, Margrete, Adam, Jacques, Hans, Maria, Liza) by no means bear exclusively French forenames. Here Brown is perhaps aiming for a universal effect in portraying the effect of war on urban or rural working-class communities. He may too, though, be hinting at the demographic upheaval provoked by pan-continental conflict, a theme more explicitly addressed in Chapter IX where two refugees from Central Europe settle in Spain. The British-set final chapters also thematize the erosive effects of empire and capital on organic communities. Thus, in Chapter XIV, the Magus's Home Counties estate is almost exclusively staffed by exiled Scots: the governess Mrs. Baillie (188), the housekeeper Mrs Stuart (191), the footman Bryce (199), and the blacksmith MacWilliam (206). Similarly, in Chapter XV, young Orcadians are increasingly tempted by 'the ample opportunities' offered by 'the vast unexploited territories of Canada, South Africa, Australia, New Zealand' (230).

At the same time, the allegorical dimension of Maurya's journey is significantly enriched in a number of ways. Firstly, Brown frames each chapter with an authorial discussion of the universal image that each explores (well, river, inn, forest, etc.) and a critical assessment of its continuing viability as a metaphor for human existence (ably analysed in Baker 98–105). Secondly, there is a greater emphasis on Maurya's pursuit of the dragon of war. First introduced, as we saw, in late drafts of the play's closing monologue, it evolves to become the narrative thread binding the novel together. It is introduced much earlier than in the final version of the play (Chapter III 'The Well'),[22] and there is some attempt to resolve the contradictions of a trajectory which, as in the earliest drafts of the play, often seems to lead Maurya away from battle. Thus, the lengthy detour through mountain and forest in Chapters V–VI is retrospectively (if perhaps unconvincingly) explained as an effort to recover a lost trail.[23]

Finally, Brown introduces the theme of female solidarity, presenting Maurya as an emblematic figure 'into whom all the world's women are gathered'.[24] This is rendered particularly explicit in Chapter IV, where the narrator insists that Maurya is 'all women, all the girl children and the old ones who have added their salt drops to the sweet on-flowing river of life, and who hate war and war-makers with a bitter hatred' (33). This is a notable development from the dramatic version of *Time in a Red Coat*, where, in all drafts up to and including the final state, Maurya provokes suspicion and hostility in the women she encounters. In the novel, conversely, they are consistently supportive of her mission to end war. In the final version of Scene III of the play, for example, the village women are certainly united in opposing the order to poison the wells but remain distrustful of the stranger and potential spy Maurya. It is a 'child' who helps Maurya evade capture while the adults are distracted. In the novel, conversely, the women clearly collude in Maurya's escape, and it is they ('in their twenty voices') who cry 'Farewell, stranger!' (30), while in the play, it is the child alone (MS 2841.1.1, f. 16). Similarly, in Chapter XIII, a 'ring of smiling women' (185) accept Maurya invitation to nurse Simon in her absence and guard him against 'a snarling fist-shaking pack of men' (183). These women are absent in the final version of the play and in earlier drafts are as vindictive as their men-folk. The novel, then, more clearly encapsulates Brown's vision of war as a 'man's game' which women see 'for what it truly is, a hideous shambles in which all youth and beauty are left to smoulder and rot'.[25]

Perhaps, though, such undoubted thematic gains are undermined by an ultimately disruptive tension between the real (historico-geographical) and allegorical dimensions of the novel. In all versions of the play, the characters that Maurya encounters—ferryman, smith, innkeeper, soldier, fisherman—exist on the same universal, archetypal plane as herself. In the novel, conversely, they are provided with a personal or communal history. Chapter V, for example, begins with an account of the innkeeper's life and marriage, and Chapter X with the thoughts of the village priest on the eve of battle. Other chapters (particularly I, III, and VIII) commence with a sketch of, or a choral commentary upon, the long evolution and seasonal rhythms of a community. If the figures that she meets are thus fleshed out, then Maurya herself becomes increasingly depersonalized and emblematic.

Dominique Delmaire 54 has complained that Maurya is not a character but a concept, representing 'la transgression du discours allégorique à l'intérieur de la diégèse'. She is not 'interprétable' within the coordinates of fictional reality itself and as such lacks 'réalité diégétique'. From a narrative viewpoint, her presence is as disconcerting as that of a cartoon character in a live action movie, and here Delmaire cites Robert Zemeckis's 1988 film *Who Framed Roger Rabbit?* (1988).

Maurya is perceived, in fact, as an otherworldly apparition throughout the novel. She is mistaken for an angel (24), a ghost (38), a fairy-tale 'snow princess' (51), a mirage (144), and, repeatedly, a statue (135, 143, and 193). The latter, in particular, underlines a paradoxical element in her characterization. For all the distance that Maurya travels, she retains a strangely static presence. Indeed rather than a voyager or visitor, she often resembles a genius loci, a 'guardian of the source' (136) or 'keeper of the well' (139). She does not so much pass through spaces, real or allegorical, as manifest herself within them. As such, rather than a quest narrative, Brown appears to present us with a series of tableaux vivants in which Maurya stages the same symbolic standoff with 'the dragon of war'. Timothy Baker 101, who notes that Maurya 'exists at the periphery of the novel's events', argues that we should interpret her as an 'observer' rather than a 'protagonist', but this, in fact, is truer of the dramatic manuscripts than the novel. A consequence of Brown's efforts to foreground and to individualize other characters in the novel, providing them with a personal or communal history, is that we now see Maurya through their eyes rather than vice versa. She is more clearly an object of observation than an observer. In the dramatic versions, though, we follow Maurya as she witnesses and investigates scenes of conflict. She often functions, in fact, as the audience's representative on the stage. Nowhere is this clearer than in Scene XIII of the final state of the play, where she steps to one side and joins us in viewing screen images of future war. When she visits the Museum of War in the equivalent chapter of the novel (XIV), however, the exhibits are presented not from her perspective but from that of the Magus and his companion Erasmus. The reader of the novel, therefore, has little sense of Maurya's journey as a learning process, an apprenticeship in the horrors of war. In the dramatic versions, particularly the earlier drafts, Maurya moves from extreme innocence to bitter experience. In the novel, she comes equipped with a foreknowledge of suffering and an innate hatred of war, which further contribute to the static nature of her character and trajectory.

At the end of the novel, Maurya nominally steps out of allegorical space into history, by marrying Simon and settling with him in Ottervoe. In the process, she acquires a community identity and, of course, a name. Yet this transition is again perhaps more effective in the final version of the play. In the play, very little dramatic time passes between the symbolic kiss that Maurya gives the wounded Simon at the end of the Napoleonic battle sequence (f. 65) and her arrival in Ottervoe (f. 73).[26] The only intervening Scene (XIII) shows Maurya at her most human, as the scenes of future slaughter provoke the anguished cry: 'O God, stop it!' (f. 70). In the corresponding 'Magus' chapter of the novel, however, she cuts an uncanny, supernatural figure, styling herself 'the lady in the white coat' (186), claiming to be 'upward of a thousand and five hundred years old', and miraculously curing her host's daughter. Indeed, the mode of the entire chapter is fantastic with the Magus himself celebrating his 222nd birthday (219) and curating a museum of future objects. It is also by some distance the longest chapter of the novel (42 pages).[27] This means that fully forty-eight pages, i.e. some twenty per cent of the novel, pass between the kiss (185) and Maurya's appearance on Orkney (233). Maurya's entrance into history is thus suspended to the point where it loses much of its force and significance, especially given how promptly she exits it once again. However one reads the final chapter, Maurya cuts a superhuman figure. If she has survived a nuclear disaster that devastates Ottervoe, it is clearly by merit of her invulnerable, immortal nature. If, conversely, she is describing a premonitory future vision, then she has powers of prophecy. It is thus difficult to refute Dominique Delmaire's contention that Maurya never truly inhabits fictional reality, remaining a transgressive invader from allegorical space. Having charted the evolution of *Time in a Red Coat*, it is perhaps more accurate to say that Brown seeks unsuccessfully to impose the historico-geographical space of the novel upon the relatively homogeneous allegorical space of the play, but the effect of incoherence remains the same.

As a final note, Edinburgh University Library's George Mackay Brown papers reveal that *Time in a Red Coat* had even more distant dramatic roots. One of Brown's first theatrical experiments, dated January 1952, is entitled *Time in a Blue Coat*.[28] An early rehearsal of one of Brown's favourite themes, the renewal of a community through an individual sacrifice,[29] it takes its title from the motto of a sundial: 'We expect time to come leisurely, in a blue coat. But it comes in a red cloak, tipsy; or in green tatters, borne on a bier' (MS 3112/4/3, f. 41). When the replenishing sacrifice is performed at the play's conclusion, a character remarks that 'time in a red cloak' has 'danced invisible through the garden, his mouth brimming with song' (f. 51). The image of time in its blood-soaked cloak clearly dances through Brown's imagination, leading to repeated attempts to give it full expression some thirty years later.

NOTES

1. Critics (e.g. Baker 95; Spear 90) generally speak *of Time in a Red Coat* covering 1500 years of history, relying on the heroine's own estimate of her age as 'fifteen centuries or thereby' (207). If, however, we accept Brown's statement that she is born 'in China at a time of Mongol invasion' ('Et in Orcadia Ego'), then the novel can begin no earlier than the thirteenth century CE. While, clearly, one cannot impose an exact chronology on an allegorical quest narrative, this reduced timescale is, in fact, more consistent with the historical indicators found in the rest of the novel.
2. Of Brown's critics, only Fergusson 247 seems aware of its origins as a play. For David Profumo, it is a 'collection of short stories uneasily run together'. For Berthold Schoene (255), it is born out of the allegorical poem with which the novel concludes (but which, in fact, first appears in the final draft of the play at MS 2841.1.1, f. 85). (For a concise overview of the Brown manuscripts held by Edinburgh University Library, see "Manuscripts of Works by George Mackay Brown", http://www.ed.ac.uk/information-services/library-museum-gallery/crc/research-resources/scottish-literature/gmbrown/mss).
3. There are two typescripts of the novel version of *Time in a Red Coat* in the Orkney Library & Archive's George Mackay Collection dated 1982 (D124/8) and 1983 (D124/9). These are clearly, however, subsequent to MS 2841.2-3.
4. As Baker 97 notes, the heroine only acquires a name in the novel's final chapter, as she at last steps into history and assumes a place in a defined community. The same is true of the final version of the play

(MS 2841.1.1, f. 81). For the sake of brevity, however, I will refer to her as Maurya throughout.

5. To date only one article (Campbell 2000) is specifically devoted to Brown's theatrical production. Otherwise critics have largely treated plays such as *A Spell for Green Corn* (1967) and *The Loom of Light* (1972) as rehearsals of themes explored more fully in his novels (e.g. Baker 68; Butter; 22, Ferguson 240). For further discussion of Brown's neglected theatrical production, see Barnaby (2013, 87–92).

6. *A Spell for Green Corn* (London: Hogarth Press, 1970), *Three Plays* (London: Chatto & Windus, 1984) (containing *The Loom of Light*, *The Well*, and *The Voyage of Saint Brandon*), and *A Celebration for Magnus* (Nairn: Balnain Books, 1987).

7. Twenty-two of the thirty-four dramatic manuscripts in Edinburgh University Library's George Mackay Brown Archive were written between 1975 and 1990.

8. Unfortunately, the manuscripts in Gen. 2134/3/3 are neither foliated nor numbered. Nor are drafts of individual scenes arranged chronologically, whether in terms of writing date or of their appearance in the play. I have thus gauged the earliness or lateness of a draft by its textual closeness to the final version of the play in MS 2841.1.1.

9. The designations 'Black Ward' and 'White Ward' remain in the final version of the play. The substitution of 'Guardian' for 'Ward' occurs during the transformation of the play into a novel.

10. 'What's this beautiful stuff?' in Gen 2134/3/3.

11. It also makes more sense that Maurya is accused of being a spy in the early versions of scene/chapter III. It is the map that awakens suspicions.

12. The windows of the inn are unlit so as not to attract soldiers. The forest is chosen as a hiding place by the party of deserters that Maurya encounters precisely because it is untouched by war. In these chapters, rather than chasing the dragon of war, Maurya seems simply to attract it wherever she goes.

13. This may also explain the 'rather aimless' appearance of her trajectory that Burns 73 regrets in the opening chapters.

14. 'Voe' is an Orcadian or Shetlandic term for a bay, inlet, or creek.

15. As Brown writes in 'Et in Orcadia Ego': 'since Hiroshima, war is a nightmare that will not leave us. At last it is within our power to eradicate history and civilization in an hour. It was that way of thinking that set me off to write *Time in a Red Coat*. The chief character was to be a young woman, and her sacred task is to get to the root of human conflict and cancel it before the final atomic flame engulfs us all'.

16. Reviewing *Three Plays*, Profumo comments that 'his stage directions are often unperformably poetic ("the burn is supple with trout")'. Similarly,

Campbell (2000) laments Brown's 'apparent lack of interest in—or, indeed, awareness of—the requirements of the professional stage'.

17. For other work by Brown written or adapted for radio, see Spear 153–55.

18. Indeed, they are part of Scene X in earlier drafts.

19. Brown's own declaration that the novel begins 'in China at a time of Mongol invasion' ('Et in Orcadia Ego') is nonetheless complicated by his use of a Mongol title, 'the great Khan' (1), for the overthrown Emperor. One of the villagers, the merchant 'Mr Tengis', also has a Mongol rather than a Chinese name. Perhaps Brown is hinting that the apparently time-less organic community violated by the 'barbarians' is itself the product of earlier incursions. There may even be a suggestion of a counter-historical universe where the Chinese overrun the Mongol Empire rather than vice versa. Where critics such as Bicket 86, Fergusson 247, and Spear 89 state firmly that the opening chapters are set in China, it may, then, be safer to follow Baker 95 and Profumo in speaking simply of an unspecified East Asian country.

20. The orthographical shift from 'ikons' in Chapter III to 'icons' in Chapter IV may indicate westward movement.

21. Poland, however, is anachronistically presented not as an independent (and Catholic) Renaissance kingdom but as a battleground for con-tending Russian and Germanic influences. The former are suggested by references to 'icons' (47 and 51) and 'roubles' (52), and the latter by Germanic names like 'Mitzi' and 'Lunzen'.

22. When village elder Ilyich reports that soldiers have burnt the bridge across the river, Maurya replies: 'I think I must go now. You've told me where the Dragon is' (28).

23. When Maurya reaches the smithy in Chapter 7, she is relieved to find that 'she was on the right road after all, having thought for a week that she had lost the spore of the dragon' (77).

24. Edinburgh University Library, MS 2841.1.4, f. 1. This is the 'suggested draft of blurb' to the novel dated 13 May 1983. It strongly resembles the 'second thoughts' on *Time in a Red Coat*, which Brown published as 'Et in Orcadia Ego', in *The Independent*, 3 August 1991. There Maurya is 'all the war-hating women who have ever lived'.

25. MS 2841.1.4, f. 1.

26. Note that f. 71 is blank.

27. The next longest is Chapter XI (23 pages).

28. It is one of a group of eight short plays written between 1949 and 1952 at MS 3112 and MS 3116. This is another uncharted period of intense theatrical activity by Brown, during which he experimented with dialogue in Orcadian.

29. The young laird Simon Knarston of Knarstonhaa appears to be on the verge of death from consumption, when, aided by gardener Andrew Goodsir, he buys and sails a lobster boat. The physical labour miraculously restores him to health but, at the play's conclusion, he dies in a storm. His doctor, Siegfried Spence, a progressive Tory with little sympathy for the island's traditional culture, is engaged to Simon's aunt Maud, and thinks that Knarstonhaa will now be his. Unknown to all, however, Simon has secretly married Andrew's daughter Hilda, and their child inherits Knarstonhaa.

WORKS CITED

Baker, Timothy. *George Mackay Brown and the Philosophy of Community.* Edinburgh: Edinburgh University Press, 2009.

Barnaby, Paul. 'Scottish Theatre Archives at Edinburgh University Library'. *International Journal of Scottish Theatre and Screen* 6:2 (2013): 87–99. Web. 3 August 2016.

Beasant, Pam, ed. *St. Magnus Festival: A Celebration.* Kirkwall: Orcadian, 2002.

Bell, Ian. 'Breaking the Silence'. Rev. of Maggie Fergusson, *George Mackay Brown: The Life. Scottish Review of Books* 2.2 (2007): n.p. Web. 28 July 2016.

Bicket, Linden. 'George Mackay Brown's Marian Apocrypha: Iconography and Enculturation in *Time in a Red Coat*'. *Scottish Literary Review* 5.2 (2013): 81–96.

Bold, Alan. *George Mackay Brown.* Edinburgh: Oliver and Boyd, 1978.

Brown, George Mackay. *A Spell for Green Corn.* London: Hogarth Press, 1970.

———. *Greenvoe.* London: Hogarth Press, 1972.

———. *Three Plays.* London: Chatto & Windus, 1984.

———. *Time in a Red Coat.* London: Chatto & Windus, 1984.

———. 'Et in Orcadia Ego'. *The Independent*, 3 August 1991: 25.

Burns, John. 'Myths and Marvels'. *The Scottish Novel Since the Seventies: New Visions, Old Dreams.* Ed. Gavin Wallace and Randall Stevenson. Edinburgh: Edinburgh University Press, 1993.

Butter, H. 'George Mackay Brown and Edwin Muir'. *The Yearbook of English Studies* 17 (1987): 16–30.

Campbell, Donald. 'Greenness in Every Line: The Drama of George Mackay Brown'. *International Journal of Scottish Theatre* 1.1 (2000): n.p. Web. 28 July 2016.

Delmaire, Dominique. 'L'Oeuvre fictionelle de George Mackay Brown: un fantastique qui laisse à désirer?' *Études écossaises* 7 (2001): 41–60.

Ferguson, Ron. *George Mackay Brown: The Wound and the Gift.* Edinburgh: Saint Andrews Press, 2011.

Fergusson, Maggie. *George Mackay Brown: The Life.* London: John Murray, 2007.
Murray, Rowena, and Brian Murray. *Interrogation of Silence: The Writings of George Mackay Brown.* London: John Murray, 2004.
Profumo, David. 'She of the Black Blown Hair'. Rev. of *Time in a Red Coat* and *Three Plays. Times Literary Supplement,* 15 June 1984: 676.
Schoene-Harwood, Berthold. *The Making of Orcadia: Narrative Identity in the Prose Work of George Mackay Brown.* Frankfurt am Main: Peter Lang, 1995.
Spear, Hilda D. *George Mackay Brown: A Survey of His Work and a Full Bibliography.* Lewiston: E. Mellen Press, 2000.

The Empty Places: Northern Archipelagos in Scottish Fiction

John Brannigan

In her review of Robert Macfarlane's *The Wild Places* (2007), Kathleen Jamie interrogated the geopolitical assumptions underpinning the recent vogue for wildness in English nature writing. While acknowledging Macfarlane's erudition and lyricism, Jamie lampoons the book as offering a familiar and conservative narrative—'Adventures, then home for tea'— which casts a wide arc around the 'wild places' far out on the peripheries of 'Britain and Ireland', but returns to the comforts of Cambridge.[1] She characterises the form of the nature book as necessarily bound up with a conservative and male literary tradition, centred on English assumptions about remoteness, adventure narratives faintly reminiscent of John Buchan, and the spiritual sensibilities of the 'lone enraptured male'.[2] The 'wildness' is inseparable from solipsism:

> In place after place, the length and breadth of the country, there is 'wildness'. There are no meetings, no encounters with intrusive folk. It is all truly empty, secret and luscious. From Sutherland to the Burren, even to Dorset and Essex, the book reveals a sense of beguiling solitude. There

J. Brannigan (✉)
University College Dublin, Dublin, Ireland

© The Author(s) 2019   71
M. Szuba and J. Wolfreys (eds.), *The Poetics of Space and Place
in Scottish Literature*, Geocriticism and Spatial Literary Studies,
https://doi.org/10.1007/978-3-030-12645-2_5

are no other voices, no Welsh or Irish or differently accented English. It
has to be thus, of course, because if we start blethering to the locals the
conceit of empty 'wild' will be lost.[3]

For Jamie, the solipsism of Macfarlane's perspective, its dependence
upon the silence of others, reprises the historical elisions and inequities of relations between England and its archipelagic neighbours. Her
use of dialect words and phrases—'blethering', 'Ach weel'—pointedly
mocks the monologism of Macfarlane's 'honeyed prose'.[4] Her critique is
instructive about the contested meanings and politics of nature writing.
Macfarlane had set out to celebrate the hidden places of wild nature, the
peripheries unknown to an increasingly globalised metropolitan society.
Jamie reads *The Wild Places* as an act of appropriation.

In her own prose essays in *Findings* (2005) and *Sightlines* (2012),
Jamie treads carefully around questions of perspective and point-of-view.
In 'Three Ways of Looking at St Kilda', she addresses the same problem-
atic concepts of 'wildness' and 'remoteness':

> Mingulay, Pabbay, Stroma, the Shiant Isles. Places with such long human
> histories, I soon came to distrust any starry-eyed notions of 'wild' or
> 'remote'. Remote from what? London? But what was London?... Being
> with the surveyors taught me to change my focus. It was like the difference
> between looking through a window pane and looking at it. Look through
> the window, and you'd see the sea, wildness, distance, isolation. Look at it,
> and you saw utility, food security, domestic management.[5]

On St Kilda, Jamie discovers a missile-tracking radar base and a National
Trust warden who is obliged to read the by-laws to which visitors must
adhere. The iconic 'street' of houses abandoned when the last islanders
emigrated turns out to be a misjudged Victorian 'improvement', too
dependent on imported resources like glass and timber to be maintained
or repaired. Remote and wild in the imagination, St Kilda turns out to
be all too modern. There is the romance of the island on the edge; there
is also the practicality that the islanders faced the same necessities of
adapting to the precarities of modernity as everyone else and chose to
leave. Jamie's essay serves to demythologise St Kilda, acknowledging the
potency and pervasiveness of the romance, the allure of enchanting the
peripheries, only then to expose its false assumptions. London is identified as the presumed source of such myths of remoteness and wildness,

just as Jamie reads Macfarlane's *The Wild Places* as inherently mediating its discoveries from southern English perspectives. As Alan Riach has argued of Jamie's poetry, the issue of nationality, and its fraught notions of 'demarcation, legalities, limits and what is beyond them', is an insistent and critical presence in Jamie's work:

> For Jamie, Scotland is contextualised with co-ordinate points that arise from the foundations of her understanding of socially gendered, power-structured identities, in which nationality is only one component and redefinable part.[6]

The 'groan' with which Jamie reads Macfarlane's quest northwards is born of these coordinate points; the 'hackles' she feels rise when Macfarlane allows a sense of enchantment to blind him to the realities of historical power struggles suggest an embodied understanding of such geopolitical structures.[7] These bodily responses are made to seem instinctive, innate, precisely because of the familiar, worn-thin conventions of representing the north as the site of 'wild places' and 'empty places', awaiting rediscovery and re-enchantment by the 'lone enraptured male'.

As Peter Davidson argues in his book, *The Idea of North* (2005), imaginative engagements with 'northness' reveal 'an idea about place that is shifting and recessive'.[8] The north seems always to recede out of reach and is wholly dependent upon the orientation of the perceiver. This is Jamie's point about the multiple ways of seeing St Kilda, of course. For Davidson, writing about literary and mythological associations of the north in Britain, Canada, China, Japan, and Scandinavia, the north may be subjective, but brings tenaciously with it a series of dense symbols and meanings:

> Everyone carries their own idea of north within them. To say 'we leave for the north tonight' brings immediate thoughts of a harder place, a place of dearth: uplands, adverse weather, remoteness from cities. A voluntary northward journey implies a willingness to encounter the intractable elements of climate, topography and humanity. In an English-language fiction, the words 'we leave for the north tonight' would probably be spoken in a thriller, a fiction of action, of travel, of pursuit over wild country.[9]

Scotland—or at least those highly mythologised regions of Scotland: the Highlands, the Islands, and the Borders—frequently occupies this imaginative terrain in the literary traditions of England. In contemporary Scottish fiction, however, the same associations with dearth, hardness, and remoteness cluster around a series of different and recessive 'norths'. In the work of George Mackay Brown, Margaret Elphinstone, and Sarah Moss, just to take three prominent examples, the north is understood in geographical terms as encompassing an expansive archipelago linking Norway to Newfoundland, taking in Scotland, Ireland, Iceland, and Greenland along the way. It is also understood historically and mythologically, however, as never wholly present to itself, always a slippage from other times, a transitional world haunted by a dark past of violence and hardship.

The history of this northern archipelago which all three writers invoke is, simultaneously, richly suggestive of alternative post-devolution geographies of a north-facing Scotland, and oddly disconnected from modern Scottish historical experience. Perhaps with the possibility of independence from that shrinking island called 'Britain', Scotland would look north instead for a more expansive and confident sense of itself as a sub-Scandinavian state, or a powerful node in a North Atlantic archipelago. Yet the north-facing fictions of contemporary Scotland perhaps risk continuing what Cairns Craig identified as a 'problematic legacy' of the historical novel in Scotland, in which the past is produced as a mythic region devoid of ideological significance in the present:

> Scotland is a place with a past but a place without a history – without a history both in the sense of there being no serious need to write histories about that past, and in the sense that the narrative of its past has no relevance to the condition of its present, to the nature of its contemporary historical experience.[10]

The three novels which are the focus of this essay—Mackay Brown's *Vinland* (1992), Elphinstone's *The Sea Road* (2000), and Moss's *Cold Earth* (2009)—all take as their historical setting, or in Moss's case, historical analogue, the Viking world of the tenth and eleventh centuries, and in particular Viking explorations of the western shores of the North Atlantic. The risk of such geographically and historically remote settings is detachment from 'contemporary historical experience'. Craig reads *Vinland*, for example, as indicative of a significant tradition in Scottish fiction of casting far outside Scotland for 'what twentieth century Scotland has failed to provide for the modern novelist – a world of significant conflict and a place where history can be witnessed in the making', a tradition in which he includes Mitchison's *The Corn King and the Spring Queen* (1931), Grassic Gibbons' *Spartacus* (1933), and Gunn's *Sun Circle* (1933).[11] Yet, it is precisely by exploring and questioning such 'remoteness' and peripherality that Mackay Brown, Elphinstone, and Moss respond to contemporary geopolitical crises.

Mackay Brown's work is deeply rooted in Orkney, where he was born and spent most of his life. His commitment to representing local settings in Orkney, and to mythology and the distant past, has resulted in some criticism for a perceived escapism. Roderick Watson attributes this to his fascination for 'timeless and mythopoeic patterns', which give the impression of 'seeking values that are only ever to be found in some other time or in the exclusion of modernity'.[12] In his best-known novel, *Greenvoe* (1972), an island has been cleared of its ancient fishing community by an ominous military installation called Black Star, a story which has sharp political resonance with the ways in which Scottish islands and coasts have been exploited as military bases, firing ranges, and nuclear facilities. Yet the novel is punctuated with a strange ritual, whereby islanders return to the island to perform a paganistic harvest blessing which seems to be timeless: 'The Lord of the Harvest raised his hands. "We have brought light and blessing to the kingdom of winter", he said, "however long it endures, that kingdom, a night or a season or a thousand ages".... The sun rose. The stones were warm. They broke the bread'.[13] Thus the novel ends and arguably draws the reader's attention away from political questions about appropriation and clearances by the state, and towards a perpetual sense of resignation to such acts as if they were seasonal cycles to be endured.

In *Vinland*, this conflict between political violence and a folk narrative of ritual communal life is dramatised through the story of Ranald Sigmundson, who begins the novel as a seafaring child who accompanies Leif Ericson on his voyages to Vinland, and ends it as an old farmer, long settled in his birthplace in Orkney, determined not to hear any news of the political machinations of the local Earls. Orkney is depicted as remote from the centres of political power in Norway and Scotland, but therefore all the more vulnerable to the whims and ambitions of contending kingdoms. Having once attended the court in Norway to bring tales of his Vinland adventures, Ranald ends his days living almost as a hermit, attending only to the passing of seasons, and oblivious of the passing of Earls and Kings. He sets his sights instead on a mythical island 'away beyond Vinland', the Celtic 'Isles of the Blessed' or Tir-nan-og, the land of eternal youth.[14] Spiritual belief in the otherworld is both informed by and appears to displace the recollections of his youthful encounter with Vinland, the land of plenty. This might also be regarded as a form of escapism, replacing politics with religion, history with myth.

Yet, Vinland is the portal through which Ranald believes he has glimpsed the possibility of a harmonious and fulfilling existence. When he is guided in his later years by the local Abbot to think of the joys of heaven as they are fleetingly apprehended on earth, the 'one moment of freedom, its sweetness and purity [which] are a part of him always', it is clear that for Ranald this moment happened in Vinland.[15] Moreover, it is a very specific moment in Vinland, when he encounters a boy about his own age among the native people, and they play and laugh together. The war dance performed by the native people to welcome Ericson and his crew is misinterpreted, however, and one of the Vikings slays a native warrior. The promise of welcome, and the possibility of settling harmoniously in the fertile land in which grapes grow, dissipates rapidly, and the 'skraelings', as the Vikings call the native people, become hostile. Ranald spends much of his later years dreaming of making reparations to the boy for the violence which marred their encounter. His sense of regret functions throughout the novel to retain in view the possibility that the symbolic dance of welcome might not have been broken by the flashing sword of history, that other futures might have materialised from that encounter.

The violence in Vinland is thus fateful of a pattern of such disastrous historical collisions, which seems to resonate down through the long, tortuous history of modernity, a pattern which nonetheless is decided moment by moment, action by action. Mackay Brown articulates this sense of the *longue durée* of modernity through the figure of Leif Ericson, who voices both the expansionist impulse of colonial conquest (discovering the 'empty spaces' which can be made prosperous) and the foresight that the Vikings have disturbed a bond between people and nature which will have disastrous consequences:

'It's a good thing,' said Leif Ericson, 'that there are still some creatures too big and strong for the greed of men to compass.'

'But I think it will come to this in the end,' said Leif later, 'that men will devise weapons to kill even the greatest whale. The skraelings, that we thought so savage and ignorant, were wiser than us in this respect. They only killed as many deer and salmon as they needed for that day's hunger. We are wasteful gluttons and more often than not leave carcasses to rot after a hunt – a shameful thing. Did you not see what reverence the Vinlanders had for the animals and the trees and for all living things? It seemed to me that the Vinlanders had entered into a kind of sacred bond with all the creatures, and there was a fruitful exchange between them, both in matters of life and death.'[16]

It is that sacred bond which Ranald dedicates his life to inculcating on his return to the homestead of his youth, laying down the roots that will become a sustainable farm and community, learning the 'land-wisdom' that he will pass on to his children before he dies.[17] There is a risk in this depiction, as there is in Heidegger's much used concept of 'dwelling' in environmental criticism, of an apparent nativism which romanticises 'closeness to the soil' and 'rootedness', as if these equate to a superior claim to belonging. For Heidegger, dwelling was both a creative and careful mode of living on the earth: 'To be a human being means to be on the earth as a mortal. It means to dwell. The old word *bauen*, which says that man *is* insofar as he *dwells*, this word *bauen* however *also* means at the same time to cherish and protect, to preserve and care for, specifically to till the soil, to cultivate the wine'.[18]

In Mackay Brown's novel, it is not just the cultivation of and care for the land which exemplify this mode of living, for Ranald learns this bond with nature at sea under Leif Ericson's guidance. Ericson talks with the boy about the nights at sea when clouds obscure the stars, and the seafarer must learn to read all the signs of nature around him: 'The skipper can hear, miles away, the smallest wave-wash on a dark cliff.... The cry and flight of a petrel, crossing the prow quickly, tells him that there is land in this direction or that. The slightest smell borne on the wind, seaweed or ice or nettles, tells him this and that'.[19] While these skills are essential to survival, they also become ingrained as a way of understanding nature not just as a resource to be exploited, but as a living force which encompasses humanity. The consequences of not doing so are also made clear by Ericson, as he observes climate change in the frequency of the ice floes around Greenland:

We must not think of the sea as constant and unchanging. Slow pulsings go through the elements of the sea and land – so slow that only a man with grey in his beard may observe them. It seems to me that this northern curve of the world may be growing colder. And if the sea has ice in it, then we may be sure that the lands round about are growing colder too, and soon the roots that nourish men and beasts may be frozen.[20]

The climate change which Ericson identifies is not, of course, the consequence of human industry, yet the novel does imply a strong sense of continuity between the failure to read the signs of natural change in the eleventh century and the reckless destruction of the earth's ecosystems in the twentieth century. In 'Shetland: A Search for Symbols' (1988), Mackay Brown made clear his understanding that the environmental crises which were becoming ever more evident in the 1980s were not just scientific or biological problems, but cultural problems too:

> the richness and strength of a people are not in oil terminals and overfishing (the breaking of the ancient treaty between man and the creatures) and literacy, but in their inheritance from the past, the riches of music and lore and imagination. We cannot know what is in store for us – some sinister symptoms are here already, acid rain, and pollution, and nuclear poison, and the death of seals and seabirds. It may be that our grandchildren will have to look even deeper into the past for meanings. We must hope that the inherited skills and knowledge and the traditional sanctities are not lost in the interim.[21]

It was the task of writers, Mackay Brown argued, to keep these meanings and riches of the imagination alive, to retain ways of knowing the land and the sea which were more than a handbook of techniques. Only in the poetry, art and lore of a place could be the richness of those traditions of life and knowledge inhere to future generations: 'I think, until fairly recently, when a Shetlander said "fish" or "bread", he meant something other than the silver-gray shape on his hook, or the crust he broke at the table'.[22] This is, of course, itself a romanticisation of Shetlanders and may indeed be complicit in a kind of agrarian nostalgia, but it is also an important corrective to the tendency to see in the northern islands and coasts a 'wildness' and 'remoteness' devoid of history and meaning.

A similar tension between the apparently distant historical past and the geopolitical problems of late modernity is evident in Margaret Elphinstone's *The Sea Road*. Elphinstone has worked mostly within the genre of historical fiction, although the first two novels she published, *Incomers* (1987) and *A Sparrow's Flight* (1989), are set within possible future worlds of ecological catastrophe and frail hopes of regeneration.

The future worlds Elphinstone imagines in these novels, however, are hardly distinguishable from the precarious and unforgiving terrain of her subsequent historical novels. *Islanders* (1994), which was the first novel she wrote, is set on Fridarey (Fair Isle) in the twelfth century and aims to tell the story of Norse society from two deliberately disorienting perspectives: the first is to show Norse society from northern perspectives (the novel begins with a map in which north is at the bottom)[23]; the second is to dislodge conventional masculine biases of the story of the Vikings by focusing on female characters. *Hy Brasil* (2002) is set on the mythical Celtic island in the mid-Atlantic, but imagines it as an island which is replete with all the conventional fictional tropes and themes of island literature, including pirate treasure, while also being exposed to the thoroughly modern historical problems of islands. *Voyageurs* (2003) tells the story of a Cumberland Quaker who gets caught up the 1812 war between Canada and the USA in the quest to find his sister, who has eloped with a fur trader into the lakelands of Michigan. *Light* (2006) is set on an island off the Isle of Man, about early lighthouse keepers. *The Gathering Night* (2009) is perhaps Elphinstone's most daring novel, set in Mesolithic Scotland, and imagining the life of a hunter-gatherer society in the aftermath of a tsunami. Adam Thorpe wrote in his review that 'the most telling achievement of *The Gathering Night* is that it persuades us to accept its entirely different value-system without a qualm, and even to regret that humanity ever thought of swapping the hunter's spear for the tiller's spade'.[24] The consistent focus of Elphinstone's work is this challenge of seeing the world from unfamiliar perspectives and the ways in which historical and geopolitical boundaries expose contending value-systems to each other.

The Sea Road is based upon the Icelandic sagas, particularly the Vinland sagas, at the beginning of the eleventh century, but in stressing political tensions in the narration of the Icelanders' encounters with other faiths, languages, and cultures, the novel is thoroughly contemporary in its themes. Gudrid's story of growing up in Iceland and Greenland, and accompanying her husband to Vinland, is narrated to a monastic scribe, Agnar, whose silence punctuates his text of Gudrid's tale (a subversion of the conventional gendered hierarchy of the Icelandic Sagas). The Icelanders live on the edge of the known world, and Gudrid's narrative is transcribed only because Cardinal Hildebrand believes it may be useful in discrediting a political rival in Rome. It survives such political exigencies only because of the power of narrative itself to connect with others:

Agnar writes at the end of his transcription, 'If you write down a person's story, there is a way in which it becomes yours'.[25] This is a kind of possession, he acknowledges, which has the potential to refigure the exigencies of the narrative to other purposes, other points of view. Rome may commission the transcription of Gudrid's narrative, as a record of the liminal outreaches of the Christian empire, but in textual form it takes on a life of its own, giving a validity and centrality to an altogether different sense of cultural geography than the view seen from Rome. Gudrid's narrative, then, subverts the map of conventional geopolitical relations between centre and periphery, just as firmly as the 'upside-down' map of the northern archipelago included in *Islanders*. That tensions between metropolitan and archipelagic conceptions of identity pertain to contemporary Scotland as much as to medieval Iceland illustrates the point that remote history may still be shown to bear legacies for, and analogies with, the present. In this manner, as Ian Campbell argues of a broader tradition of the historical novel in Scottish fiction, Elphinstone's writings can be read as being '*about* Scotland even when their immediate subject matter may not be the country itself', writings which 'by startling revision and re-visioning of the reader's assumptions through their use of space and time, achieve ... a sharpening and refocusing of insight by distancing perception from received opinion'.[26]

In contrast to the glorification of violence and conquest in the sagas, Elphinstone's novel, just like Mackay Brown's *Vinland*, revisits the westward expansion of the Viking settlements as 'a wicked voyage'. For Gudrid, the entry of the Vikings into the western lands is the transgression of a bond between people and land:

> Black crags towered over me, but I was walking through sweet young grass. I stopped by a stream bordered by celandines and river beauty, and looked down into the water clear as air. I looked at the path under my feet, and I thought, 'This path is twelve years old. That's how old we are in this country. And this place, lovely as it is to my eyes, has been here since the nine worlds were made. From the beginning of time it has been like this for the glory of God alone.' Our world is made out of the empty places, Agnar, and we'll never touch anything but the fringes of the unknown. That seems to prove to me that it wasn't made for us.[27]

Vinland itself is such an unknown place, with rivers, islands, woods, and hills, 'all empty and unnamed'.[28] Encounters with the 'savages' who live there are brief and brutal. Whereas Agnar's record of Gudrid's narrative bears the dates and place-names of his transcription, Vinland is defined by its absence of any such records or marks:

> The heart of Vinland is old; the seasons have followed one another here since the world was made, but no time has passed; no one has measured the years that have gone by. No one knows the boundaries of this country; its shores stretch on and on, far into the south of the world, and no one has sailed to the end of them. And no one at all has travelled inland to the heart of the country. There is no way in.[29]

It is not clear from whose perspective such italicised passages in the novel are told—they may be dreams or memories of Gudrid's past, or those of an omniscient narrator. In the context of a novel which constantly focuses our attention on questions of authority, transcription, translation, and voice, however, the question of who is mediating this view of an empty space, apparently boundless, timeless, and nameless, is never innocent. Gudrid's narrative is one of blurred boundaries, of the coexistence of contradictory world views—Christian and pagan, and as Monica Germanà argues, the tension between them is the central dramatic device in the novel.[30] The novel ends with the destabilisation of Agnar's own certainties about Roman perspectives on the farthest reaches of the Christian world.

The liminal spaces of human habitation in the deep north are also the setting for Sarah Moss's first novel, *Cold Earth*. Moss's novel differs from Elphinstone's *The Sea Road* and Mackay Brown's *Vinland*, in that it is set in contemporary Greenland, with a group of archaeologists researching a Viking settlement, yet their camp is haunted by the troubled history of that settlement, and the distant past seems to leak ominously into their present. The novel begins with the first-person narrative of Nina, an English Literature Ph.D. student who has volunteered to help on the archaeological dig, but as she struggles to sleep in the midnight sun, she is increasingly disturbed by visions of the violent end of the Viking community. In her visions, the settlement has been raided by marauding sailors, some of the inhabitants are locked in a burning church, the women have been kidnapped, and the children murdered: '*Screams carry a long way across the quiet sea*'.[31] Nina becomes convinced that the ghosts of this community are disturbed by the archaeologists, and she hears and feels their presence around the camp. As none of her colleagues will believe her, she becomes more isolated, stops eating, and remains in her tent. As the dig progresses, and bodies are unearthed which testify to violent deaths, Nina's visions begin to seem more credible, and the others begin to notice strange occurrences also.

The ingredients of a compelling ghost story are all assembled, yet the power of Moss's novel comes not just from haunting scenes of a violent past, but from its increasingly eerie depiction of the vulnerabilities of the present. Equipped with tinned foods, satellite phone, and satellite Internet access, the expedition begins with all the securities of modern technology. It enables them not just to live in the site long vacated of human habitation, but to believe that they can do so without leaving any traces behind, to live there in precisely the ways that the Greenlanders could not: 'No rubbish, no fires, no soap. No picking anything that grows and no planting anything that doesn't. Good thing the Greenlanders didn't think like that, isn't it, there'd be nothing here for us to find'.[32] The dream of a clean, Godlike modernity, able to study the lives of distant others from a safe and privileged vantage point, begins to fall apart, however. By email, they learn that the few isolated cases of a killer virus which had struck before they left have now become a pandemic. The satellite phone does not work, so they cannot call anyone, including the people responsible for taking them home. The Internet stops working, and they are left wondering if the pandemic has decimated global society. Their food is depleted, they are too far from any habitation to walk or make contact, and tensions between them threaten to turn violent. The vulnerability of modern society to catastrophe is shown to be as thin as the Viking settlement they have come to exhume.

All of the archaeological team have come in quest of an experience of wilderness, to answer questions about the remote past and the conditions of bare life in barely inhabitable environments. Nina is inspired by Victorian conceptions of the far north as a wild place. Ruth is attempting to grieve the loss of her partner: 'I thought wilderness and unspoilt scenery might cure me … but the healing power of natural beauty turns out to be one of those popular myths'.[33] For Jim, the 'real Arctic' is a vision of 'creation on rewind, back towards darkness and the void', but the romance of this notion is exposed when it becomes apparent that they are thoroughly unprepared for the onset of winter.[34] Catriona, on the other hand, has come for the light, an artist familiar with the wet seascapes of Skye, who wishes to paint 'proper ice'.[35] Wilderness turns out to be something different than they had imagined, however: it is neither aesthetically pleasing nor therapeutic, neither distant nor empty.

They learn to see wildness not as the object of a spiritual quest, but in ways which are akin to Kathleen Jamie's observations that wildness is 'a force requiring constant negotiation.... to give birth is to be in a wild place, so is to struggle with pneumonia.... you can look down a microscope, and marvel at the wildness of the processes of our own bodies, the wildness of disease'.[36]

The wild spaces of the north in these fictions turn out to be places with their own dense histories of habitation, meaning, and conflict. The idea of a land of enchantment, or plenitude, or tranquillity, is exposed in each novel as a fantasy, masking the social, gender, and ethnic power struggles of the past and the present. The stories told in the work of Mackay Brown, Elphinstone, and Moss of the 'empty spaces' of the north, and the lines of connection once traced by Norse settlers and raiders across the northern archipelago, reorient our attention away from mythic tropes of adventure and conquest, and focus instead on histories of violence, exclusion, and appropriation. The historical tensions between contending ideologies, between peripheral settlements and political centres, take radically different forms in different ages, but nonetheless resonate with the inequities and strains of contemporary relations between Scotland and England. The northern archipelago at once offers both an alternative geographical perspective on Scottish national identity, beyond the troubled legacies of the Union, and a reminder of the powerful myths at stake in cultural conceptions of 'wild' or 'empty' spaces, for as Peter Davidson writes in *The Idea of the North*, 'In any Scottish context "wilderness" is a fraught term, a political time bomb'.[37]

NOTES

1. Kathleen Jamie, 'A Lone Enraptured Male', *London Review of Books* 30:5 (6 March 2008), 25–27.
2. Ibid., 25.
3. Ibid., 26.
4. Ibid., 26.
5. Kathleen Jamie, 'Three Ways of Looking at St Kilda', *Sightlines* (London: Sort of Books, 2012), 143, 158.
6. Alan Riach, 'Mr and Mrs Scotland are Taking a Vacation in the Autonomous Region', in *Kathleen Jamie: Essays and Poems on Her Work*, ed. Rachel Falconer (Edinburgh: Edinburgh University Press, 2015), 21, 21–31.

7. Jamie, 'A Lone Enraptured Male', 25, 27.
8. Peter Davidson, *The Idea of North* (London: Reaktion Books, 2005), 19.
9. Ibid., 9.
10. Cairns Craig, *The Modern Scottish Novel: Narrative and the National Imagination* (Edinburgh: Edinburgh University Press, 1999), 117–18.
11. Ibid., 135.
12. Roderick Watson, *The Literature of Scotland: The Twentieth Century*, 2nd edition (Basingstoke: Palgrave, 2007), 131.
13. George Mackay Brown, *Greenvoe* (Harmondsworth: Penguin, 1976), 249.
14. George Mackay Brown, *Vinland* (Edinburgh: Polygon, 2011), 258.
15. Ibid., 208.
16. Ibid., 27.
17. Ibid., 176.
18. Martin Heidegger, 'Building Dwelling Thinking', in *Poetry, Language, Thought*, trans. Albert Hofstadter (New York: HarperCollins, 2001), 145.
19. Mackay Brown, *Vinland*, 26.
20. Ibid., 26–27.
21. George Mackay Brown, 'Shetland: A Search for Symbols', in *Northern Lights: A Poet's Sources*, ed. Archie Bevan and Brian Murray (Edinburgh: Polygon, 2007), 250.
22. Ibid., 271.
23. Margaret Elphinstone, *Islanders* (Glasgow: Kennedy & Boyd, 2008), xx.
24. Adam Thorpe, 'Love in the Mesolithic Era', *The Guardian*, 25 July 2009, 8.
25. Margaret Elphinstone, *The Sea Road* (Edinburgh: Canongate, 2001), 243.
26. Ian Campbell, 'Disorientations of Place, Time and "Scottishness": Conan Doyle, Linklater, Gunn, Mackay Brown and Elphinstone', in *The Edinburgh History of Scottish Literature*, Vol. 3, ed. Ian Brown (Edinburgh: Edinburgh University Press, 2007), 106, 106–113.
27. Elphinstone, *The Sea Road*, 119.
28. Ibid., 194.
29. Ibid., 194.
30. Monica Germanà, *Scottish Women's Gothic and Fantastic Writing: Fiction Since 1978* (Edinburgh: Edinburgh University Press, 2010), 35.
31. Sarah Moss, *Cold Earth* (London: Granta, 2010), 2.
32. Ibid., 15.
33. Ibid., 104.
34. Ibid., 184.
35. Ibid., 37.
36. Jamie, 'A Lone Enraptured Male', 27.
37. Davidson, *The Idea of the North* 242:7. "Greenock-Outer Space: Place and Space in Ken MacLeod's *The Human Front* and *Descent*".

WORKS CITED

Brown, George Mackay. *Greenvoe*. Harmondsworth: Penguin, 1976.

———. 'Shetland: A Search for Symbols'. *Northern Lights: A Poet's Sources*. Ed. Archie Bevan and Brian Murray. Edinburgh: Polygon, 2007. 237–303.

———. *Vinland*. Edinburgh: Polygon, 2011.

Campbell, Ian. 'Disorientations of Place, Time and "Scottishness"': Conan Doyle, Linklater, Gunn, Mackay Brown and Elphinstone'. *The Edinburgh History of Scottish Literature*, Vol. 3. Ed. Ian Brown. Edinburgh: Edinburgh University Press, 2007. 106–13.

Craig, Cairns. *The Modern Scottish Novel: Narrative and the National Imagination*. Edinburgh: Edinburgh University Press, 1999.

Davidson, Peter. *The Idea of North*. London: Reaktion Books, 2005.

Elphinstone, Margaret. *The Sea Road*. Edinburgh: Canongate, 2001.

———. *Islanders*. Glasgow: Kennedy & Boyd, 2008.

Germanà, Monica. *Scottish Women's Gothic and Fantastic Writing: Fiction Since 1978*. Edinburgh: Edinburgh University Press, 2010.

Heidegger, Martin. 'Building Dwelling Thinking'. *Poetry, Language, Thought*. Trans. Albert Hofstadter. New York: HarperCollins, 2001. 143–59.

Jamie, Kathleen. 'A Lone Enraptured Male'. *London Review of Books* 30:5 (6 March 2008). 25–27.

———. 'Three Ways of Looking at St Kilda'. *Sightlines*. London: Sort of Books, 2012. 131–63.

Macfarlane, Robert. *The Wild Places*. London: Granta, 2007.

Moss, Sarah. *Cold Earth*. London: Granta, 2010.

Riach, Alan. 'Mr and Mrs Scotland are Taking a Vacation in the Autonomous Region'. *Kathleen Jamie: Essays and Poems on Her Work*. Ed. Rachel Falconer. Edinburgh: Edinburgh University Press, 2015. 21–31.

Stegner, Wallace. *Where the Bluebird Sings to the Lemonade Springs*. London: Penguin, 1992.

Thorpe, Adam. 'Love in the Mesolithic Era'. *The Guardian*, 25 July 2009. 8.

Watson, Roderick. *The Literature of Scotland: The Twentieth Century*, 2nd edition. Basingstoke: Palgrave, 2007.

'Keep Looking, Even When There's Nothing Much to See': Re-imagining Scottish Landscapes in Kathleen Jamie's Non-fiction

Ewa Chodnikiewicz

"It was probably nothing, so I said nothing, but kept looking. That's what the keen-eyed naturalists say. Keep looking. Keep looking, even when there's nothing much to see. That way your eye learns what's common, so when the uncommon appears, your eye will tell you" (*Sightlines* 66–67). This is what Kathleen Jamie, a Scottish nature poet and non-fiction writer, expresses in one of her collections of essays *Sightlines: A Conversation with the Natural World*. With her attentive eye and naturalist's affinity for the natural places, Jamie presents a new insight into the natural surroundings of her native country, Scotland. Jamie's way of writing about the natural world encourages readers to look at well-known places afresh and discover them often from unusual perspective. As a result, Jamie's writing about nature may be referred to as "The New Nature Writing". The term was first used by Richard Kerridge in his essay "Ecological Hardy". He argued that "environmentalism calls for a new nature writing, clearly

E. Chodnikiewicz (✉)
University of Gdańsk, Gdańsk, Poland

© The Author(s) 2019   87
M. Szuba and J. Wolfreys (Eds.), *The Poetics of Space and Place in Scottish Literature*, Geocriticism and Spatial Literary Studies,
https://doi.org/10.1007/978-3-030-12645-2_6

differentiated from the conservative tradition and aware of its appeals and dangers" (138). However, the term was formally coined by Jason Cowley in the British literary magazine *Granta*. Studying the recent environmental literature, he remarked that the new nature writers "share a sense that we are devouring our world, that there is simply no longer any natural landscape or ecosystem that is unchanged by humans. But they don't simply want to walk into the wild, to rhapsodize and commune: they aspire to see with a scientific eye and write with literary effect" (9).

Nowadays, the environmental crisis is transforming the natural world, which, simultaneously, is changing the concept and understanding of nature. As a result, the way writers reflect on the natural environment needs to be different. Kenneth White believes that nature writing in Scotland needs to establish a new relationship with nature that is distinct from "rural bucolic" of English tradition (14). In *The End of Nature*, Bill McKibben strongly emphasizes humans' negative impact on the environment as well as the way it changes the understanding of "nature":

> When I say "nature", I mean a certain set of human ideas about the world and our place in it. But the death of those ideas begins with concrete changes in the reality around us – changes that scientists can measure and enumerate. More and more frequently, these changes will clash with our perceptions, until, finally, our sense of nature as eternal and separate is washed away [...]. (7)

Tim Dee also argues that new understandings of nature are far from those presented in the past:

> Country diaries survive in some newspapers but DDT, species losses, and Ted Hughes' gore-poetics saw-off the nice in the 1970s, while nature itself- under the human heel – has been pushed, bloodied, shrunken and ruined to the front of the stage ever since. There, even enfeebled, it has called for new descriptions, fresh thoughts. (22)

Morton, however, suggests that nature is something "other": "[...] there is a 'thing' called nature that is 'out there' (183). It might be assumed that nature is "not all primroses and otters" (25) as Jamie writes in *Sightlines*. It can be everything that concerns humanity, and it is closer than we realize. The most important is experimenting with different ways of looking at the natural world, and I believe that this is what Jamie does in her essays.

To produce the collections of essays *Sightlines* and *Findings* Jamie walked and sailed many miles. She had conversation with experts at visual artists, pathologists, curators and ornithologists. However, she shows a number of times that to notice the beauty of nature sometimes it is just enough to listen to it around our houses during everyday domestic duties: "[...] I chanced to look out of the window and saw the male osprey himself. [...] then the osprey was gone and I turned back to the dryer, looking for matching socks" (*Findings* 45–46). Natural landscapes, highland areas and their beauty co-exist in Jamie's Scotland together with animals, birds and human bodies. In my essay, I would like to present three aspects of Jamie's perception of the natural world of Scotland which is not only "primroses and otters" (*Sightlines* 24–25).

The first point I would like to highlight is the way Jamie writes about the places she visits. Reading the collections of essays *Sightlines* and *Findings* we are taken for a vivid trip around the islands of Scotland, mainly to the Hebridean islands of St Kilda, Rona, and to the Orkneys where Jamie reflects on darkness and light. She also takes readers to the gannetry off the coast of Scotland and follows the corncrakes' remarkable sounds on Coll. Jamie does not only focus on the aesthetic values of places, but she also presents them from a different perspective than it may be expected, putting emphasis on details. Furthermore, her both physical and mental journeys around Scotland adopt more scientific features than only down-to-earth ones. The first example illustrating this argument is Jamie's visit to St Kilda. She attempts to reach the island three times and unfortunately the two of them are unsuccessful because of the strong wind. She sees the island from the yacht and when anchoring on a cliff bay, which enables her to see St Kilda, as she says "fleetingly" (*Sightlines* 106) and to feel its abandonment wondering "how rarely we stand still for an hour watching" (*Sightlines* 103). Fortunately, the third visit is lucky as she goes there with the group of surveyors doing research on the buildings called cleits which are very unique to St Kilda. However, at the beginning of the trip, Jamie cannot understand the surveyors' enchantment with the cluster of old buildings regarded as a "cultural landscape":

A 'cultural landscape' they called it, but up on the island's heights, giddied by the cloud shadows over the turf, and by sea and sky, and distracted everywhere by birds, you could be forgiven for asking where, in this wild place, was the culture? But soon I understood that, ranged along the cliff tops, camouflaged by stone and turf, were yet more cleits. They were everywhere. The more you saw, clinging to steep slopes or perched on rocky tables, the more there were. (*Sightlines* 113)

Jamie does not understand the artistic values of the view. She is able to notice more obvious things for her at first glance—birds. She wonders what can be more beautiful than the natural view without any human contribution. Nonetheless, looking more attentively, Jamie becomes fascinated with the uniqueness of the place and changes the way of looking at the surroundings:

> Being with the surveyors taught me to change my focus. It was like the difference between looking through the window pane and looking at it. Look through the window, and you'd see the sea, wildness, distance isolation. Look at it, and you saw utility, food security, domestic management. (*Sightlines* 117)

Jamie's observation explains the way she learns to watch and feel the world around her—the essence is to look deeper than we usually do. When observing nature, we should open to different interpretations and learn to view the world from a different angle. This is the reason why in her essays Jamie writes about three ways of looking at St Kilda. Her experience shows that even if you are not able to physically make a trip around the place, you can feel it in a different way. Jamie's third time on St Kilda does not focus on the pure beauty of the place itself. She changes her perspective and finds the essence in cleits. Even when she considers staying for more days on the island herself, she states: "Ach, Enough. I went to get ready. [...] To linger on St Kilda just for the sake of it would merely have been romance" (*Sightlines* 120). Jamie does much more than just a visit and feeling sentimental in a place. She is a deep thinker on the human condition and nature, especially the strong relationship between the two. This example may be followed by the observation of a moth on the Lochan moor. After eating breakfast at the moor's side, Jamie goes to the water to rinse the bowl when suddenly a moth catches her attention. It is floating captive between three rocks, so Jamie attempts to make it free and put it on the rock by the use of the spoon. Unfortunately, helping the moth is not an easy task, as it made the wings wet. The encounter with the moth makes Jamie see the natural environment from other perspective. What is more, her intervention shows how much she is sensitive to nature. While looking at the moth's wings through a magnifying glass, she gives a detailed description of its behaviour and appearance, worried that she could do it more harm than good. Later on in the essay, Jamie admits that she was supposed to write about something different that she actually did. Nevertheless, this situation amazes her:

> I had been absorbed in the miniscule: a moth's eye, a dab of lichen; been granted a glimpse into the countless millions of tiny processes and events that form the moor. Millions! Tiny creatures, flowers, bacteria, opening, growing, dividing, creeping about their business. It's all happening out there, and all you have to do, girl, is get your foot out of your eye. (*Sightlines* 128)

Jamie's reflection proves that it is crucial to look deeper into the land to present its real beauty. There are millions of creatures in it and they make the landscape unique and picturesque. Jamie's looking at Scotland is realistic and presents a detailed perspective which urges readers to look at the natural world anew. By the heartbreaking encounter with a moth, readers of Jamie's essays find themselves constantly re-examining and reassessing the views concerning their place on the earth. It shows how much sensitive and attentive we should be in order to notice the real beauty of the natural world. However, apart from being a careful observer, Jamie is also an excellent thinker. Her trip to the Orkneys to experience "real, natural, starry dark, solstice dark [...] (*Findings* 5) supports this point. Being puzzled by the metaphors of darkness and light, she decides to check if they are true: "Pity the dark: we're so concerned to overcome and banish it, it's crammed full of all that's devilish, like some grim cupboard under the stair. But dark is good. We are carried in the darkness, are we not?" (*Findings* 3). Jamie writes that it were Christians who created the metaphorical dark which is often associated with death, whereas the light is the way of new life and salvation. Jamie believes that to experience the real dark we have to abandon the clichés and be open to new interpretations in order to create refreshed ideas: "We couldn't see the real dark for the metaphorical dark. Because of metaphorical dark, the death dark, we were constantly concerned to banish the natural dark" (*Findings* 10). Unfortunately, her attempts to experience the real darkness of the Orkneys while swimming on a ship was unsuccessful because of the full moon. The visit to Maes Howe was the last chance. Maes Howe is a Neolithic chambered cairn and passage tomb on Mainland, Orkney. The builders of the tomb were aware of the regular movement of the sun in the sky which is indicated by the fact that during the winter solstice the sun's rays fall directly into the tomb. Jamie wants to see this "trick of the light" (*Findings* 23) unfortunately, to no effect. However, she is amazed by the lights of lasers used by the surveyors who were carrying out some research at that time:

> My ventures into light and dark had been ill-starred. I'd had no dramatic dark, neither at sea nor in the tomb, and no resurrecting beam of sunlight. But lasers are light, aren't they? Intensified, organized light. I'd crept into Maes Howe at solstice, hoping for Neolithic technology; what I'd found was the technology of the 21st century. Here were skilled people making the measurements by light and time. That thought pleased me. (*Findings* 24)

Jamie's final reflection on the play of light and darkness is that in truth it is not the real metaphorical darkness people overcame, but only the possibility to see in the dark:

> We have not banished death, but we have banished the dark. We have light we have made, we can see that there are, metaphorically speaking, cracks. We are doing damage, and have growing sense of responsibility. [...] We look about the world, by the light we have made, and realize it's all vulnerable, and all worth saving, and no one can do it but us. (*Findings* 24)

This thought might explain the reason why Jamie connects the general beliefs and metaphors of dark and light with Christmas time when the shops and streets are decorated with colourful lights. When writing about nature, she always manages to find connections with everyday domestic situations. Furthermore, Jamie's different aspects of looking at darkness and light can be followed by her experience of silence while watching icebergs on the sea:

> That's what we see. What we listen to, though, is silence. Slowly we enter the most extraordinary silence, a radiant silence. It radiates from the mountains, and the ice and the sky, a mineral silence which presses powerfully on our bodies, coming from very far off. It's deep and quite frightening, and makes my mind seem clamorous as a goose. I want to quell my mind but I think it would take years. I glance at the others. Some people are looking out at the distant land and sea; others have their heads bowed, as if in church. (*Sightlines* 11)

In comparison with the experience of darkness and light, it may be stated that silence may be more terrifying than darkness. As a result, all Jamie's experiences mentioned above prove that there are more fascinating things to notice when you observe the world with a great insight.

However, sometimes Jamie's encounters with natural creatures lead to sad discoveries. When she visits the river Braan, she observes salmon leaping against the weight of tremendously fast water. Jamie wonders if their attempts to clear the fall are a matter of a technique or instinct. Standing among other fascinated viewers—tourists and photographers, she is amazed by the effort of the salmon to jump into the water. When one of the fish leaps, everyone shows their excitement shouting "Ho!": "Birch leaves were twirling down into the water. The rocks in the middle of the river were patted with their gentle shapes. The leaves twirled down, landed on the water, then were swept merrily over the falls and away. There was a lull, then Ho! – a leaping fish" (*Findings* 73). However, after a conversation with her neighbour Robin, she realizes that the river Braan is not a natural salmon river and there are hatcheries upstream created to examine the hatchlings, how they disperse and survive. After this revelation Jamie changes her attitude to fish and thinks ironically about the fascinated viewers who came to the river specially to watch the leaping salmon which according to them replenish their souls:

> I'd written about watching the salmon leap before Robin's revelation, but after that I put the work aside, because something had changed in my attitude to the fish. Now I knew a secret, something the salmon didn't, that whether it be instinct or technique it didn't matter, their effort was all hopeless. I thought about the little passing audience, the sheer goodwill of the viewers from the balcony; the photographer with his 'wildscapes' and the old man from Kirkcaldy, and the mild ladies who said, 'Are they here? We'd heard they were here. We came specially.' Replenishing our souls. Joke. Ho Ho. Could I replenish my soul by watching the salmon try to leap the falls, knowing all the while that it was useless? (*Findings* 79–80)

The way Jamie writes about the people watching leaping salmon changes as well as her attitude towards this show. She writes about the salmon with a great sympathy presenting humans in a bad light. Moreover, Jamie makes us aware of the fact that what we sometimes consider to be beautiful and natural in the environment may appear disappointingly artificial and humans are responsible for this destructive intervention:

They say the day is coming – it may already be here when there will be no wild creatures. That is, when no species on the planet will be able to further itself without reference or negotiation with us. When our intervention or restraint will be a factor in their continued existence. Every creature: salmon, sand martins, seals, flies. What does this matter? (*Findings* 79)

This may even lead to the assumption that in the future there will be no natural beauty. Timothy Clark claims that "in the limited sense of places unaffected by human activity there is no nature as such left on the planet but there are more environments, some more pristine than others" (6)—this is what Jamie also highlights in her observations—it is significant to look deeper.

The second aspect of Jamie's representation of the natural world is her keen eye on what is happening around her home in Fife. Jamie reflects on nature while observing birds, cobwebs or the changing colours of the moon from her attic window. She is amazed by the variety of shapes and colours it adopts during the eclipse:

By its shadow, the earth had been revealed as massive and mineral, but the lifeless moon, on entering into that shadow was changing color. It looked as though becoming less barren, more like a living thing. Further, because the reddish coloration of the moon's lower side deepened as it curved away out of sight, it showed that the moon was a sphere. No longer a silver plate hung in the sky, the moon was turning into a bruised ball. The moon was a sphere [...]. Now the whole of the moon was painted with coppery reds, weal-reds. They were mammalian colours, the shades of an incarnation, colours liable to pain [...] Here was the moon becoming fruit or flesh; she looked like the one fruit in a vanitas painting, the one soft globe among the peaches and pomegranates which is already beginning to darken toward decay. (*Sightlines* 95–96)

Jamie observes the moon with an extraordinary attention being absorbed in every detail of its transformation, which makes the impression that the moon lives. Playing with colours and their movements on the moon, Jamie makes readers imagine it clearly in their minds. She also writes that the eclipse influences the animals as the dogs start barking and are more watchful as if they knew about the changing moon.

Observing cobwebs around her home leads Jamie to deeper conclusions. She writes about cobwebs in the context of her husband's illness trying to compare them with human lungs:

What are we to imagine, the breathing area of our lungs, the 600 million of alveoli? Spread out like what? Tarpaulin? Frost? A fine, fine cobwebs, exchanging gases with the open air? And what are our nerves? There are hundreds of miles of neurones in our brains. I tried to imagine it, all that nerve, all that awareness and alertness spread out around me. All that listening. (*Findings* 104–05)

Jamie never literally compares the structure of lungs to the cobwebs. However, writing about her ill husband who is about to die, she reflects on both cobwebs and spiders juxtaposing their fleetingness with human life: "The young hatch and then disperse 'by climbing onto a vantage point, spinning a silk thread and waiting for the wind to catch it and whisk them away" (*Findings* 113). Writing about the natural world around her house, Jamie demonstrates that we do not need to go far to discover the uniqueness of nature. The essence is not to perceive what we expect and what we are accustomed to, but it is important to look at the world with a fresh eye and a looser mind, so the familiar may become new. Jamie's keen observations make her aware of everything which happens near her house. For instance, she writes that every year in the third week of February, she observes a natural play of light which comes back, because winter's blackness and darkness disappears although the trees are still bare and stark. She provides readers with a vivid and gentle description of natural processes visible from her window:

The sun is still low in the sky, even at noon, hanging over the hills southwest. Its light spills out of the southwest, the same direction as the wind: both sunlight and wind arrive together out of the same airt, an invasion of light and air out of a sky of quickly moving clouds, working together as a swift team. The wind lifts the grasses and moves the thin branches of the leafless trees and the sun shines on them, in one movement, so light and air are as one, two aspects of the same entity. The light is razor-like, edging grasses and twigs of the willow and apple trees and birch. The garden is all left-leaning filaments of light, such as you see on cobwebs, mostly, too hard to be called a sparkle, too metallic, but the whole garden's being given a brisk spring-clean. (*Sightlines* 72)

Jamie encourages her audience to see the world with great precision, especially around domestic places. In this passage, she brings forth the spirit of a place making it familiar to readers. Furthermore, she demonstrates that nature is harmonious and all its components work together. One movement is followed by another creating a splendid view.

When reading *Findings* it can be assumed that bird-life seems to be Jamie's favourite—observable from home while doing domestic chores or walks, she often combines nature with her everyday life:

> Between the laundry and fetching the kids from school, that's how birds enter my life, I listen. During a lull in the traffic, oyster catchers. In the school playground, sparrows [...]. There are old swallows' nests up there. It's late April, but where are the swallows? The birds live at the edge of my life. (*Findings* 39)

What is more, Jamie describes in details the life of peregrines, ospreys and cranes engaging a lot in their life and watching how they behave, live and nest. For instance, she watches the peregrine falcon which has nested near her home:

> Terribly, lecherously, his eye fell on every passing bird. He checked the sky constantly. In a single minute, he shifted his gaze twenty times, left, right, directly overhead, more often than a Formula One driver changes gear. Here's a line I think of whenever I glimpse a bird of prey on a fence post, or watch a kestrel hovering. If you've seen the hawk, be sure, the hawk has seen you. (*Findings* 32)

Jamie's careful observations show how much it is possible to see in nature and how birds' lives differ from ours: "I like knowing these things I like being able to glance up from my own everyday business, to see the osprey or the peregrine going about hers" (*Findings* 43). With her interpretation of the natural world, she makes a well-known area a fresh and new place. In addition, Jamie emphasizes the fact that the knowledge is not necessary to observe the natural environment because "there are things which cannot be said – not by scientists, anyway" (*Findings* 98). She encourages us to discover the world naturally on our own and understand in the way we see it:

> This is what I want to learn: to notice, but not to analyze. To still the part of the brain that's yammering. 'My god, what's that? A stork, a crane, an ibis? – don't be silly, it's just a weird heron.' Sometimes we have to hush the frantic inner voice that says 'Don't be stupid,' and learn again to look, to listen. You can do the organizing and redrafting later, the diagnosing and indentifying later, but right now, just be open to it, see how it's tilting nervously into the wind, try to see the colour, the unchancy shape – hold it in your head, bring it home intact. (*Findings* 42)

Jamie expresses her belief that the natural environment is home for humans and they should take advantage of its goods. She also believes that some places and natural phenomena cannot be expressed in any words because they are so remarkable that they leave us speechless:

> I made notes, but the reason I've come to the end of the road to walk along the cliffs is because language fails me there. If we work always in words, sometimes we need to recuperate in a place where language doesn't join up, where we're thrown back on a few elementary nouns. Sea. Bird. Sky. (*Findings* 164)

Jamie also notices birds with a considerable sensitivity even when walking in Edinburgh: "The only birds visible were herring gulls resting on chimneypots, or cruising over the rooftops like pieces flaked off from the city's skin" (*Findings* 155). Jamie treats the streets of Edinburgh as human landscapes—she comes to the same conclusion when observing salmon in the Braan river, the conclusion that nothing exists in isolation and the signs of human intervention are everywhere: "We have a crisis because we have lost our ability to see the natural world, or find it meaningful. There had been a break-down in reciprocity. Humanity had taken a wrong path, had become destructive and insulated" (*Sightilnes* 24). Perhaps, this is why Jamie decides to write about herself, her family and everyday activities while writing about nature—as an observer, she never allows herself to forget her own place in the environment and as a human, sometimes she is unaware of the negative influence to the natural environment. This is why by her remarkable style of writing, she tries to raise our awareness by looking for the smallest details, even these not seen with the naked eye.

The last aspect concerns Jamie's observation of the internal parts of human body, which change her understanding of the term "nature". Frustrated after an environmental conference that she attended, she meets Professor Frank Carey, clinical consultant in pathology at Ninewells Hospital in Dundee. Then, she realizes that "There's our own intimate, inner natural world, the body's weird shapes and forms [...]. There are other species, not dolphins arching clear from the water, but the bacteria that can pull the rug from under us" (*Sightlines* 25). During the meeting, Jamie takes a guided tour into human bodies to see what can destroy them inside. She looks at the liver cancerous cells through the microscope and discovers completely different landscapes than she saw around Scotland:

> I was admitted to another world, where everything was pink. I was look-
> ing down from a great height upon a pink countryside, a landscape. There
> was an estuary, with a north bank and a south. In the estuary were wing-
> shaped river islands or sandbanks, as if was low tide. It was astonishing, a
> map of the familiar; it was our local river, as seen by a hawk. (*Sightlines* 30)

Jamie presents another view on nature—it is not only what can be noted outdoors, but there is much more than that. Returning home after the meeting with the professor, she contemplates on the river which she drives along. She relates it with what she saw under the microscope wondering how many things are undiscovered in the natural world because they are not able to be seen with our eyes:

> I drove home along the river I'd fancied I'd seen in the poor man's liver
> cells. The tide was in, no sandbanks. The inner body, plumbing and land-
> scapes and bacteria. The outer world also had flown open like a door, and
> I wondered as I drove, and I wonder still, what is it that we're *just not see-
> ing*? (*Sightlines* 35)

Another example is Jamie's visit to the Surgeons' Hall in Edinburgh, which leads her to the same conclusion. Humans are strongly connected to nature in many ways and the outside environment resembles inside environment. Watching the collections of human body parts, she is amazed by the beauty of some specimens and realizes one more time that nature is inside us. She says: "We consider the natural world as 'out there', an 'environment', but these objects in the jars show us the forms concealed inside, the intimate unknown. [...] 'in the midst of this city, you think you are removed from nature, they say – 'but look within'" (*Findings* 141). A number of times in her essays she states that everything in the world is a wholeness. When looking at the specimens in the jars, she compares them to the outside environment and finds them beautiful and fascinating like the landscapes of Scotland which she has admired before:

> Many of the specimens are beautiful. One of the earliest is what looks like
> bracket fungus, but it is actually a fine slice of kidney into which the then
> preservator has introduced mercury. Silver threads of mercury fan through
> the tissue, illustrating blood vessels. It is quite lovely, one could wear it as
> a brooch. You think 'bracket fungus', and the tiny veins around an ectopic
> kidney are identical to dried lichen. There are bezoars – hard masses of

indigestible material like hair or straw, which people have swallowed, and which over time have mixed with mucus and moulded to the shape of the stomach, so when removed they resemble peaches or bird's nests. (*Findings* 140–41)

Moreover, when she looks at the stalagmites in a cave, where the walls are covered with Neolithic animal paintings, describing them she adds: "We have entered a body, and are moving through its ducts and channels and states of processes. The very chamber we stand in is streaked with iron-red; it's like the inside of a cranium, a mind-space, as though the cave were thinking us" (*Sightlines* 121). Jamie shows one more time how many similarities can be found between our bodies and the outside environment. When observing more carefully, there is a range of similarities to be noticed. When Jamie visits Bergen Natural History Museum, she enters the hall with the skeletons of whales and becomes enchanted by their enormousness, saying that it is "less an animal, more a narrative" (*Sightlines* 74). After watching the skeletons, she concludes: "Whales is what we were. This is what we are. Spend a little time here and you too feel how it is to be a huge mammal of the seas, to require the sea to hold you, to grow so big at the ocean's hospitability" (*Sightlines* 75). Jamie emphasizes the fact that to know other living creatures means to know ourselves. Additionally, exploring the skeletons makes her identify with the whales: "Despite the size, you could, with a minimum of effort, extend your sense of self, and imagine this was your body, moving through the ocean. You could begin to imagine what it might feel like, to be a blue whale (*Sightlines* 88)."

In conclusion, the three aspects presented in my essay reveal a complex view of the natural world in the light of "The New Nature Writing". In the collections *Sightlines* and *Findings*, Jamie emphasizes the uniqueness of places going through their smallest components observable even in everyday activities, and finally discovering nature inside the human body. Jamie's ability to combine Scotland with her personal and scientific observations on nature makes that nature a different, new place. I believe that Jamie wants us to change our perception and the way we interpret the natural environment. The most crucial thing is to look deeper and try to find the unusual. She also expresses her great concern about human negative intervention to the natural environment where more and more things become artificial: "Maybe five thousand years from now we will indeed be living among replicas. We may be replicas ourselves.

It's not impossible. But I have my doubts" (*Findings* 25). In both collections, Jamie proves that nature is not only flowers and landscapes. Her technique not only re-imagines the landscapes of Scotland showing them in complex and unusual ways, but also urges humans to take care of their natural habitat.

WORKS CITED

Clark, Timothy. *The Cambridge Introduction to Literature and Environment.* New York: Cambridge University Press, 2011.

Cowley, Jason, ed. *Granta 102: The New Nature Writing.* New York: Granta Publications, 2008.

Dee, Tim. 'Nature Writing'. *Archipelago* 5 (Spring 2011): 21–30.

Jamie, Kathleen. *Sightlines: A Conversation with the Natural World.* London: Sort of Books, 2012.

———. *Findings.* London: Sort of Books, 2015.

Kerridge, Richard. 'Ecological Hardy'. *Beyond Nature Writing: Expanding the Boundaries of Ecocriticism.* Ed. Karla Armbruster and Kathleen R. Wallace. Charlottesville and London: University Press of Virginia, 2001. 126–42.

McKibben, Bill. *The End of Nature.* London: Penguin, 1990.

Morton, Timothy. *Ecology Without Nature, Rethinking Environmental Aesthetics.* The United States of America: President and Fellows of Harvard College, 2007.

Greenock-Outer Space: Place and Space in Ken Macleod's *The Human Front* and *Descent*

Jessica Aliaga Lavrijsen

Introduction: The Spatial (Transmodern) Turn in Literature

Traditionally, Scotland has been considered a relatively small nation with strong local interests. However, the truth is that contemporary Scotland is by no means provincial or insulated from the rest of the world. Quite the contrary, the Scottish nation and its cultural production have been considered to be rather international and innovative, especially since the cultural revival of the twentieth century—that is, since the Scottish Renaissance, commenced and lead by Hugh MacDiarmid, among other writers and thinkers such as George Douglas, Lewis Grassic Gibbon, Edwin Muir or Neil M. Gunn (Aliaga 8). As their writings showed once and for all, the use of the vernacular and the love for the local, for what is specific to a certain space (and time), do not make a nation's literature small, but distinctive and multiform instead (Korzeniowska 37). The distinctiveness or uniqueness of both the Scottish character and

J. Aliaga Lavrijsen (✉)
Centro Universitario de la Defensa, Zaragoza, Spain

© The Author(s) 2019
M. Szuba and J. Wolfreys (eds.), *The Poetics of Space and Place in Scottish Literature*, Geocriticism and Spatial Literary Studies, https://doi.org/10.1007/978-3-030-12645-2_7

the Scottish landscapes is not something newly discovered, whether one agrees with the idea of the Caledonian Antisyzygy—or the "polar twins of the Scottish Muse" mentioned by Smith in his seminal work *Scottish Literature, Character and Influence* (Smith 20)[1]—or not. After all, geographic place and social space matter a lot, despite the fact that "place" has not been studied as a central literary aspect until quite recently.

Edward S. Casey stated that, in the period of modernity, "place has come to be not only neglected but actively suppressed. Owing to the triumph of the natural and social sciences in this same period, any serious talk of place has been regarded as regressive or trivial" (Casey xiv). In this line, Thomas Brockelman has pointed out that "in the past two centuries to embrace place has meant to resist the 'abstract' character of modern life" (Brockelman 36). The idea that to be modern implies to give up the sense of place—more associated with the late medieval hierarchical world (Brockelman 36)—in favour of time and space, could make us believe that place studies reject modernity. However, it is my insight that it is not a drastic rejection of modernity but an integration of it, and that it has been the rise of Transmodernity—term used by Rosa María Rodríguez Magda in 1989 to refer to the theoretical configuration of the change of paradigm of the late twentieth century and the beginning of the twenty-first century (Rodríguez Magda, "Transmodernidad" 1–2)—that which has finally allowed space to find its place in literary theory.

It is necessary to briefly focus on the concept of Transmodernity, as it will help us to understand the spatial turn that some critics have observed in sociocultural anthropology and literary theory in particular, replacing the earlier interest on the paradigm of time (Hess-Lüttich 3). It will contextualize as well as the current interest in the "glocal" or in the concept of "glocalization", a term popularized by sociologist Roland Robertson to refer to the simultaneity of both universalizing and particularizing tendencies of contemporary globality.

Transmodernity is thus a concept used to demarcate a change of paradigm that is presently taking place. Rodríguez Magda has used the term "Transmodernity" (1981) to refer to the synthesis of Modernity and Postmodernity that would describe a globalized, rhythomatic, technologic society, developed in the countries of the first world, which opposes otherness while at the same time penetrating and assuming it, trying to transcend this surrounding, hyperreal and relativistic closure (Rodríguez Magda, "Transmodernidad" 2–3). According to Rodríguez Magda, the industrial societies found its correspondence in modern culture, postindustrial societies in postmodern culture, and our present-day globalized—or rather we should say glocalized—society in the trans-modern culture, which is characterized by its fluid hybridity (Rodríguez Magda, "Transmodernidad" 7–8). In Transmodernity—regarded as virtual, transnational, trans-ethnically cosmopolitan, connective, strategic, transubiquitous, etc. (Rodríguez Magda, *Transmodernidad* 34)—time is instantaneous; that is, it has become a present which is continuously being updated, and space is created between the momentary attraction to the local and the surrounding set that includes the specific (Rodríguez Magda, "Transmodernidad" 10).

Frederick Jameson, in his book *Postmodernism*, defines this "spatialization of the temporal" as a hallmark of a new paradigm: "A certain spatial turn has often seemed to offer one or more productive ways of distinguishing postmodernism from modernism proper" (Jameson 154). And this new paradigm would correspond to Rodríguez Magda's Transmodernity, which is linked to new conceptualizations of space and time, as we shall see.

The concept of glocalization is a key to understand the transmodern. Robertson does not understand the local as opposed to the global, but rather he views both tendencies as dialectical forces that transcend polarity (Robertson 29). Rather, he states that the local is "an aspect of globalization", as our sense of home is not being destroyed by globalization, but instead, "globalization has involved the reconstruction [...] of 'home', 'community' and 'locality'" (Robertson 30 and Abu-Lughod). The local is constructed on trans- or super-local basis (Robertson 26), and thus cannot be understood without the global. The particular and the universal are inextricably interrelated.

Giddens has argued that "the concept of globalization is best understood as expressing fundamental aspects of time-space distanciation. Globalization concerns the intersection of presence and absence, the interlacing of social events and social relations 'at distance' with local contextualities" (Giddens 22). It is a dialectical intersection of presence and absence, not only spatial, but also temporal. Robertson believes that when discussing globalization, we should pay more attention to the intimate links between temporal and spatial dimensions of human life, as "there has been little attempt to connect the discussion of time-and-space to the thorny issue of universalism-and-particularism" (Robertson 26).

With all this in mind, it becomes essential to understand the transmodern experience and its representations of space. As Hess-Lüttich has
suggested, "a contemporary understanding of 'space' under the sign of
a balance of tension of globalization and regionalization, of non-located
medial networks and local assertion of identity", is crucial when analysing literary texts, understood as media of cultural-specific codes and sym-
bolizations of space (Hess-Lüttich 2).

SCIENCE FICTION: TRANSCENDING THE EUCLIDEAN-SPACE PERSPECTIVE INTO A NEW SPACE PARADIGM?

Historically, we have been perceiving the universe from an Euclidean
perspective, which regards space as consisting of three dimensions, and
time as consisting of one dimension. Classical or Newtonian Mechanics
used the notion of Euclidean space instead of the later-developed relativistic concept of "space-time", because it conceived time as being universal; that is, time had a constant rate of passage that was independent of
the state of motion or the observer. However, the theory of relativity—
which refers to Albert Einstein's theories of Special Relativity and
General Relativity—made a break in the Newtonian understanding of the
universe and presented a whole new understanding of space and time.

It is necessary perhaps, despite the literary scope of this essay, to
briefly describe "the space-time continuum"—also known as the fourth
dimension or fourth-dimensional space-time—roughly defined as the
dimensions of space combined by or rather intertwined with the dimension of time, as science fiction usually deals with this concept assuming
that readers all are at least familiar to it, ignoring the fact that, most possibly, our perception of space-time does not match or maybe just hasn't
been updated yet to this new information about our fourth-dimensional existence. Albert Einstein came to the revelation of discovering
the hidden connection of space and time through complex mathemati-
cal equations—something already recognized by primitive cultures such
as the Incas[2] by means of intuition—and he stated in *General Relativity*
(1915) that in the space-time continuum events are defined in terms of
four dimensions: three of space and one of time, with one coordinate
for each dimension. In this context, time cannot be separated from the
three dimensions of space, because the observed rate at which time
passes for an object depends on the object's velocity, which is relative to
the observer, and on the strength of the gravitational fields. According to

Einstein's theory of Special Relativity, if something would travel in space at a very high speed, let's say almost at the speed of light, time would actually slow down for that object, subjectively and objectively. Time thus depends on the relative distance—space—of object and subject. And here we run into a big problem when trying to conceptualize the fourth dimension: perception.

We cannot experience the space-time continuum as described by Einstein directly. And by this I am not referring to the fact that we cannot travel at rates close to that of the speed of light—299,792,458 m/s—but, most importantly, to the reality that we, three-dimensional human beings, cannot perceive the four dimensions empirically. It seems that three-dimensional organisms perceive the world visually in only two dimensions, the same as a two-dimensional organism would only perceive one dimension—as the satiric science fiction novel *Flatland. Romance of Many Dimensions* (1884), by Edwin Abbott Abbott, ingeniously illustrates. Therefore, we cannot even picture this three-dimensional world, but we only perceive it mathematically, or through the use of our imagination.

However, perception of space-time is being altered not by theoretical science but mostly by our use of technology, as Postmodernism already showed. Postmodernism, as opposed to Modernism, was "characterised as the site of pure immanence, immediacy, stasis and above all a disorientating and disempowering realm of space" (Skordoulis and Arvanitis 106). The technical revolution would produce changes in the social and economic spheres, and they would involve a change in the spatial paradigm. According to Jameson, in late capitalism, spatial logic is simultaneously homogeneous and fragmented, and produces what he called "hyperspace", which characterizes the inability of the subject to locate him/herself physically/spatially within the world. Later, the new geographers and theorists such as Lefebvre,[3] Foucault and Soja challenged contemporary conceptions of space insisting on the fact that space is not given but produced. They argued that space is an essential quality of humanness and that social beings are produced by the ontological triad of space, time and society (Rick 5).

In Transmodernity, and as the technological revolution has continued with its steady progression, space becomes even a more complex issue, as already anticipated in the previous section. The particle "trans-" implies that this movement reaches beyond; it is not just an inter-territory, it means something "further than". With the particle "trans-", another

new territory is created. Boundaries are not crossed here, but transgressed, penetrated, and even transformed. In addition, the contents of
those spaces are also affected by this "trans" movement, and the perspective of the subject in relation to the object also changes, as we shall see in
our analysis.

Science fiction, as part of the speculative fiction, is an ideal literary
genre to explore transmodern representations of the space-time continuum, as its scientific background allows readers to experience representations of new configurations of space and time. Not in vain, the term
"science fiction" was coined by Hugo Gernsback in 1929 to describe
pulp magazine stories of *space*men and *time* travel written in the first decades of the twentieth century. Many pulp short stories as well as other
post-World War I novels explored—possibly influenced by Modernism—
new ways of treating space, time and experience in their narrative other,
sometimes dystopian, worlds. Between the 1930s and late 1950s, during what has been named The Golden Age of science fiction, the genre
grew out of its cheap magazine beginnings and entered the general public's awareness, and worlds of space travel and adventure provided readers with stories dealing with the advances in the technology of the time.
From 1960 onwards, New Wave stories are marked by experiments in
form and content as well as a transition away from "hard" science, such
as physics and engineering, to "soft" science like psychology and anthropology (Tambasco). Two decades later, contemporary science fiction has
transitioned away from the New Wave, and books are more influenced by
later technological development and factors such as the expanding avail-
ability of information and deep environmental concerns. Along with the
dramatic changes in computer technology, contemporary science fiction
has also been strongly influenced by the incredible discoveries in genetics
and medicine (Tambasco). The quick development of the World Wide
Web, as well as the use of electronic media and digital devices, and the
creation of social networks, as well as online access to news in the late
1990s and in the first two decades of the twenty-first century, have, of
course, encouraged science fiction to enlarge its scope even further away.

KEN MACLEOD'S WRITING AND ITS SENSE OF PLACE

Ken MacLeod—born in Stornoway in 1954—is a leading figure in contemporary Scottish science fiction, and a key member of what has been
called the "British Boom", a loose designation applied to the rise of

a group of young British science fiction writers in the mid-1990s and continuing well into the twenty-first century (Booker 49). MacLeod's writing style has been praised because of his "combination of deftly employed hard science fiction concepts with sophisticated meditations on the potential social and political implications of those concepts" (Booker 165–66). He has written fifteen acclaimed novels and several short-story collections, and the majority of his novels are at least partly set in Scotland.

As stated in the introduction, Scotland has traditionally been associated with rural and romantic landscapes and, later, in contemporary literature, also to the postindustrial city. It is clear that the past seems to be imbedded in those landscapes and keeps speaking through those places. So one may ask oneself: But what about the future? Is it possible in Scotland? Ken MacLeod explains his use of Scottish places in his writings, as well as insights into this issue, as follows:

[T]he majority of my novels are at least partly set in Scotland, or have protagonists whose sometimes far-flung adventures begin in Scotland. And it made me wonder why there haven't been more. With its sharply varied landscape, turbulent history, and the complex, cross-cutting divisions of national and personal character which Scottish literature has so often explored, Scotland may inspire writers of SF, but as a location it features more often in fantasy. The result is that there have been many Scottish writers of SF —including Orbit's very own Michael Cobley, Charles Stross, and the late and much missed Iain M. Banks— but not many SF novels have been set in Scotland. (MacLeod, "Ken MacLeod" 1)

But, of course, the distinction between fantasy and science fiction makes only sense if one conceives them as different temporal and stylistic approaches to reality. Fantasy, it seems to me, would be understood as a more romantic genre, focusing especially on timeless stories, on old myths, whereas science fiction focuses especially on the future or possible futures of humanity.

Ken MacLeod's fiction is proof that a science fiction novel, a futuristic novel, can be placed in any town or city of Scotland and still, or precisely because of this, remains credible. His novels have been set both in rural landscapes and in urban landscapes, from the "bleak rocky moors of Duirinish and Balmacara" to postindustrial Glasgow (MacLeod, "The Future" 1).

On the landscapes of MacLeod's childhood days in Lewis, Miavaig—
in Uig—Lochcarron or Plockton, the author has "inflicted science fiction. Made them the battlefield of wars both guerrilla and global.
Crashed flying saucers and tactical nukes into them. Crushed under them
the mechanical sprawl of runaway artificial intelligences. Choked them
with mutant jungles. Made them sea-lochs ring with the din of spaceship
yards" (MacLeod, "The Future" 1). And he has also represented urban
landscapes where he has lived during his adulthood, such as Greenock,
Edinburgh, Glasgow, the Clyde, the Firth of Forth (MacLeod, "The
Future" 1). Mostly, these town and villages are very familiar to the
writer, but he uses them in an estranging way, as they might appear in
other worlds that are not the Earth. For example, we can find hints of
the Pear Tree in Edinburgh—a well-known pub near to university—
being humorously portrayed in his fiction as "a garden where the bat-
winged aliens get drunk on the alcohol from over-ripe fruit" (MacLeod,
"The Future" 2).

However, MacLeod's power of suggestion also recreates these com-
monplaces as he imagines these cities enduring, as part of the future,
including both possible and unlikely prospects: "Edinburgh reinvent
itself as a biotechnology capital, West Lothian flourish as Carbon Glen,
and the University of Glasgow sail on through dark centuries as an ark of
reason" (MacLeod, "The Future" 1). There is also an implicit political
stance or ideological requirement behind these representations: Scotland
must be made visible.

Place, as understood by MacLeod, is enriched by its use in fiction—
an idea already employed by Alasdair Gray, when he complained about
the inexistence of Glasgow in literature through Duncan Thaw's lament
on the fact that "nobody imagines living" in Glasgow, since "if a city
hasn't been used by an artist not even the inhabitants live there imaginatively" (Gray 243). Existence requires a mind to conceive as well as
to perceive something. A place cannot exist if it's not been imagined, if
it's not been perceived, as Gray wrote; but MacLeod goes a step further
by emphasizing the need not only to perceive and represent it, but to
recreate and to re-imagine these Scottish places in its possible futures.
As stated in his essay "The Future Will Happen Here Too" (2010),
"[t]he real life of a place is added to if it's lived in imagination, including in the imaginations of people who've never been there" (MacLeod,
"The Future" 2). So science fiction has an extra commitment in the
reconfiguration of plausible futures, "science fiction can add an extra

shiver of significance by saying of a place: the future will happen here, too" (MacLeod, "The Future" 2).

So, MacLeod summarizes his reasons for using Scottish places in his science fiction in four: firstly, the use of these places in fiction provides them with a certain recognition and respect that he thinks they deserve; secondly, his deep and specific knowledge of those places allows him to gain a higher realism; thirdly, his love for these places; and fourthly, his intimate identification with the landscape that has shaped him as the person he is: "Scotland's streets and mountains, lochs and rain have shaped my own mind just as a geological processes have carved the landscape itself" (MacLeod, "The Future" 2). And, contrary to the old pessimistic laments that view Scotland was a "damaged land" and an "artistic wasteland"—from T. S. Eliot in "Tradition and the Individual Talent" (1919) to Irvine Welsh in *Trainspotting* (1993)—MacLeod actually believes that Scotland is a great place to inhabit, physically as well as imaginatively: "[t]his land I live in is still the place I visit in dreams. I owe it that forming, that weathering, that uplift" (MacLeod, "The Future" 2).

With all this in mind, I will now focus on the use of place and space, in the past, present and in the near future, in Ken MacLeod's *The Human Front* and *Descent*.

THE HUMAN FRONT AND DESCENT: AN ANALYSIS OF PLACE IN THE TRANSMODERN SPACE-TIME CONTINUUM

I have chosen Ken MacLeod's novella *The Human Front*, published in 2001 and later again with three other short texts—two short essays, titled "Other Deviations: The Human Front Exposed" and "The Future Will Happen Here, Too", and an interview with the author, titled "Working the Wet End"—in 2013, and the novel *Descent*, published in 2014, as they both share some key narrative-setting elements related to place, which is our main interest in this essay, and they have similar intradiegetic narrators.

In *The Human Front*, the narration often focuses on the description of what readers will identify as typically Scottish places and landscapes, of the land with an extreme "disproportion between natural attraction and sentimental attachment" (MacLeod, *The Human* 7). Especially important is the representation of Greenock, the place where the *novella*'s main character, John Matheson, grew up as a child after having moved from Lewis. The place is described as "an industrial town on the Firth of Clyde" (MacLeod, *The Human* 13). However, readers do not get the impression that the child is describing a depressing place—quite the contrary, it is described as an exciting place that was full of life:

> It was another world. In the mid-1960s the Clyde was booming, its shipyards producing naval and civilian vessels in almost equal proportion, its harbours crowded with British and American warships, the Royal Ordnance Factory at Bishopton working around the clock. Greenock, as always, flourished from the employment opportunities upriver —beginning with the yards and docks of the adjacent town of Port Glasgow— and from its own industries […]. The pollution from the factories and refineries was light, but fumes from the heavy vehicular traffic that serviced them may well explain the high incidence of lung cancer in the area. (My father's death, though outside the purview of the present narrative, may also be accounted. […]) (MacLeod, *The Human* 13)

We can see some nostalgia in these sentences—an almost ironic or even bitter nostalgia—as moving to Greenock was for John shocking in different ways; not only the location changed, the landscape, but, most importantly, the whole place was different, with its people and its customs. As John explains, anticipating the preoccupations he will have as a grown-up man: "Class division shocked me: after growing up among the well-fed, if ill-clad, population of Lewis, I saw the poorer eight-tenths of the town as inhabited by misshaped dwarfs" (MacLeod, *The Human* 13).

Space and place inevitably change with time. And, in the future, Scotland will be different to what we know; as time passes, probably its landscapes will change profoundly due to the advance of civilization and technology, or even due to possible future wars. There is a deep ecological awareness in this passage that demands a careful consideration that exceeds a local preoccupation. The ecological crisis brought about by capitalism cannot be understood in binary terms, as it not only affects Scotland, but the whole world. Despite the fact that the causes are local, it is a global problem affecting the whole planet.

Sometimes it is the character of the people, shaped by history and landscape, what constitutes a place. As John narrates, "Scotland is not a good country for rural guerrilla warfare, having been long since stripped of trees and peasants. Without physical or social shelter, any guerrilla band in the hills and glens would be easily spotted and picked off, if they hadn't starved first" (MacLeod, *The Human* 47). However, the Scottish guerrilla would not be stopped by this change of the landscape, and they try to find advantage in other elements of nature that they identify with and that will offer them some protection: "Night, clouds and rain, gullies, boulders, bracken, isolated clumps of trees, the few real forests, burns and bridges and bothies all provide cover. [...] Deer, sheep and rabbits abounded, edible wild plants and berries grew everywhere, and vegetables were easily bought or stolen" (MacLeod, *The Human* 47). Despite the change in the landscape through the years, one gets the impression that the later dystopic landscapes are as Scottish as the traditional moorlands and glens where peasants could live in peace in the past. But the exactitude of descriptions of place contrasts with the vagueness of the description of time. Through the abundance of space descriptions readers know very well the story is taking place in Scotland, but *when-where* is it taking place?

The Human Front starts with the following lines: "Like most people of my generation, I remember exactly where I was on 17 March 1963, the day Stalin died" (MacLeod, *The Human* 1). However, as far as we know, Joseph Stalin died on 5 March 1954, not in 1963. So, this story offers readers an alternate history or a world in a parallel universe where things have happened differently to what we know has happened in our world: Moscow, we learn, was destroyed by atomic bombing in 1949—in Operation Dropshot[4]—and, as an indirect consequence, the Communist Movement has emerged to lead a unified, militant global uprising—"the Human Front" (MacLeod, *The Human* 15)— against Western imperialism. The location where the story takes place is Northern Scotland, but Scotland must be different here, as in *this* near-future Scotland, US bombers shaped like an aluminium disk or a flying saucer hover in the cloudy skies.

The *novella*'s protagonist, John, a young boy from the Scottish island of Lewis, lives in a world where the Third World War is taking place. At very young age, he witnesses an accident by a US saucer-shaped anti-gravity bomber, one of the advanced high-altitude bombers (AHAB) that are allowing the Americans to win the war. As he grows up, John finds out that no AHAB technology has filtered down to any other products, and starts questioning himself where the technology has come from and who is using it. As a young man, John joins the Soviets and he becomes part of the fifth column against the British—"the Brits"—and the Americans—"the Yanks"—(MacLeod, *The Human* 44). However, his revolutionary career changes abruptly when he shoots one of these saucers down, taking its pilot prisoner and discovering that, like the pilot he saw as a child in the AHAB accident, this man was in fact not a man, but a Grey alien: "It was a perfectly healthy, normal body, but it was not human" (MacLeod, *The Human* 45).

Indeed, one of the central themes in *The Human Front* is the secret of the AHAB flying saucers and the UFO lore, and despite the fact that not many science fiction stories have been set in Scotland, as Ken MacLeod has stated in "As if You Lived in the Near Future of an Undecided Nation" (MacLeod, "As if" 1). It is not true at all that the Scottish imagination dwells only on the past and cannot conceive speculative stories such as the visiting of aliens. In fact, the paranormal as well as science-fictional ideas have always been very much present in the Scottish mind: from haunted castles, strange creatures that only cryptozoology takes seriously, stones and glens with magical powers, poltergeists or spooky apparitions, to mind telepathy, supra-human powers and flying saucers. Some people have publicly assured that they have seen UFOs and strange lights in the skies Scotland. In fact, and according to several newspapers, after a request under the Freedom of Information Act, "Defence chiefs have revealed a string of X-Files-style UFO sightings in Scotland" (Daily Record). So it seems that flying saucers and other strange phenomena do not avoid Scottish skies after all.

In many aspects, *The Human Front* also shows resemblances to the first book of *The Engines of Light* trilogy,[5] *Cosmonaut Keep* (2000), as this novel also has unique take on the UFO *mythos* and one of its two alternating timelines is set in a near-future Edinburgh, in an alternate world where a neo-Soviet Russia has defeated the USA and installed socialism in Europe. The other alternating timeline of *Cosmonaut Keep* is set in another star system, on planet Mingulay, five or six centuries later. So, the novel alternates almost oscillate between these two faraway places and times: Scotland in the near future, and the vast universe in the farther future. We will see that this swinging between the local scale and the universal scales is especially remarkable in *Descent*, Ken MacLeod's latest science fiction novel.

Descent is also set in Scotland in the near future—*circa* 2040s—like other of his novels such as the above-mentioned *Cosmonaut Keep*— whose first timeline is set in 2048; *The Execution Channel* (2007)— which takes place on the early decades of the twenty-first century; *The Night Sessions* (2008)—set in the year 2037; or *Intrusion* (2012)—also set in the 2040s. *Descent* tells the story of 16-year-old Ryan Sinclaire, a middle-class boy living in Greenock with his family, who has an over-whelming experience: after having seen a UFO in the sky while having a walk in the hills, one night he is—or he believes he has been—abducted by extraterrestrial beings, more specifically by Greys.

The novel's plot shows here obvious resemblances to that of *The Human Front*, as both children live in Greenock when they have an experience with flying saucers[6]—which look like silver spheres—and Grey aliens. While having a walk with a friend on the hills, Ryan spots a light in the sky: "The light became a bright sphere, shimmering and expand-ing" (MacLeod, *Descent* 20). Later they discover that they have no fur-ther recollection of that light and that they have missed an hour and a half—something that is quite habitual in the encounters with UFOs—and they suspect it might have been a time warp (MacLeod, *Descent* 40) or, after a vivid hallucination that Ryan experiences in his bed, an alien abduction: "Someone, or something, was standing at the foot of the bed. [...] Terrified, but not surprised. The creature was a cliché, your average working alien, a bog-standard Grey" (MacLeod, *Descent* 44). This unexplainable episode, as well as the technological progress that is taking place—in a world in crisis where "we live from day to day with-out knowing what's going to happen tomorrow or even what's just happened unless we check our phones every few seconds" (MacLeod, *Descent* 34)—will disrupt his understanding of space-time altering his world paradigm. Later, Ryan goes to university and a few years back, he becomes a postgraduate student in Scotland—although, and we shall see, the world does not seem to have boundaries anymore, as one can see anything one would desire, regardless of the remoteness of the place. Moreover, the rapidly changing society also forces citizens to change the traditional and pre-transmodern conceptions of space and time, that is, of perception and reality itself. As we shall see, in *Descent*, a new space-time paradigm, where past, alternative presents and futures overlap and place manifest itself as glocal space, that is, as a synthesis of the global and the local, an in-between space highlighting the relativity of trans-modern locality.

This overlapping and coexistence of both local and global spaces and places are one of the characteristics of Transmodernity, as mentioned in the introduction. Glocalization, which views the local and the global as dialectical forces that transcend polarity, is a key element to under-stand this homogenizing and heterogenizing phenomenon. According to Roland Robertson, "[m]uch of what is often declared to be local is in fact the local expressed in terms of generalized recipes of locality" (Robertson 26). In fact, globalization has involved the production of renewed ideas such as "home", "community" and "locality" (Robertson 30). Therefore, the local can be regarded "as *an aspect* of globalization" (Robertson 30). As the coiner of the term "glocalization" affirms, "the concept of globalization has involved the simultaneity and the interpenetration of what are conventionally called the global and the local, or —in more abstract vein— the universal and the particular" (Robertson 30).

Robertson precisely complains about the fact that, despite the increasing interest in spatial considerations and the intimate links between temporal and spatial dimensions of human life, these considerations have made little impact on the topic of globalization. In particular, he states, "there has been little attempt to connect the discussion of time-and-space to the thorny issue of universalism-and-particularism" (Robertson 26).

So with his in mind, the analysis of Ken MacLeod's chosen novels will focus on the interconnectedness of space, which, like time—or rather we should say like "space-time"—is relative, as both the ideas of locality and globality are relational; that is, they are relative and cannot be understood in monomythical or unidirectional terms. Space, like time, has expanded: "As the sense of temporal unidirectionality has faded so, on the other hand, has the sense of 'representational' space within which all kinds of narratives may be inserted expanded" (Robertson 32).

Both *The Human Front* and *Descent* show, in their multiple settings, that the local and the universal are inextricably linked in Transmodernity. As commented above, both texts are set in Scotland in the near future, which is, of course, even more globalized and technologized than our present day. In both texts, the main characters use a special type of glasses that are very similar, although a bit more advanced, to those we have already seen announced on some technological sites: digital glasses. For example, Google glass and iGlass—created in 2014, the same year *Descent* was published—are different models of an optical head-mounted display in the shape of a pair of eyeglasses that work as a ubiquitous computer. Actually, the narrator refers to these devices as "iGlasses" (MacLeod, *Descent* 3). Naturally, they are worn over the eyes, so the user does not see the external material world that surrounds him or her, but instead he or she watches a—chosen—digital reality on a LED illuminating display. So, in a sense, these devices distance us from what we used to consider (unique) reality, incorporating virtuality to our experience of the world.

However, this does not mean that by using those digital displays we are entering the "postmodern *simulacrum*", as Baudrillard could say, but rather, as Rodríguez Magda would affirm, that we are moving a further step from the modernist conception reality and entering the "transmodern virtuality" (Rodríguez Magda, "Transmodernidad" 8). Besides, this virtuality does not have any space limits; actually, it creates space at will, no matter what size, as it can represent space at any place in any scale: "'Great,' said Calum. 'Put your glasses on and I'll show you.' He put his own glasses on, and conjured space in the space between us: a four-sided wedge of vacuum and atmosphere, wide at the top in low Earth orbit and narrowing to a point at the ground" (MacLeod, *Descent* 266). With an app called SkEye—which would "amount to real-time Google Earth" (MacLeod, *Descent* 266)—they will be able to "[m]ake a virtual visit anywhere on Earth" (MacLeod, *Descent* 267). Space becomes potentially everywhere ubiquitous.

However, this new perception of space-time does not imply that the characters are witnessing a substitution of reality. The virtual images are part of their reality too, as Ryan realizes when he witnesses a mission that is being sabotaged, almost causing the death of hundreds of people in Edinburgh: "A shape familiar from maps and satellite-pic apps filled the screen. My glasses reinterpreted what was in front of my eyes at the moment my brain did the same. Right in front of us, right below the rocket, was Edinburgh" (MacLeod, *Descent* 328). This transmodern space as created by these near-future technological devices is rather an overlapping of realities of a different nature—of reality and virtuality—of different spaces that coexist at the same time depending on the perspective taken on them.

In the following extract, we can see how, through the use of the iGlasses, the intradiegetic narrator in *Descent* interweaves different space-times and realities into one single experience:

[A]s I walk up the Mound and down the High Street, the alternative Edinburghs I distract myself by calling up in rapid succession on my glasses aren't just the standard historicals, entertaining though it is to stroll the main drag of Hume's and Smith's Athens of the North and watch the chamberpots tipped from upstairs windows to splatter heads below; or to scroll the city's growth from Neolithic settlement to modern capital, or let the smoke of Victorian lums and Edwardian slums rise to swap the streets and then, with quite surprisingly suddenness, disperse the miasma with a wave of the Clean Air Act. (MacLeod, *Descent* 4)

Space-time here multiplies and opens itself up to other timelines that are not exclusive but inclusive. In this way, Ryan Sinclair has access through his iGlasses to a multifold world. The particular does not exclude other possibilities, so to say. "In the perspective of contradiction the tension between, for example, the universal and the particular may be seen either in the dynamic sense of being a relatively progressive source of overall change or as a modality which preserves an existing global system in its present state" (Robertson 33). In this line, Wallerstein argued that the relation between the universal and the particular is basically a product of expanding world-systemic capitalism, an idea that Rodriguez Magda's "transmodern virtuality" seems to support.

Well-known places in near-future Edinburgh—which is extremely similar to the present-day Edinburgh known by locals as well as by visitors—are playfully confronted with other past and future Edinburghs in this narrative, producing an entertaining kind of estrangement in readers. As the narrator himself explains, this transmodern reality is a palimpsest that expands both towards the future and towards the past: "I play with overlays of alternate pasts and possible futures, with steampunk and cyberpunk, utopia and dystopia" (MacLeod, *Descent* 4). The palimpsest—a concept first used by Thomas De Quincey in 1845, defining it as an involuted phenomenon where otherwise unrelated texts are interwoven, competing with and infiltrating each other, and later developed by critical thinkers such as Sarah Dillon (Dillon, "Reinscribing" 243–44)—has an intricate structure that illuminates and advances modern thought, refiguring concepts such as history, subjectivity, temporality, metaphor, textuality and sexuality (Dillon, The *Palimpsest* 27). In this line, the palimpsest both questions and combines both modern and postmodern interests, and is considered to be transmodern in that sense. Not only Edinburgh, but the whole Scotland has become a "transmodern palimpsest", as the following description denotes:

> Layers in and imbricated with the new [future Edinburgh of sun-powered vehicles and loitering drones], of course, are the strata of earlier looks and times: diesel-belching buses, petrol-burning taxis, trouser suits and short skirts and jeans and skip cars and bare heads and bare legs, [...] and so on and on, but here is nonetheless, an iffy skiffy future like none I would or could have imagined in my teens.
> Oh, wait. That's reality. (MacLeod, *Descent* 7)

As Ryan further narrates: "Looking down towards Waverly Station, I replace its long sheds with the Nor Loch, stagnant and stinking. [...] The vista along George IV Bridge gets an instant make-over as a Blackshirt mob storms the National Library, then I time-shift the street to the metropolis of concrete, glass and steel the agitators fancied themselves fighting for" (MacLeod, *Descent* 4). By moving temporally, space is also transformed.

In his novel *Intrusion*, published in 2012, Ken MacLeod already used virtual space to explore the transmodern tensions of the near future between the local and the global. Hope Morrison, the female main character in this SF novel, also has a pair of iGlasses which she uses mainly for her job: "She made a coffee, hung up her apron, sat down at the kitchen table, opened her glasses and started working in China but not in Chinese" (MacLeod, *Intrusion* 12). She is able to log herself in and out of a virtual space that is also real, as it has become part of the place she works at, both in Britain and in China *at the same time*: "One p.m. Back to China", she says to herself while sipping her coffee in her own familiar kitchen (MacLeod, *Intrusion* 15).

In *Descent*, this tension between the local and the global is brought further than the limits of planet Earth, expanding the transmodern palimpsest to the whole universe, as China is no longer exclusively located in Asia, nor on Earth, but has now extended into the rest of our solar system: "with their Moon and Mars bases and their space stations and Jovian expeditions and deep-sky astronomy satellites and [...] orbital hotels [... and a]steroid mining" (MacLeod, *Descent* 304). It seems thus that in the near future, the world will expand even further, and we will be able to move quicker; but also, the local will be as present as always, or even more (if we bear in mind the nostalgia for the local present in late capitalism) and the past won't be lost. Both past and future, the local and the global, will continue coexisting.

Personally, I find the assumption that human beings can populate or even conquer or exploit the unknown universe—as depicted in many of Ken MacLeod's novels—as disturbing as imagining a first contact with extraterrestrial beings—as in *The Human Front* and *Descent*, among other novels—; perhaps because both imply a radical change in our current, already outdated, paradigm, in our perception of space, place, scale and perspective. When everything changes, so will we. And I believe this is a key to the impact of the representations of space and place in the analysed novels: the relative locality-globality of the transmodern space-time paradigm forces us to reconsider (Euclidean) space and try to understand space-time in a more contemporary way where our position will have changed. Naturally, this space shift, if one assumes it with all its implications, can result as shocking as an alien encounter.

Conclusions

As we have seen, the transmodern experience and representations of space in the novels by Ken MacLeod that have been analysed show that modern interest in time and postmodern "hyperspace" have given way to what could be called the transmodern space-time paradigm. Transmodern space-time creates a new territory where the glocal and the virtual playfully meet in a new multifold reality. Thereby, space-time boundaries are transgressed and transformed, as the contents of those spaces, as well as the perspective of the subject—both taken individually and collectively—are also affected by this "trans" movement.

The virtuality present in the transmodern space-time paradigm, which encompasses the glocal—as it is also based on the tension of globalization and regionalization—produces a multiplicity of spaces that unfold and contract in a single space we refer to as reality. Further analysis of transmodern space-time and place will determine how the contemporary experience of space-time, as well as identity, is being modified by these changes. In the meanwhile, science fiction will give us ideas about the future paths that the world and human beings, including non-Earthlings, will take. There is still a long way to go for Scottish speculative fiction, a lot of places and times to imagine.

Acknowledgements The research carried out for the writing of this article is part of a project financed by the Spanish Ministry of Economy, Industry and Competitiveness (MINECO) in collaboration with the European Regional Development Fund (DGI/ERDF) (code FFI2017-84258-P), and a project financed by the Centro Universitario de la Defensa Zaragoza (CUD2017-01). The author is also thankful for the support of the Government of Aragón and the European Social Fund (ESF) (code H03_17R).

Notes

1. Actually, some authors, when discussing Ken MacLeod's Scottishness, refer to this "divided consciousness" as "being peculiarly Scottish" (Butler viii).
2. The Incas regarded space and time as a single concept, named *pacha*. "*Pacha* is a univocal word that denotes space (length, width and depth)

and time (the fourth dimension). This connection of two conditions—a static one and a dynamic one on the same level—besides connecting the cosmic space of 'sky', also shows a concept of time in history that reveals the sequence of autonomous and dynamic loops that can generate themselves. Such a pattern reveals itself by means of the conjunction of the term *urin* (as ancient and no-visible zone), *janan* (as recent and visible zone) and *ñawpa* a word that alludes to 'ancient time' and to the 'time that will come towards us'" (Manga Qespi 155).

3. Lefebvre, in his *Unitary Theory of Space* (1991), brought together all the three elements he considered in space: *physical* (real/material) space, *mental* (imagined/conceptual) space and *social* space. What Lefebvre calls the *perceived*, the *conceived* and the *lived* (Rick 10–12).

4. "Operation Dropshot" was the code name of a real US contingency plan for a possible nuclear war against the Soviet Union and its allies, prepared in 1949 and declassified in 1977.

5. Consisting also of the second volume, *Dark Light* (2001) and a third and closing title, *Engine City* (2002).

6. It must be noted that Greenock is only 40 miles away from the most important UFO-sightings hot spot in the world: Bonnybridge. As sated in the Scotsman, "part of the 'Falkirk Triangle', whose other two points are formed by Stirling and Fife, Bonnybridge averages 300 sightings a year" (*The Scotsman*, web). Also, numerous UFO-sightings have been spotted in Inverclyde. As reported by *Greenock Telegraph*, "unidentified flying objects were recorded in the skies above Inverclyde by a special Air Command department of the Armed Forces" ("UFO", web). From 1999 onwards, many citizens have seen these strange objects flying over the roofs of their homes: "The Ministry [of Defense] also recorded a sighting above Greenock on 15 February 2005. A man reported a large yellow conical craft in the sky while walking his dog just after 1am" ("UFO", web).

WORKS CITED

Abbott Abbott, Edwin. *Flatland. Romance of Many Dimensions*. London: Seely, 1884. Print.

Abu-Lughod, J. 'Going Beyond Global Babble'. *Culture, Globalization and the World-System*. Ed. Anthony King. London: Macmillan, 1991. Print.

Aliaga Lavrijsen, Jessica. 'Contemporary Scottish Literature and the Problematics of Identity'. *The Fiction of Brian McCabe and (Scottish) Identity*. Oxford: Peter Lang, 2013. 3–32. Print.

Booker, Keith M. *Historical Dictionary of Science Fiction in Literature*. London: Rowman & Littlefield, 2015. Print.

Brockelman, Thomas. 'Lost in Place? On the Virtues and Vices of Edward Casey's Anti-modernism'. *Humanitas* XVI:1 (2003): 36–55. Print.

Butler, Andrew M. 'Introduction: The True Knowledge?' *The True Knowledge of Ken MacLeod*. Ed. Andrew M. Butler and Farah Mendlesohn. Reading: Science Fiction Foundation, 2003. vii–xiii. Print.

Casey, Edward S. *Getting Back into Place: Toward a Renewed Understanding of the Place-World*. Bloomington: Indiana University Press, 1993. Print.

Dailyrecord. 'MoD Admit They Probed Claims of UFOs Over Greenock and Renfrewshire'. 1 July 2012. http://www.dailyrecord.co.uk/news/uk-world-news/mod-admit-they-probed-claims-of-ufos-1106682#XKpcdo1R0WcY-DiFI.97. Web.

Dillon, Sarah. 'Reinscribing De Quincey's Palimpsest: The Significance of the Palimpsest in Contemporary Literary and Cultural Studies'. *Textual Practice* 19:3 (2005): 243–263. Print.

———. *The Palimsest: Literature, Criticism, Theory*. London: Bloomsbury, 2007. Print.

Eliot, T. S. 'Tradition and the Individual Talent'. *The Sacred Wood*. London: Methuen, 1920 (1919). Print.

Giddens, A. *Modernity and Self-Identity*. Oxford. Polity, 1991. Print.

Gray, Alasdair. *Lanark: A Life in Four Books*. Edinburgh: Canongate Books, 1981. Print.

Greenock Telegraph. 'UFO Sightings Probed by MOD'. 28 June 2011. http://www.greenocktelegraph.co.uk/news/13999863.UFO_sightings_probed_by_MOD/?commentSort=score. Web.

Hess-Lüttich, Ernest W. B. 'Spatial Turn: On the Concept of Space in Cultural Geography and Literary Theory'. *Journal for Theoretical Cartography*, Vol. 5, 2012. Print.

Jameson, Frederick. *Postmodernism, Or the Cultural Logic of Late Capitalism*. London: Verso, 1991. Print.

Korzeniowska, Aniela. '"Scotland Small? Our Multiform, Our Infinite Scotland Small?" Scotland's Literary Contribution to the Modern World'. *Colloquia Humanistica* 2 (2013): 37–58. Print.

MacLeod, Ken. *Cosmonaut Keep* (*The Engines of Light*. Book 1). London: Orbit, 2000. Print.

———. *Dark Light* (*The Engines of Light*. Book 2). London: Orbit, 2001. Print.

———. *Engine City* (*The Engines of Light*. Book 3). London: Orbit, 2002. Print.

———. *The Execution Channel*. New York: Tor Books, 2007. Print.

———. *The Night Sessions*. New York: Prometheus Books, 2008. Print.

———. 'The Future Will Happen Here Too'. *The Bottle Imp*, Vol. 18, 2015 (2010). http://asls.arts.gla.ac.uk/SWE/TBI/TBIIssue18/MacLeod.pdf. Web. 11 November 2016.

———. *Intrusion*. London: Orbit, 2012. Print.

————. *The Human Front*. Oakland: PM Press, 2013 (2001). Print.

————. *Descent*. London: Orbit, 2014. Print.

————. 'Ken MacLeod on Scotland in Science Fiction'. 19 November 2014. http://www.orbitbooks.net/2014/11/19/ken-macleod-descent-scottish-science-fiction/. 2014. Web. 12 December 2017.

Manga Qespi, Eusebio Atuq. 'Pacha: Un concepto andino de espacio y tiempo'. *Revista española de Antropología Americana* 24 (1994): 155–189. Print.

Radstone, Susannah. 'What Place Is This? Transcultural Memory and the Locations of Memory Studies'. *Parallax* 17:4 (2011): 109–123. Print.

Rick, A. 'What Space Makes of Us: Third Space, Identity Politics, and Multiculturalism', UCLA, *American Educational Research Association Conference*, Chicago. 1997. http://files.eric.ed.gov/fulltext/ED409409.pdf. Web. 28 October 2016.

Robertson, Roland. 'Glocalization: Time-Space and Homogeneity-Heterogeneity'. *Global Modernities*. Ed. Mike Featherstone, Scott Lash, and Roland Robertson. London: Sage, 1995: 25–44. Print.

Rodríguez Magda, Rosa María. 'Transmodernidad: Un nuevo paradigma'. *Transmodernity. Journal of Peripheral Cultural Production of the Luso-Hispanic World* 1.1 (2011): 1–13. Print.

————. *Transmodernidad*. Barcelona: Anthropos, 2004. Print.

Skordoulis, Constantine, and Eugenia Arvantis. 'Space Conceptualisation in the Context of Postmodernity: Theorizing Spatial Representation'. *The International Journal of Interdisciplinary Social Sciences* 3:6 (2008): 105–113. Print.

Smith, Gregory. *Scottish Literature, Character and Influence*. London: Macmillan, 1919. Print.

Tambasco, Brandi. 'Science Fiction: Spanning Space, Time, and Genre'. *Notes. The New York Society Library* 18:4 (2011). https://www.nysoclib.org/sites/default/files/pdf/news2011_11.pdf. Web. 17 December 2016.

The Scotsman. 'They're Out There'. 26 July 2007. http://www.scotsman.com/news/they-re-out-there-1-910687#ixzz47aZOM37c. Web. 17 December 2016.

Wallerstein, Immanuel. 'The National and the Universal: Can There Be Such a Thing as World Culture?' *Culture, Globalization and the World-System*. Ed. Anthony King. London: Macmillan, 1991: 91–106. Print.

Welsh, Irvine. *Trainspotting*. London: Secker and Warburg, 1993. Print.

PART III

Figuring Land, Figuring Self: Poetics

"The Wider Rootedness": John Burnside's Embodied Sense of Place

Monika Szuba

In his extensive body of poetry, John Burnside recurrently explores human interactions with the flesh of the world, emphasising the groundedness and embodiment of his poetic subjects. Burnside's poems are phenomenological in that they describe discrete features of things and events, experienced by the self through the senses. "The body is the vehicle of being in the world and, for a living being, having a body means being united with a definite milieu,"[1] writes Maurice Merleau-Ponty in *Phenomenology of Perception*; the embodied self is "an inter-corporeal being" grounded in the world, and sensually fused with its elements. Burnside's explorations of the spatio-temporal *Umwelt* ("environment") of a poetic subject are complemented by his concerned with dwelling on the earth. His work is thus also profoundly ecopoetic in the sense that it evokes what lies at the root of this word, composed of two Greek terms, where *eco-*, coming from the word *oikos*, means home and *poesis* suggests creation. Preoccupied with home making in a sense of finding how to dwell properly on the earth, Burnside's writing delves into the human relation with the world, examining the possibilities of a

M. Szuba (✉)
University of Gdańsk, Gdańsk, Poland

© The Author(s) 2019   125
M. Szuba and J. Wolfreys (eds.), *The Poetics of Space and Place in Scottish Literature*, Geocriticism and Spatial Literary Studies, https://doi.org/10.1007/978-3-030-12645-2_8

meaningful existence. It focuses on the condition of the modern human subject, and the alienation experienced in the Anthropocene era, as some call the age in which we live,[2] with a longing for the interconnectedness of beings.

The role and significance of place has been extensively discussed from various perspectives in recent years. In her study *Sense of Place and Sense of Planet: The Environmental Imagination of the Global*, Ursula Heise writes about "eco-cosmopolitanism," or what she calls, "environmental world citizenship."[3] For Heise, cosmopolitanism should no longer be understood as "an alternative to nationality based on forms of identity" but one that "confronts more local attachments."[4] While it is difficult to disagree with these conclusions and Heise's suggestion that globalisation has ushered in a new way of thinking about place, "the emergence of new forms of culture that are no longer anchored in place,"[5] it is nonetheless necessary to point out that a reverse movement also occurs in contemporary literature. More and more, authors seem to recognise something which Merleau-Ponty has described as a reversible, chiasmatic relation between humans and the environment, a relation that is about enfolding of mutually entwined elements: "the landscape makes its impact upon me and produces feelings *in* me...it reaches me *in* my uniquely individual being"[6] (emphases added). Despite (or perhaps because) the fact that in contemporary world of modern transport and communication technologies, we spent our lives mostly "unplaced," as Tim Dee suggests,[7] in recent writing there is visible a direction towards retrieving place, an attempt at expressing re-enchantment with place, as the title of a collection of essays and poems edited by Gareth Evans and Di Robson suggests; this is by no means the only publication raising this subject (cf. Bennet 2001; Maitland 2012; Macfarlane 2008, 2015; Dee 2018).[8] The contributors of the collection *Towards Re-enchantment of Place* including Robin Robertson, Kathleen Jamie, Robert Macfarlane, and Alice Oswald among others evoke a fragile sense of belonging, through memories, meditations in response to various landscapes in Britain. Even though John Burnside did not contribute to the collection, his whole work attests to similar concerns. In effect, place is central to Burnside's poetic work: his poems often begin in a place which constitutes an abode of intimate spaces, the source of enchantment and wonder. The lyric, as he argues, is aimed at "conveying the timelessness of the chosen place...focusing very specifically on the moment (i.e. on transience, which is the space in which linear time disappears."[9]

Celebrating an aesthetics of proximity, many poems emerge from a sensual experience of place, a direct, corporeal experience. They are also about being in motion, passing through various places, demonstrating how dynamic, sensory tempo-spatial knowledge affects the evaluation of a lived moment. In this chapter, I wish to argue that Burnside's poetry is anchored by place, exploring the experience of the authentic, or what Merleau-Ponty calls wild being, which is possible when the world is accessed through the lived body, as place appears "by way of body," according to Edward S. Casey.[10] My argument is that place in Burnside's writing is frequently a site of enchantment in contemporary life for the self, focusing on the interconnectedness of beings and the reversible intertwining of the self with landscape. Heise's metaphor of an anchor evoking an image of a temporary mooring is useful for suggesting an aspect of Burnside's preoccupation with transience and intermittence; however, much Burnside's poetics dismisses the notion of anchoring. Following a consideration of this image, my analysis will include an attempt to follow the poet's mapping of extensive territories of the globe in the context of the problem of proper dwelling, and how it mediates place in a phenomenological relationship.

Pace Heise, many of Burnside's poems evoke a state of "unplacedness" in a number of ways, expressing a yearning for home, an attempt to retrieve the ability to dwell properly, meaningfully. His poetic subjects long to inhabit places deeply, at times achieving this in phenomenological glimpses of Being. Burnside's understanding of poetry emphasises the significance of place as he considers the lyric poem "the point of intersection between place and a specific moment or moments."[11] Among Burnside's collections, three are particularly preoccupied with place: *The Asylum Dance* (2000), *The Light Trap* (2002) and *The Good Neighbour* (2005); thus, my discussion will focus on a selection of poems from these volumes. Each offers a meditation on home and dwelling, and each proposes a slightly different approach. For instance, in *The Asylum Dance* the sense of intermittence is particularly pronounced. A recurrent preoccupation in *The Light Trap* is gravity, the pull of the earth, primal, fundamental, embedded, song of the earth, while sharing the world dominates *The Good Neighbour*.

The experience of place is suspended in a dialectics of material and spiritual, something that is powerfully present in Burnside's works. As Tom Bristow puts it, Burnside shows "what it might be like to reconcile mind and matter, and being and world" as his "anti-dualist epistemology...endeavours to harmonize reason and revelation via an ecological-metaphysical poetic compound."[12] The phrase "the wider rootedness" (l. 2) used in the title of this chapter comes from a poem titled "Appleseed,"[13] where it suggests soul or spirit, which is 'wild and single' (l. 8). The title of the poem refers to the story of Johnny Appleseed, a hero of American folklore who is said to have walked barefoot with a sack of apples to plant a tree everywhere he stopped. This is "one of those stories gathered from the wild" (l. 21), which explains the origin of things. The ending of the poem returns to the concept of "the wider rootedness": "what, in code, we sometimes call the soul/is out there, growing, rooted in the stars" (ll. 23–24). The prepositional phrase "out there" points to the outside, an unknown, uncharted region of space, while the verb "rooted" in the same line suggests an embeddedness, a depth. The word "root" from Old Norse, figuratively meaning "cause" or "origin," is the invisible source from which everything begins. Rootedness encourages thinking of what is underground and acknowledging things taking place under the surface. Yet the final line of the poem suggests a counter-intuitive movement where reaching the roots is not directed downward but into the stars in a form of a holdfast clasping the earth and the sky in an image of the fourfold. Coined by Martin Heidegger, the concept of the fourfold describes earth, sky, divinities and mortals, which are gathered in a "simple oneness of the four"[14] by a bridge thus unifying human beings together with the divinities on the surface of the earth and beneath the sky. Being in relation, things "unfold themselves ecstatically, opening relations with the world beyond them."[15] In his 1954 essay, "Building Dwelling Thinking," Heidegger writes, "[H]uman being consists in dwelling and, indeed, dwelling in the sense of the stay of mortals on the earth. But 'on the earth' already means 'under the sky.' Both of these also mean 'remaining before the divinities' and include a 'belonging to men's being with one another.' By a primal oneness the four—earth and sky, divinities and mortals—belong together in one."[16] Humans stay on earth, under the sky with other mortals and things, interconnected with 'gods', which represent customs and traditions, "the world-as-fourfold appears to be an integrated combination of nature (earth and sky) and culture (divinities and mortals)."[17]

"The wider rootedness" thus also evokes a rhizomatic growth, an image of a network of interrelations that reaches wide and deep. Along the word "rooted," which appears twice in the poem, "wild" equally recurs twice is suggestive of a concept of "wild being," which Merleau-Ponty sketched in *Working Notes* to denote an authentic being accessed briefly in moments of epiphany. A term borrowed from Husserl, brute, or wild being describes the originary source of the sense. It is an attempt to access the infinity of the *Lebenswelt* ("lifeworld") through uncovering "a whole series of layers of wild being,"[18] associated with and apprehended as coming from the domain of pre-reflective experience. Wild being is a form of "a silent knowing," "a pre-meaning," or "a pre-knowing,"[19] which occurs at the level of the human body. As Merleau-Ponty assures us, being immersed in the "environment of brute existence and essence is not something mysterious: we never quit it, we have no other environment."[20] Sensually immersed in the world, we experience it with our bodies, remaining in relation with other beings and things.

Thinking of Being brings dwelling to the fore, which in Burnside's writing, informed by Heideggerian thought, occupies a central place. As Jeff Malpas suggests, Martin Heidegger's philosophy constitutes "perhaps the most important and sustained inquiry into place to be found in the history of Western thought."[21] Dwelling is understood as the meaningful inhabitation of the earth and, in general as sense and world making. The term "dwelling" was first used by Heidegger in *Being and Time* to "capture the distinctive manner in which *Dasein* is *in* the world" gains an important role in his later writings, made philosophically central to our understanding of Being."[22] Dwelling means making oneself at home, having a place in the world. In a more specific approach, dwelling is poetic habitation: "'Earth is the serving bearer, blossoming and fruiting, spreading out in rock and water, rising up into plant and animal... The sky is the vaulting path of the sun, the course of the changing moon, the wandering glitter of the stars, the year's seasons and their changes, the light and dusk of day, the gloom and glow of night, the clemency and inclemency of the weather, the drifting clouds and blue depth of the ether."[23] By employing what might best be understood as poetic rather than a strictly philosophical register in the above passage, Heidegger suggests that humans dwell principally poetically, which he takes after Hölderlin. Thus, for Heidegger, our relation is felt rather than logically deduced.

Heidegger returns to the ontological properties of poetry in "The Thinker as Poet" when he states "poetry that thinks is in truth the topology of Being."[24] This seems to express a truth to which Burnside's own poetry adheres. Burnsides refers to Heidegger implicitly through his poetry and explicitly in his essays, arguing that in dwelling we inhabit the poetic. In an essay titled *Otro mundo es posible: Poetry, Dissidence and Reality TV: A Poet's Polemic*, Burnside argues that "[w]hat he [Heidegger] was demanding from poets was a special quality of attention, a special quality of dwelling that would rescue the world from those who would reduce it to endless and homogenous stacks of produce."[25] In opposition to the "age of consummate meaninglessness,"[26] as Heidegger puts it, the poet according to Burnside needs to be present and grounded, paying attention, dwelling properly. These qualities stand in opposition to modern world of mechanical reproduction and uniformity. What poetry offers instead is "[a] world of dwelling" as "[e]very good poem proposes this world and, to that extent, every *published* poem is a political act...not merely to include, but to revolve around a question of right dwelling."[27] Right or proper dwelling comes with poetic Being which enables sense and home making on earth which in turn arises from a "special quality of attention," an embodied presence. For Burnside, "proper" dwelling requires an acute awareness of other beings, a sensual, especially auditory immersion. "When we consider poetry as an ecological discipline – that is, as a *scientia* of dwelling – we see that what it makes happen is *listening*,"[28] he writes. Poetry is a manifestation of listening, of making listening visible and so exposing the self to the song of the world. The privileged role of the lyric was also noticed by Jacques Derrida, who said, "I wonder if philosophy, which is also the birth of prose, has not meant the repression of music or song. Philosophy cannot, as such, let the song *resonate* in some way."[29] Poetry makes listening happen, and through listening, it creates an alertness to place and its topology.

How much grounding and listening matter is evidenced in a creation myth cited by Burnside whereby the heart of a reindeer is buried underneath the earth's surface:

> In the beginning, says the Sami myth, the god who made all things took the beating heart of a two-year-old reindeer and set it at the centre of the earth. The rhythm of this heart is the rhythm of the world, the pulse of life, the source of all being. When times are difficult, the people have only to press their ears to the ground and listen: if they hear the beat of the reindeer's heart, all will be well, they will emerge from the hard times. If they do not, they are doomed.[30]

The sound of the song of the earth is a guarantor of continued existence: as long as the people could hear the beat of the heart, they know they are safe. According to the poet, the heartbeat is not heard; it is either because it stopped beating or because the sound is muffled by all the noise that we make.[31]

If, in modern times, listening and paying attention are essential for proper dwelling, and so is "remembering complexity and diversity."[32] Noticing and reminding oneself of the entanglement is a task which Burnside's speakers set themselves in many of his poems, often containing catalogues of plants and animals. The speaker frequently invokes a taxonomy that is singular, inasmuch as it is not connected by the relation between objects and phenomena. Hence, it is not *Linnaean taxonomy* that would scientifically objectify the world as masterable through the economy of scientific naming, but inasmuch as what the speaker encounters, sees, hears, is what 'makes' the self in the poem. The self appears through the list the self constructs. At times, the sense of the present in which the self is immersed is mingled with memories of inhabiting a place, once, usually in childhood as if attempting to fix a fleeting world. "Memories are motionless, and the more securely they are fixed in space, the sounder they are," writes Bachelard.[33] Frequently, in Burnside's poems a memory re-places the present, becoming more concrete and "real." Childhood appears as a time when Being was rooted in the world. Burnside's Heideggerian legacy is particularly visible in the volume *The Light Trap*, most ostensibly in the title of a poem "Being and time,"[34] the poem which is concerned with childhood as a unique moment when knowledge of things comes intuitively:

we knew without knowing, as we knew

that everything was finite and alive,
cradled in warmth against the ache of space. (ll. 14–16)

Open space is juxtaposed with inner space, which offers safety and intimacy. The place is determined by the phenomenal events: "wet afternoons" (l. 7), "the slink of tides, the absolutes of fog" (l. 8). The collective subject, which occurs in this and a number of poems, creates a sense of community dwelling in the same place and sharing experience. Childhood is a recurrent theme in Burnside's work, where it provides a grounding for the poetic subject, a first attachment to a place "our adult life is so dispossessed of the essential benefits, its anthropocosmic ties have become so slack, that we do not feel their first attachment in the universe of the house."[35] Returning to childhood brings memories of a preverbal, corporeal knowing ("the knowledge we kept in the bones," l. 6); recreating this first attachment, it reunites the poetic subject with the world. Yet the poem does not promote an idealised version of an innocent time. The bloodroot mentioned in the penultimate stanza (l. 17) augurs a grim kind of knowledge, a reminder of the finite nature of Being and the frailty of the transitory lives of biological creatures. "Human beings are time binders and our ecological niche is time," as Max Oelschlaeger argues.[36] Bloodroot is a plant which emerges in early spring and blooms for a brief period. Its white, delicate flowers conceal an underground poison. The juice that flows from the root is toxic, and when it comes in contact, it stains the skin orange. The juice promotes cell death, dissolving the tissue and scarring it deeply. The image of children digging the bloodroot in the woods, then carrying the stain on the fingers "through snow and miles of sleep" (l. 19), offers this deep-buried knowledge of the underlying danger, with a hint of mythical the woods as a site of menace. The final line evokes the bloodroot poison, which enters the body like the knowledge of death, "a sliver of fate" (l. 20), "unstitching its place in the marrow, and digging in" (l. 21). In this image, the realisation of finitude sinks into and fuses with the body, reaching the very core: the bone marrow. The knowledge dissolves what used to be solid, it undoes what seemed certain.

In a brief essay titled "A Science of Belonging: Poetry as Ecology," Burnside underlines the fact that "what we know of life" is limited to phenomenal things and "we need to remember above and beyond all our other concerns […] that this is the real world, this is our enduring mystery."[37] But where is "the real world"? Burnside's speakers vacillate between temporal and spatial planes, recognising that presence is about being emplaced, being there yet unable to decide where stress falls. The dialectics between 'here' and 'there' has preoccupied the poet since the early collections. This concern is overt in the collection *The Good Neighbour*, which is divided into two parts, "Here" and "There." This division brings to mind Bachelard's divagations concerning the expression "being there": "Where is the main stress…in *being-there* (être-là)," asks Bachelard, "on *being*, or on *there*?"[38] And further: "In *there* – which it would be better to call here – shall I first look for my being? Or am I going to find, in my being, above all, certainty of my fixation in a *there*?"[39] In this expression, there may occur "a geometrical fixation"[40]

if the adverb "there" is stressed more, which "might easily relegate intimate being to an exteriorized place."[41] Burnside's "here" and "there"
function as markers of place which is internalised in poems focused on
experience rather than representation.

Place, essential in Burnside's writing, is present through its topographical features as well as names of the local flora and fauna. The
employment of topographical images and topological motifs enables
Burnside to moor experience temporally. He evokes various locations
from the British Isles to different parts of Europe and Americas, yet one
location returns with regularity. It is not a specific location but rather
designates a direction: the north. The idea of north occupies an important place in Burnside's writing. As Peter Davidson writes, "Everyone
carries their idea of north within them."[42] An attempt to grasp it in its
multifarious nature is for instance a poem titled "A Duck Island Flora."[43]
Finding himself at the edge of the earth, he passes sites where "a common beauty thrives"; he observes the landscape with humility for the vast
terrain, as "north – further north, Arctic north – represents a place of
extremes that is also a place of wonders."[44] "A Duck Island Flora" is one
of Burnside's poems on the move, in which the speaker passes through
places on the way to the Brensholmen ferry to Botnhamn, a small village in Norway north of the Arctic Circle. He notices names in two
languages, one line beneath the other, which label these places and translate them into codes which can be deciphered by humans. The need to
name, which, although ambivalent as suggested above, is inevitable and
is expressed in a line from a poem from the same collection, and also
set in the north, titled "On Kvaloya."[45] In the first section "Learning
to talk," through naming the elements of the vegetal world—"I gloss
uncertainties" (l. 8)—the speaker orients himself, achieving temporary,
fleeting mooring. The opening stanza states this urge explicitly: "This
is our game for now, rehearsing words/ to make the world seem permanent, and ours" (ll. 1–2). The speaker then proceeds to enumerate
the things that they pass on the way. The naming concerns "all we can
see" (l. 4)—a common plant, three kinds of birds—thus foregrounding the sense of sight. Vision is combined at the end of the stanza with
the sense of hearing as the black-backed gull appears "at the rim of the
sound" (l. 6). The impossibility to know a place in its entirety, always
slipping from grasp where words for known things run out: "It never
ends; there's always something else" (l. 13). An apparition of a blackbird,
a messenger between worlds, disrupts a cosy illusion and "everything we

know is strange again" (l. 16). There is often this sense of the uncanny in Burnside's poems, a powerful eeriness which imbues place. The lines ending this section—"finding and naming, one thing at a time:/ field-fare, redshank, cranesbill, alchemilla" (ll. 26–27)—emphasise this paramount need to find oneself through language which designates and classifies as well as having the poetic function, expressed in the sound of words, the rhyme and rhythm. As the speaker states at the beginning, this is just a game played by humans which tames place, making it familiar and creating an illusion of permanence.

Burnside's musings about the concept of place and the relationship that people have with it through language return in a short essay titled "In Arizona," in which he asks, "what is place, anyway? How do we know where one place ends and another begins?"[46] and further he poses one more question "Do we find, or do we make it?" to which he immediately replies "Perhaps both: we find a place, we give it a name – our name – and we begin to change its intrinsic nature, more often than not transforming it into property."[47] We treat places as our property, we appropriate them, "One of the main reasons for changing a place is to facilitate this process of acquisition. Our first relationship to place, then, is a betrayal. After that, the only question is: where do we build the wall?"[48] People betray place by thrusting names on it and claiming ownership. Appropriation and acquisition are anthropocentric gestures, no doubt. Yet, as the first lines of Robert Frost's poem titled "Mending Wall" suggest

> Something there is that doesn't love a wall,
> That sends the frozen-ground-swell under it,
> And spills the upper boulders in the sun;
> And makes gaps even two can pass abreast. (ll. 1–4)[49]

Burnside uses Frost's poem as one of the epigraphs to the first section in *The Good Neighbour* yet he focuses on the final lines. These opening lines offer a non-human reaction to wall with a returning line, "Something there is that doesn't love a wall," which foregrounds the contrast between an unnamed entity which disrupts human-made constructions. Frost's speaker seems to empathises this perspective as well, sceptical about the necessity to rebuild the wall. The adverbial phrase "there is" simply states an existence of "something," acknowledging other beings without trying to pinpoint or name them, respecting the "enduring mystery" of place.

Preceded by an epigraph from Lucretius's *De Rerum Natura*,[50] "Birth Songs"[51] is composed of six sections. The epigraph indicates that the order of things is affected by their passing in the process of becoming: where change affects the world, one thing gives place to another: a new cycle of birth follows decay, the process of destruction is inextricably bound with creation. The nature of the whole world relies on the atomic flowing where everything is in flux. Such processual vision of the world is present in Burnside's lyric, evoked by his "phenomenologically modulated lexis of mutability."[52] In the first section titled "Lullaby," place is transformed by the eeriness of night time which creates an oneiric atmosphere, so favoured by Burnside. In "a realm of shades / and fairy rings" (ll. 17–18), the speaker has a sense of mystery, aware of other beings "somewhere in the grass/ an insect sings" (ll. 23–24). The indefinite phrasing occurring throughout the poem introduces a sense of vagueness and lack of specificity. For instance, in the lines cited above the pronoun "somewhere" suggesting an unspecified place is followed by a general name of a group of invertebrates. Something is suggested indirectly, giving a slight indication of presence. When vision fails, other senses prevail. In the final section of "Birth Songs" titled "Catalogue," the air is filled with a subtle scent, "hints of gorse and tar" (ll. 11–12). More specific names appear—"spiraea, mallow, buckthorn, guelder rose" (l. 14), all indicating common plants, widely cultivated as garden ornamentals, "near-native plants," which situate the speaker. They are also familiar, reliable plants "that anyone might trust/ to bloom, in time, like bodies" (ll. 15–16). Likening plants to bodies further enhances this familiarity and closeness, foregrounding human welding with the environment. The house is "open to the air," the outside entering it, leaving traces in the form of pollen and light. The openness of the house stands for the shimmering self in Burnside's poems, a self which is unfinished, unconstituted and which responds to landscape in a constant process of becoming. As Merleau-Ponty, drawing from Malebranche and Husserl, argues the world is the *field* of our experience, and if we are nothing but a view of the world, for in that case it is seen that the most intimate vibration of our psycho-physical being already announces the world, the quality being the outline of a thing, and the thing the outline of the world. A world which, as Malebranche puts it, never gets beyond being an "unfinished work", or which, as Husserl says of the body, is "never completely constituted", does not require, and even rules out, a constituting subject.[53]

In "Birth Songs," there is, as often in Burnside's poetry, a sense of uncertainty, of a subject as if hesitantly emplaced. The self is in an unfinished state, never fixed, remaining in a relational being with the world. The title of the poem "Viriditas"[54] means vitality, lushness though as Burnside's speaker suggests in the first section, it is better not to understand but to sense it, "catching the hint of leaf/in a map or a place-name" (ll. 7–8). In the first section, "It's buried in the flesh/ with avocet and lizard and the last/ glimmer of rock-salt/ravelled in the spine" (ll. 20–23). What do these lines mean? What is it that is buried? The word "it" returns "but never think it;/ let it go unnamed" (ll. 23–24). "It" is viriditas, something that cannot be fully understood or named, but poetry may open it up: "By means of poetic language, waves of newness flow over the surface of being. And language bears within itself the dialectics of open and closed. Through *meaning* it encloses, while through poetic expression, it opens up."[55] It cannot be fully named or comprehended because it is process rather than product, becoming rather than being, and in its ineluctability, it exceeds any static condition or presence that could be gathered under a name. Viriditas hints at "unexpected depths" (l. 3), suggesting a rootedness that connects animal, vegetable and mineral, foregrounding that dwelling is about connectedness with other beings. The words such as "the hint," "a ghost," emphasise the ungraspable, transient and mutable aspect of Being. Transformation of matter returns in the second section where autumnal decay depicts an opportunity for renewal with the inrush of "new sugars/in the blood" (ll. 11–12), the rotting windfall suggestive of the approach of winter. The poetic subject makes a brief presence in the collective "we know" in the seventh line yet is there throughout the whole poem in the things perceived and sensed such as "the crushed-plum and rainwater scent/ in the outer fence" (ll. 5–6). Similarly, in the third section the plural subject watches for snow, perceiving and experiencing the states in-between, things taking place "somewhere in the gap between" (l. 8). This suspension is a characteristic feature of Burnside's poetry, his signature, "something like guesswork/happens amongst the leaves" (ll. 11–12).[56] The transformative nature of the world is emphasised in the final two couplets:

> threads of sycamore
> and blackened rain
>
> becoming mildew, slut's hair,
> random birds. (ll. 17–20)

Divided into four parts, the poem follows the seasonal cycle, beginning with a hint of deep-buried green and ending with the evergreen. Like the evergreen plants—holly, ivy, shrubs forming a hedgerow—the self exists as an ideal form, "uninterrupted" (l. 13). Significantly, throughout the whole poem, and indeed in many other poems, Burnside maintains the first person plural, which emphasises the coexistence with others, an intersubjectivity which extends towards other consciousnesses. How this occurs, "[w]e always wondered" (l. 7). Wonder returns twice in this last section, the final words being "lost in wonderment" (l. 18).[57] The honeyed, powerful fragrance of wintersweet the blooming of which in the middle of winter may surprise and delight. The speaker likens "the smell of distance" (l. 5) to the scent of wintersweet, "clinging to our hands" (l. 6). It suggests an intertwining of the senses: vision, touch and smell come together in experience of place. The poetic subject experiences the world in a temperate climate with distinct seasonal changes which enhances a regularity inherent to Being where "everything is circuitous, roundabout, recurrent."[58]

In "Field Mice,"[59] a "tidy street" (l. 2) is contrasted with the wild, or what Yi-Fu Tuan calls a "carpentered" habitat, constructed along straight lines as opposed to a "noncarpentered" one, lacking in regularity.[60] The "wild," this uncultivated, untamed place is contrasted with the "civilised," with neat and tidy space. Yet, as Oelschlaeger points out, it seems "contemporary wilderness philosophy represents more than an extolling of the recreational value of wild nature, retrograde romanticism, or mystical escape from an overpopulated, industrialized, anxiety-ridden, polluted, and violent world."[61] The poem does not propose a simple contrast between wilderness and civilisation but rather suggests an interpenetration of the two. What we think of as the wild blends with the space of the house. The street evokes a sense of sterility, enhanced further at the end of the second stanza in the image of "talk-shows and the news" (l. 10), the noise of which obscures the sound of the wind. The wild is out there in "that odour" (l. 3), "these shreds" (l. 4), volatile and discrete. This is not wildness that is distant or exotic but one that is near. The second line—"The closest we come to wild"—offers a paradox in the form of a reversal as in effect the image created in the poem suggests that the field mice come to the places inhabited by humans. "In wildness lies the preservation of the world," writes Henry David Thoreau in his essay "Walking" (1892).[62] The poem abounds in references to minute, often intangible particles, which leave traces. These are things hidden underneath the surface, as in the following lines:

a hidden stream
of warmth and dread, alive beneath the home
we only half possess. (ll. 10–12)

These insubstantial things are emotions shared with "them," suggesting complementary dwelling which is not exploitative. The notion of the house entails boundaries: a threshold, doors and windows separate the outside from the inside. Yet these boundaries are permeable, which enables making the house open. The word "home" reappears in many poems, oftentimes combined with another word—"sense"—to form an expression "a sense of home" as if home was only possible when mediated, never experienced directly. The phrase "a half-forgotten dream" (l. 7) marks a recurrent theme in Burnside's poetry, which is filled with oneiric spaces, affecting the experience of place and creating "the unfathomable store of daydreams of intimacy."[63]

Burnside's poetry abounds in "thin places," a concept from Celtic cultures meaning "borderline between this world and the other."[64] In "Animism,"[65] the house abounds in non-human animals inhabiting it together with the human dwellers: bees, starlings, lacewings, frogs, a civet. Yet before the physical animals are "discovered" in the nooks and corners of the house, the opening two lines suggest the existence of a hidden, "secret animal." The speaker's "[a]s if this house contained/ a secret animal/ I keep watch" (ll. 1–2) Animism, from the title of the poem, indicates a belief that places possess a spiritual essence, filled with innumerable spiritual beings influencing humans. Rooted in the prehistoric era and belonging to "the older forms of prayer" (l. 9), the animistic worldview is contrasted with Christianity. The bible is "open forever/ at Leviticus" (ll. 6–7), a phrase which suggests that it is not read actively, but merely left there. This is contrasted with the vitality, the spiritedness of the place imbued with life beneath the surface, out of sight, stitched into the fabric of the house, "a thin song in the walls" (l. 19). Once again Burnside returns to the necessity to listen, as listening "is dissident work, and it carries no reward, other than a dark, live murmur that, in the small hours, or in some far place, reveals itself, for minutes at a time, as the song of the earth."[66] Listening to the "thin song" is a responsibility of the human dweller.

The prepositions used in the poem emphasise the dialectics of surface and depth, visible and invisible. The dialectic is particularly pronounced by the preposition "in," which recurs throughout in such expressions as "in the roof" (l. 10), "in a trap" (l. 12), "in the snow" (l. 16), "in the walls" (l. 16), as well as other prepositional phrases as "into built into the stair" (l. 21) and "beneath the outhouse floor" (l. 14), that in turn suggest an inner intimacy and depth, the preposition at once marking a surface and at the same time, passing through, allowing access or passage through those surfaces given as nouns. They foreground that which is hidden from sight but nonetheless sensed or heard. Embedded in the place, contained by it, other beings are there, always present "built into the stair" (l. 21). Sharing the house with all the other animals, the speaker expresses a yearning for a community of all beings.

The first part of the collection *The Good Neighbour* titled "Habitat" is preceded by Paul Shepard's words: "What is meant here is something more mutually and functionally interdependent between mind and terrain, an organic relationship between the environment and the unconscious, the visible space and the conscious, the ideas and the creatures."[67] Burnside's poetic subject often expresses a longing for unity, in the hope that there must be, then, corresponding to this open unity of the world, an open and indefinite unity of subjectivity. Like the world's unity, that of the *I* is invoked rather than experienced each time I perform an act of perception, each time I reach a self-evident truth, and the universal *I* is the background against which these effulgent forms stand out: it is through one present thought that I achieve the unity of all my thoughts. What remains, on the hither side of my particular thoughts, to constitute the tacit *cogito* and the original project towards the world, and what, ultimately, am I in so far as I can catch a glimpse of myself independently of any particular act? I am a field, an experience.[68]

The intertwining of self with the world is powerfully evoked in a poem ending *The Light Trap*, titled "A Theory of Everything."[69] The indefinite pronoun in the title of the poem mitigates the totalising aspect of the noun and pronoun. The enjambment, a poetic device favoured by Burnside, creates a flowing rhythm and rhyme, but also foregrounds the hesitance hinted at in the title, by creating micro pauses at the end of lines. One place name appears in the poem: *Mirtiotissa*, a beach on Corfu, a path leading to the sea. Faced with the ungraspability of things, the speaker declares "I'll settle for that reach of sunlit track/ that led out to the sea" (ll. 4–5). The phrase "I'll settle for" suggests a compromise, a decision reached when faced with a large number of options. The experience of that place in that moment makes a sense of unity possible: "for this is how the world /occurs: not piecemeal /but entire."

There is for the speaker that one moment in time experienced in that one place which brings him closer to wild being, a glimpse of something genuine is revealed, when what Heidegger calls unconcealedness takes place. Burnside's poetry is a poetry of unconcealment, of crossing the surface to the reveal the depth, the spirit inside the form of place. His poems often arise from glimmers, fleetingly observed through peripheral vision, while passing through a place, the speaker experiencing being in "the instantaneous."[70] Burnside's attunement to place stems from sensory, embodied responses to the world, whereby the self is "wedded to the earth" (l. 51).[71] Place evoked in Burnside's poetry is fused with time, being a sequence of overlapping sights unveiled for an instant, revealing fragments of the invisible field.

NOTES

1. Maurice Merleau-Ponty, *Phenomenology of Perception*, trans. D. A. Landes (London and New York: Routledge, 2002), 84.
2. As Robert T. Tally and Christine M. Saville argue in the introduction to *Ecocriticism and Geocriticism: Overlapping Territories in Environmental and Spatial Literary Studies*, 'anthropocene' may not be the most helpful term, drawing as it does so much of its rhetorical power from the sense that a distinctive *anthropos* could exert such influence over a planetary geological domain. Critics of the term have noted that, in its quasi-scientific appearance, the concept of an anthropocene elides any consideration of specific agents or structures beyond the "human," which are responsible for environmental destruction. Worse, some would argue that such a notion intentionally covers up and thereby excuses the bad actors' (London: Palgrave, 2016), 6.
3. Ursula Heise, *Sense of Place and Sense of Planet: The Environmental Imagination of the Global* (Oxford: Oxford University Press, 2008), 10.
4. Ibid.
5. Ibid.
6. Merleau-Ponty, *Phenomenology of Perception*, 472.
7. Tim Dee, ed., *Ground Work: Writings on People and Places* (London: Jonathan Cape, 2018), 1.
8. Jane Bennett, *The Enchantment of Modern Life* (Princeton: Princeton University Press, 2001); Robert Macfarlane, *The Wild Places* (London: Granta, 2007); Robert Macfarlane, *Landmarks* (London: Hamish Henderson, 2015); and Sara Maitland, *Gossip from the Forest: The Tangled Roots of Our Forests and Fairytales* (London: Granta, 2012).

9. John Burnside, 'Poetry and a Sense of Place', in *Proceedings of the Writing and a Sense of Place Symposium*. Tromsø, 15–18 August 1996. Ed. Astrid Sollid Brokke, Rolf Gaasland, Sandra Lee Kleppe, and Henning Howlid Wærp. *Nordlit* No. 1 (1997) https://septentrio.uit.no/index.php/nordlit/article/view/2208/2060, accessed 1 March 2018, 201.
10. Edward S. Casey, *The Fate of Place: A Philosophical History* (Berkeley and London: University of California Press, 1998), 202.
11. Burnside, 'Poetry and a Sense of Place', 201.
12. Tom Bristow, 'Negative Poetics and Immanence: Reading John Burnside's "Hommage to Henri Bergson"', *Green Letters: Studies in Ecocriticism* 10:1 (2009): 50–69, 51, http://dx.doi.org/10.1080/1468 8417.2009.10589044, accessed 1 March 2018.
13. John Burnside, *The Good Neighbour* (London: Jonathan Cape, 2005), 32.
14. Martin Heidegger, *Poetry Language Thought*, trans. Albert Hofstadter (New York: Harper Perennial Modern Thought, 2013), 148.
15. Andrew J. Mitchell, *The Fourfold: Reading the Late Heidegger* (Evanston: Northwestern University Press, 2015), 3.
16. Heidegger, *Poetry Language Thought*, 351.
17. Michael Wheeler, 'Martin Heidegger', *The Stanford Encyclopedia of Philosophy* (Fall 2017 edition), ed. Edward N. Zalta, n.p., https://plato.stanford.edu/archives/fall2017/entries/heidegger/, accessed 1 March 2018.
18. Maurice Merleau-Ponty, *The Visible and the Invisible: Followed by Working Notes*, trans. A. Lingis (Evanston: Northwestern University Press, 1968), 178.
19. Ibid.
20. Ibid., 117.
21. Jeff Malpas, *Heidegger and the Thinking of Place Explorations in the Topology of Being* (Cambridge: MIT, 2006), 3.
22. Wheeler.
23. Heidegger, *Poetry Language Thought*, 351.
24. Ibid., 12.
25. John Burnside, *Otro Mundo es Posible: Poetry, Dissidence and Reality TV: A Poet's Polemic* (Edinburgh: Scottish Book Trust, 2003), 8.
26. Martin Heidegger, *Nietzsche: Volumes Three and Four*, ed. David Farrell Krell (San Francisco: Harper & Rowe, 1991), 163; cit. Burnside, *Otro Mundo es Posible*, 8.
27. Burnside, *Otro Mundo es Posible*, 10.
28. Ibid., 6.
29. Jacques Derrida, *Points…Interviews 1974–1994*, ed. Elisabeth Weber, trans. Peggy Kamuf et al. (Stanford: Stanford University Press, 1995), 394.
30. Burnside, *Otro Mundo es Posible*, 3.

142   M. SZUBA

142 M. SZUBA

31. Ibid.
32. Ibid., 11.
33. Gaston Bachelard, *The Poetics of Space*, trans. M. Jolas (Boston: Beacon Press, 1994), 9.
34. John Burnside, *The Light Trap* (London: Jonathan Cape, 2002).
35. Bachelard, *The Poetics of Space*, 4.
36. Max Oelschlaeger, *The Idea of Wilderness from Prehistory to the Age of Ecology* (New Haven: Yale University Press, 1991), 30.
37. John Burnside, 'A Science of Belonging: Poetry as Ecology', in *Contemporary Poetry and Contemporary Science*, ed. Robert Crawford (Oxford: Oxford University Press, 2006), 91–106, 107.
38. Bachelard, *The Poetics of Space*, 213.
39. Ibid.
40. Ibid.
41. Ibid.
42. Peter Davidson, *The Idea of North* (London: Reaktion Books, 2005), 8.
43. Burnside, *The Light Trap*, 59.
44. Ibid., 9.
45. 'Whale Island' in northernmost parts of Norway which also provides a setting for Burnside's novel, *A Summer of Drowning*.
46. John Burnside, 'In Arizona', in *Ground Work: Writings on People and Places*, ed. Tim Dee (London: Jonathan Cape, 2018), 54–63, 56.
47. Ibid., 57.
48. Ibid.
49. Robert Frost, *The Collected Poems* (London: Vintage Books, 2013), 33.
50. 'Mutat enim mundi naturam totius aetas, ex alioque alius status excipere omnia debet, nec manet ulla sui similis res: omnia migrant' (l. 828–830); 'For time changes the nature of the whole world, and one state of things must pass into another, and nothing remains as it was: All things move, all are changed by nature and compelled to alter' (Garani 2007, 201).
51. Burnside, *The Light Trap*, 45–51.
52. Thomas Bristow. *The Anthropocene Lyric: An Affective Geography of Poetry, Politics, Place* (London: Palgrave Macmillan, 2015), 49.
53. Merleau-Ponty, *Phenomenology of Perception*, 472.
54. Burnside, *The Light Trap*, 78–82.
55. Bachelard, *The Poetics of Space*, 222.
56. Burnside, *The Light Trap*, 81.
57. Ibid., 82.
58. Bachelard, *The Poetics of Space*, 213–14.
59. Burnside, *The Light Trap*, 15.
60. Yi-Fu Tuan, *Topophilia: A Study of Environmental Perception, Attitudes, and Values* (Englewood Cliffs: Prentice-Hall, 1974), 75.

61. Oelschlaeger, *The Idea of Wilderness from Prehistory to the Age of Ecology*, 2.
62. William David Thoreau, 'Walking'.
63. Bachelard, *The Poetics of Space*, 78.
64. Burnside, 'In Arizona', 62.
65. Burnside, *The Light Trap*, 16.
66. Burnside *Otro Mundo es Posible*, 3.
67. Paul Shepard, *Thinking Animals: Animals and the Development of Human Intelligence* (Athens: The University of Georgia Press, 1978), 35.
68. Merleau-Ponty, *Phenomenology of Perception*, 473.
69. Burnside, *The Light Trap*, 83.
70. Ibid., 14.
71. Ibid.

WORKS CITED

Bachelard, Gaston. *The Poetics of Space*. Trans. Maria Jolas. Boston: Beacon Press, 1994.
Bennett, Jane. *The Enchantment of Modern Life*. Princeton: Princeton University Press, 2001.
Bristow, Thomas. *The Anthropocene Lyric: An Affective Geography of Poetry, Politics, Place*. London: Palgrave Macmillan, 2015.
Bristow, Tom. 'Negative Poetics and Immanence: Reading John Burnside's "Homage to Henri Bergson"', *Green Letters: Studies in Ecocriticism* 10:1 (2009): 50–69, 51. http://dx.doi.org/10.1080/14688417.2009.10589044. Accessed 1 March 2018.
Burnside, John. 'Poetry and a Sense of Place'. *Proceedings of the Writing and a Sense of Place Symposium*. Tromsø, 15–18 August 1996. Ed. Astrid Sollid Brokke, Rolf Gaasland, Sandra Lee Kleppe, and Henning Howlid Wærp. *Nordlit* 1 (1997). https://septentrio.uit.no/index.php/nordlit/article/view/2208/2060. Accessed 1 March 2018, 201.
———. *The Light Trap*. London: Jonathan Cape, 2002.
———. *Otro Mundo es Posible: Poetry, Dissidence and Reality TV: A Poet's Polemic*. Edinburgh: Scottish Book Trust, 2003.
———. *The Good Neighbour*. London: Jonathan Cape, 2005.
———. 'A Science of Belonging: Poetry as Ecology'. *Contemporary Poetry and Contemporary Science*. Ed. Robert Crawford. Oxford: Oxford University Press, 2006. 91–106.
———. 'In Arizona', in *Ground Work: Writings on People and Places*. Ed. Tim Dee. London: Jonathan Cape, 2018.
Casey, Edward S. *The Fate of Place: A Philosophical History*. Berkeley and London: University of California Press, 1998.
Davidson, Peter. *The Idea of North*. London: Reaktion Books, 2005.

Dee, Tim, ed., *Ground Work: Writings on People and Places*. London: Jonathan Cape, 2018. 54–63.

Derrida, Jacques. *Points...Interviews 1974–1994*. Ed. Elisabeth Weber. Trans. Peggy Kamuf et al. Stanford: Stanford University Press, 1995.

Frost, Robert. *The Collected Poems*. London: Vintage, 2013.

Global. Oxford: Oxford University Press, 2008.

Heidegger, Martin. *Nietzsche: Volumes Three and Four*. Ed. David Farrell Krell. San Francisco: Harper & Rowe, 1991.

Heidegger, Martin. *Poetry Language Thought*. Trans. Albert Hofstadter. New York: Harper Perennial Modern Thought, 2013.

Heise, Ursula. *Sense of Place and Sense of Planet: The Environmental Imagination of the Global*. Oxford: Oxford University Press, 2008.

Macfarlane, Robert. *Landmarks*. London: Hamish Hamilton, 2015.

———. *The Wild Places*. London: Granta, 2007.

Maitland, Sara. *Gossip from the Forest: The Tangled Roots of Our Forests and Fairytales*. London: Granta, 2012.

Malpas, Jeff. *Heidegger and the Thinking of Place Explorations in the Topology of Being*. Cambridge: MIT, 2006.

Merleau-Ponty, Maurice. *Phenomenology of Perception*. Trans. D. A. Landes. London and New York: Routledge, 2002.

———. *The Visible and the Invisible: Followed by Working Notes*. Trans. Alphonso Lingis. Evanston: Northwestern University Press, 1968.

Mitchell, Andrew J. *The Fourfold: Reading the Late Heidegger*. Evanston: Northwestern University Press, 2015.

Oelschlaeger, Max. *The Idea of Wilderness from Prehistory to the Age of Ecology*. New Haven: Yale University Press, 1991.

Shepard, Paul. *Thinking Animals: Animals and the Development of Human Intelligence*. Athens: The University of Georgia Press, 1978.

Tally, Robert T., Robert T. Battista, and Christine M. Saville, eds. *Ecocriticism and Geocriticism: Overlapping Territories in Environmental and Spatial Literary Studies*.

Tuan, Yi-Fu. *Topophilia: A Study of Environmental Perception, Attitudes, and Values*. Englewood Cliffs: Prentice-Hall, 1974.

Wheeler, Michael. 'Martin Heidegger'. *The Stanford Encyclopedia of Philosophy*, Fall 2017 Edition. Ed. Edward N. Zalta. n.p. https://plato.stanford.edu/archives/fall2017/entries/heidegger/. Accessed 1 March 2018.

"Under the Saltire Flag":
Kei Miller's Spatial Negotiations of Identity

Bartosz Wójcik

"It is in fact mainly the postcolonial imagination, with its contested relation to Eurocentric discourses (...)", as keenly observed by Carla Sassi (12), "that has taught us to reassert spatiality as a factor that bears the same impact over human activities as temporality" (12). For that reason, drawing succinctly on Jahan Ramazani's theorised notion of "transnational poetics" (2009) and on Philip Nanton's concept of "the frontiers of the Caribbean" (2017), the essay attempts to investigate how Kei Miller, a Jamaican-born and sometime Scotland-based poet and prose writer, creatively explores the nexus of (transatlantic) geographic translocation, identity transition and cultural transference, as evidenced by a selection of his poems and essays, many of which originated as his blog posts (http://underthesaltireflag.com/) that the present text owes its title to.

Starting from the close reading of "In This New Country", the opening section of his second volume of verse—*There Is an Anger That Moves* (2007), the article zooms in on Miller's pluralised narratives of the

B. Wójcik (✉)
Centre for the Meeting of Cultures, Lublin, Poland

© The Author(s) 2019   145
M. Szuba and J. Wolfreys (eds.), *The Poetics of Space and Place
in Scottish Literature*, Geocriticism and Spatial Literary Studies,
https://doi.org/10.1007/978-3-030-12645-2_9

Caribbean[1], Scotland and beyond with a view to among others focusing on, in his own words, "a complex interaction and negotiation between notions of local and foreign" (*Writing* 45), on their interrelatedness and ingenious interplay frequently producing a third space of meaning— a creolised identity that is informed by and replenished through an administered (and sought-after) selection of Caribbean produce (daily provisions and interconnected doses of island-specific smells, flavours, textures and colours), products (music), phenomena (sunnier climes) as well as speech acts. After all, in among others Glasgow "you say *bombo-clawt /* softly, like a prayer, like Amen" (*There Is* 14), turning this common Jamaican expletive into a hushed incantation, into "something to sustain you/in this country" (14)—your (temporary) home away from home. This whispered swear word barely leaves the inner space of the migrant persona's lungs, yet, as it is transformed into a supplication, it acquires the capacity to, one hopes, alter the harsh outside world—the new Old World that the Caribbean newcomer has just found himself in. The word thus belongs to the toolbox/toolkit of spatial survival to be deployed abroad so as to make his diasporic existence more bearable. Or, in other words, to Caribbeanise Scotland—a space whose cultural landscape simultaneously, due to the country's present legislation and its socio-historical trajectory, offers same-sex couples not just fewer instances of "proscriptions, banishments, ostracisms and (...) extreme violence [than the Antilles]" (Glave 1), but a place to call (and make) their home.

Written under a set of saltire flags (Jamaican, Scottish, English/ British), Miller's poems "outstrip single-state or single-identity affiliations" (Ramazani 31) and as "[l]iterary representations of 'postcolonial' topographies are suffused with tropes of migration, mobility and displacement"[2], which remain, however, predominantly filtered through the culture, geography, cuisine and folklore inhabiting the space of the Caribbean island of his origin. Self-avowedly identifying primarily as a Jamaican and "always commenting on that landscape and that literature" (Miller 2014), in all his volumes, though to a varying degree, Miller advocates a poetics of inclusiveness, a thematically national and transnational hybrid[3] that allows for the depiction of "the so-called simple life (...) in all its stunning complexity" (*Writing* 21), as symbolically illustrated by "the folk (...) hold[ing] an iPad in one hand, and a mango in the other" (21). The verse of the Scotland-domiciled Miller, whose poetic personae navigate their way through the territory of the erstwhile British Empire and negotiate their own presence both in the English language and on the land that—to evoke Jamaican Louise

Bennett—"[has been] coloniz[ed] in reverse" (Markham 63), constitutes an example of modern literary production that "reconceives widely
disparate geo-cultural spaces and histories in relation to one another"
(Ramazani 163). This practice provides evidence to support Curwen
Best's assertion that "[t]he Caribbean is never alone; there are always
cross-cultural and intertextual relations between Caribbean and other
cultures" (56), which Miller transplants onto the space he occupies in
the UK. Interestingly, the spatialised condition of an immigrant—and in
particular the condition of a non-white newcomer in a predominantly
white society/space, as the "In This New Country" cycle of poems
shows—is portrayed by Miller with recourse to a number of opposites
that correspond to "slavery and post-emancipation society and its construction of a range of binary oppositions" (Best 67).

2

Caribbean writing, given the prolonged history of exile its practitioners
have been conditioned and affected by, constitutes a form of travel literature—one that constantly expands the radius of the Caribbean frontier,
providing "a useful foil to the nationalist representation of history [and
the present]" (Nanton 25). "The exile", as Barbadian novelist and essay-
ist George Lamming asserts in his 1960 classic text on cultural translocation and the challenges facing Caribbean creative diaspora, "is a universal
figure" (Lamming 253) that, one could argue, accompanies human existence regardless of the particulars of one's residence (living in the country
of one's origin or abroad), as "[w]e are [all] made to feel a sense of exile
by our inadequacy and our irrelevance of function in a society whose past
we can't alter, and whose future is always beyond us" (Lamming 253).
Wary of ensuing generalisations and aware of the pitfalls of biographical
criticism, one could justifiably claim that Miller's writing aims to, among
others, illustrate Lamming's verdict: "[t]o be an exile is to be alive"
(253) and to record this human condition in print.

Historical, political and personal differences aside, Miller's translocation to the UK follows the trajectory pioneered by fellow Caribbean
writers,[4] who—not unlike Guyanese Martin Carter—did

> understand the full implications of the choice that had to be made,
> between leaving the region in order to find publishers, an audience, the
> possibility of commercial success – but at the cost of that sense of exile
> and alienation so many Caribbean writers of that period [and beyond]

expressed – or to stay and feel his ambitions frustrated by the narrowness of life in a post-colony, the parochialism, the lack of a developed literary culture, the sense of being, as he [Carter] puts in one of his essays, 'a displaced person' in the very society he has stayed to serve. (Brown, xvi)

Furthermore, migration and ensuing instances of border crossings and identity shaping engaged not only Miller (or his personae) but scores of West Indian creatives as well in not yet "another boundary challenge" (Nanton 8), but in becoming physical and textual representatives of Caribbean space abroad, and/or actors contributing to the shifting of the Caribbean frontier.

In contrast with Carter, however, Miller emigrated from the Caribbean, making Manchester and subsequently Glasgow his home, perhaps corroborating in effect Jamaican Andrew Salkey's pronouncement: "it's as though the economy fashioned us rather than anything else. The economy is the Bible that fashioned us, not the folk culture" (Birbalsingh 37). Interestingly, Miller's writing chronicling his life abroad abounds in strategies of domesticating the foreign locale and making him a less displaced person in the very society whose ancestors,[5] as historian Sir Tom Devine reminds us in *Recovering Scotland's Slavery Past: The Caribbean Connection* (2015), were infamously instrumental in the proliferation of the Caribbean servitude of enslaved Africans.[6]

If, as maintained by fellow Jamaican writer Ishion Hutchinson, "[m]an's hardest divorce is from the sea" (22), then in Scotland, surrounded by the North Sea in the east and by the Atlantic in the west, the author of *Augustown* should feel at home. Un-divorced from the sea, which—as Derek Walcott proclaims in his poem—"is History" (137–39), Kei Miller weaves a poetic, transnational tale of migration and diasporisation. Poems constituting two series, namely "In This New Country" (published in 2007) and "A Short History of Beds We Have Slept in Together" (published in 2010), are—respectively—records of a geographic translocation: they trace the journey undertaken by Miller's persona—from being culturally (and spatially) marooned in England, to sailing across the global seas of Creolisation, to eventually dropping anchor in Scotland.

Read alongside his verse, essays written during that period and published, among others, in *The International Journal of Scottish Literature* provide explicit footnote-like references to the Caribbeanisation of the space of Glasgow. This is how Miller introduces a crucial caveat—the limited first-hand experience of a newcomer[7]—in "But in Glasgow, there are Plantains":

I map out that timeline to make the simple point that this is all new to me. I know that in me and my biography there is now an undeniable Scottish-Caribbean connection. I know that I'm looking at Glasgow and understanding it through Caribbean eyes, but I'm not sure the few observations I've made in six months can come with any real depth or profundity. This is necessarily an essay of first impressions. (*Writing* 43)

The then *still* foreign city is domesticated not only in the course of the momentous 2008 Beijing Olympics, as recounted in "Imagining Nations", where Scotland acquires some of the tastes, aromas, hues, sounds and ambience of Jamaica when "the previously colonized subject (...) is confidently imagining his nation onto the colonizer's land. In a world characterized by the breaking down of transnational boundaries, innovations in containerised shipping, and a market-driven economy, what has emerged are niche markets – diasporic communities with culturally specific tastes and longings – and nowadays with money to spend" (*Writing* 52). This comes as no surprise as any migrant, unless affected by amnesia, "arrives and travels with the memory" (Lamming 253) and, in the case of arrivals from former dependencies, also with "the habitual weight of a colonial relation..." (253), which imposes further demands on newcomers and complicates their connection with the space they are learning to cope with and eventually inhabit.

The paradox of exile, to use Lamming's phrase that reverberates across the universe that is Anglophone Caribbean literature (and, truth be told, seems apposite to the migrant condition as such), is that "the West Indian writer abroad (...) hungers for nourishment from a soil which he (as an ordinary citizen) could not at present endure" (260). This is evident in Miller's second collection, and the first published after his settlement in the UK. Jamaica abroad, as illustrated by "In This New Country", a sequence of poems opening Miller's *There Is an Anger That Moves*, is summoned up by the expedient of an Internet shopping delivery service, which domesticates the still unknown and alien European residence:

[Y]ou might be desperate enough
to buy plantains online – after all,
you do not know what is what
or where to find things like ground
provisions, or heat, or the sounds of your people. (*There Is* 10)

This tactile connection with homeland, as suggested by the enjambment that bifurcates the expression "ground provisions" and allows the land to take precedence over the produce cultivated in/on it, is provided by the mediated presence of Jamaica: by the digital manifestation of the island's physical space, its palpable climate, its audible phonetics, its meaningful semantics and its human geography. Represented graphically by the enjambment (the visual and aural split of the fixed phrase and its continuation after the line break), the potential indeterminacy of diasporic existence (separation followed—at best—by the prospect of an almost Odyssean return) is hinted at in the poem, which seemingly literalises the "cross-geographic experience [of being] enjambed between the (post) colonies and the Western metropole" (Ramazani 163–64); this is also suggested by the etymology of the poetic device itself—the French verb "enjamber" means, among others, "to straddle" and "to span".

Produced by the arrival, alienation, uncertainty and despair—"you might be desperate enough" (*There Is* 10)—trigger coping mechanisms, such as the strategy of *online* re-modelling one's novel environs— the new *offline* living space in the Old World. To do so, assisted by e-commerce—an example of "an array of technological resources and creative products claiming to free human life from the tyranny of the 'real'" (Paul 626), the persona resorts to the familiar and internalised. The highly idiosyncratic ("your people") and personalised (degree of heat, volume of sound)—if not, given the mercantile basis of the exchange and its transactional nature, customised, i.e., custom-built and customer-oriented, relationship of the speaker with his homeland stems from the fact that "the Caribbean, as much as it is a place, is also an idea" (Jelly-Schapiro 6). Not a monopolist—"In this, the Caribbean is not unique. Any good geographer will tell you that" (6), the Caribbean, or—to be precise—Jamaica is ideated from life—from the former life back home that the persona endeavours to re-enact: "[t]he ways that we humans develop our sense of place – the ways in which we vest location with meaning – have to do always, in some sense, with experience and memory" (6).

As a digital nomad, hindered only by the time zone constraints and fuelled by perseverance, Miller's personae—not unlike the "transnational" poems as such—strive to "cross national borders" (Ramazani 181) as well as "the borders of nation-states, regions and cultures" (181). Available on select websites, almost—the speaker hopes—at his fingertips, the online Caribbean experience may seep offline:

At nights you look through the hopeful window
of a computer screen, waiting for Jamaica
to come falling through and fill your flat.
It will happen, you think, if you stay
awake, keep the channels open,
google the right word, like kumina,
pocomania or Elverine, your mother's name; (*There Is* 10)

The success of the technological endeavour hinges on the end-user's spiritual expertise—"kumina" and "pocomania" are significant instances of folk religious practice in Jamaica (Alleyne 101–102)—and on his emotional attachment (invocation of the parent). The physicality of the transatlantic connection is assured by its anchorage in the fertile Jamaican soil—as implied by "a hand of plantain" (*There Is* 10), evocative of "the yellow insistence of morning / food, as if the sun rose from your small plate" (10). These banana cultivars, the fond memories of which (not to mention their exoticised Latin name i.e., *Musa paradisiaca*) convey the impression of the homeland as paradisal island space, which can be—with the aid of props (home-delivered tropical perishables and the simulacrum of sunshine)—staged in his flat in the North.

In the country he is yet physically unaccustomed to, Miller's persona aims to erect a bunker against cold, to create a buffer zone, to build an embassy, to insulate himself, to find shelter against the storm of culture shock, if only by means of signifiers of home in the shape of (once) colonial goods. Not unlike other diasporic writers, including Trinidadian-British Roger Robinson, whose "The Immigrant's Lament" contains "prayers (…) to the god of warmth" (26) comprised of "phrases like *the coral reef / of my soul* and *the rumshop / of my conversation*" (26), Miller at first evokes rudimentary binaries: the North–(global) South divide, freezing cold vs life-cultivating warmth, light/dark:

> In Glasgow my flat is red and orange and green; people who enter say, with delight, what bright Caribbean colours! They are Ikea colours – but it's true, I have been trying to make the place warm with more than just the heat from Scottish Gas. I've been trying to conjure up an Island in that tiny flat. (*Writing* 44)

His is a predominantly frontier position: as the body of literary evidence shows, he occupies a place typified by "[an] outpost status"

(Nanton 34)—his constantly re-established link with the homeland makes him a proactive Jamaican envoy to Scotland who avoids an identity crisis. Perhaps even, for Miller, as "[f]or Walcott, meaning and affect occur at the space of the in-between of the many lines of narrative, voice, colour and time" (Antoine-Dunne 80).

As a result, Jamaica in Scotland is—if not regained—then at least re-connected and its presence (not to mention the writer himself) is nursed back to safety: "[s]ometimes in this country, the only thing far away / is this country" (*There Is* 13). Arguably, this re-enactment of the desirable Antillean experience (heterotopia) and its imposition on the Auld Country questions the distinctiveness of the cultural landscape of England, Ireland, Scotland, and Wales, as a similar sleight of imagination could be successfully performed all over the UK—if not, market forces permitting, anywhere in the North.

However, Miller's persona is no mere tourist in reverse, a Jamaican student variant of, say, a British middle-class holidaymaker craving Waitrose frozen yoghurt while in Barbados. Experiencing poverty, he willy-nilly practises culinary creolisation, as in "How quickly you grow":

> In this country, when you can't afford
> more than one tin of ackee
> you might use mushrooms to stretch the pot. (*There Is* 16)

Necessitated by the economic reality he experiences, his food production and "consumption can be defined as a performative act that not only fulfils a concrete purpose, but also serves as a medium to construct identities and to express one's position in relation to society, class, nation, religion, and culture" (Beushausen 16). This is the third space of meaning—the "neither here nor there" cultural position of a migrant and an example of the shift of the Caribbean frontier.

In fact, it is through the performance of the daily ritual of cooking that Miller's persona not only provides himself with the sensualised Caribbean gratification but, most importantly, familiarises himself—often through acts of intellectual serendipity—with the transnational space of the imaginary, with the global interconnectedness that we are all part of at present:

In Glasgow, I buy plantains from a little shop on Great Western Road called Solly's, and there you can also find scotch bonnet peppers, which I'd never reflected on before – these peppers I've always thought of as Jamaican peppers, but which had obviously reminded someone long time ago, about something he saw in Scotland. These connections go both ways! (*Writing* 47)

Rather than merely lining the walls of his stomach cavity with some faux Caribbean sustenance or desperately emulating the aromas and tastes of his island home in a fit of nostalgia, Miller's persona calibrates the sense of the self and re-discovers his identity:

In Glasgow I am learning how to cook the Caribbean. It is not really that some sudden wave of homesickness has come over me, or that I never cooked before. I've always loved cooking but in the Caribbean I had never tried to cook mackerel rundown, or gungo peas soup, or escoveitch fish, partly because so many people could do it better than I could ever even attempt. In Scotland the Caribbean becomes a cuisine that I can master – and as I said before, I find this is often the case, that we can become our home-selves most in places away from that home. (*Writing* 46)

In effect, changed by the outside space of the Scottish reality (and the provisions it provides) as well as by the internal re-valorisation of his Jamaican memory banks, he understandably advocates fusion cuisine, a product of a cultural meeting in time and space that he himself has grown to symbolise:

So it is, in my current cooking and the smells that come from my kitchen, I am self-identifying with the Caribbean – but also, it must be said immediately, with Scotland. You see, it is not enough to learn how to make red peas soup – if you are good, you must make it your own, with your own special touch. I am learning to cook the Caribbean with Scottish ingredients, and dare I say, I'm becoming good at it. I think I now prefer my Johnny cakes to anything served at that house in Hope Pastures – something about the self-rising flour from Lidl, the sprinkle of fine cornmeal from the delicatessen on Great Western Road, all these combine to make a fried dumpling so much softer and lighter and sweeter than the version my mother made. When I tell my mother the things I've been making, she says that I am becoming stoosh – because sometimes I can't find the exact things I need so I make do. (*Writing* 47)

3

In Miller's writing, Jamaica abroad, as illustrated in "Always Under Your Breath", is expressed among others by its "landscape of sound" (Miller 2009), conjuring "the Caribbean [that] exists far beyond the Caribbean" (Miller 2009):

> you leave the CD playing all day
> hoping it will witness to the empty flat, a gospel
> of warm. (*There Is* 11)

Such Jamrock is a point of constant return while in Scotland, serving as a lifeline that keeps his speaker's spirit afloat in the brand new Old World. A fixture and a fix, it is both a feature and a bug: referencing the homophobic lyrics of Buju Banton's hit song (*killa* tune) "Boom Bye-Bye", Miller's persona "say[s] boom-bye-bye to the weatherman/insistent on his bab-ylon creed of chill and wind, / saying there is no such thing as Heat" (*There Is* 11). On the one hand, "joining / the chorus of a reggae tune almost illegal / here" (11) reminds one of the existences, to borrow Benedict Anderson's term (2006), of an "imagined community" abroad that has its roots in the fellowship cemented back home—in the space they call their own:

> For like the realisation that confronts Jamaicans as they simmer in traf-fic, wet with the heat of the sun – banker next to barrister, clerk behind courier – there's an overarching framework that unites them despite the class divisions and social fissures that threaten to split the Rock into a loose association of fiefdoms ruled by corrupt politicians, ruffneck drug lords and cliché spouting lecturers at university. The framework is reggae, a form as strong and supple as bamboo. (Channer 14)

The choice of this particular Jamaican track, whose influence has since its release reached beyond the shores of the Caribbean archipelago, points to "the historic significance of music and sound" (Antoine-Dunne 82) to the African population residing in the West Indies and in the Americas in general, as analysed by Kamau Brathwaite (Brathwaite 1995; Antoine-Dunne 82), and to the importance of the oral tradition as a means of dis-semination of culture within the Caribbean (82). Construed perhaps as a form of aural environment or—to once again evoke the poet—a carry-on "landscape of sound" (Miller 2009), the song does not just provide the persona with a very *sound* grounding, but facilitates his sure-footed walk through alien topography and climate.

Resonating with reggae, the alien space of a foreign country is transformed into an acoustic intertextual space, filled with the politics of carnivalesque appropriation that are nuanced, ambiguous and multilayered. Introduced in "Always Under Your Breath", the song choice may be construed as the harbinger of the issue of Jamaican heteromatrix (Kitliński and Leszkowicz 2005), not abstracted, but, as expanded upon in "A Short History of Beds We Have Slept in Together", a poem that tellingly culminates in Scotland. Obviously, humming in exile the very same lyrics of "a reggae tune almost illegal here" (*There Is* 11) that hem him/her in at home constitutes an instance of appropriation of hate speech, of reclaiming demonising signifiers and defusing them in a land that is more hospitable to his sexual identity but whose climate still remains inclement. Miller's persona aptly expresses his own critical orientation towards the foulness of the climate affecting him on the British Isles. This is indeed an instance of cultural transference, a third space of meaning, a liminal zone and a state of in-betweenness where Miller's persona signs a tactical alliance with an enemy who happens to be a fellow Jamaican. Additionally, the reference to "Boom Bye-Bye" summons the Gordian knot of being aesthetically enamoured of a performer while concurrently aghast at his/her ideology and agog at one's continued admiration for the craft of the artist in question.

Altogether, the six poems constituting "A Short History of Beds We Have Slept in Together" are set in the parts of the world that reflect Miller's personal itineraries of 2002–2009, chronicling his life in Jamaica,[8] an excursion to Trinidad, and eventual relocation to Glasgow. Also, if one assumes that Jamaica in "A Short History of Beds We Have Slept in Together" is rendered a generator of absences, a covert commentary on the offshoring of affective alterities to sites outside of the Caribbean: the consecutive poems trace leaving one's home island, making temporary home in a foreign land ("Apsley Street, Glasgow, 2008") and buying a flat there ("A Prayer at Squire Street, 2009").

The final pair is particularly of interest here as it falls within the very topical remit of the present paper. Both are set in Glasgow, which unsurprisingly is conspicuous by its absence; after all, the poems treat of the intimate interior of one's or—to be more precise—the couple's home sweet home. Extraterritorial, this is a place to rent and share together, if not yet to call their own, even if their own sensations of the place (their mediation of the space inside) seem to differ, as in "Apsley Street, Glasgow, 2008".[9] Meta-textual, addressing the speaker's partner and reflecting upon his difference of opinion, the poem negotiates the lived intimacy and its individual representation:

> I know you will say, isn't it magic enough
> that we fall asleep in the tangle of fingers,
> that we sometimes dream a single dream. (*A Light* 58)

Correspondingly, the notion of mysticism also permeates "A Prayer at Squire Street, 2009", a house-warming poem that transforms a recently purchased space into a space experienced and internalised as their own:

> Bless the stairs that our door opens to,
> may we always ascend into our home
> in peace. (*A Light* 59)

Conceived as a means of enchanting reality and providing protection against the onset of daily decrepitude of love life, this fitting benediction—"[t]his used to be a church" (59)—introduces the motif of building one's nest in Glasgow. Although the construction metaphor does not play any role in Miller's poem, the subject resurfaces in "In Defence of Maas Joe", an autobiographical essay, in which the writer states that he "live[s] in a converted church; the design there is slick, the floors wooden, the art collection forever growing, and the stock of wine forever being emptied and then replenished" (*Writing* 24). Doubly consecrated—first by the Church and then by the poet, the space of the former house of worship is testimony to the change of the Scottish religious landscape, hinting at a transformation that Miller's diasporic persona undergoes in the space of "A Short History of Beds We Have Slept in Together".

Still, otherworldly idealisation of Scotland does not transpire in Miller's writing. Truth be told, in stark contrast with Jamaica/Jamrock—that cultural cornerstone of the author's literary framework—a country in which a homosexual is not only symbolically stigmatised but potentially stoned as well, Scotland—or the British Isles for that matter—is not as insular, offering more freedom of movement, more room to breathe, more *living* space and a third space of meaning. Still, the poem contains a textual disclaimer suggesting that the relationship, which matured outside of Jamaica, may eventually head for the rocks, as the Scottish/ Glaswegian utopian space is undercut by "Epilogue", the sixth verse that closes "A Short History of Beds We Have Slept in Together". Here, the fantasy of a home sweet home narrative culminates in a reality check, which lays bare the possible exhaustion of affection:

> Let us not repeat the easy lies about eternity
> and love. We have fallen out of love
> before – like children surpassing
> the borders of their beds, woken
> by gravity, the suddenness of tiles. (*A Light* 60)

"A Short History" constitutes a chronicle of past love, of loves lost as well as a projected (and de-territorialised) resurrection into love. This is no implosion of space but a reboot, the re-furnishing of the interior.

4

With the exception of a passage in "But in Glasgow, There are Plantains", the great Scottish outdoors[10] does not, however, constitute any particular focus of Miller's writing. Still, in contrast with England, whose landscape in "How we became the pirates", a poem opening the "In This New Country" sequence, is as "restrained" (*There Is* 9) as "hate in this place" (9), Scotland is not a contestable nor inimical space. In fact, just as St Lucian Pitons provide constant solace to Derek Walcott and offer an azimuth for his transnational writing, so does the Scottish landscape constitute a source of comfort for Miller's persona. On condition, however, that it remains filtered through the prism of the Caribbean, through the lens of nostalgic territorial marketing,[11] as it were:

> In Glasgow, you cannot always see the mountains – but they are there, the Highlands rise magnificently to the north of the city. And the fact of mountains reminds me of the Caribbean I've known. The popular Haitian proverb goes, 'behind the mountains are more mountains', which speaks of course to the never ending of trials some people have had to go through for generations – but for me it was always a simple description of the landscape of the Greater Antilles, so that I can remember vividly as a child visiting the United States, and seeing for the first time, an uninterrupted horizon on every side, feeling suddenly uncomfortable, afraid, exposed, knowing then that I'd always need mountains to hem me in. (*Writing* 45)

By comparison, his Glaswegian poems are similarly devoid of Scottish nature, countryside or places outside of the city. There is no interaction with the country save the country of the self, fashioned out of the Caribbean staples discussed earlier on. This somehow repeats the critical assumption echoed throughout Guyanese-British photographer Ingrid Pollard's 1988 *Pastoral Interlude* series: "as if the Black experience is only lived within an urban environment" (*Postcards Home* 21).

In fact, throughout the poems constituting the "In This New Country" cycle human interaction (human geography) is limited, as locales are reduced to confined spaces, shops, flats, kitchens and living rooms which the single individual frequents or occupies. Perhaps, to Miller's persona, as to countless others, "space becomes invested with an existential dimension only when it remains in a living relation to a human being, when it asks the human being questions about the self" (Sławek 4), which is not the case with regard to Scottish nature and the nature of the diasporic existence ventriloquised by the poet. One could also infer that Miller's poetic persona is more "concerned with cultural landscapes, with the pastoral rather than wilderness" (Goodbody and Rigby 2–3), i.e., with the controllable space/controlled environment, which corresponds to the textual avenues of terraforming his life and shaping his living space abroad.

5

Much as the personae inhabiting the poems and prose under discussion endeavour to Caribbeanise Scotland, the present essay attempts to Scotlandise the reception of Miller's work, to put his oeuvre on the map of Caledonian-Caribbean connections and, by doing so, to contribute to the existing body of scholarship on the subject.[12] While one could convincingly repeat after Ramazani that at present "[t]he poetry of the African diaspora in Britain (…) is neither homebound nor homeless, neither rooted nor rootless" (163) and, in general, reflective of what Bauman terms the liquid modernity (2007), the Scotland-themed creative output of Miller is all the more compelling for its brevity and transitoriness. As the writer's later collections and blog posts show, the textual presence of Scotland has been radically diminished since the author's relocation to London.

Regarding the development of the present chapter, the next, perhaps logical, step would be to map the intertextual cartographies offered by a wider selection of West Indian writers. Their interest in Scotland ranges from the historical to the topical, as expressed in "A Visit from Scotland", a recent poem by Jean "Binta" Breeze in which her persona dialogises with a Rasta elder on the subject of independence, nationhood, social consequences of political emancipation and being "caught somewhere / mid-atlantic" (*Verandah*, 33) in the space of temporal and physical liminality:

> Who better to ask
> than someone who spend so much time in Britain
>
> Yuh really tink it right
> For Scotland to ask for freedom? (33)

Another task at hand would be to focus on a literary atlas of spatial representation engendered by the network of Celtic-Caribbean trajectories and nexuses, so as to include the space-images offered by Wales and Ireland as well. As corroborated by existing research,[13] these interconnections are too numerous and too important to be overlooked. In this context, Miller's Glaswegian period and his Caribbean spatialisation of Scotland provide a springboard for further critique and contextualisation of inter-continental cultural practices, offering also a potential for the development of global Creolisation studies in the light of breakthrough research conducted by such insightful critics of the Anthropocene as Anne Elvey, Axel Goodbody, Timothy Morton, Kate Rigby and Kate Soper.

NOTES

1. "Caribbean", not unlike any other geographic term denoting a region, is an ambiguous byword for a group of individual island states vying for unquestioned, singular cultural identity, political independence as well as economic autonomy, without losing a sense of interconnection, shared history, regional coherence and significance as an archipelago in the post-colonial era. It is "a moniker in which lie many of the torturous turns that made its islands as they now exist" (Jelly-Schapiro 7), including the Middle Passage/the triangular trade, commodification of natural resources, mass tourism and their effect on the cultural practices, human geography and the re-spatialisation of the entire region, which historically has been imagined by filmmakers as places "without identity

or personality (...) only as sites of pleasure, savagery or sexual release" (Antoine-Dunne 182).

2. Taken from the abstract of Annika McPherson's unpublished article entitled "Narrative Absorptions of Place, Space and Diaspora in *The Amazing Absorbing Boy and Pigeon*".

3. Miller's essay manifesto "In Defence of Maas Joe" critiques the elitism of the constructed self of "the cosmopolitan writer and reader from the Caribbean" (*Writing* 24), characterised by the "insiste[nce] on locating our intelligence and our savvy in a rejection of ourselves and what we perceive as the embarrassing smallness of our cultures" (24).

4. In a broader sense, this is how in "Imagining Nations" (originally published in 2008), an essay written at the beginning of his residence in Glasgow, Miller reflects on the shared fate befalling West Indians in the diaspora: "I have begun to wonder how it is the Caribbean immigrant in Britain survives the distance. The answer is sometimes a sad one: many of us haven't. The highest incidence of patients suffering from schizophrenia in the United Kingdom has for many years been among West Indian migrants. At other times the answer is a simple one: because we had to. The flight from England to the Caribbean fetches a steep price, and so frequent connection with the countries of our birth is economically impossible for most of us. But beyond the question of affordability, there is a further hesitation: we are, after all, children of exodus. In some way or the other, we escaped something and many feel conflicted about going back to countries whose reputations declined even further after we left" (*Writing* 51).

5. Unsurprisingly, given the historical Scottish-Caribbean relationship which dates at least to the mid-seventeenth century—to the times of Oliver Cromwell and his edict of the deportation of Scots to the New World colonies, Miller is by no means the first West Indian writer interested in Scotland. Although the literary representation of the Celtic Fringe, Scotland including, is neither as vast nor as imprinted on the Caribbean collective consciousness as that of the "mother country" that England was once hailed as, it still offers engaging tropes worth more than a cursory analytical approach. These include "Country Dance", a poem by Edward Baugh—Miller's one-time mentor, and "Recompense", a prose poem by Tanya Shirley, whose work Miller featured in *New Caribbean Poetry* (2007), an influential anthology he edited.

6. The theme of a Scottish ancestor of a contemporary Jamaican girl is explored by Shirley: "[i]n 18-something her great great great somebody step off a boat and dig up her great great great somebody out of the cane field to test the sweetness of local sugar (no sense buying puss in a bag) and she not letting Scotland get away scot-free" (*Merchant* 15).

7. Demonstrably, one should not fall into the trap of receiving autobiographic prose as naïve, unconstructed life writing, as Caroline Jones reminds us in her essay on literary imaginings of Edinburgh, "like map makers, (...) authors have their own agendas behind what they choose to display, to bring to the attention of the reader, and what they wish to be ignored, unnoticed, hidden" (50).

8. The fact that there was no room for the male lovers' bed in Kingston, Jamaica is implied by the contrast with Hull, a city and port in the North-East of England, where "Hull, Student Accommodation, October 2007", the second poem of the sequence (and the first after leaving the Caribbean), takes place, and whose full geographic name is "Kingston Upon Hull". It is here that the couple, no longer lying low but sharing a single bed together—so small "that could not fit / our torsos side by side" (*A Light* 56), continues their love story in six acts, founded for the first time on the bedrock of a mattress and linen and not on the *rockstone* of the fear of stones.

9. Upon onomastic research, the name of the Glaswegian street reveals a potential reference to Apsley George Bent Cherry-Garrard (1886–1959), an English explorer of Antarctica, whose textual presence seems apposite in the context of the Miller's personae itinerant life.

10. Gladly/glibly appropriated by the tourist industry, the phrase "great outdoors" covers a multitude of sins, among others the "violent political and economic subordination of this region and its cultural silencing by the British state" (Sassi 11), which gave rise to the Highland Clearances and the resultant "correlative objective of the appealing emptiness, the eerie absence of human life that characterise such landscape-images" (Sassi 11). This fact may not be addressed directly by Miller, yet the very presence (not to mention interaction and negotiation) of his Jamaican persona(e) in the post-colonial landscape of Scotland echoes historical parallels between countries and the imperial treatment of their respective (cultural) landscapes.

11. Interestingly, comparisons between the geography of the Antilles and Scotland, whose "landscape has been one of the privileged symbols [with regard to nation-building and identity-shaping]" (Sassi 11), were not lost to the actors in the Scottish independence media debate. Referring to the country's potential post-referendum character and its international marketability, Jay Pond-Jones of &&& Design Agency suggested that since tourism constitutes such a major ingredient of the country's gross national product, then—as a sovereign territory "made up of 790 islands" (Delaney)—Scotland "could rebrand [itself] as northern Europe's very own Caribbean" (Delaney). This, given Pond-Jones' assumption that Scotland "with its popularity among the royals, (...) [has] always been

a bit of a playground for the rich and famous" (Delaney), would situate Scotland, not unlike the Caribbean tourist resorts and secluded islets, considerably out of reach of the local residents. Still, analogously to Miller's re-imagining his Scottish flat and/or surroundings as (a simulacrum of) Jamaica, this leap of imagination, is utopian by default. Such *imaginary* Scotland constitutes "an expression of desire" (Carey xi): it is a "utopia [that] always needs to remain unfulfilled in order to serve the human purpose of dreaming and hoping" (Aidnik and Hviid Jacobsen 158).

12. See Covi et al. (2007).
13. See Donnell et al. (2015).

Works Cited

Aidnik, Martin, and Michael Hviid Jacobsen. 'Not Yet: Probing the Potentials and Problems in the Utopian Understandings of Ernst Bloch and Zygmunt Bauman'. *Beyond Bauman: Critical Engagements and Creative Excursions*. Ed. Michael Hviid Jacobsen. London: Routledge, 2017. 136–62.

Alleyne, Mervyn C. *Roots of Jamaican Culture*. London: Pluto Press, 1989.

Anderson, Benedict. *Imagined Communities: Reflecting on the Origin and Spread of Nationalism*. London: Verso, 2006.

Antoine-Dunne, Jean. *Derek Walcott's Love Affair with Film*. Leeds: Peepal Tree Press, 2017.

Baugh, Edward. *Black Sand: New and Selected Poems*. Leeds: Peepal Tree Press, 2013.

Bauman, Zygmunt. *Liquid Times: Living in an Age of Uncertainty*. Cambridge: Polity Press, 2007.

Best, Curwen. *Culture @ the Cutting Edge: Tracking Caribbean Popular Music*. Kingston: University of the West Indies Press, 2004.

Beushausen, Wiebke, Anne Brüske, Ana-Sofia Commichau, Patrick Helber, and Sinah Kloß. 'The Caribbean (on the) Dining Table: Contextualizing Culinary Cultures'. *Caribbean Food Cultures: Culinary Practices and Consumption in the Caribbean and Its Diasporas*. Ed. Wiebke Beushausen, Anne Brüske, Ana-Sofia Commichau, Patrick Helber, and Sinah Kloß. Bielefeld: Transcript Verlag, 2014. 11–24.

Birbalsingh, Frank, ed. *Frontiers of Caribbean Literature in English*. London: Macmillan Caribbean, 1996.

Brathwaite, Edward Kamau. *History of the Voice: The Development of Nation Language in Anglophone Caribbean Poetry*. London: New Beacon Books, 1995.

Breeze, Jean 'Binta'. *The Verandah Poems*. Hexham: Bloodaxe Books, 2016.

Brown, Stewart, and Ian McDonald. 'Introduction: The Poems Man'. *Poems by Martin Carter*. Ed. Stewart Brown, and Ian McDonald. London: Macmillan Caribbean, 2006. xiii–xxv.

Carey, John. 'Introduction'. *The Faber Book of Utopias*. Ed. John Carey. London: Faber and Faber, 1999. xi–xxvi.

Channer, Colin. 'Preface'. *Wheel and Come Again: An Anthology of Reggae Poetry*. Ed. Kwame Dawes. Leeds: Peepal Tree Press, 1998. 13–15.

Covi, Giovanna, Joan Anim-Addo, Velma Pollard, and Carla Sassi. *Caribbean-Scottish Relations: Colonial and Contemporary Inscriptions in History, Language and Literature*. London: Mango Publishing, 2007.

Delaney, Sam. 'Could Scotland Be Northern Europe's Caribbean?' *The Guardian*. 20 May 2011. http://www.theguardian.com/uk/2011/may/20/northern-europe-caribbean-scotland-rebrand. Accessed 15 September 2015.

Donnell, Alison, Maria McGarrity, and Evelyn O'Callaghan, eds. *Caribbean Irish Connections: Interdisciplinary Perspectives*. Kingston: University of the West Indies Press, 2015.

Glave, Thomas, ed. *Our Caribbean: A Gathering of Lesbian and Gay Writing from the Antilles*. Durham: Duke University Press, 2008.

Goodbody, Axel, and Kate Rigby, eds. *Ecocritical Theory: New European Approaches*. Charlottesville: University of Virginia Press, 2011.

Hutchinson, Ishion. *Far District*. Leeds: Peepal Tree Press, 2010.

Jelly-Schapiro, Joshua. *Island People: The Caribbean and the World*. Edinburgh: Canongate, 2017.

Jones, Caroline. 'Mapping Edinburgh'. *Boundless Scotland: Space in Contemporary Scottish Fiction*. Ed. Monika Szuba. Gdańsk: Gdańsk University Press, 2015. 45–58.

Kitliński, Tomasz, and Paweł Leszkowicz. *Miłość i demokracja. Rozważania o kwestii homoseksualnej w Polsce*. Kraków: Wydawnictwo Aureus, 2005.

Lamming, George. 'The Occasion for Speaking'. *The Routledge Reader in Caribbean Literature*. Ed. Alison Donnell and Sarah Lawson Welsh. London: Routledge, 1996. 253–60.

Markham E. A., ed. *Hinterland: Caribbean Poetry from the West Indies and Britain*. Newcastle: Bloodaxe Books, 2001.

Miller, Kei. *There Is an Anger That Moves*. Manchester: Carcanet, 2007a.

———. 'Interview'. *Iota*. No. 83 and 84 Spring, 2009. 67–70. www.poetrymagazines.org.uk/magazine/record9cf9.html?id=24192. Accessed 19 September 2015.

———. *A Light Song of Light*. Manchester: Carcanet, 2010.

———. *Writing Down the Vision: Essays and Prophecies*. Leeds: Peepal Tree Press, 2013.

————. 'Kei Miller: Next Generation Poets—Interview'. *Poetry Book Society*, 2014. https://www.youtube.com/watch?v=UGrs8QoHI-Y. Accessed 28 September 2015.

Miller, Kei, ed. *New Caribbean Poetry*. Manchester: Carcanet, 2007b.

Nanton, Philip. *Frontiers of the Caribbean*. Manchester: Manchester University Press, 2017.

Paul, Annie. 'LOG ON: Toward Social and Digital Islands'. *The Routledge Companion to Anglophone Caribbean Literature*. Ed. Michael A. Bucknor and Alison Donnell. London: Routledge, 2014. 626–35.

Pollard, Ingrid. *Postcards Home*. London: Autograph, 2004.

Ramazani, Jahan. *A Transnational Poetics*. Chicago: University of Chicago Press, 2009.

Robinson, Roger. *The Butterfly Hotel*. Leeds: Peepal Tree Press, 2013.

Sassi, Carla. 'Foreword'. *Boundless Scotland: Space in Contemporary Scottish Fiction*. Ed. Monika Szuba. Gdańsk: Gdańsk University Press, 2015. 11–12.

Shirley, Tanya. *The Merchant of Feathers*. Leeds: Peepal Tree Press, 2014.

Sławek, Tadeusz. 'Być z przestrzenią'. *Autoportret* 41: 4–9, 2013.

Walcott, Derek. *Selected Poems*. Ed. Edward Baugh. New York: Farrar, Straus and Giroux, 2007.

A World of Islands: Archipelagic Poetics in Modern Scottish Literature

Alexandra Campbell

Throughout its etymological history the word 'island' has commonly signified isolation and has frequently become attached to narratives of sovereignty and individualism. Synonymous with the romantically remote, literary island space is classically far flung from the reaches of continental civilisation. Within such narratives, islands are 'deemed remote, exotic, and isolated by their continental visitors' and are subsequently relegated to the realm of myth and colonial fantasy (DeLoughrey 2007, 2). The recent emergence of Island Studies and the associated rise of the Blue Humanities has sought in part to counteract this belittling and insular view of island cultures by challenging 'topologies of "island thinking" that reproduce the binary opposition of "island-mainland"' by offering alternative readings of island spaces as interactive sites of cultural and ecological interconnectivity (Allen et al. 2017, 13). Instead of focusing on discourses of 'singularity, isolation, dependency and peripherality', these 'archipelagic' models consider how island space 'might be experienced in terms of networks, assemblages,

A. Campbell (✉)
The University of Edinburgh, Edinburgh, UK

© The Author(s) 2019
M. Szuba and J. Wolfreys (eds.), *The Poetics of Space and Place in Scottish Literature*, Geocriticism and Spatial Literary Studies, https://doi.org/10.1007/978-3-030-12645-2_10

filaments, connective tissue, mobilities and multiplicities' (Stratford et al. 2011, 114). Within such scholarship, the archipelago becomes a critical tool through which to consider the 'limits of nationalism' and the 'influence of world systems of small cultural and geographical territories' (Allen et al. 2017, 8). This chapter proposes that the archipelago serves as an important model for considering the decentralising movements of contemporary Scottish literature. Examining a range of modern and contemporary writing from the Scottish Islands (the Hebrides and Shetland in particular), the chapter considers how the early writings of Hugh MacDiarmid serve as an originary moment in the establishment of an archipelagic mode of writing that has come to the surface of contemporary poetic works by Angus Peter Campbell and Jen Hadfield. Across their collections, these poets offer a perspective of island cultures which actively explores the tension between insular national contexts and increasingly ecologically minded 'planetary' perspectives.

Arriving at the Archipelago: Hugh MacDiarmid's *The Islands of Scotland*

In 1975, the historian J. G. A. Pocock called for a new methodology for constructing British history that consciously responds to the 'problem of nationality' (607). For Pockock, this 'problem' concerns the 'writing of history so Anglocentric that "British history" itself has in the past denoted nothing much more than "English history" with occasional transitory additions' (Pocock 2005, 77). Pocock's subsequent coining of the term 'Atlantic archipelago' hoped to aid scholars to 'construct a new ordering of historical consciousness' that avoided the biases of terms such as 'British Isles' or 'United Kingdom' by bringing attention to the 'plural history of a group of cultures situated along an Anglo-Celtic frontier' (1975, 606). Since Pocock's initial plea, the term 'Atlantic archipelago' has been seized by a range of literary scholars and historians who have adopted the term in the hopes of 'stripping away modern Anglocentric and Victorian imperial paradigms to recover the long, braided histories played out across the British-Irish archipelago between three kingdoms, four countries, divided regions, various ethnicities, and religiously determined allegiances' (Kerrigan 2008, 2). Writing in a post-devolution landscape, John Kerrigan's study *Archipelagic English* (2008) works to present an alternative history of these islands in a way that is attentive to conflicting narratives of national identity and long histories of cultural interconnection through more neutral, plural, and relational terms that have previously been available. While both Pocock's and Kerrigan's work attends to early-modern Anglophone literatures and histories, their critical attention to the fluidity and mobility of the archipelago has inspired a recent swell of writing that considers the significance of 'fugitive alliances [...] between and among islands' in modern literature (Allen et al. 2017, 3).

In relation to modern Scottish literature, the spatial imaginary of the nation has been central to scholars examining questions of belonging, community, and attachment. For archipelagic scholars, it is the connective seas between, rather than the distinct terrestrial islands, that serves as an important means of addressing these questions of relation. While the constitutive island spaces of the Atlantic archipelago are linked through the flows of history, capital, and culture, they are also connected through deep geological movements, thriving biotic communities, and oceanic currents. John Brannigan's recent exploration of island relations in *Archipealgic Modernism* (2015) urges us to conceive of the seas and oceans as a 'space of connection and communication' rather than as boundaries and borders between distinct national spaces (p. 11). Importantly, the adoption of such archipelagic modes of reading does not do away with the category of 'nation', but enables the consideration of an interactive range of scale-framings, from the national to the transnational, the local to the global, the planetary and the regional. For the modern and contemporary Scottish poets examined here, the islands and their surrounding seas are re-imagined as sites of ongoing cosmopolitan connection and communication. Their exploration of the social and ecological connections that proliferate across the land and seascapes of the archipelago test the limits of purely nationalist spatial framings and actively prompt the adoption of new 'vocabularies of habitation, new geographies of connection and living between the islands' (Brannigan 2015, 183).

This chapter traces the emergence of a distinct archipelagic poetics back to the modernist works of Hugh MacDiarmid and considers how the archipelago has served Scottish authors as a dynamic means of reassessing Scotland's place within the wider world. MacDiarmid's collection *Stony Limits* (1934) and his travelogue *The Islands of Scotland* (1939) serve as an important moment in the development of contemporary archipelagic perspectives. MacDiarmid's experimental interrogation of the relationships between local landscapes and languages provides a critical framework through which to consider more recent Scottish poetry collections such as Angus Peter Campbell's *Aibisidh* (2011) and Jen Hadfield's T. S Eliot award-winning *Nigh-No-Place* (2008) and the more recent *Byssus* (2014). Importantly, these poets acknowledge the local intimacies of their island environments, but do so with a conscious projection of these localities into cosmopolitan frameworks which criss-cross a whole world of islands. Their poetic 'inquiries open the local out into a network of environmental links that span a region, a continent, or the world' (Heise 2008, 56) and gesture towards the emergence of an environmentally tuned 'planetary consciousness' that actively draws from the topographies and ecologies of Scottish islandscapes (Gairn 2008, 81).

The Islands of Scotland occupy a provocative and important space within MacDiarmid's poetry and critical thought, and have been a recurring physical site of habitation throughout his lifetime. Across his works of the 1930s, MacDiarmid's poetic and political eye is simultaneously drawn to the internal forces of secessionist movements while also addressing Scotland's position within a wider geopolitical frame. The ambiguous and paradoxical position of the islands as isolated and yet interconnected spaces provides MacDiarmid with the opportunity to envision new forms of cultural identity and relation. As Edna Longley suggests, within Scottish and Irish literatures islands 'more often symbolise national separatism than archipelagic commonalities' as both 'islands and poems are, of course, locally distinctive' (2010, 146). For Longley, the local distinctiveness of islands and island poems is most easily located in MacDiarmid's 1930s travelogue *The Islands of Scotland* in which he describes an island as 'an almost startlingly entire thing, in these days of the subdivision, of the atomisation of life' (1939, 26). Seen in such a light, it is tempting to understand MacDiarmid's island poems as reservoirs of 'linguistic, cultural and racial purity' which in turn fuel discourses of an isolating and insular nationalism (Brannigan 2015, 39). Yet this solitary and insular perspective is not the driving political message behind *The Islands of Scotland*, rather MacDiarmid asks us to speculate on 'the very different course not only Scottish, and English, but World history would have taken if the whole of the mainland of Scotland had been severed from England and broken up into the component islands of a numerous archipelago' (1939, 8). Indeed, MacDiarmid further acknowledges the striking differences between Scotland's island spaces where 'Islands as like each other as two peas [...] can nevertheless give rise to the most unaccountable variations' (1939, 95) and urges his readers to make 'due allowance for the number, let alone the individual and group differences, of [Scotland's] islands' (1939, 8). By remaining attentive to the internal distinctiveness of the islands, MacDiarmid avoids the production of homogenising narratives of place. Across his early collections, the variety of the islands' geographic, linguistic, and cultural dimensions serve as a means of resisting 'British centralisation' and present the means through which to 'politically challenge a metropolitanism that subsumes difference and patronises or ignores what it terms the provinces' (Lyall 2006, 135–36). Through his poetic explorations of the 'connection between solitude and universality' (MacDiarmid 1939, 6), MacDiarmid's writing of the 1930s works to identify a new national identity that makes a 'virtue of the marginal' and embraces the interactive nature of the archipelago (Lyall 2006, 136).

Stepping ashore on the island of Whalsay in 1933, MacDiarmid was seen by many to be 'sailing against the tide of urbanised modernity' (Lyall 2006, 116). However, his movement from the city to the sea proved to be the most formative in terms of his poetic voice and is often cited as a major influence in the development of his experimental synthetic scots and vehement fascination with Gaelic language and culture. Yet I suggest that the literature produced during this period is far more than a mere resistance to the modernist, metropolitan, and mainstream. Working in line with a tradition of earlier travel writing,[1] *The Islands of Scotland* presents its readers with a collage of interlaced cartographic, geographic, and poetic explorations of place in which Scotland, and it's seemingly 'fringe' spaces, is positioned at the forefront of not only artistic representation, but of geopolitical relations and international networks. In focusing on the history, anthropology, and material geology of the islands, MacDiarmid's traversal of Scotland's islandscapes creates a drastic re-imagining of these previously isolated and romanticised spaces. Indeed, John Brannigan argues that 'in contrast to nationalist appropriations of islands as cultural and racial repositories of pre-modern "purity", and imperialist figure of islands as symbolic origins, the literature of islands in the 1930s [...] is inherently connective, relational and material' (2015, 146). Thus, while MacDiarmid's engagements with island spaces perhaps originate in states of solitude in the hopes of providing a 'natural base for our national life' (1939, 27), they do so with a conscious projection of 'small' island cultures into the wider realms of global systems of communication and culture. Through patterns of transmission and travel, the island becomes a porous and interconnected space and for MacDiarmid fuels an emergent archipelagic poetics that emphasises interconnection and interaction. This sentiment is most fully presented in his poem 'In the Shetland Islands' when he states: 'I am no further from the "centre of things" /In the Shetlands here than in London, New York, or Tokio' (1939, xv). Shifting the critical and creative axis away from 'megapolitan madness' of other modernist writing of the period, MacDiarmid's residence in Whalsay allows for a new a connective 'world-consciousness' to emerge from the deep rich waters of the Shetland isles and expands to include 'the Orkney and the Western Isles, and then [...] Scotland as a whole, and beyond that to all the world, through all time' (1939, xv).

Questions of community and isolation reverberate throughout MacDiarmid's poetry of the 1930s. His 'Shetland Lyrics' sequence taken from his earlier collection *Stony Limits* (1934) best displays this bleak and materially attentive aesthetic. While critics have noted that this sequence tends towards 'solitary revelation in the North Sea from which Shetlanders earn a living' (Lyall 2006, 139), I suggest that the lyrics are not merely concerned with conditions of isolation and exile, but are fascinated by the new forms of ecological community and connection that the Shetland environment provides. In 'With the Herring Fishers', MacDiarmid is struck by the close community ties that wind their way across both land and sea. Commenting on the jovial sing-song voices of the fishermen, MacDiarmid declares 'it ane o' the bonniest sichts in the warld/To watch the herrin' come walkin' on board/In the wee sma' 'oors o' a simmer's mornin' (1993, 437). Notably, across the 'Shetland Lyrics' sequence, MacDiarmid's poetic speaker is located at the margins of this tight-knit community. His lyrical explorations of place occur at an objectifying distance which effectively likens the Shetlanders to their own catch. In 'Deep Sea Fishing', the 'gapin' mooths and gogglin' een/O' the fish' (1993, 437) are mapped onto the 'animal forms/And primitive minds' of the fishermen who draw them from the sea (1993, 438). The apparent unity of the fishermen with the land and seascapes of Shetland leads MacDiarmid to declare that their 'coarser lives' more 'naturally' possesses the 'Omnipotence o' God than a fribble like me' (1993, 438).

This romanticisation of the 'so-called primitive life' (MacDiarmid 1939, xi) is of course problematic; however, it does reveal MacDiarmid's underlying interest in 'a way of living which seems harmonious with the natural world' (Brannigan 2015, 162). Across the sequence, MacDiarmid's solipsistic lyrics attempt, with varying levels of success, to access the different strands of relation that thread together both human and non-human communities. It is not only the fish and the fishermen that catch MacDiarmid's poetic attentions in this sequence, but a range of seabirds that gently float above the islandscape. In 'Gruney' (the name of an uninhabited island), the poetic figure declares 'I'll be like these white birds/Sittin' facin' the ocean' (1993, 439) and in subsequent poems finds unity with the flight of the Great Scua, Shags, Bonxies, and Sea Eagles. Adopting a literal bird's-eye perspective, the poetic voice takes flight and declares 'Guid-bye to mankind' (1993, 440) preferring instead the company of 'angels, archangels, devils and gods' (1993, 440). For Nancy Gish, this conscious separation of the poetic voice from the people and land below reflects the 'artist's struggle and MacDiarmid's personal sense of separateness and artistic destiny' (1984, 152). The sequence as a whole is concerned with contrasting visions of community and isolation, in which the poet's dramatic flights of fancy effectively detach him from the coarse realities of the 'primitive' island community.

Despite this tension, the sequence frequently displays the fundamental relationship between poet and place. While he feels little connection between himself and the Shetlanders, MacDiarmid finds a deep sense of relation with the geological histories of the Shetland landscape. In 'On a Raised Beach', MacDiarmid explores the ways in which geological time, rather than social time, provides the means through which to comprehend man's place in the world. Positioned as but one element of a wider ecological system that includes stones and birds, the human figure understands the brevity of human existence in relation to the deep histories of geological time: 'Already I feel all that can perish perishing in me/As so much has perished and all will yet perish in these stones' (MacDiarmid 1993, 424). As Scott Lyall has suggested, 'On a Raised Beach' most likely derives is inspiration from a 'three-day stay alone on the uninhabited West Linga, with its raised beach at Croo Wick, an island west of Whalsay', and further draws 'sustenance from the 1933 geological survey of Shetland' which MacDiarmid notes he participated in as an avid novice (2006, 121). Through his sustained geological attentions, MacDiarmid highlights the infinitely varied physicality of Shetland's environment with its 'incomparable scenery' and 'vivifying [...] geological elements' (1939, 2). The deep geological histories of the landscape become a way through which the poet is able to form a sense of connection with the world around him. As Lyall suggests, 'On a Raised Beach' emphasises MacDiarmid's engagement with a developing form of 'eco-Marxism' in which the physical earth provides a common ground for the formation of community (2006, 122). For MacDiarmid, the Islands of Scotland are thus not only 'linked together by comings-and-goings' of various migrants and travellers, but are deeply linked through a subterranean geological history that runs the length of the Atlantic coasts, joining 'Cornwall, the Hebrides, and the Orkneys and the Shetlands' (1939, 2).

While MacDiarmid's nationalist project inevitably shapes the majority of his island configurations, the scope of his poetry is continuously cosmopolitan, drawing the meshwork of Scottish island spaces outward across the globe through a 'renewal of Scandinavian connections' and continual references to other archipelagos in Greece, Greenland, Ireland, Iceland, and Tahiti (1939, 43). MacDiarmid closes *The Islands of Scotland* on a message of cosmopolitan interconnection in which island spaces are seen as infinitely connective:

> There are invisible bridges from every one of the Scottish islands, I think, that cross as far as the mind of man can go and reach across whatever space lies between us and anything that has ever been or ever will be apprehensible by the minds of men. (1939, 136)

MacDiarmid's examination of these island–island relations is indicative of an early archipelagic consciousness within modern Scottish poetry. Connected through shared 'oceanic vistas, wind and rain, cliffs, rocks and hard places, bogs and moors, seabirds and seals', MacDiarmid's early works reveal the island regions of Scotland to be incredibly mobile not only in terms of their migratory human populations, but their ecological characteristics and creative potential (Longley 2010, 146).

ISLAND CONSTELLATIONS: 'PLANETARY CONSCIOUSNESS' IN CONTEMPORARY SCOTTISH LITERATURE

A similar fascination with the relationship between land and sea, community and isolation occurs in the contemporary works of the Scottish Gaelic author and poet, Angus Peter Campbell. Perhaps best known for his award-winning Gaelic text *An Oidhche Mus Do Sheòl Sinn* (2004), Campbell's works operate within the same fluid 'world-consciousness' of MacDiarmid's archipelagic landscape. Campbell's poems exhibit a similar fascination with the varied scales of time and place that looking to the archipelago unveils. As Peter Mackay noted in an introduction to Campbell's poems in 2012, his work 'bridges the age of the plough and the age of the space-shuttle, with an awareness that – in his own words – that bridge can be rickety, frayed, and ad-hoc' (npag). Constantly skipping from Scotland to places in the wider world, Campbell's poetic works are not unlike the skimming stones which are a central trope in *An Oidhche Mus Do Sheòl Sinn*. His collections originate in the waters around his birthplace of South Uist before being cast out through the entire Hebridean chain and beyond into seas of distant archipelagos such as Japan and New Zealand.

Roving from the granular to the intergalactic, Campbell's collection *Aibisidh* (2011) engages an itinerant and transient perspective of place in which the poetic figure is positioned 'on board/between two ports' (2011, 3), crossing bridges and 'hopping from branch /to branch' (2011, 7). The collection as a whole explores how the inherent ambiguity of place and the 'dissolution of certainties challenges us to discover new connections – between individuals, communities and cultures' (2011, Book Cover). These poems are '"born between the Cuillin and the Minch."/In the cradle of the sea' but reach out 'from Berwick/and Baden Baden/and Buenos Aires yonder' into the 'dust and stars' (2011, 17, 25, 41, 83). Through his close attention to the shifting dimensions of the Hebridean landscape, Campbell's poetry aligns the uncertainty of place with the wider geopolitical disruptions across the globe, moving from the intimate examination of 'Pebbles/on the shore. Sea-worn smooth' (2011, 17) to other geological fragments formed through the dismantling of the Berlin Wall, the Vietnam War, and the fall of the Twin Towers. While Campbell's poems originate in the cool salty waters of the Hebrides, they consciously extend outwards in the creation of a poetics of relation which flows from the personal to the universal. Campbell's poems allow us to see how the archipelago as a conceptual framework is as much attuned to planetary currents as it is to local 'turbulences, whirlpools, clumps of bubbles, frayed seaweed, sunken galleons, crashing breakers, flying fish, seagull squawks, downpours, night-time phosphorescences, eddies and pools' (Benitez-Rojo 1996, 2). Akin to MacDiarmid's continuous invocation of various island chains, Campbell's island movements drive towards cross-current connections with cityscapes in London, Berlin, and Rome.

Travel and movement are thus a core feature of this collection. Throughout these poems, Campbell's poetic vantage point aligns with various forms of transportation including boats, ferries, planes, and aerial balloons. The poem 'Fragments 1' addresses the seeming isolation of a 'tiny island' formed from 'fragments of peat and sand' that is opened outward through the installation of 'a pier and an airport' (Campbell 2011, 9). The opening of the poem focuses on questions of scale declaring: 'It was not a world/ we inherited but an island, /even though the island was a world' (Campbell 2011, 9). Despite the seemingly diminutive scale of the islands, the poem reveals how these tiny spaces are interlinked with one another, not only through the different transport networks that wind their ways across the skies and oceans, but through the movement of story: 'and many stories returned, about how big the trees were,/ and how high the mountains, and how wide/ the rivers' (2011, 9). The poem in many ways aligns with schools of thought that are integral to contemporary Island Studies perspectives, particularly the work of Epeli Hau'ofa. Hau'ofa's seminal essay 'A Sea of Islands' identifies similar spatial politics at work in Western perspectives of the Pacific:

> There is a gulf of difference between viewing the Pacific as 'islands in a far sea' and as 'a sea of islands'. The first emphasises dry surfaces in a vast ocean far from the centres of power. When you focus this way you stress the smallness and remoteness of the islands. The second is a more holistic perspective in which things are seen in the totality of their relationships. (1993, 7)

The fragmented construction of Campbell's poem echoes this 'holistic perspective' of island cultures. Snippets of sentences float freely on the page, but importantly work in concert with the surrounding text to form an archipelagic mode of writing. This sense of holistic connection is emphasised through the poem's attention to different travel networks across air and sea, which enable the singular island to forge narratives with spaces beyond the boundaries of the 'tiny island' opening this landscape outwards to new 'big', 'high', and 'wide' topographies beyond the Hebrides (Campbell 2011, 9).

Interestingly, MacDiarmid's early poems exhibit a similar fascination with the aesthetic and cultural potential of flight. Throughout *The Islands of Scotland*, MacDiarmid frequently adopts an aerial vantage point as a means of highlighting the vastly interconnected nature of Scotland's islands. Indeed, it is only from certain geological vantage points that MacDiarmid is able to discern the full scale of the archipelago, noting how 'The Ward Hill of Hoy is the highest in Orkney, 1565 feet, and from its summit the whole archipelago can be seen' (1939, 77). Standing atop another peak in Shetland MacDiarmid exclaims: 'A most extensive view is obtained; the whole west coast of Shetland stretches out before us, like a continent of no mean dimensions; and several of the islands of Orkney can be distinctly discerned' (1939, 9). This recognition of the archipelagic interconnections presents within Scottish culture is in many ways tied to the modern advancement of not only the geological sciences, but modern machinery. As MacDiarmid states:

> It is only now, with the use of an aeroplane, that the Scottish islands (I am thinking particularly of the Hebrides) can be seen effectively at one and the same time in their individual completeness and in all their connections with each other and with the mainland. (1939, 8)

Aerial vantage points offer these poets the means through which to physically and politically reorientate their critical and creative attentions. Across both Campbell and MacDiarmid's works, the ability to view this world of islands from above, below, and within allows for the emergence of an archipelagic sense of connection that emphasises an understanding of the archipelago as an active, orbital, constellation of 'fluid cultural processes, sites of abstract and material relations of movement and rest, dependent upon changing conditions of articulation or connection' (Pugh 2013, 11).

For both Campbell and MacDiarmid, these changing conditions of articulation and connection are not only influenced by the local language of the islands, but are directly altered through shifting scales of time and distance. While the Gaelic language is vitally important to both poets artistic and political projects,[2] the question of spatial framing is equally significant. Campbell has recently remarked upon the importance of '[o]rientation' in his work, noting how his childhood spent on the Hebridean island of South Uist 'gave [him] a very early awareness of what you might call "spatial geography" – a sense that your way of life was framed (like a painting) by your physical environment' (2015, npag). As Timothy Baker has recently suggested, in 'Campbell's works the Hebrides are a place of constant variation' in which the 'variability of the landscape necessities continually shifting relationships between the individuals and the community' (2016, 36). The shifting scales and landscapes of Campbell's collection seek to navigate personal and political narratives of belonging and exile which arise in the wake of the 'fragmentation of language and identity in our modern global age' (2011, Book Cover). The collection's concern with fragmentation and globalisation is offset by a continued fascination with the minutely local dimensions of the text where pebbles, puddles, and grains of sand are frequently juxtaposed with wider planetary dimensions of stars, oceans, and vast skyscpaes. This tension between 'cosmic and regional' (Gairn 2008, 9) perspectives of place is increasingly common within contemporary Scottish writing and reflects a growing understanding of place that is both 'locally grounded but at the same time involved in a network of cultural exchange' (Allen et al. 2017, 12). Thus, while archipelagic writings highlight the cultural interconnectivity of closely linked island–island chains, they also expose how these sites and cultures are tethered to wider currents and networks of relation that circulate around the globe.

An awareness of the shifting relationship between the local environment and global discourses is commented upon by MacDiarmid who in a commentary on his poem 'In Memoriam James Joyce' writes: 'Our consciousness is beginning to be planetary. A new tension has been set up between the individual and the universe. [Arising from] the response provoked in the writer in relation to his own language and his own environment' (1992, 224). In *The Islands of Scotland,* he notes how island perspectives are vital for the formation of a 'World-consciousness', declaring that 'the idea that by going to islands one cuts oneself off from the forces of civilisation is one against which I cannot protest too strongly' (1939, xv). Using archipelagic frameworks as a basis for understanding new modes of relation and connection, both MacDiarmid's and Campbell's works gesture towards a form of 'planetary consciousness' which draws on an intensely 'vivid and intimate sense of the local, a shared heritage of memories, traditions and meanings embedded in the Scottish landscape [and] Scots vocabulary' (Gairn 2008, 83) while simultaneously being aware of the wider forces of globalisation.

The relationship between the local and the global has long been a key point of concern for literary critics attempting to negotiate place-specific literature in an age of globalisation. Ursula Heise suggests that it is particularly within the twenty-first century that the concept of globalisation has become *the* organising discourse through which we consider 'current politics, society, and culture in the humanities and social sciences' (2008, 4). In her work *Sense of Place and Sense of Planet* (2008), Heise suggests that due to the spatial and temporal distortions evinced by globalisation, the 'advocacies of place' drawn from 'individual's existentialist encounters with nature and engagements with intimately known local places' are increasingly inadequate in their ability to address the scale of global environmental change (2008, 55). Thus, while the conjunctive 'and' of her title suggests that both scales of (local) place and (global) planet must be addressed when comprehending the Anthropocene, her argument ultimately implies a sense of 'or' that incurs an abandonment of the local in the face of the global. Further to this, despite her recognition that the move towards the global may incur a 'neglect of political and cultural heterogeneity', Heise's conception of 'eco-cosmopolitanism' tends towards a troubling utopian and homogenising vision (2008, 63). Encompassing plural identities and fluid environments, the archipelago does not limit itself to a 'narrow' or rooted sense of space but rather acknowledges the reciprocal relationship between the regional and the planetary, highlighting 'how human impact affects and changes this connectedness' (Heise 2008, 28). In the final half of this chapter, I therefore want to outline how modern Scottish poets engage with their archipelagic environments in the creation of an environmentally relational 'planetary consciousness' which 'charges every act, every entity, with the largeness of the cosmic and planetary and adds meaning to it' without losing site of the local (Shiva 1993, 60). By turning towards the cosmic and cosmopolitan, I suggest that archipelagic frameworks not only foster new forms of interrelation and connection between island spaces, but actively encourage an ecologically attuned planetary perspective which stems from a deeply attentive relationship to the local.

The emergence of this planetary perspective can again be traced to the early poetic works of MacDiarmid who frequently moves from the regional to the cosmic in his earlier collection *Sangschaw* (1925). Within these poems, the position of the globe is a cause of concern for MacDiarmid. For MacDiarmid, the image of the Earth is at once transcendent and troubling. Either the cause of God's tears in 'The Dying Earth', a neglected child in 'The Bonnie Broukit Bairn', a great trembling rock in 'The Eemis Stane' or a 'bare auld Stane [that]/ Glitters beneath the seas o' Space, /White as a mammoth's bane' in 'Au Claire de la Lune' (1993, 24). Wrapped in MacDiarmid's iconic Scots language, the Earth oscillates between the galactic and the local, at one moment a glittering figure against a pitch-black night and at another a grounded, sooty, and fragile rock. In each poem, the 'orb' of the Earth is personified and made fragile, the figure of God slowly drawing away and leaving the 'bare auld stone' (1993, 24) to the mercy of the human race. Across these poems, the planet becomes a relational object caught within the movements of a wider universe while still drawn to the gravity of local environments through the particularities of language. Louisa Gairn has noted how MacDiarmid's planetary perspectives are often drawn between 'the universal and the particular' where his 'sometimes unsettling global view' is contrasted by resolutely grounded perspectives that are rooted in local landscapes and languages (2008, 82–83).

Similar movements between intimately local environments and planetary dimensions occur in the recent works of the Shetland-based poet, Jen Hadfield. Her award-winning second collection *Nigh-No-Place* is at once a telescopic and magnifying collection which roves between the cosmic and the regional, tracing a journey from the vast Canadian landscape, to her adopted home of Shetland, before delving into the intimate folds of the Isle of Burra. Akin to the spatial attentions of Campbell and MacDiarmid, there is a constant mediation of domestic and galactic scales within her collection where poems such as 'Canis Minor' transforms the constellations overhead into the form of a friend's dog with 'scruffy mohican' and 'haunches like a telescope' (2008, 13). Within the poem, the overhanging 'stars […] rising through peacock dust' are directly grounded in the quotidian canine image who 'scours his butt and licks my elbow' (2008, 13) forging a direct link between the intricacies of home and the wider universe.

The opening poem of the '*Nigh-No-Place*' sequence, 'Witless/Aa' similarly mediates domestic and planetary dimensions where a young child playing on the kitchen floor becomes a 'triangulation point that punctuates infinity' (2008, 30). The infant perceived as 'cosmic collateral, pyramidal, just *apparently* small' (2008, 30, emphasis in original) is shown to be the centripetal force around which the mother figure orbits while she questions her relationship with both child and universe. The scale of the poem zooms in and out moving 'Cell by cell /Saturn to Sedna' (2008, 30) widening the aperture of vision from the homely space of the kitchen to the wider external 'universes' (2008, 30) and subsequently transposing maternal feelings of care from the figure of the child, to the rest of the world. This planetary consciousness is enhanced by the visual construction of the text which, roughly circular in shape, is arranged as if to trace the outline of continental landforms on a globe. Working in the style of concrete poetry, the construction of 'Witless/aa' accentuates the ability of Hadfield's poetic eye/I to mediate several scales of attention at once. Moving inwards and outwards from the domestic to the galactic, the typographic form of 'the fat poem' is a conscious construction that 'hangs like a planet in the outer/inner space of the white page' (Hadfield 2010, n.p.).

This interplay of local and planetary conceptions of 'home' continues with a more distinct ecological edge in the poem 'Burra Moonwalk'. Like 'Witless/aa', the poem 'Burra Moonwalk' relies on textual and typographic play as it navigates the 'split or dual nature of the geographical landscape from which the title of the poem is taken: Burra, in Shetland, is comprised of two islands that have a collective name' (Yeung 2015, 71). In the poem, the verses are aligned in two columns which can be read both vertically and horizontally:

> the fancy moon   the coarse crumb, Sirius
> the chapped lower lip   the Fair Isle bonnet.
> (Hadfield 2008, 32)

As the poem progresses, the tight stanzas begin to fragment, with the distance between the columns broadening as the lines stretch to fill the space of the page. The widening lines mimic the languid leaps and bounds of zero-gravity movement as Hadfield's poetic eye hopscotches across 'the fancy smalls' of the 'asteroidal island' from 'the Fair Isle bonnet' to a quick 'glinder at Foula' (Hadfield 2008, 33). Tracing the specific bioregion of Burra, the topography of the island meshes itself into the typographical landscape of the poem. The poem engenders a progressive and active concept of place through its engagement with different scales and modes of relation. The focus on the domestic spaces of 'the honeyed windows of home' and the 'uncan neighbours' (2008, 33) further emphasises a mode of interconnection that is not inhibited by the island's physical geography, but is instead responsive to the different modes of relation that such spaces generate.

The closing sequence of 'Seven Burra Poems' in many ways chimes with MacDiarmid's earlier 'Shetland Lyrics' through Hadfield's attention to the idiosyncrasies of Shetlandic dialect, island geology, and birdsong. The opening poem of the sequence 'Burra Grace' locates the speaker within a set of environmental relationships which are botanical ('daffodil' 'rosy'), geological ('basalt' 'granite'), and animal ('wimbrel' 'shalder') in nature (Hadfield 2008, 52). The image of the 'coarse crumb, Sirius' from 'Burra Moonwalk', is invoked in a later Burra poem, 'Burra Grace', in which the poetic speaker is seen to 'bide on this bit/of broken biscuit –', where the image of the 'broken biscuit' invokes the split topography of Burra (Hadfield 2008, 52). Importantly, within these Burra poems, the islandscape is not shown to be fully separated. Across both poems, the discrete geographies of East and West Burra are connected by the flight of 'lapwings tumbling', or the 'sobbing wimbrel' whose closing call of 'peew-t,/ peew-t || peew-t,/peew-t' flows across the blank white page, forging a mobile connection between the two seemingly separate page halves (Hadfield 2008, 32, 52–53). Each poem becomes but one fragment of an interlacing whole, much as an island is but one piece of an archipelago.

Hadfield builds on this intimate interweaving of poem, person, and place in her latest collection *Byssus*. Across this collection, language and place continually inform one another through an 'An ambiguous rustling', where the meaning of place can only be understood by 'listening in' (Hadfield 2014, 37). Much as the 'sea returns whatever you give it, more so, realler', across this sequence Hadfield transforms seemingly known and familiar objects: a cat, brisket, mackerel, a pig, puffballs a puffin, an orange, etc. into forms that are familiar yet altered, reflecting the idiosyncrasy of both language and place through unexpected and refreshing juxtapositions (Hadfield 2014, 36). Across *Byssus*, this sense of place as formed through assemblage and interconnection is invoked through the trope of the bursting, sporous, puffball (*Vascellum pratense*). In 'The Puffballs', Hadfield describes the fungus as 'irregular pearls', 'blowing bubbles', a 'white roe;/ the flesh that fries/ to a savoury foam' (Hadfield 2014, 27). The use of oceanic language continues throughout in the poem, aiding the diasporic action of the puffballs whose 'anchor and bowls/ forever brewing buboes' will soon spew forth a mass of spores from its 'blackened blowhole' (Hadfield 2014, 28). Hadfield's lines attempt to trace the movement of the spores, where the diasporic action of the puffball is traced in the form of the poem. Akin to 'Witless/Aa', Hadfield's use of concrete-style typography works to mimic the circular form of the puffball, whose bulbous, contained, spherical form slowly unravels into a 'peripatetic' poetic form (2014, 31). The stream of letters and words that spew forth from the 'blackened blowhole' the 'pocked sphincter' (Hadfield 2014, 31) of Hadfield's poetic puffball prompts the reader to take an active role in the poem's construction, whereby the reader is forced to scan back and forth across the text in order to connect the final lines of the poem that are (Fig. 1) (Hadfield 2014, 28–29).

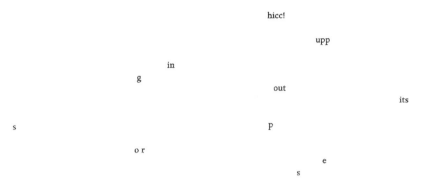

Fig. 1 'The Puffballs' (Hadfield 2014, 28–29)

In 'Puffballs', this diasporic action continues where the fungus is imbued with an inherently cosmopolitan character. Described as 'Mork eggs -/ you Finns, you eyeless / Dia de Meurtos/ skulls', the puffballs, much like the contents of the rock pools in *Nigh-No-Place*, engage different cultural coordinates of place beyond the confines of the Shetland landscape (Hadfield 2014, 31). This sense of cosmopolitanism is extended through the communicative action of the puffballs who 'sing to blurt/ your spore-mass/ from your ragged/ moue!', their cells caught by 'the wind' are 'broadcast' across the ocean 'like smoke/ like spice' (Hadfield 2014, 31). Able to move across both land and sea, Hadfield combines oceanic and terrestrial terms in her contemplation of the puffballs; possessing both a sphincter and a blowhole, the land-bound fungi is also a sea-going cetacean (Hadfield 2014, 31). Noting how its growth is akin to '*Löragub*' (the Shetlandic term for 'sea-haze, expanding foam') on the verge of going 'nova', the poem is fuelled by the dynamics of dispersal in which the bursting image of the puff-ball mediates the poetic movement between intimate local environs and wider planetary scales of connection (Hadfield 2014, 31).

In tracing the material connections that form across island spaces through lines of bird flight, puffball spores, or weird weather, Hadfield's work aligns with an active and progressive sense of place as outlined by Doreen Massey, in which place is viewed as an active process, 'constructed out of a particular constellation of social relations, meeting and weaving together at a particular locus' (Massey 1991, 28). These island–island poems connect with one another without losing their own specific shape and colour so that while it is true that 'everywhere rubs up against the islands' (Hadfield 2014, 8), they still retain a sense of precise locality. Whether she is perched at the shifting edges of the shoreline, continually punched off-balance, or precariously lying at a cliff edge, Hadfield's poetic I/eye encourages us to alter our perspective when engaging island places. Her lyrical works are 'built for flexibility in a coarse/ sea' and present the archipelago as a continually shifting and responsive site in which the 'ruddy/conglomerate' of global discourses are fragmented and filtered into local scales of place attachment (Hadfield 2014, 46, 8). Roaming between stars and sand her poems are 'written out within a planetary context and yet this context is not ignorant of moments of solitude in private places – the domestic space, familial relations, and idiosyncratic and regional inflections' (Bristow 2015, 8). Across her works puffball spores float in on the breeze, sea life becomes a 'violet nebula stranded and spun/ by the current', and beaches are linked by the arrival of ocean plastics (Hadfield 2014, 21). Importantly, it is not that Hadfield's planetary scales of attention seek to speak for *all* planetary subjects (both human and non-human), rather her positioning of the dynamic between island and ocean alerts us to the fact that archipelagic space is by its very nature inherently linked to wider discourses and global dimensions of environmental crisis.

Coda: Coastal Connections

At its core archipelagic criticism and forms of writing help us to open previously closed island imaginings which have for so long focused on insular spatial conceptions derived from the borders and boundaries between land and sea, or island and mainland. Instead, the archipelago emphasises 'connections between "island and island"' and prompts us to seriously consider how this new spatial assemblage might unsettle 'static tropes of singularity, isolation, dependency and peripherality that presently dominate how islands are conceptualized in [...] literature' (Pugh 2013, 11). As demonstrated, for these poets thinking with the archipelago enables the consideration of alternative narratives of belonging and modes of relation that directly question 'entrenchments of national identity, reminding us that such moments exist within fluid constellations of identity and relation, constellations that are as diversely networked beyond the traditional borders of the nation-state as they are variegated within those borders domestically' (Allen et al. 2017, 10). Fuelled by experiences of migration and displacement, the archipelago provides the means through which to find and foster new resonances, alliances, and communities. At a time when nostalgic and reductive imperialistic discourses are on the rise across both sides of the Atlantic Ocean, the creative and cultural potential of the archipelago is increasingly valuable in its ability to produce new forms of relation that are plural, connective, and constantly on the move. Able to navigate multiple scales and forms of relation, from the bioregion to the biosphere, archipelagic literatures remind us of the inherent fluidity and plurality of place in an increasingly bordered world. Marked by the tidal flow of arrival and departure, these collections position the 'local' as a constantly shifting place. The environmental dimensions of these texts emphasise that place is not static and remind us that while each island has its own particular and specific topographical form, they are all linked to one another through a range of interactive histories, languages, and ecologies.

NOTES

1. Edna Longley notes the similarities between MacDiarmid's Hebridean poems and the Anglo-Irish poet, Louis MacNeice's earlier travelogue *I Crossed the Minch* (1936) alongside earlier Irish island texts such as J. M. Synge's *The Aran Islands* (1906) (2010, 143–50). Scott Lyall further suggests that MacDiarmid's travelogue 'can be seen as a nationalist response to *A Journey to the Western Islands of Scotland* (1775), topographically extending yet ideologically troubling the assured Enlightenment metropolitanism of Johnson and Boswell's tour of lonely places incompatible with British civilisation' (2006, 136).

2. Angus Peter Campbell is a native Gaelic speaker and has written variously on the significance of the Gaelic language in his work. While not a native speaker, MacDiarmid has frequently drawn from the languages and traditions of the Gaidhealtachd in his political and poetic works, viewing Gaelic as a rich cultural reserve from which to rejuvenate wider Scottish culture. As Louisa Gairn notes, the concept of the 'Gaelic Idea' 'developed and matured during MacDiarmid's time in Shetland, resurfacing with renewed poetic power in *Stony Limits* as "Lament for the Great Music"' (2011, 92). During the early 1930s, MacDiarmid cultivated a long friendship with the great Scottish Gaelic poet, Sorely MacLean who aided MacDiarmid in translating Gaelic poems for inclusion in *The Golden Treasury of Scottish*

Poetry (1940). For MacDiarmid, Gaelic language and culture offers 'a potent image of a distinct Scottish identity and a point of resistance against English cultural ascendancy' (Gairn 2011, 93). For MacDiarmid, the connections that run along the geopolitical edges of 'Cornwall, the Hebrides, and the Orkneys and the Shetlands' (MacDiarmid 1939, 2) are thus not only linked through deep geological histories but a linguistic history that supplies MacDiarmid with 'ammunition against British centralisation' (Lyall 2006, 130).

BIBLIOGRAPHY

Allen, N., N. Groom, and J. Smith. 'Introduction'. *Coastal Works: Cultures of the Atlantic Edge*. Ed. Nicholas Allen, Nick Groom, and Jos Smith. Oxford: Oxford University Press, 2017. 1–21.

Baker, T. 'The Lonely Island: Exile and Community in Recent Island Writing'. *Community in Modern Scottish Literature*. Ed. Scott Lyall. Leiden: Brill, 2016. 25–42.

Benitez-Rojo, A. *The Repeating Island: The Caribbean and the Postmodern Perspective*. Trans. James. E. Maraniss. Durham: Duke University Press, 1996.

Brannigan, J. *Archipelagic Modernism: Literature in the Irish and British Isles, 1890–1970*. Edinburgh: Edinburgh University Press, 2015.

Bristow, T. *The Anthropocene Lyric: An Affective Geography of Poetry, Person, Place*. Basingstoke: Palgrave Macmillan, 2015.

Campbell, A. *Aibisidh*. Edinburgh: Polygon, 2011.

———. 'Inheriting Islands—An interview with Angus Peter Campbell'. *Island Review*, 2015. June 1. http://www.theislandreview.com/island-books-angus-peter-campbell. Accessed 19 July 2017.

DeLoughrey, E. *Roots and Routes*. Honolulu: University of Hawai'i Press, 2007.

Gairn, L. *Ecology and Modern Scottish Literature*. Edinburgh: Edinburgh University Press, 2008.

———. 'MacDiarmid and Ecology'. *Edinburgh Companion to Hugh MacDiarmid*. Ed. Scott Lyall and Margery Palmer McCulloch. Edinburgh: Edinburgh University Press, 2011. 82–97.

Hadfield, J. *Nigh-No-Place*. Edinburgh: Bloodaxe Books, 2008.

———. 'Interview with the Poet Jen Hadfield: Humble, Sincere, Honest'. *The Midnight Heart*, 2010. September 6. http://blogs.warwick.ac.uk/zoebrigley/entry/interview_with_the. Accessed 19 July 2017.

———. *Byssus*. London: Picador, 2014.

Hau'ofa, E. 'Our Sea of Islands'. *A New Oceania: Rediscovering Our Sea of Islands*. Ed. Eric Waddell, Vijay Naidu, and Epeli Hau'ofa. Suva, Fiji: The University of the South Pacific, 1993. 2–17.

Heise, U. *Sense of Place and Sense of Planet: The Environmental Imagination of the Global.* Oxford: Oxford University Press, 2008.

Kerrigan, J. *Archipelagic English: Literature, History, and Politics 1603–1707.* Oxford: Oxford University Press, 2008.

Longley, E. 'Irish and Scottish "Island Poems"'. *Northern Lights Northern Words. Selected Papers from the FRLSU Conference, Kirkwall 2009.* Ed. Robert McColl Millar. Aberdeen: Forum for Research on the Languages of Scotland and Ireland, 2010. 143–61.

Lyall, S. *Hugh MacDiarmid's Poetry and Politics of Place: Imagining a Scottish Republic.* Edinburgh: Edinburgh University Press, 2006.

MacDiarmid, H. *The Islands of Scotland: Hebrides, Orkneys and Shetlands.* London: Batsfod, 1939.

———. *Selected Prose.* Ed. Alan Riach. Manchester: Carcarnet, 1992.

———. *Complete Poems: Volume 1.* Ed. Alan Riach. Manchester: Carcanet, 1993.

Mackay, P. 'Introduction to a Reading by Angus Peter Campbell at the Pleasance, Edinburgh, on National Poetry Day', 2012. October 4. http://www.anguspetercampbell.co.uk/angus-peter-campbell. Accessed 19 July 2017.

Massey, D. 'A Global Sense of Place'. *Marxism Today* 38:1 (1991): 24–29.

Pocock, J. G. A. 'British History: A Plea for a New Subject'. *The Journal of Modern History* 47:4 (1975): 601–21.

———. *The Discovery of Islands: Essays in British History.* Cambridge: Cambridge University Press, 2005.

Pugh, J. 'Island Movements: Thinking with the Archipelago'. *Island Studies Journal* 8:1 (2013): 9–24.

Shiva, V. 'The Greening of the Global Reach'. *Global Visions: Beyond the New World Order.* Ed. John Brown Childs and Jill Cutler Jeremy. Brecher. Boston: South End Press, 1993. 53–61.

Stratford, E. et. al. 'Envisioning the Archipelago'. *Island Studies Journal* 6:2 (2011): 113–30.

Yeung, H. *Spatial Engagement with Poetry.* New York: Palgrave Macmillan, 2015.

From "Pictish Artemis" to "Tay Moses": Visions of the River Tay in Some Contemporary Scottish Poems

Robin MacKenzie

Thy silver streams and vernal banks, O Tay!
Inspire my soul, and swell the muses lay:
O cou'd my verse rise equal to my theme,
Wind with thy shores, and warble with thy stream.
No more should Thames triumphant flow along,
Nor Pope nor Windsor shou'd transcend my song. (Glas 3)

This paean to the River Tay, penned by a certain Alexander Glas and published by R. Morison and Son, Booksellers, in Perth in 1790, is only one among many poems to celebrate the charms, and sometimes the storms, of Scotland's longest river. The most famous (or notorious) of these is no doubt William Topaz McGonagall's lament for the victims of the Tay Bridge Disaster in 1889, but the river's poetic pedigree extends much further back—at least as far as Arthur Johnston's neo-Latin lyric, "Taodunum", from the early seventeenth century.[1] In this article, I want

R. MacKenzie (✉)
School of Modern Languages,
University of St Andrews, St Andrews, UK

© The Author(s) 2019   187
M. Szuba and J. Wolfreys (eds.), *The Poetics of Space and Place
in Scottish Literature*, Geocriticism and Spatial Literary Studies,
https://doi.org/10.1007/978-3-030-12645-2_11

to look at how the River Tay appears in poems by three rather more contemporary Scottish poets, Douglas Dunn, Robert Crawford and Kathleen Jamie, each of whom demonstrates in their work a close familiarity with the natural and cultural history of the river.[2] The poems in question—Dunn's "Here and There" and "Memory and Imagination", Crawford's "Mary Shelley on Broughty Ferry Beach", and "The Tay Moses" and two of the "Five Tay Sonnets" by Jamie—explore some of the Tay's various intertextual associations and resonances; they thus offer rich pickings for the kind of geocritical approach adopted in this essay.

Robert T. Tally, in the introduction to his translation of Bertrand Westphal's *La Géocritique*, outlines two ways in which geographically minded critics can give spaces meaning (thereby transforming them into places):

> Westphal intends for geocriticism to be an exploratory critical practice, or set of practices, whereby readers, scholars, and critics engage with the spaces that make life, through lived experience and through imaginary projections, meaningful. (xii)

I want to focus especially on our poets' "imaginary projections" as expressed in the intertextual dimension of their poems—the cultural, historical and mythological allusions they draw on in their evocation of the Tay—since intertextuality plays a crucial role in the contrasting visions of the river they offer.

According to Westphal, intertextuality is one of the "four cardinal points of the geocritical approach" (122), together with multifocalisation, polysensoriality and stratigraphy. Prieto reiterates the point in more critical mode in his comparison of geocritical and ecocritical approaches:

> [D]espite his insistence on the referential function of literature and the interface between fiction and the real, Westphal seems to be leaving us with an interface between some texts and other texts. Or, to put it another way, Westphal's theory of reality amounts to a theory of intertextuality. (27)

Westphal expands on the role of intertextuality in an earlier essay, arguing that it offers the principal means by which literature can invest places with an imaginary dimension, or indeed translate into literary form the imaginary dimension places already possess.[3] The place of intertextuality in geocriticism can be further elucidated with reference to two of the other "central tenets". The link with multifocalisation is evident in Prieto's account of the latter:

> In order to escape from the perspectival limitations of a single author or interpretive community, the geocritic will consult as many texts, and as many different *kinds* of texts, as possible. [...] The goal is to develop a polyphonic or dialogical understanding of the place in question, one that incorporates the widest array possible of perspectives. (24)

The juxtaposition and comparison of such a range of texts would certainly count as a mode of intertextual analysis if we adopt a broad definition of the concept, akin to what Gérard Genette calls "transtextuality" ["la transtextualité"] in his massively influential study, *Introduction à l'architexte*.[4]

The second link—with what Eric Prieto calls "the stratigraphic perspective"—is particularly crucial for my discussion of the Tay poems. Prieto gives a brief but lucid explanation of the term: "Westphal uses the term stratigraphic to emphasise the extent to which a given place is composed of an accumulation of past moments, an archaeological layering of successive historical phases" (25). Westphal himself outlines the relationship between stratigraphic and intertextual in an elegant metaphor: "La stratification temporelle de l'espace humain est en partie déterminée par sa valence intertextuelle" (7). "Valency" here is used in quite a precise sense: originally a term from chemistry, it is defined by OED as "the combining power of an element, especially as measured by the number of hydrogen atoms it can displace or combine with". The intertextual valency of a place, then, would consist in the number of intertextual connections it can generate, the density of the intertextual web in which it is situated; this, according to Westphal, partly determines how multilayered what he calls the temporal layering or stratification—the traces of history in a particular place (or "human space")—will be.

Although Glas (from the eighteenth century) and Johnston (from the seventeenth century) are mentioned in the opening and closing sections, the stratigraphic dimension of this study lies not so much in the chronological spread of texts examined, which were all produced over the last thirty or so years, as in their content. All three of our poets, in spite of the clear differences in their historical visions and modes of imagining the past, attach great importance to the depth of historical and cultural references in their work—the "accumulation of past moments" and "archeological layering of successive historical phases" mentioned by Prieto. A focus on intertextuality can therefore—to borrow a concept made famous by the ethnographer Clifford Geertz—help to build up a "thicker" description of the place evoked, adding extra layers of meaning and association—historical, cultural and indeed personal—to the purely physical or sensory depiction of a particular site.

THE RIVER TAY

If we trace it back to its headstream, the Tay is Scotland's longest river, measuring around 120 miles from its source on the slopes of Ben Lui in the Highlands, thirty miles or so from Oban, to the point where it meets the North Sea. Known initially as the Fillan Water and then the River Dochart, it flows east, passing through several smaller lochs before entering Loch Tay at Killin; emerging at the other end of the loch under its own name, it runs past Aberfeldy before looping round and heading south past the small cathedral town of Dunkeld towards the city of Perth. There it becomes tidal, turns east and broadens out to form the Firth of Tay. Dundee, Scotland's fourth city, stretches along the northern shore of the Firth not far from where it flows into the North Sea, between Buddon Ness on the north side and Tentsmuir Point on the south.

As even this brief roll call of place names indicates, the Tay is not short of historical associations. The medieval cathedral town of Dunkeld, the ancient Scottish capital of Perth and the great nineteenth-century commercial and industrial centre of Dundee are all built on or beside the river; not far from its banks we can also find Scone Palace, the ruined medieval abbeys of Lindores and Balmerino, and Birnam Wood (no longer so mobile nowadays as it was in Macbeth's time). The natural history of the river is similarly rich, with its salmon, otters, beavers and pearl mussels; the Tay has been designated a SAC (Special Area of Conservation) by the Scottish Government.

The settings for our poems—insofar as they can be precisely identified—are all to be found along the Firth of Tay, downstream from Perth. Broughty Ferry ("Mary Shelley") and Tayport ("Here and There") lie roughly opposite each other near the mouth of the estuary, on the north and south bank, respectively. We can safely assume that the riverscape in "Memory and Imagination" is also to be found near Tayport (where Dunn lived at the time), especially given the reference to Buddon Ness in the poem. Jamie's river of creels and rushes and sandbanks is perhaps a little less easy to locate with precision but it would be reasonable to place it not too far from Newburgh, where the poet lives; we know that this is where the excavation of the log-boat in the fourth Tay Sonnet takes place. It must be said, though, that the web of allusions and intertexts woven by our poets lends much greater variety to their riverscapes than would be found in the "unembellished" description of a geographer. From Michael Scot to Mary Shelley, "Pictish Artemis" to "Tay Moses", the Tay of the poets is haunted by a vivid cast of characters, drawn from history and legend.

"Here and There"

The Tay appears in a number of Dunn's poems, especially around the time of *Northlight* (1988), the first collection he wrote after returning to Scotland to live in Tayport. The most direct evocation of the river occurs in "Tay Bridge", its three stanzas offering a series of impressions (almost in the painterly sense)—"a long train floats/ Through a stopped shower's narrow waterways/ Above rose-coloured river" or "Mud's sieved and drained from pewter into gold". In the poem I want to examine first, "Here and There", the poet's gaze is less sharply focused on the Tay itself but the evocation of the surrounding landscape (and village of Tayport on the shore of the Firth) is more complex and multi-layered.

"Here and There" is a long dialogical poem which could justifiably be regarded as the centrepiece of *Northlight*: the poet-speaker writes from (and about) Tayport and environs ("here"), engaging in discussion and debate with an interlocutor based in a southern and metropolitan "there" (presumably London, though the city's name does not in fact appear in the poem). The argument that structures the poem and gives it its dialectical impetus centres on the poet's decision to leave the metropolis and return to Scotland to settle in rural North Fife. The interlocutor—whom Dunn identified in an interview for the *Scottish Review of Books* as his fellow-poet, editor and friend, Ian Hamilton (17)—accuses the poet of retreating into a safe and complacent parochialism, which will have catastrophic effects on his poetry (and his career as a poet, which is perhaps not quite the same thing). The poet defends his choice over the poem's twelve stanzas, arguing that his move to Fife will serve his poetry, leading to a healing and regeneration of the self and a renewed openness to experience and capacity to love (a word that occurs seven times in the poem). As Margitta Rouse argues, the dialogue between the two speakers moves towards a "dissolution of antagonisms [that] involves the binaries of centre and periphery [...], province and metropolis [...], country and city [...], and Scottishness and Englishness" (63).

The predominantly descriptive mode we saw in "Tay Bridge" is still very much in evidence in the opening lines of "Here and There":

> You say it's mad to love this east-coast weather –
> I'll praise it, though, and claim its subtle light's
> Perfect for places that abut on water
> Where swans on tidal aviaries preen their whites.

Several critics—foremost among them Sean O'Brien and W. N. Herbert—have emphasised the pastoral element in the poem. Herbert situates the poem, both structurally (in its dialogical form) and thematically, firmly in the Horatian tradition—"Dunn [...] presents us with a new synthesis: the British poet in Horatian mode" (124)—and goes on to identify intertextual links to the odes and satires Horace addressed to his patron Maecenas from his (Horace's) Sabine farm.[5] It is tempting at this point to paraphrase the most famous line in the poem and claim that Tayport is Tibur as well as Trebizond... O'Brien is more ambivalent about Dunn's use of the pastoral; he observes that "[h]aving it both ways is one of the functions of pastoral" (65), a laconic statement that could itself perhaps be read in more than one way. If we take it to mean that the pastoral, by framing or containing an evocation of nature within a conventional cultural form, blurs the boundaries or subverts the opposition between nature and culture, then even those elements of "wild" nature dramatised by Dunn—"I love the rain and winds that magnify it"—take on a veneer of literariness, a kind of intertextual halo or aura.

These literary resonances are increasingly noticeable as the poem goes on: the first and perhaps most striking instance is the famous comparison, or indeed identification, of Tayport with Trebizond I alluded to above. This is often (and I think justifiably) read as a lyrical assertion of the cultural and existential richness and value of the local. Hans-Werner Ludwig articulates this well:

> [T]he homely Tayport becomes the exotic Trebizond – fabulous orien-
> tal city famous for its wealth and splendour and its tournaments, a "lit-
> erary city" conjured up in English literature from the fourteenth- and

fifteenth-century romances, from Marlowe to James Joyce, from *Paradise Lost* to Gibbon's *Decline and Fall of the Roman Empire*. (205)

But if we look at the passage more closely, it begins to appear somewhat less straightforward, formally and syntactically, than one might expect:

> So spin your globe: Tayport is Trebizond
> As easily as a regenerate
>
> Country in which to reconstruct a self
> From local water, timber, light and earth...

The bold enjambment across the stanza break throws considerable stress on both "regenerate" and "[c]ountry", which counterbalances the resounding emphasis on (Tayport as) Trebizond. Moreover, the apparently straightforward equation between the two alliterating towns is strangely modified by the comparison that follows. We might have expected a clearer opposition between "Trebizond" and the second term—"as easily as some worthless provincial backwater" or something similar—whereas what we get is two different types of positive, as it were: the legendary and exotic glamour of Trebizond is counterposed to, or juxtaposed with, a place, however modest and provincial, where poetry can be written and the self heal and become whole again.

Things become yet more complex and nuanced if we reflect on the historical implications of the comparison. Trebizond was rich, exotic and famed in legend and literature—as Ludwig says—but for long periods could hardly be described as central in geopolitical terms. In Roman times, though prosperous in the period after Hadrian, it was really quite remote from the political, economic and cultural centres of Empire (first Rome, then Constantinople). Its political importance in medieval times—as one of the successor empires to Byzantium after the latter was sacked during the Fourth Crusade in 1204—was relatively short-lived. This becomes more interesting, perhaps, with the mention of Byzantium later on in the poem—"The Pax Britannica's/ Dismissed, a second-rate Byzantium"—which introduces the theme of post-imperial decline that features quite prominently elsewhere in Dunn's poetry, in *Northlight* and beyond ("Stories" in *Elegies* is a notable example). The Trebizond and Byzantium references, taken together, could perhaps be read as complicating Dunn's historical narrative: the poet's retreat to the periphery, emotionally and imaginatively fulfilling though it promises to be, takes place against a backdrop of broader political and cultural decline: perhaps Tayport-Trebizond stakes its claim as (or after) the power of the centre (London-Byzantium) begins to erode.

The Trebizond-Byzantium motif might seem to be taking us quite far from the Tay, even though the intertextual superimposition of Black Sea coast or Hellespont upon the topography of the northern Firth holds out a tantalising (if disorientating) prospect to the reader. Once we get to the sixth stanza, though, we find a flurry of allusions—literary, historical and folkloric—which are more directly linked to the Tay itself. Given the plethora of these cultural references, it makes sense to quote the relevant lines in full:

> A ferry town, a place to cross from… Verse
> Enjoys connections: fugitive Macduff
> Escaped Macbeth by it. Lacking his purse,
> He paid in bread – The Ferry of the Loaf…
> *'Ferries? Fairies! That's medieval farce!'*
> The wizard, Michael Scot, was born near here…
> *'I might have guessed you'd more like that, and worse…'*
> … Alchemist, polymath, astrologer
> To the Holy Roman Empire; Tayport's son
> Mastered all knowledge, too controversial
> For Dante who invented his damnation
> In the *Inferno*: 'Tayport Man in Hell,'
>
> They'd say in the *Fife Herald* – 'Sorcerer
> From Tayport Slandered by Tuscan Poet.'

This is a complex passage which repays close reading. The dominant motif is that of "crossing", with its various metaphorical derivatives, which appears in the first line—"A ferry town, a place to cross from…". We would, I think, be justified in seeing an allusion here to the mythological topos of Charon ferrying the shades of the dead across the Styx to Hades, prefiguring the reference to Dante's *Inferno* at the end of the stanza; more directly, though, the ferry motif introduces a series of crossings (or shifts or transitions) that structure the stanza. First, there is the reflexive turn towards writing—"Verse/ Enjoys connections…"—which is one of several such moves in a poem very much concerned with the activity of writing and the conditions of its production. This leads on, by way of local folklore (the story of Macduff and the Ferry of the Loaf), to the first of two major literary references (to *Macbeth*, of course); a single allusion thus encompasses the native folkloric tradition and the Shakespearean summits of English literature. Next we return to linguistic (and implicitly reflexive) forms of transition: this time, though, the interlocutor's rejoinder—"*Ferries? Fairies! That's medieval farce!*"—is motivated by wordplay, by phonetic resemblance rather than semantic content. Could we read the interlocutor's rather desperate pun as a sign of exasperation, or even an indication that he is beginning to lose the argument?

The "fairies" pun provides the link to the next motif: the undercurrents of witchcraft in the Macduff/ *Macbeth* reference rise to the surface with the mention of Michael Scot, a figure who likewise combines and condenses elements from native folklore with the cosmopolitan (in political-historical terms) and the canonical (in the literary sphere). The historical Michael Scot was indeed "astrologer to the Holy Roman Empire", thus exemplifying the archetypal figure of the peripatetic Scot—*Scotus vagans*, in Herbert's phrase (130)— who ends up in one of the political and cultural centres of Europe: the Sicilian court of Frederick II, with its astonishingly cosmopolitan assembly of scholars and artists. In more literary guise, "Magister Michael" famously makes a brief appearance in Dante's *Inferno*, the work of another towering figure in post-classical European literature, in which he is consigned as a soothsayer to the Fourth Bolgia (trench or ravine) of the Eighth Circle of Hell.[6] Significantly, it is Scot's dual identity—ontologically divided between historical actor and legendary figure—that makes him such a fitting emblem of the connection, and also tension, between local and cosmopolitan cultures in Dunn's poem.

This tension finds a different kind of expression in the shift of tone towards the comic in the last lines of Stanza VI (continuing into Stanza VII)—"Tayport Man in Hell" and "Sorcerer/ From Tayport Slandered by Tuscan Poet". On the one hand, we could read this as a rather conventional mode of portraying the local—"priming a parish pump" by inventing headlines for the local newspaper—which, instead of elevating the apparent insignificance of local things ("Tayport is Trebizond"), ends up in something more like what was traditionally known as travesty.[7] Thus an incident in the *Divina Commedia*, the major philosophical/ theological poem in the Western tradition, is reduced to the level of a local newspaper headline. From another perspective, however, this bold act of cultural transposition could be taken as a sign of confidence in the local: the demotic voice—and what could be more demotic than the *Fife Herald*, that most local of local newspapers?—can itself assimilate, "trope" and thereby transform figures and motifs from cosmopolitan "high" culture.

As these comments indicate, "Here and There" is a complex work which explores large ethical, political and aesthetic questions, involving selfhood, nationhood and artistic creation. Dunn is concerned to do various things in the poem: to evoke a landscape in all its specificity, to argue that this apparently peripheral place encourages a regeneration (creative and emotional) of the poet's self and thereby to challenge his interlocutor's unexamined assumptions about the values of the local and "parochial" as against the metropolitan. The Tay is a persistent presence in the poem, described with Dunn's characteristic attentiveness to sensuous detail but also haunted by figures from literature, history and legend. Both spatially and temporally, Dunn's poetic riverscape is complex and multi-layered; motifs from local history and legend are linked through a multitude of intertextual references to the broader cosmopolitan narratives of European culture, thus subverting (as Rouse and Ludwig have argued) the hoary and unexamined old oppositions of centre and periphery.

"MEMORY AND IMAGINATION"

There are, if anything, even more connections made between local elements and images from further afield (usually the Mediterranean) in our next poem from *Northlight*, "Memory and Imagination". Like "Here and There", this poem takes the form of an ode, though not a Horatian one: the form is closer to the irregular "Pindaric" version popular among later seventeenth-century and eighteenth-century English poets and adopted most famously by Wordsworth for the Immortality Ode. The poem outlines a rather more systematic poetics than we find in "Here and There", centring on the two nouns that occur in the title, which correspond to the twofold source of the poet's "raw material": broadly speaking, memories of sense impressions on the one hand, and the reserves of the European tradition, its storehouse of collective cultural memory, on the other.[8]

Like "Here and There", "Memory and Imagination" opens with a vivid description of the river and its surroundings:

> Metre's continuum
> Articulates
> An artless view of water, sky and slates.
> Rhythmical memory,
> Archival drum,
> Its hammer beats with primitive decorum
> Over the roofs, past chimneypots
> Toward the river's tidal pulse...

Perhaps the most striking feature here is the prominence of metaphors from the arts (primarily poetry and music) to describe the concrete details of the scene: "metre's continuum", "rhythmical memory", "archival drum". (A little later on we have "Paint, pencil, three struck chords" as well.) As Silvia Mergenthal argues, the perception of reality, and indeed reality itself, is frequently translated into linguistic terms in the poem and thereby takes on a poetic form (60).[9] This habit of portraying natural phenomena in textual, linguistic or aesthetic terms is in fact a recurring trope in *Northlight*, as we see in the frequently quoted opening lines of "Abernethy":

> Air-psalters and pages of stone
> Inscribed and Caledonian
> Under these leaf-libraries where
> Melodious lost literature
> Remembers itself!

The poet's impressions of the Tay in "Memory and Imagination" are often quite specifically linked to other, distant waterways, through the "displacement" effected by memory and imagination:

> But mind can change
> Uncertain waterscapes.
> That coloured pool could be
> The Serchio's
> Displaced to Tay by quick
> Sight-echoes.

Such spatial leaps in "Here and There" were usually triggered by historical or literary allusions (Trebizond, Byzantium, Michael Scot) rather than fleeting visual or sensory echoes. But "Memory and Imagination" too has its share of cultural references, especially to figures from myth and legend, even though the mode of presentation is rather different. If one of the dominant Tay-related motifs in "Here and There" is that of crossing, as we saw in the "Ferry of the Loaf" stanza, the river in "Memory and Imagination" is often evoked through images of fusion and indeed confluence: this is most strikingly exemplified in the following passage, where the poet conjures up a syncretic mythological scene of Greek, Egyptian and native Pictish deities swimming or sailing together in the waters of the Tay:

> Poseidon rises from where fresh meets salt
> Into the arms of Tutha, Tay's goddess,
>   North-water's Pictish Artemis
>   Among her swimming stags,
>   Otters,
>   Seals and swans,
> Columban saints who navigate on stones.
>   Osiris with his black
>   Nilotic fleet
>   And attic biremes on
>   The water-street
>   Glide on by muscled slavery...

This fusion (or confluence) of traditions is enacted on the verbal level in the description of Tutha as "Pictish Artemis", which condenses the two main mythological strands in the poem in one phrase. The geographical feature that is the River Tay is transmuted in the poet's mind, fed by the streams and tributaries of cultural memory and the European (or rather Mediterranean) cultural heritage; rather than being triggered by a motif from local folklore or history, this scene seems to emerge in that unmediated act of vision which Dunn refers to as "imagination's second sight".

But in spite of these differences of mode, the ideological implications are broadly similar to those in "Here and There". The remote northern River Tay, far from the centres of European history and culture, is nevertheless shown to be very much bound up with them in imaginative terms; the gods of the Classical and Egyptian pantheons, as well as other Continental cultural "icons" ("Mozart's strings/ Encourage echoed songs"), are clearly at home on or beside the chillier and more turbulent waters of the Firth of Tay.

"Mary Shelley on Broughty Ferry Beach"

Our third poem was written by Robert Crawford, a poet from a younger generation than Dunn. "Mary Shelley on Broughty Ferry Beach", from the 1992 collection *Talkies*, presents an imagined scene from the famous novelist's life. Whether Mary Shelley witnessed a dismembered whale on Broughty Ferry beach is not recorded—though, given Dundee's status as a major whaling port at the time, it is hardly an unlikely scenario— but we do know that she spent time in Broughty Ferry as a guest of the Baxter family. She even mentions this period in the "Introduction" to *Frankenstein*:

> I lived principally in the country as a girl, and passed a considerable time in Scotland. I made occasional visits to the more picturesque parts; but my habitual residence was on the blank and dreary northern shores of the Tay, near Dundee. [...] It was beneath the trees of the grounds belonging to our house, or on the bleak sides of the woodless mountains near, that my true compositions, the airy flights of my imagination, were born and fostered. (20)

The episode evoked in Crawford's poem takes place against the historically realist backdrop of the flensing of the whale and the whalers' domestic lives, in which objects derived from whaling (their wives' corsets, their children's toys) are ubiquitous. The text itself builds towards a moment of grim inspiration which (it is hinted) implants the germ of an idea that will lead to *Frankenstein*, as the young Mary Shelley "sneaks past a leftover eye/ Flung on the sand, and other small last bits/ Of monster littering the promenade". In certain respects, Crawford seems close to Dunn in his poetic inscription of the Tay and environs within the context of a wider literary and cultural history. But the way in which he does this is rather different: the poetic mode adopted is dramatic rather than discursive, very much based on showing rather than telling (to use a well-worn critical distinction). Whereas Dunn's cultural allusions and intertextual references in "Here and There" and "Memory and Imagination", vividly evoked though they often are, frequently serve to make a point and underscore an argument, Crawford is primarily concerned to dramatise an episode (blending poetic invention and historical realism) in the aspiring novelist's biography. His portrayal of Mary Shelley on the beach not only recreates in a few brushstrokes the material conditions of a particular way of life at a specific historical moment but also hints at contrasts in social position and psychological make-up (or emotional response): unlike the Broughty Ferry whalers, the future novelist comes from a relatively wealthy and educated bourgeois family and her reaction to the spectacle of the dismembered whale is more coloured by emotion (she's "sad") and takes its place within a wider range of intellectual and imaginative concerns.

In spite of these obvious contrasts in poetic mode, however, there is a similarity in what we might call the ideology underlying the two poets' uses of history in these poems. Like Dunn, Crawford is interested in tracing links and establishing connections between what have often been seen in cultural terms as Scottish periphery and English or European centre. In Crawford's case, this has fed into the project of "devolving English literature" (to quote the title of perhaps his most influential work of literary criticism) and "Mary Shelley on Broughty Ferry Beach" can, among other things, be read as a poetic contribution to that endeavour.

Tay Sonnets: "Excavation and Recovery" and "Doing Away"

If there were a Tay makar—a poet laureate of the river—our third poet, Kathleen Jamie, would have a very strong claim to the title. Jamie lives in Newburgh, a little town on the southern shore of the river, and the Tay forms the backdrop to much of her writing, in verse and prose.[10] She has even made a short radio programme about a kayaking trip on the river, and the impressions and reflections arising from the experience, which was broadcast on Radio 4 on 18 August 2016 as one of a series of five programmes by different speakers entitled "The River". In her talk she recounts (among other things) the events which gave rise to the poem "Excavation and Recovery", the fourth of the five Tay Sonnets from her 2012 collection, *The Overhaul*.[11]

The object of the excavation and recovery of the title is a Bronze Age log-boat, which archaeologists are attempting to raise from the river bed. This laborious undertaking prompts the poet-spectator to imagine the original boatmen and their relationship with the river; in an imaginative move characteristic of Jamie's writing, the textures and activities of everyday life—the material substratum of human existence—form a bridge to scenes and figures historically remote, as we see (or hear) most strikingly in the use of current colloquial Scots to transcribe the Bronze Age boatmen's words: "Ca' canny, lads!" Equally striking, though, is the contrast between contemporary technological civilisation, with its "hi-viz jackets" and its capacity to measure the discharge of the Tay Estuary into the sea, and the life-world of the Bronze Age peoples who saw the Tay as a goddess, whose name and its meaning—"the Flowing(?), the Silent One(?)"—are shrouded in uncertainty for us. As Louisa Gairn observes, "[t]he question marks are significant. The possibility for language to reconcile us with the natural world is an open-ended question which recurs throughout Jamie's poetry and prose" (141). We could also read the question marks as pointing to the gap between our knowledge and experience and that of the ancient inhabitants who presumably did know what the name they gave to the river meant. As for the three variants of the river's name that the poet lists—"Tay/ Toi/ Taum"—they could perhaps be heard as a faint echo of the giant's blood-curdling cry in "Jack and the Beanstalk"—"Fee-fi-fo-fum"—hinting at the child-like fear the Bronze Age boatmen might have felt when faced with the elemental power of the river goddess. Not all readers will be convinced by this reading but those who are will see it as yet another instance of Jamie's subtle gift for imaginatively exploring a world view and mode of experience very far removed from her own. The figure of the Tay goddess shows clear affinities with Dunn's image of "Tutha", the Pictish Artemis, in "Memory and Imagination"; the differences, however, are equally marked and typical of the two poets' respective visions: Dunn's cavalcade of figures from myth and history draws widely on the dramatis personae of European cultural memory, while Jamie's Tay goddess is a more elusive figure in visual terms, indissolubly linked with the natural forces she personifies.

As we might expect from a poet so attentive to the natural world—the first of the Tay Sonnets describes the return of a pair of ospreys to nest—the echoes of history and legend in Jamie's evocation of the river are typically embedded (like the log-boat) in layers of vivid and detailed physical description. A slightly different manifestation of this can be found in the fifth of the Sonnets, entitled "Doing Away". Whereas "Excavation and Recovery" maintains a steady focus on the material vestiges of the historical past, the folklore motif in "Doing Away" is slipped in quite unobtrusively and yet it resonates throughout the poem: it is introduced in the glancing description of the Tay when the tide is out "shining like an Elfland", before reappearing in the final lines in a subtle contemporary variation on the traditional theme of abduction by the fairy folk, as the poet muses on the possibility of abandoning her car "a mile from home", where it will be found with the "engine thrumming quietly". As Rachel Falconer has remarked, "[r]eferences to Celtic fairy-lore have always had a place in Jamie's poetry [...]. A number of poems articulate the lure of fairyland. Sometimes the speaker succumbs (as in 'Glamourie'), sometimes she stays just this side of what might have proved to be a fatal enchantment (as in 'The Wood' and 'Whales')" (163). Indeed, the title of Jamie's subsequent collection, *The Bonniest Companie*, is taken from the epigraph to the famous Border ballad, "Tam Lin", which tells of the eponymous hero's rescue from the clutches of the Queen of Elfland. Jamie herself acknowledges the influence of the ballad tradition in her comment on "Glamourie" on the Scottish Poetry Library website:

> I love the supernatural or fairy element in the old ballads, like "Tam Lin" and "Thomas the Rhymer", where the fairy-folk are powerful; and I did wonder, when I was wandering in the wood, if when eventually the spell broke and I found my way out, seven years might have passed. Seven is the magic number. Both Tam Lin and Thomas the Rhymer spent seven years in fairyland before being rescued or released. [...] It pleased me to write the poem, to bring the Scottish fairy tradition with us into the 21st century.[12]

"The Tay Moses"

The merging of motifs from folklore and myth with acutely observed contemporary details and textures, both physical and emotional, is a recurring element in Jamie's writing, from early period work such as "The Queen of Sheba" onwards. Our next poem is one of the better-known examples, drawing on cultural sources very different from the native folkloric traditions of the ballads mentioned above. "The Tay Moses", from Jamie's 1999 collection *Jizzen*, combines the intertextual resonances of the well-known biblical episode with the intimately personal in theme and mood. As well-nigh every critic and commentator explains, "jizzen" is a Scottish word for "childbed" (in the sense of "lying in childbed" or giving birth), and it comes as no surprise that "The Tay Moses" does indeed engage, in quite an unexpected way, with the childbirth theme. The poem is essentially an imaginative exploration of the poet-mother's anxiety that she will not establish an emotional bond with her baby when it arrives. If all goes well, the baby will be carried upstream where it will be "held safe/ in eddies"; if not, the infant will drift downriver on the ebb-tide "to snag/ on reeds".

Jamie herself explains what is at stake in her introduction to the poem on the Poetry Archive website:

> Before my boy was born – I didn't know it was a boy obviously – but before this child was born I was frightened that I might not like this child who was going to come and live with us. I think this is a thing a lot of expectant mothers fear but you're not allowed to say it. And I thought this person's going to come and live with us for, maybe, twenty years and what if we just don't like each other? But I live by the Tay which has huge reed beds so I thought well if the worst comes to the worst I can always make a wee basket which of course I didn't. Instead I wrote this poem called 'The Tay Moses'.[13]

Perhaps the most striking feature of the poem is the delicate balance maintained between elements or impulses that might seem to be in tension with one another. On the one hand, the situation described is in many respects a very down-to-earth one, which dramatises what Jamie acknowledges to be quite a common anxiety among expectant mothers; on the other, it takes on an archetypal resonance through its biblical intertext, which not only refers to the famous scene from the Book of Exodus but is also an instance of the much more widespread mythological motif of the newborn child abandoned to the waters. The tension is perhaps more apparent than real: as in much medieval art and literature, the poem seems to intensify the immediacy of the biblical story by embedding it within an everyday contemporary setting. We find this conjunction in other poems in *Jizzen*— most notably, perhaps, in "The Barrel Annunciation" with its allusion to that most archetypal of maternal figures, the Virgin Mary. The symbolism of the vessel or container, touched on by Juliet Simpson in her essay "Birth, Being and Belonging in *Jizzen*", further underlines the biblical resonances of the childbirth theme in both poems:

> [I]n both 'The Barrel Annunciation' and 'The Tay Moses', the 'vessel' as bearer carries a density of wood and sensory texture, intimately evocative of a physical and spiritual birthing. [...] And when the vessel is empty in

'The Tay Moses', it is experienced in a wrenching fullness of unexpected loss [...], as a movement of matter or an echo of a more ancient biblical flight. (73–74)

The riverscape itself—the setting for the emotional drama—is evoked in a series of spare but vivid details—"a woven/ creel of river-/ rashes, a golden/ oriole's nest"—that convey a strong sense of geographical root-edness. The indigenous connotations of "creel", the use of the vernac-ular word "rashes" ("rushes")—and (more subtly) the "golden oriole's nest"—anchor the poem firmly in a specific natural and linguistic setting. Simpson teases out some of the oriole's connotations: "Yet even here, the arresting choice of species, not 'thrush' but 'golden oriole', captures a mood at once domesticated (in its nested presence) and rare; protect-ing and wild – in the oriole's bright passage: an exotic migrant to Tay shores – which is distinctively Jamie's voice" (74).

If links to what we might be tempted to call "official" literary and cul-tural traditions are very much to the fore in Dunn and Crawford, some-thing rather different seems to be at stake in Jamie's poem. The only conspicuous intertext—the allusion to Moses in the bulrushes—is hardly very recondite and seems designed not so much to situate local events within broader historical narratives and cultural contexts as to allow the exploration (through symbol and myth) of a perennial emotional state: that of the mother anxious about whether she will be able to bond with her baby and perhaps, as Timothy Baker argues (64–65), concerned for the child's future more generally.[14]

Conclusion

Unsurprisingly, perhaps, none of our contemporary poets eulogises the Tay in quite such a straightforward (and indeed conventional) way as Alexander Glas in 1790. Nor, in spite of the ghostly presence of the Nile in two of our poems, have any of our poets set the Tay in dialogue with as far-flung a river as the Ganges, as Bashabi Fraser has done in a long ("epic") composition entitled *From the Ganga to the Tay*, published in 2009. But each has drawn on intertextual elements to situate the Tay and environs in broader cultural and imaginative contexts, showing what Westphal would describe as a stratigraphic cast of mind, alert to the histor-ical substrata beneath the surface of contemporary life. For Dunn in the two poems we examined, the river and its environs call forth numerous elements of local history and legend which connect this apparently remote and peripheral region to the cultural monuments and historical centres of Europe and indeed the world. In "Here and There" in particular, this serves both a personal and a political purpose: a renewal of the poet's creative self and a dismantling of complacent metropolitan cultural assumptions. Crawford's poem likewise positions his Tayside evocation of Mary Shelley within a broader cultural context, indicating its putative significance for English literary history while making sure to convey a vivid sense of place at a specific historical moment. Jamie's river provides the setting for everyday scenes, evoked in precise material detail but opening out on to images of the archaic and the archetypal; in "The Tay Moses" in particular, the intertextual resonances give an aura of universality to the poet's personal (though by no means unusual) emotional predicament. Alexander Glas in 1790 attempted to present the Tay as a rival to those other great Continental rivers, the Danube and the Tiber; Dunn, Crawford and Jamie find other, perhaps subtler and less explicit, ways to link Scotland's longest river to the world beyond our shores.

NOTES

1. For a translation of "Taodunum" into modern English, see Robert Crawford's version in *Apollos of the North* (94–95).
2. It is no doubt worth mentioning in this context that all three poets are or have been part of the distinguished stable of writers attached to the School of English at St Andrews University: Crawford is currently Professor in the School, Dunn is Emeritus Professor and Jamie was Reader before her appointment as Professor of Poetry at the University of Stirling.
3. "Pour une approche géocritique des textes" (6): "[L]es espaces humains ne deviennent pas imaginaires en intégrant la littérature; c'est la littérature qui leur octroie une dimension imaginaire, ou mieux: qui traduit leur dimension imaginaire intrinsèque en les introduisant dans un réseau intertextuel".
4. Here is the relevant passage, in the translation by Jane E. Lewin: "The text interests me in its textual transcendence – namely everything that brings it into relation (manifest or hidden) with other texts. I call that transtextuality, and I include under it intertextuality in the strict (and, since Julia Kristeva, the 'classical' sense) – that is, the literal presence [...] of one text within another" (81–82).

5. Herbert quotes specifically from *Sermones* 2:6, ll. 70–76, in the English translation by Gilbert Highet (124).
6. See Dante, *Inferno*, XX, 115–17.
7. Travesty—the opposite of mock-heroic—is defined in the *Oxford Dictionary of Literary Terms* as "a mockingly undignified or trivializing treatment of a dignified subject" (340).
8. Silvia Mergenthal gives a lucid and succinct account of this in her article on *Northlight*: "Während 'memory' im Gedicht als eine Erinnerung an eine Sinneserfahrung beschrieben wird […], kann 'imagination' die Sinneserfahrung durch Rekurs auf das kollektive kulturelle Gedächnis transzendieren" (62).
9. "In der Literatur […] wird die Beobachtung der Wirklichkeit, wird damit die Wirklichkeit selbst, versprachlicht; natürliche Phänomene werden in Sprache 'übersetzt', erhalten eine poetische Form" (60).
10. See, for instance, the chapters "Peregrines, Ospreys, Cranes" and "Fever" in *Findings*, and "Pathologies" in *Sightlines*, where, in an unusual metaphorical displacement, the internal organs of the body, seen through a microscope, take on an uncanny resemblance to the Tay riverscape.
11. I focus on the fourth and fifth of the "Tay Sonnets" here because of the more obvious presence in them of elements from history and folklore. In the first three, the emphasis falls predominantly on natural phenomena—birds, floods, the coming of spring—as indeed their titles would suggest ("Ospreys", "Spring", "May"). We might, however, detect a hint of the Elfland motif in "Ospreys", in which the poet exhorts the birds to "claim your teind from the shining/ estates of the firth" (5).
12. This passage is taken from the Scottish Poetry Library website; details are given in "Works Cited" at the end of the article.
13. This quotation is from the Poetry Archive website (details in "Works Cited").
14. Baker reads the poem as essentially concerned with the mother's "eventual separation from her child […]. While the speaker [poet] can offer the child access to the natural world, […] as the child grows he will enter a human, social world over which she has no control and in which she plays no part" (64–65).

Works Cited

Baker, Timothy L. "'An Orderly Rabble'": Plural Identities in *Jizzen'*. *Kathleen Jamie: Essays and Poems on Her Work*. Ed. Rachel Falconer. Edinburgh: Edinburgh University Press, 2014. 62–70. Print.

Baldick, Chris. *Oxford Dictionary of Literary Terms*, 3rd edition. Oxford: Oxford University Press, 2008. Print.

Crawford, Robert. *Talkies*. London: Chatto & Windus, 1992. Print.

Dante. *The Divine Comedy: Vol. 1. Inferno*. Trans. Mark Musa. Harmondsworth: Penguin, 1984. Print.

Dunn, Douglas. *Northlight*. London: Faber & Faber, 1988. Print.

——. 'Douglas Dunn: The SRB Interview'. *The Scottish Review of Books* 4:1 (2008): 16–18. Print.

Falconer, Rachel. 'Midlife Music: *The Overhaul* and *Frissure*'. *Kathleen Jamie: Essays and Poems on Her Work*. Ed. Rachel Falconer. Edinburgh: Edinburgh University Press, 2014. 156–67. Print.

Fraser, Bashabi. *From the Ganga to the Tay*. Edinburgh: Luath, 2009. Print.

Gairn, Louisa. '"Connective Leaps": *Sightlines* and *The Overhaul*'. *Kathleen Jamie: Essays and Poems on Her Work*. Ed. Rachel Falconer. Edinburgh: Edinburgh University Press, 2014. 134–45. Print.

Genette, Gérard. *The Architext: An Introduction*. Trans. Jane E. Lewin. Berkeley, Los Angeles, and Oxford: University of California Press, 1992. Print.

Glas, Alexander. *The River Tay: A Fragment*. Perth: R. Morison Junior, 1790. Print.

Herbert, W. N. 'Dunn and Dundee'. *Reading Douglas Dunn*. Ed. Robert Crawford and David Kinloch. Edinburgh: Edinburgh University Press, 1992. 122–37. Print.

Jamie, Kathleen. *Jizzen*. London: Picador, 1999. Print.

——. *Findings*. London: Sort of Books, 2005. Print.

——. *Sightlines*. London: Sort of Books, 2012. Print.

——. *The Overhaul*. London: Picador, 2012. Print.

——. '"The Tay Moses": Poem Introduction'. http://www.poetryarchive. org/poem/tay-moses. Web. 29 June 2016.

——. 'Glamourie'. http://www.scottishpoetrylibrary.org.uk/poetry/poems/ glamourie. Web. 8 February 2018.

Johnston, Arthur. 'Taodunum'. *Apollos of the North*. Trans. Robert Crawford. Edinburgh: Polygon, 2006. 94–95. Print.

Ludwig, Hans-Werner. 'Regional Identities in Contemporary British Poetry: North (and South)'. *Critical Dialogues: Current Issues in English Studies in Germany and Britain*. Ed. Isobel Armstrong. Tübingen: Narr, 1995. 188–208. Print.

Mergenthal, Silvia. '"You'll Twist Your Art on the Parochial Lie": Douglas Dunns Gedichtband *Northlight*'. *Literatur in Wissenschaft und Unterricht* 25:1 (1992): 53–68. Print.

O'Brien, Sean. *The Deregulated Muse: Essays on Contemporary British and Irish Poetry*. Newcastle upon Tyne: Bloodaxe, 1998. Print.

Prieto, Eric. 'Geocriticism Meets Ecocriticism: Bertrand Westphal and Environmental Thinking'. *Ecocriticism and Geocriticism: Overlapping Territories in Environmental and Spatial Literary Studies*. Ed. Robert T.

Tally Jr. and Christine M. Battista. Houndsmills, Basingstoke, and New York: Palgrave Macmillan, 2016. 19–35. Print.

Rouse, Margitta. *The Self's Grammar: Performing Poetic Identity in Douglas Dunn's Poetry 1969–2011*. Heidelberg: Universitätsverlag Winter, 2013. Print.

Shelley, Mary. *Frankenstein*. Ed. Johanna M. Smith. Boston, MA: Bedford Books of St Martin's Press, 1992. Print.

Simpson, Juliet. '"Sweet-Wild Weeks": Birth, Being and Belonging in *Jizzen*'. *Kathleen Jamie: Essays and Poems on Her Work*. Ed. Rachel Falconer. Edinburgh: Edinburgh University Press, 2014. 71–82. Print.

Westphal, Bertrand. *Geocriticism: Real and Imagined Spaces*. Trans. Robert T. Tally Jr. New York: Palgrave, 2011. Print.

———. 'Pour une approche géocritique des textes'. *SFLGC* (*Vox Poetica*). 30 September 2005. Web. 20 November 2015.

Derick Thomson's *An Rathad Cian* (*The Far Road*, 1970): Modern Gaelic Poetry of Place Between Introspection and Politics

Petra Johana Poncarová

Lucy Lippard defines a place as "a portion of land/town/cityscape seen from the inside, the resonance of a specific location that is known and familiar" and maintains that "places are entwined with personal memory, known or unknown histories, marks made in the land that provoke and evoke".[1] The inside perspective is essential. Poetry of place is then poetry written about these meaningful locations and also poetry where the place serves as a paradigm by means of which something else is discussed and interpreted. According to Christopher Tilley,

This work was supported by the European Regional Development Fund-Project "Creativity and Adaptability as Conditions of the Success of Europe in an Interrelated World" (No. CZ.02.1.01/0.0/0.0/16_019/0000734).

P. J. Poncarová (✉)
Department of Anglophone Literatures and Cultures,
Charles University, Prague, Czechia

© The Author(s) 2019   209
M. Szuba and J. Wolfreys (eds.), *The Poetics of Space and Place in Scottish Literature*, Geocriticism and Spatial Literary Studies,
https://doi.org/10.1007/978-3-030-12645-2_12

through an act of naming and through the development of human and mythological associations such places become invested with meaning and significance. Place names are of such vital significance because they act so as to transform the sheerly physical and geographical into something that is historically and socially experienced. The bestowing of names creates shared existential space out of a blank environment. [...] By the process of naming places and things they become captured in social discourses and act as mnemonics for the historical actions of individuals and groups.[2]

Human perception is essential in the creation of places. Places, in turn, also contribute to the creation and maintenance of human identity, both personal and collective, so the relationship, as Tilley points out, is reciprocal:

> The place acts dialectically so as to create the people who are of that place. These qualities of locales and landscapes give rise to a feeling of belonging and rootedness and a familiarity, which is not born just out of knowledge, but of concern that provides ontological security. They give rise to a power to act and a power to relate that is both liberating and productive. [...] Human activities become inscribed within a landscape such that every cliff, large tree, stream, swampy area becomes a familiar place. Daily passages through the landscape become biographic encounters for individuals, recalling traces of past activities and previous events and the reading of signs – a split log here, a marker stone there.[3]

They are important both for the creation and development of personal identity and for the functioning of society, they play an essential role in the construction and maintenance of private and public histories. As Edward Casey notes, it is the "stabilizing persistence of place as a container of experiences that contributes so powerfully to its intrinsic memorability. [...] We might even say that memory is naturally place-oriented or at least place-supported".[4]

However, in the modern world, the attachment to place has become problematised—Tim Cresswell writes about the "general condition of creeping placelessness marked by an inability to have authentic relationships to place" and about the widespread inability to become "existential insiders".[5] It seems that despite (or perhaps precisely because of) the "multicenteredness"[6] of the modern world where people move and travel extensively and do not become locally attached, the attraction of the local place, what Lippard calls "the lure of the local", seems to increase.[7]

This essay discusses poems by Derick Thomson that discuss places that already have been established, carve places out of space, and where the place serves as a cognitive paradigm, as a means of seeing and interpreting the world. More often than not, these places have names and can be located on the map. By incorporating places in his works, Thomson also contributed to the perpetuation of the place, to its performative becoming, and sometimes endowed it with an entirely new meaning. Place names, the results of this process, appear frequently in poems about places and present a number of interesting theoretical problems. As Alan Gillis suggests, regional places in Scottish and Irish poetry have two basic functions: "they can create an effect of verisimilitude, rooting a poem in the actual and making it concrete" and they become "a means of asserting the cultural and artistic validity of erstwhile marginalised places and traditions".[8] Both these aspects are at play in Thomson's writing.

Places occupy a conspicuous position in the Gaelic poetry from early on. The reasons of this propensity may include the unique natural, cultural and linguistic environment of the Highlands and Islands, and the historical, social and political circumstances which caused a great number of people from the Gàidhealtachd to leave their home behind, both forcibly and voluntarily, creating a powerful tragic attachment to places no longer available.

In traditional praise poetry addressed to the chieftain, the lord is frequently addressed in connection with the places he rules over, identifying the person with the territory.[9] In the eighteenth century, which is often perceived as the first golden age of Gaelic poetry, all three greatest Gaelic poets—Alexander MacDonald (Alasdair mac Mhaighstir Alasdair), William Ross (Uilleam Ros) and Duncan Bàn MacIntyre (Donnchadh Bàn Mac an t-Saoir), composed poems in praise of places, characterised by detailed observation and carefully wrought description. This deep interest in places was further stimulated and transformed by the turbulent history of the region in the eighteenth and nineteenth centuries, featuring massive migration from the Highlands and Islands to the lowland cities, emigration to America, Canada and Australia, and the Clearances. In the nineteenth century, the poetry of *cianalas*, longing for home, comes forward as a way of dealing with this experience.[10] Most of the great nineteenth-century poets, including Mary MacPherson (Màiri Mhòr nan Òran) and William Livingstone (Uilleam MacDhunlèibhe), wrote about places influenced by dislocation and the drastic social changes which affected the Gàidhealtachd in this period.

Places feature prominently also in modern Gaelic poetry, albeit in a rather different manner, as poets writing about places in the twentieth century turns mainly towards "the problems of identity and location".[11] The important difference between the traditional poetry and the so-called new poetry (*nua-bhàrdachd*) resides in both in tone, as the poetic subjects delve into explorations of their intimate feelings and memories and often discuss and ambiguous relationship to the place, while in most of the traditional verse where the poet was often speaking on behalf of the community, and in structure, for in contrast with the linear older poetry focused on description, the modern poetry is non-linear, fragmented and often more oblique and difficult to approach.[12]

Most of the great modern Gaelic poets, including Sorley MacLean (Somhairle MacGill-Eain), George Campbell Hay (Deòrsa Mac Iain Dheòrsa), Ian Crichton Smith (Iain Mac a' Ghobhainn) and Donald MacAulay (Dòmhnall MacAmhlaigh), engaged with places in their writing. The last of the so-called "great five", Derick Thomson (Ruaraidh MacThòmais), was extensively preoccupied with his native island, Lewis, especially in his first three collections, and this ambiguous, obsessive relationship to Lewis is one of the chief themes Thomson gets associated with. As Michel Byrne puts it, "no other Gaelic poet has explored the theme in such depth or developed such an extensive poetic vocabulary for treating it without resorting to cliché".[13] It is not so well-known that in his later collections, Thomson also devoted a great deal of attention to Glasgow and is acknowledged as one of the most important Scottish poets of this city in the twentieth century.

Derick Thomson (1921–2012) was one of the most universal personalities of the Gaelic world in the twentieth century as a university lecturer, scholar, translator and "the father of modern Gaelic publishing".[14] He also contributed to modern Gaelic literature a total of seven poetry collections: the first one, *An Dealbh Briste*, was published in 1951; the last one, *Sùil air Fàire*, appeared in 2007. Most of the numerous activities he undertook during his long and productive life were aimed at the preservation and promotion of Gaelic as a viable, versatile language.

Born in Lewis but "educated out of the island" and spending most of his life in Glasgow, Thomson was, in MacAulay's words, one of the poets "who have been transplanted out of their native communities into the ubiquitous outside world" and have thus "become bicultural and it is this situation, a notoriously uneasy one, which creates the tension from which a great deal of their poetry derives".[15] Undoubtedly, many of Thomson's poems arise from precisely this tension between the years he spent on the island, surrounded by Gaelic and what was at that time still a rather traditional community, and the subsequent experiences of living in a city where immigration and popular culture had started to challenge the older notions of Scottish identity.

The large and varied body of Thomson's poems about places may be seen as advancing in three general directions. The first would include the psychological explorations of childhood memories of Lewis and the effects of leaving the island. The second group could be defined as revolving around Glasgow, while the third would comprise poems engaging with the political issues of Lewis, of the Gàidhealtachd and of Scotland as a whole, through the paradigm of place. This essay focuses on Thomson's third poetry collection, *An Rathad Cian* (The Far Road), which appeared in 1970 and is devoted entirely to Lewis.

The dedication introduces the book "mar thiodhlag do eilean m' àra-ich, Leòdhas" (as an offering to the island of my upbringing, Lewis).[16] The book contains fifty-six poems exploring different aspects of the island, its landscape, history and people. The local rootedness of the collection is also manifested in the language, for Gaelic has a very fine shading of local accents and dialects, delineating not only islands but even villages, and the colouring in terms of recognisably Lewis Gaelic is fairly strong in the collection.[17] Thomson pointed out that at the time when the collection emerged, in the 1960s, he was realising that despite Lewis being central to his experience, he was unlikely to return to it in the physical sense.[18] The collection comes across as an attempt to sum up all the aspects of Lewis and of the poet's relationship to it, so that it could be moved aside and become one concern among others, not an overwhelming obsession. *An Rathad Cian* is a moving, delicate exorcism of a deep-seated love for one's native place.

The opening poem, "An Uilebheist" (The Monster) and the final one, "An Ceann Thall" (The Far Side) frame the collection as a conversation with the island. The attempted dialogue—for the speaker does not get any answer form the island—and the address are two prevailing modes of the sequence. As Whyte notes, "there is a sense in which Lewis stands behind all the poems in the sequence as their ultimate referent or tenor, while different aspects of the island's history and geography also function as vehicles for individual items", so that the island Thomson comes from can be signifier and signified at one and the same time.[19] This obsessive unity, combined with an astonishing variety of imagery, tone and point of view, make *An Rathad Cian* such an original, haunting sequence and one of Thomson's major achievements.

"An Uilebheist" sets up three essential characteristics of the whole sequence: its religious dimension, the ambiguous relationship to the island and the therapeutic function of the collection:

Ag èirigh à muir uaine
[...]
o uilebheist mo dhomhain,
tha mi tighinn thugad le m' adhradh,
le mo shùilean prabach, leis a' chainnt
a dh'ionnsaich mi aig d' altair

As you rise from the green sea
[...]
o monster of my world,
I come to you in worship,
with red-rimmed eyes, a language
learnt at your altar[20]

The direct, intimate address to the place and the word "uilebheist" is, rather unusually,[21] treated as feminine in terms of grammatical gender, so it might suggest that the island becomes a feminine entity—later in the collection, it is indeed addressed as a mother and a lover. Lewis is thus first invoked as a monster[22] arising from the sea, which is a fitting image for an island, especially given the dark brown colour of Lewis, but it also reveals the speaker's ambiguous emotions: the island is at once terrifying and captivating. Indeed, from the opening poem, the island emerges as an all-pervasive influence, the language of the poem is that which the speaker learnt at the monster's altar, the words are consecrated to its service. Yet the words consecrated to the monster's service are not going to be ones of easy praise, as the rest of the poem makes clear:

leis a' mheirg air mo bhilean,
leis a' ruithleum, leis a' bhàs
a dh'fhuiling mi air do sgàth,
leis a' bhrèig, leis an taise,
[...]
leis an fhuidheall dhe mo ghràdh dhut.

the rust on my lips,
the élan, the death
I suffered for your sake,
the lies, the sentiment,
[...]
remnant of my regard for you.

The conflicted relationship to the place is proclaimed at the very beginning. In the list of items, the speaker acquired from the island/monster and which he brings to its shrine, one finds gifts and blessings, but also restrictions, injuries and deceit. "An fhuidheall dhe mo ghràdh dhut" (remnant of my regard for you) indicates the uneasiness, the gradual sobering up and tearing the ties of the obsessive concern; the relationship with Lewis is, in accordance with the author's comments, portrayed as a love affair. But the remnant of the regard is still powerful enough to fuel the fifty-six poems of the collection, which are passionate, tender and sometimes bitterly critical, but never indifferent.

In the next poem, "Na Freiceadain" (The Watchmen), the perspective zooms in from the island viewed as arising in the distance and offers a closer view of the individual landmarks of the Lewis landscape. The speaker names several specific places in Lewis which are "'nam freiceadain nuair thilleas m' anam" (the watchmen when my soul returns).[23] As the poet points out, Chicken Head (Aird Chirc) and Kirk Head (Rubha na Circe) are one and the same—the Norse name, referring to a church, became misinterpreted in Gaelic (*cearc*, gen. *circe*—Gaelic for "hen"). Bayble is a Norse name, containing the Norse word for "monk".[24] The place names thus conjure images for the one who is able to read their semantics: the name Bayble brings to the speaker's mind an image of priests singing a mass in Latin, cheekily reminding the sternly Presbyterian Lewis of its forgotten Catholic past.[25]

In poem 4, "Leannan M' Òige" (Sweetheart of My Youth), the moorland-covered island is personified as a girl with "cuailean donn" (brown hair) and "sùilean dorcha" (dark eyes) and its landscape with mounds and hollows becomes a body of a woman, of a lover the speaker has fallen away from.[26] He looks back on those features of "her" he did not know and feel, so the remembering of the place becomes intensely physical and intimate. The image of the island/lover reappears in poem 9, "Chaill Mi Mo Chridhe Riut" (I Lost My Heart to You). This time, the erotic meanings are displayed in full. The movement of the seasons and the changes of the place are paralleled with the progression of a relationship, from the promises of spring to the disillusion and loss of autumn.

Personification of the island recurs in poem 7, "Dh'fhairich Mi Thu le Mo Chasan" (I Got the Feel of You with my Feet), but this time, Lewis appears as a mother allowing a child to find peace and security. The poem moves between the island past and the city present. The difference in lifestyle, environment and age is summed up in the memory of going barefoot: "Dh'fhairich mi thu le mo chasan / ann an toiseach an t-samhraidh; / m' inntinn an seo anns a' bhaile / a' strì ri tuigse, 's na brògan a' tighinn eadarainn" (I got the feel of you with my feet, / in early summer; / my mind here in the city / strives to know, but the shoes come between us).[27] In this poem, the possible reconciliation with the place is hinted at:

is bhon a tha an saoghal a bh' againn	*and since the world we knew*
a leantainn ruinn chon a' cheum as fhaide	*follows us as far as we go*
chan fhiach dhomh am poll sin a ghlanadh	*I need not wash away that mud*
tha eadar òrdagan a' bhalaich.	*from between the boy's toes.*

There is no need to "wash away the mud": to forget the island childhood is impossible and the memories can moreover provide warmth, even when the speaker has grown up and left the place. A similar image appears in poem 34 "Na Canadh Duine" (Let No One Say) where the island again assumes the guise of a mother. The relationship between the speaker and the island is imagined as a cord through which he still receives sustenance, so the bond has not been torn altogether and can still provide nourishment. The bond here becomes much less oppressive and the poem expresses the idea that it is not beneficial to be breaking the cords. The fact that something which might be a resolution of the conflicting relationship occurs very early in the collection (the seventh poem out of fifty-six) points to the non-linear structure of the sequence: *An Rathad Cian* does not present a story of gradual abandonment, of finding a solution. It is tied together by repetitions and motifs that are picked up across the fifty-six poems. This tidal movement of coming closer and withdrawing, praise and critique, love and hate, obsession and disillusionment, allows the speaker, in the end, to leave the monster's temple.

The sequence contains a number of personal poems which inspect the effects of the island and its voluntary abandonment. Poem 50, "Nuair a Thilleas Mi" (When I Come Back), discusses the disillusionment connected with an imagined return to the island. The first stanza presents an idyllic picture—the potato flowers blooming, bees humming, cows lowing to milking. Yet, in the second and third stanzas, coldness creeps in and the voice of the cuckoo is heard wailing, probably as a symbol of the passing years and sorrow. When the speaker awakes in the last stanza after a night spent on the island, the illusion is broken—"bidh 'n fhàinne sgealbt' / is a' bhò gun bhainn' aice, / 's an t-eilean riabhach mar bu chiad aithne dhomh" (the ring will be shattered / and the cow dry / and the dark-brown island as I first knew it).[28] In "Reangan an Eathair" (The Ribs of the Boat), the past is symbolised by a decaying boat and although the speaker is advised by a local woman to let the boat alone, he confesses his fear of what the effect of such a radical step may be: "tha eagal orm / lasair o m' eanchainn a chur ris an t-seann chrannlach ud"

(I am afraid / to set a torch from my brain to that old timber).[29] "Am Mac-stròdhail a' Bruidhinn ri Tìr a Bhreith agus Àraich" (The Prodigal Son Speaking to the Land of His Birth and Upbringing.) presents leaving the island as the choice of a prodigal son, yet the moral is not clear: the speaker refuses to return (and does not want to have his portion of salted meat sent to Glasgow) and acknowledges that it is equally possible that his choice could have been right or wrong.

""Bùrn is Mòine's Coirc"" ("Water and Peat and Oats"), poem 6, for the first time introduces the city as a counterpoint to the island, as a place where the remembering of Lewis takes place. The overheard words of a stranger, "water, peat and oats", represent some of the most essential daily realities of island life and instantly trigger old memories. This automatic reaction of the speaker, that a few words suffice to transport him back to the place he left long ago, appears to him as "boile" (madness): "an cridhe gòrach / a' falpanaich mu na seann stallachan ud / mar nach robh slighe-cuain ann / ach i" (the foolish heart, / lapping along these ancient rocks / as though there were no sea-journey in the world / but that one).[30] His own attachment to the place seems extreme to him, yet he cannot help the spontaneous reaction of his emotions: for his heart, there is still no sea journey in the world but the one leading to Lewis. At the end of the short poem, Thomson uses a very specific, very physical and local image and plain, everyday words that would have been common in the village to communicate the painful attachment. The heart is tied to a tethering post,[31] "car ma char aig an fheist / 's i fàs goirid" (round upon round of the rope / till it grows short), and the mind is free, yet its freedom has been achieved at a great cost: "is daor a cheannaich mi a saorsa" (I bought its freedom dearly). The dearly bought freedom suggests that bicultural Gaelic intellectuals may have considered the prize they had to pay for education and living outside the Gàidhealtachd to be very high, perhaps too high.

The juxtaposition of the city and the island appears again and more pronouncedly in "An Glaschu" (In Glasgow). The speaker walks the Glasgow streets in the evening, "anns an t-saoghal ùr" (in the new world) and seems to be rather excited about his situation.[32] However, someone asks him: "Eil fada bho nach d'fhuair sibh bhon taigh?" ("Is it long since you heard from home?") and immediately, the question provokes a surge of memories. Suddenly, Glasgow is not the exciting new world, but a place of exile and the tie with the island is painful and able to destabilise the speaker's contented existence in the city. The following

poem, ""Bheil Cuimhn' Agad...?"" ("Do You Remember...?"), develops
the same theme. The speaker is reminded of peat-cutting back home by a
friend or relative, and is once more, against his will, brought back:

'Na mo chuis-bhùirt ann am meadhon Ghlaschu,	*Making an ass of myself in the middle of Glasgow,*
[...]	*[...]*
'na mo shuidh air prugan a' toirt riamhaichean calcais às a chèile	*sitting on a tuft of moor-grass teasing out peat fibres*[33]

He feels the power the island exerts over him as uncomfortable. His
current position, far away from his Lewis childhood, is stressed by the
resolutely defined location in time and space: in the middle of Glasgow
(earlier on, Sauchiehall Street is mentioned), in the middle of Scotland,
in the middle of his life. Yet, the simple question drags him back to the
moorland, to his own embarrassment, and this shift is also emphasised
by the distinctly Lewis words related to the island's natural environment:
"prugan" and "riamhaichean calcais".

The theme of exile is not treated by Thomson only as a private situation through adopted personae, but as a situation of other Lewis people
and as a process which has been shaping the history of the island. "Na
Lochlannaich a' Tighinn air Tìr an Nis" (The Norsemen Coming Ashore
at Ness) presents an unusual view of the Scandinavian incomers to the
Western Isles and adds another important piece to the overall tapestry
of Lewis which *An Rathad Cian* unfolds: the Scandinavian influence on
the Gaelic world which is so strong especially in Lewis, in place names
and also in the local dialect of Gaelic. In this poem, just as in many later
ones,[34] Thomson provides parallels with the Gaelic situation. This time,
it is not the Gaels who come ashore to settle in a new strange land, an
image abundant in the emigration song, but the Norsemen. Apart from
disrupting the stereotypical image of the Scandinavian incomers as plun-
derers by presenting them as people who were afraid and later settled
down as farmers, Thomson also, contrary to many a song and poem of
the Gaelic tradition, suggests that people can get used to their new environment and be content with it—that the homesickness will go away
after some time ("agus dh'fhalbh an cianalas").[35] As the poet himself
explained, he used the image of the Norsemen to show that the "displaced person goes through various experiences, and if he is realistic,
[he] realises at the end of the day that he is going to settle down, too,
he's going to make a life where he is now, to acclimatise".[36] Poem 17,

"Air Mòinteach Shuardail" (On Swordale Moor), also comments on exile and settling down: a man who had moved from Lewis to live in Chile has returned to the island again and now walks the moor in the Point of Lewis, recalls the pampas and the forests, and speaks to his dog in Spanish. It is not only Lewis that is missed: there are people in Lewis longing for other places.

An Rathad Cian is a deeply personal and introspective collection, but in its all-pervasive concern with the island it also addresses some broadly political issues, especially the impact of religion on the local life and the social and economic situation in Lewis.

One of Thomson's main objections was that the evangelical churches often strove to suppress the traditional folk culture and in consequence weakened language: "The evangelical religion arrived somewhat late in Lewis, but we have accounts from the third and fourth decades of the nineteenth century of evangelical ministers stamping as hard as they could on local culture".[37] This point of view is expressed most strongly in "Am Bodach-ròcais" (The Scarecrow), which describes a situation when a black man, i.e. an evangelical minister or preacher, arrives to a ceilidh house where people are sitting round the fire and engage in traditional community amusements. The image of the minister draws on a tradition of portraying the representatives of evangelical churches in the Highlands as sinister ominous dark figures opposed to joy of any sort.[38]

The poem has an almost filmic quality to it or it could very easily serve as a subject for a painting: the moment the black figure enters the cosy house, everything freezes, cards fall down and the chatter dies out. In spite of the derogatory title of the scarecrow, the man's presence is powerful and transformative—the music loses its goodness, all the activities cease. The black man is also giving, not only taking away, yet the gifts are destructive:

thug e òran nuadh dhuinn,	*he gave us a new song,*
[...]	*[...]*
is sprùilleach de dh'fheallsanachd Geneva,	*and fragments of philosophy from Geneva,*
is sguab e 'n teine à meadhon an làir	*and he swept the fire from the centre*
's chuir e 'n tùrlach loisgeach nar broillichean.	*of the floor*
	and set a searing bonfire in our breast.

The strength of the poem lies in the striking visual image it conveys and also in the ironic correlations between the traditional folk culture and the imported culture of evangelic Christianity: the richness of Gaelic songs is replaced by a new song, which is an echo of Psalm 40,[39] the tales of ancient kings and heroes by Biblical stories, and the community and its solidarity by fragments of Calvinist philosophy. The word "sprùilleach", i.e. crumbs, fragments or refuse, indicates that what the scarecrow brings is not even a proper philosophical system which would replace the traditional mindset but debris which could have been twisted and misinterpreted on the way.

The final image of the change from the homely fire in the middle of the ceilidh house which drew the people together and provided light and warmth for the assembled community to the individual searing bonfires of fear of damnation in the breast of each individual, a divisive flame of fanaticism, is an especially powerful one. The bonfire could also associate the widespread image of a fire used for burning musical instruments by converts seized by the evangelical zeal.[40]

The poem "Is Dubh a Choisich Thu Latha" (Black You Walked Through the Day) addresses Lewis in the guise of a pious woman mourning the deaths of local men returning from World War I who drowned within the sight of home when HMS *An Iolaire* was wrecked on the Beasts of Holm on 1 January 1919. The title refers to the traditional song "Is Dubh a Choisich mi 'n Oidhche", a lament in which a man tells of coming to see the girl he loved, only to find that she is dead, and he pleads with God to prevent him from going mad with grief. There is recording of Thomson's own rendition of the song, so the echo is surely intentional.[41] The disaster had a profound effect on the community, as it killed a substantial part of the male population in some areas and also presented a great challenge to the ideas of Calvinist theology: "Is thubairt thu gur h-e toil Dhè a bh' ann / gun deach am bàta sin air na Biastan, / a' dìochuimhneachadh na chual' thu às a' chùbainn: / gun robh Abharsair nan iomadh riochd a sàs unnad" (And you said it was God's will / that the ship went on the Beasts, / forgetting what you heard from the pulpit: / that the Adversary of many guises was working on you).[42] The woman might interpret the terrible ironical and useless deaths of men who survived the world war as God's decision, but this could, according to the speaker, actually be devil's talk.

A more humorous and tongue-in-cheek take on the island's religion is presented in the poem "A' Cluich air Football le Fàidh" (Playing Football with a Prophet). The poem begins with the speaker's statement that when one has ever played football with a prophet, it is an unforgettable experience. The surprising discovery that there are prophets in other churches than the established one (even among the Catholic clergy!) and in other places in Lewis is a satirical hint to the sectarian strains in Highland religion and also to the rivalry between the individual islands.

<table>
<tr><td>agus beag air bheag thuig mi</td><td>*And bit by bit I came to know*</td></tr>
<tr><td>nach robh tròcair an Tighearna air a'</td><td>*that the Lord's mercy is not confined*</td></tr>
<tr><td>cuingealachadh</td><td>*by creed or region,*</td></tr>
<tr><td>ri creud no ceàrnaidh</td><td>*or even language.*</td></tr>
<tr><td>no eadhon cànan.</td><td>*The greatest sin /*</td></tr>
<tr><td>'S e 'm peacadh as motha</td><td>*is to pile all of the Grace in your own*</td></tr>
<tr><td>a bhith càrnadh a' ghràis gu lèir 'na do</td><td>*creel.*</td></tr>
<tr><td>chliabh fhèin.</td><td></td></tr>
</table>

The final conviction about the unlimited range and reach of divine grace, expressed through particular and very day-to-day image of the creel, as if mercy came into the world in peat turfs, is at the same time amusing and poetically convincing. In spite of these critical comments, Thomson was not an anti-religious poet[43] and in some later poems, such as in "Àirc a' Choimhcheangail" (The Ark of the Covenant), he expresses a great deal of sympathy for the Lewis manifestations of Christianity—however, this sympathy seems to be directed mainly at the common believers, their strength and human dignity, never at the dogmas.

The sequence also contains several poems aimed at political and social issues in Lewis, with criticism is directed both to the outside, i.e. to the Scottish Lowlands and England, for their intrusions into the Gàidhealtachd and their exploitation of the area and lack of concern for its well-being, and also inside, at the Gaels themselves, for being unable to resist these pressures and for sinking into passivity.

Several of these poems address the withering of the Gaelic language and culture. The poem "Fàs is Taise" (High Summer) starts with the description of a peaceful scene in the countryside, everything in nature is moist and growing. After the lush opening comes the startling question "Cò chanadh gu bheil am baile seo ri uchd bàis?" (Who could guess this village is at death's door?) This death is a death of culture and language:

Tha nighean bheag, le sùilean sgèanach,	*A little girl, with frightened eyes,*
a' cluiche air tricycle.	*plays on a tricycle.*
Dh'fhalbh an liùdhag	*No rag-doll now –*
is thàinig an dolla à Hong Kong,	*plastic from Hong Kong –*
[...]	*[...]*
's bidh a' chreathail a' breothadh anns an	*and the cradle will rot in the new barn*
t-sabhal ùr le mullach zinc air.	*with its zinc roof.*

The words such as "tricycle" and "zinc" stand out of the poem, and Thomson pointed out that the old word for a doll, "liùdhag", is contrasted with the borrowed "doll", and the contrast is even starker as the doll is manufactured and imported, not home-made. The poem describes "the break-up of Gaelic tradition on the island, not the break-up of Lewis itself or Lewis society, but certainly of a Gaelic one".[44] The place can be lush and green and full of natural life, but the cradle, a symbol of new life and new generations, is rotting in a barn sealed with a new zinc roof. The criticism here is not directed at technological advancement such as zinc roofs, but on the suffocating and deadening effect of the rapid changes on the weakened Gaelic world.

Other poems, such as "Na Tràlairean" (The Trawlers), focus on economic issues. It starts with a plain statement that trawlers, boats which pull fishing nets behind them at the bottom of the sea, sweep the ground clean. Fishing with trawlers is naturally more effective than individual fishing boats which just cast nests, but can in consequence be damaging both to the sea environment and to the local economy. Again, there is the image of outside intrusions threatening the economy of the Gàidhealtachd and culture, for it is evident from Thomson's journalism he realised that there would be no cultural and linguistic revival without sound economy in the region. The speaker then ironically lists a number of local subjects which he would like the Secretary of State to consider, such as schools in Uig, a tweed-mill in Shawbost, or a seaweed factory in Keos, but which in implication is unlikely to happen. The poem ends in an ironic parody of the way the government and the development boards address the locals and try to hoodwink them into thinking they are not actually being robbed of their resources. The locals can get food enough from the trawlers, but other sources of sustenance they may require, such as local schools, are disregarded.

There are also several poems focusing on the poor and downtrodden of Lewis, such as "Murdag Mhòr" ("Mucka") and "Bha Do Shùilean

Ciùin" (Your Eyes Were Gentle, That Day). In the latter, the speaker addresses an old "every-woman" whom he imagines walking the roads of Russia and sitting on the banks of the Ganges.[45] By this address, although the literal reference is to China, Tibet and India, he commemorates some of the historical sins committed against the Gaelic people—the land machinations, contemptuous attitudes to the traditional culture, obliteration of language and the abandonment of the poor in their need during the eighteenth- and nineteenth-century evictions. In spite of its international scope, the poem ends with a distinct island image—the sins of the fathers are piled on the woman's back in a creel, as if they were slices of peat, with crumbs of grace falling through its apertures. When commenting on the poem, Thomson mentions that in the poem, he employed the figure of the "archetypal old woman", who is seen in Tibet, Russia, India or Scotland, who is contrasted with the representatives of imperialism who would seek to obliterate the language of the neighbouring community.[46] Camels which receive the Lord's inheritance while people are dying of consumption are intended as parallel to sheep in the Highlands at the time of the Clearances.[47]

These politically charged poems are not usually associated with *An Rathad Cian*—the sequence is famous mostly for poems discussing the different shades of internal and external exile, and those in which the spell of the native place is at the same time reinforced and overcome. However, they form an important layer of Thomson's portrayal of Lewis.

Last but not least, an essential part of the delineation of Lewis in the sequence is her people. Some of these poems are celebratory recollections of distinct personalities and their gifts, such as "Murchadh Moireasdan, 1872–" (Murdo Morrison, 1872–) or "Cotrìona Mhòr" (Catherine the Elder), a moving homage to the dignity and strength of a local lady who used to work as a cleaner in a school where Thomson's father taught. The collection also features several poems that do not fit into the main thematic groups outlined above, such as "Stèidhichean Làidir" (meaning literally "strong foundations" but titled simply "Lewis" in the poet's own translation) which is one of the more traditional celebratory poems, praising the strength and beauty of the island.

As has been mentioned already, the resolution, perhaps even mutual absolution between the place and the speaker, is woven into the sequence, so it does not appear as a surprise at the end. Poem 47, "Tachais an t-Slànachaidh" (The Healing Itch), depicts the absence from the island as a physical wound, as a healing itch in the speaker's heart. The wound has stopped leaking, the speaker has removed "plàsd nam bliannachan" (the plaster of many years' standing) and is ready to resume his life's journey.[48] However, just before the end of the collection, two poems present the relationship to Lewis as inescapable. In "Ged a Thillinn A-nis" (Though I Were to Go Back Now), the speaker confirms that has realised some unpleasant truths about the place, but still is not able to resist looking back at it: "Thàinig firinn thugam / mu innis na firinn; / chuimhnich mi air Bean Lot, / 's an dèidh sin, an dèidh sin, / tha mi gu bhith 'na mo charragh-cuimhne" (A truth came to me / about the righteous isle; / I remembered Lot's wife, / and yet, and yet, / I am going to be a memorial-pillar).[49] The dangerous glance back is again emphasised in poem 54, "Mo Chùl ri Mo Cheann-uidhe" (My Back Turned to My Destination), in which he is not facing the direction his life is moving in and is therefore unable to control its course, as he remains hypnotised by the past. However, the next poem is entitled "An Eileatrom" (The Bier) and it mentions the well-known places in Lewis, Mùirneag, Barvas hills and Hòl, as clothed in a shroud. The speaker grasps the bier-poles and embarks on a funeral procession which will see his obsessive love for Lewis laid to rest. In "An Ceann Thall", he emerges from the monster's temple, ready to move on, albeit still carrying a deep emotional wound:

thàinig mi mach às do theampall,	*I have come out of your temple,*
[...]	*[...]*
le mo bilean loisgte,	*with my lips burnt,*
le mo dhrùis coisgte,	*with my lust abated,*
[...]	*[...]*
is thriall mi maille	*and gone on my way*
ris a' chridh a chailleadh.	*with the heart I have lost.*[50]

Indeed, in the following collections, Lewis does not loom as large, although it continues to be present to the very end of Thomson's career as a poet. It becomes one theme among others, not a monster of the poet's world. *An Rathad Cian* remains one of the most remarkable and original twentieth-century contributions to the Gaelic poetry of place, deftly combining echoes of the tradition with modern introspective lyric, comments on history and sociology, humour with wrenching farewell to a lost world.

NOTES

1. Lucy Lippard, *The Lure of the Local: Sense of Place in a Multicentered Society* (New York: The New Press, 1997), 7.
2. Christopher Tilley, *A Phenomenology of Landscape: Places, Paths and Monuments* (Oxford: Berg, 1994), 18.
3. Tilley, 26.
4. Edward Casey, *Remembering: A Phenomenological Study* (Bloomington: Indiana University Press, 1987), 186–87, quoted in Cresswell, 86.
5. Tim Cresswell, *Place: A Short Introduction* (Oxford: Blackwell Publishing, 2004), 44.
6. Lippard, 5.
7. Lippard, 7.
8. Alan Gillis, 'Names for Nameless Things: The Poetics of Place Names', in *Modern Irish and Scottish Poetry*, ed. Peter Mackay, Edna Longley, and Fran Brearton (Cambridge: Cambridge University Press, 2011), 204.
9. John MacInnes, 'The Panegyric Code in Gaelic Poetry', in *Dùthchas nan Gàidheal: Collected Essays of John MacInnes*, ed. Michael Newton (Edinburgh: Birlinn, 2006), 277.
10. "In the Highlands and Islands, the natural landscape had been blighted by clearance and social change, and could not be accepted at face value any longer. Poets who celebrated their homelands (an increasingly dominant theme among the exiles) tended to look back longingly to a pre-clearance ideal when the natural rhythms of the community were positive and inclusive. The re-imagined homeland thus came to incorporate, or indeed to represent, a set of emotional and moral values which provided a new focus for eulogy, and also a potent stimulus for political activism by the last quarter of the century". Donald E. Meek, ed., 'Introduction', in *Caran An-t-Saoghail / The Wiles of the World: An Anthology of Nineteenth Century Gaelic Verse* (Edinburgh: Birlinn, 2003), xxxiii.
11. Donald MacAulay, 'Introduction', in *Nua-bhàrdachd Ghàidhlig / Modern Scottish Gaelic Poems*, ed. Donald MacAulay (Edinburgh: Canongate Books, 1995), 49–50.
12. Derick Thomson, *An Introduction to Gaelic Poetry* (Edinburgh: Edinburgh University Press, 1989), 279.
13. Michel Byrne, 'Monsters and Goddesses: Culture Re-energised in the Poetry of Ruaraidh MacThòmais and Aonghas MacNeacail', in *The Edinburgh History of Scottish Literature, Vol. 3. Modern Transformations: New Identities*, gen. ed. Ian Brown (Edinburgh: Edinburgh University Press, 2007), 178–79.
14. Ronald Black, ed., 'Introduction', in *An Tuil: Anthology of 20th Century Scottish Gaelic Verse* (Edinburgh: Polygon, 1999), xl.

15. MacAulay, 'Introduction', 47–48.
16. Derick Thomson, 'Dedication', in *An Rathad Cian* (Glasgow: Gairm, 1970), page not numbered. The other dedicatee is the poet's deceased mother and, as Thomson mentions in the interview with Whyte, the death of his mother was an important impulse for the creation of *An Rathad Cian*. The maternal and funeral imagery is very prominent in the collection.
17. Christopher Whyte, 'Interviews with Ruaraidh MacThòmais', in *Glaschu: Baile Mòr nan Gàidheal*, ed. Sheila Kidd (Glasgow: Roinn na Ceiltis, Oilthigh Ghlaschu, 2001), 253. Thomson for example mentions that while he grew up speaking Bayble Gaelic, his mother retained the Gaelic of her native Ceòs.
18. Whyte, 'Interviews with Ruaraidh MacThòmais', 242.
19. Christopher Whyte, 'Derick Thomson: The Recent Poetry', *Aiste* 1 (2007), 27.
20. Derick Thomson, *Creachadh na Clàrsaich* (Edinburgh: Macdonald, 1982), 126–27.
21. As far as Gaelic dictionaries are concerned, both Edward Dwelly and Colin Mark list "uilebheist" as a solely masculine noun, Angus Watson includes both possibilities.
22. As D. A. MacDonald makes an interesting point in his review of *An Rathad Cian* when he says that Lewis becomes the speaker's "Midgardsormr, his world-encircling monster". 'Review of *An Rathad Cian*', *Scottish Gaelic Studies* XII (September 1971): 133.
23. *Creachadh na Clàrsaich*, 126–27.
24. Whyte, 'Interviews with Ruaraidh MacThòmais', 249.
25. Whyte asked Thomson in the interview: "Did you have fun bringing specifically Catholic references into a Lewis poem?" Thomson answered: "I think that is the truth of the matter. But this has again an etymological significance, because Bayble, a Norse name, is thought to mean 'priest's dwelling', 'papa', so it is an easy move to *sagart* from that. It gave me great pleasure to call the Free Kirkers and what-not of Bayble *sagart*" (249).
26. *Creachadh na Clàrsaich*, 128–29.
27. *Creachadh na Clàrsaich*, 130–31.
28. *Creachadh na Clàrsaich*, 170–71.
29. *Creachadh na Clàrsaich*, 148–49.
30. *Creachadh na Clàrsaich*, 130–31.
31. The image of being tethered can be traced back to the poem "Sgòthan" from *Eadar Samhradh is Foghar*.

32. *Creachadh na Clàrsaich*, 154–55.
33. *Creachadh na Clàrsaich*, 156–57.
34. For example, "Feòrag Ghlas, tuath air Braco" (Grey Squirrel, North of Braco) from *Meall Garbh*.
35. *Creachadh na Clàrsaich*, 160–61.
36. Whyte, 'Interviews with Ruaraidh MacThòmais', 290.
37. Thomson, *Taking You Home*, 97.
38. For a discussion of this image, see Donald Meek, 'Saints and Scarecrows: The Churches and Gaelic Culture in the Highlands Since 1560', *Scottish Bulletin of Evangelical Theology* 14 (1996): 3–22.
39. 'Is òran nuadh do chuir am bheul', *The Gaelic Psalms 1694* (Lochgilphead: James M. S. Annan, 1934), 68. I realised this reference thanks to Meek, 'Saints and Scarecrows', 5.
40. For a discussion of this image, see Meek, 'Saints and Scarecrows', 18.
41. Recording nr. 21229, *Tobar an Dualchais*, http://www.tobarandualchais.co.uk/en/fullrecord/21229/1, 20 October 2016.
42. *Creachadh na Clàrsaich*, 136–37.
43. "I remember as a teenager, probably as a fairly young teenager, becoming sceptical of religious attitudes, particularly of the narrower religious attitudes. In a place like Lewis, where you have several Presbyterian sects, some are particularly narrow, almost vicious, and that aspect of things struck me as preposterous at a fairly early age. [...] By my middle teens I was aware that religion was a wide-embracing thing, was a catholic thing if you like, with a small 'c'". Whyte, 'Interviews with Ruaraidh MacThòmais', 247.
44. Whyte, 'Interviews with Ruaraidh MacThòmais', 279.
45. Thomson mentions he developed a great interest in Tibet and India, and the challenge of the Everest when at Aberdeen. 'A Man Reared in Lewis', in *As I Remember: Ten Scottish Authors Recall How Writing Began for Them*, ed. Maurice Lindsay (London: Robert Hale, 1979), 137.
46. Whyte, 'Interviews with Ruaraidh MacThòmais', 265.
47. The strange aspect of the poem is the inclusion of China and the reference to the obliteration of China's language (which one?), overlooking the Chinese occupation of Tibet and the brutal attempts to obliterate the local culture and traditions. Logically, China should have been included in the imperial camp.
48. *Creachadh na Clàrsaich*, 166–67.
49. *Creachadh na Clàrsaich*, 172–73.
50. *Creachadh na Clàrsaich*, 174–75.

WORKS CITED

DERICK THOMSON'S POETRY COLLECTIONS

An Dealbh Briste. Edinburgh: Serif Books, 1951.
An Rathad Cian. Glasgow: Gairm, 1970.
Creachadh na Clàrsaich. Edinburgh: Macdonald, 1982.
Eadar Samhradh Is Foghar. Glasgow: Gairm, 1967.
Meall Garbh / The Rugged Mountain. Glasgow: Gairm, 1995.
Saorsa agus an Iolaire. Glasgow: Gairm, 1977.
Sùil air Fàire/ Surveying the Horizon. Stornoway: Acair, 2007.
Smeur an Dòchais / Bramble of Hope. Edinburgh: Canongate, 1991.

SECONDARY SOURCES

Byrne, Michel. 'Monsters and Goddesses: Culture Re-energised in the Poetry of Ruaraidh MacThòmais and Aonghas MacNeacail'. *The Edinburgh History of Scottish Literature, Vol. 3. Modern Transformations: New Identities.* Ed. Ian Brown. Edinburgh: Edinburgh University Press, 2007.

Cresswell, Tim. *Place: A Short Introduction.* Oxford: Blackwell Publishing, 2004.

Dwelly, Edward. *The Illustrated Gaelic-English Dictionary.* Glasgow: Gairm, 1993.

Gillis, Alan. 'Names for Nameless Things: The Poetics of Place Names'. *Modern Irish and Scottish Poetry.* Ed. Peter Mackay, Edna Longley, and Fran Brearton. Cambridge: Cambridge University Press, 2011.

Lippard, Lucy. *The Lure of the Local: Sense of Place in a Multicentered Society.* New York: The New Press, 1997.

MacAulay, Donald. 'Introduction'. *Nua-bhàrdachd Ghàidhlig / Modern Scottish Gaelic Poems.* Edinburgh: Canongate Books, 1995.

MacDonald, D. A. 'Review of *An Rathad Cian*'. *Scottish Gaelic Studies* XII (September 1971).

MacInnes, John. *Dùthchas nan Gàidheal. Collected Essays of Dr John MacInnes.* Ed. Michael Newton. Dùn Èideann: Birlinn, 2006.

Mark, Colin. *The Gaelic-English Dictionary.* London: Routledge, 2003.

Meek, Donald E., ed. *Caran An-t-Saoghail / The Wiles of the World: An Anthology of Nineteenth Century Gaelic Verse.* Edinburgh: Birlinn, 2003.

Meek, Donald E. 'Saints and Scarecrows: The Churches and Gaelic Culture in the Highlands Since 1560'. *Scottish Bulletin of Evangelical Theology* 14 (1996): 3–22.

Smith, Iain Crichton. 'Review of *An Rathad Cian*'. *Lines Review* 36 (March 1971).

The Gaelic Psalms 1694. Lochgilphead: James M. S. Annan, 1934.

Thomson, Derick S. 'A Man Reared in Lewis'. *As I Remember: Ten Scottish Authors Recall How Writing Began for Them*. Ed. Maurice Lindsay. London: Robert Hale, 1979.

―――. *An Introduction to Gaelic Poetry*. Edinburgh: Edinburgh University Press, 1989.

―――. *Taking You Home: Poems and Conversations*. Ed. Iain Crichton Smith and Andrew Mitchell. Argyll: Argyll Publishing, 2006.

Tilley, Christopher. *A Phenomenology of Landscape: Places, Paths and Monuments*. Oxford: Berg, 1994.

Watson, Angus. *The Essential English-Gaelic Dictionary*. Edinburgh: Birlinn, 2005.

Whyte, Christopher. 'Derick Thomson: The Recent Poetry'. *Aiste* 1 (2007).

―――. 'Interviews with Ruaraidh MacThòmais'. *Glasgow: Baile Mòr nan Gàidheal / City of the Gaels*. Ed. Sheila M. Kidd. Glasgow: Roinn na Ceiltis, Oilthigh Ghlaschu, 2007.

Glaswegian and Dundonian: *Twa Mither Tongues* Representing the Place and Space of Tom Leonard and Mark Thomson

Aniela Korzeniowska

Glasgow-born Tom Leonard and Mark Thomson from Dundee are two contemporary Scottish poets inextricably linked through the use and promotion of their *mither tongues* with the places—and spaces— they come from. It is through their poems, written, respectively, in Glaswegian and Dundonian, that we can see the significance of their writing for Scottish poetry today and for bringing to the foreground the very essence of where their origins lie.

It is thanks to a small selection of their works, in particular Tom Leonard's groundbreaking series of poems 'Six Glasgow Poems' and 'Unrelated Incidents', as well as the poem 'right inuff' from 'Ghostie Men', which can be found in his *Intimate Voices. Selected Work 1965–1983* (1995), and Mark Thomson's 'Mind Yir Lang-Widge', 'Thi Language Barrier', and 'Thi Mither Tongue' from his debut collection *Bard fae thi building site* (2007) that we can see how very significant these individual voices are when highlighting what is part and parcel of not only the owners of those working-class voices, but also when

A. Korzeniowska (✉)
University of Warsaw, Warszawa, Poland

© The Author(s) 2019   231
M. Szuba and J. Wolfreys (eds.), *The Poetics of Space and Place in Scottish Literature*, Geocriticism and Spatial Literary Studies,
https://doi.org/10.1007/978-3-030-12645-2_13

representing large groups of people who make up and identify with one large city on the west coast of Scotland and another, somewhat smaller one, on the east coast of the country.

Tom Leonard was born in 1944 into a Glasgow working-class Catholic family, his father being an Irishman from Dublin and his mother from Ayrshire, albeit of Irish lineage. He is one of Glasgow's best known poets, also highly influential among the city's critics and writers. What put Leonard initially onto the literary map of Glasgow, Scotland and the UK generally was his use of the Glasgow vernacular in his poetry, his interest in and concern with language, also as a representation of identity. This led him to highlight the position of dialect and different language varieties contra the standard form obligatory in education, which of course has its reflection in the majority of societies, not only Scottish. This in turn was closely connected with his politics generally, his long-lasting concern with education, especially that of Scotland, as well as with power and class.[1]

It goes without saying that Leonard was not the first to use a local vernacular in literary works, whether prose or poetry. He was not even the first in Glasgow (here, we cannot forget about Ian Hamilton Finlay [1925–2006][2] or Stephen Mulrine [b. 1938])[3] but it was definitely Leonard who was to add intellectual horizons to this mode of writing. The philosophical and political issues he was to address were to be of primary importance not only to the writer himself, but also to the vernacular literary output coming from the city of Glasgow as a whole. What is also characteristic of Leonard's writing is his rendering of Glasgow speech forms in his own phonetic transcription, which does not follow any standard rules and which is also interspersed with words written according to the standard forms of English. The same system of notation can be observed in the written form of the younger poet's work, although the transcription here is according to Mark Thomson's Dundonian phonetics.

By the late 1960s, when Leonard's first published collection *Six Glasgow Poems* (1969) first appeared, illustrating his experimental use of the Glasgow vernacular, it could be seen that, on the one hand, it related to what Edwin Morgan had suggested in reference to moving on and beyond Hugh MacDiarmid's introduction of a recreated Lowland Scots—or *Lallans*—in the 1920s, or of what came to be known as synthetic Scots:[4] '[the] MacDiarmid "renascence" of a general synthetic Scots [...] can still be felt, and learned from [...] the move should now be towards the honesty of actual speech' (Morgan 1974, 178). On the other hand, Leonard's poetic voice illustrated in his verse was his own invention, albeit based on his authentic Glasgow voice.[5] It was used not only to subvert or replace English in accordance with his views concerning education and language, but initially also to mock 'the insularity', as Gerard Carruthers put it, of such people as MacDiarmid (67).[6] This is clearly visible in his 'poster-poem' 'Makars' Society' which contains one, but very telling, sentence: 'Grand' meetin' the nicht tae decide the spellin' o' this poster' (*Intimate Voices...*, 53). His irony addressed to the *makars* of the first half of the twentieth century and their inability to decide on a standard orthographic form for the language they wished to introduce to literary writing[7] is all too evident. However, it is also interesting to see how he represented the speech of his Glasgow community and why this form of expression was so important to him.

It has to be remembered that the urban dialects—or speech forms— in Scotland have always been accompanied by a certain stigma that is not perceived in connection with the different rural varieties of Scots. They are also strictly linked with the working classes which, in Glasgow, for example, started to form a linguistic variety characteristic only to them. Due to the Industrial Revolution of the late eighteenth and the nineteenth centuries, there was an influx of immigrants to Glasgow from other parts of Scotland, especially from the Highlands after the Clearances, from Ireland as a result of the potato famine, and then, somewhat later, from other European countries and the Commonwealth. This demographic explosion led to what McClure called 'the obliteration of the native dialects' (4) which in turn led to:

> the emergence of an urban patois differing in many respects from the original dialect of the area, in which the traditional vocabulary of agricultural life was superseded by a new and often inventive and colourful word-stock reflecting the habits and preoccupations of the urban proletariat. (*Language, Poetry and Nationhood*, 167)

In one of his essays, 'Literature, Dialogue, Democracy', Leonard speaks on the same subject, referring specifically to the complexity of locality and national culture, in the following manner:

> It was not a simple matter of locality and national culture. For with the Industrial Revolution had come the emergence in Britain of the proletarian urban dictions, and diction had become [...] what it has never been since:

not simply a matter of locality, but of class. The proletariat of the West of
Scotland, Protestant or Catholic – freethinking or of any other religion,
of immigrant stock or not – all could be seen as forming linguistically a
colony within a colony. [...] The contempt that was heaped on the speakers of the new urban diction of the West of Scotland was based on class,
and sometimes religious, prejudice as much as a desire for a return to the
mythical "pure" diction of a pure race of pre-proletarian Scottish folk.
(53, emphasis added)[8]

Although these observations—and ever-present anger—were expressed
in 1990, i.e. many years after his first poems were published, they also
appear to be true today. At the same time, even if he argues that 'urban
dictions' are a matter of class and not locality, if he is using the Glasgow
'urban diction' in his writing, it is as a representation of the Glasgow
working class. It is that community's voice that is being brought to the
foreground, albeit the ideas underlining his writing do refer to more
global issues, definitely going beyond the poet's immediate locality, in
this case Glasgow.

It is Glasgow, not only through the series' title but also its linguistic representation of the city together with its characteristic sound
and rhythm that we are introduced to in his earliest poetic works, the
above-mentioned *Six Glasgow Poems*. The first of these poems, the most
frequently anthologized 'The Good Thief',[9] is a very strong manifesto
challenging convention. We are confronted with how one of the thieves,
crucified alongside Christ, might have addressed the Lord if he had been
from twentieth-century Glasgow, and also in a style and language never
used in such topics before. This is especially visible in the last stanza, for
example, in which the thief is regretting missing the football game that
is about to start at 3 o'clock: 'heh jimmy/ lookslik wirgonny miss thi
gemm/ gonny miss thi GEMM jimmy/ nearly three o cloke thinoo'.
His concluding note, however, is in quite a positive tone. Although it is
already dark, it is a good job there are lights (*Intimate Voices...* 9).[10]

Leonard's confronting convention and breaking with it here concerns
both presenting one of the most tragic and dramatic events of the New
Testament—and of paramount importance to Christianity—in a manner
that was totally contrary to the norm, and in a linguistic form that was
highly depreciated at the best of times. Although Glaswegian and the
language of the Scriptures do not appear to go hand in hand, Leonard's
poetic language and the poem's 'enduring power', as McClure illustrates,

continues 'to puzzle, intrigue and shock, [this being] visible on several levels' (*Language, Poetry and Nationhood*, 169). The first levels, which are most relevant here and are worth quoting, are:

> First, the almost opaque spelling, a quasi-phonetic transcription of the short, disjointed phrases, pronounced with a high degree of ellipsis of unstressed syllables, characteristic of uneducated Glasgow speech: *yawright* "are you all right" [...]. Next, the phonological distinctness of the dialect from either traditional Scots or Scottish standard English: neither *gaunt ae* nor *going to* but *gonny* [...] and the rapier-like accuracy with which the writing evokes the cadences of the Glasgow basilect [...]. (169)

Furthermore, Jesus is addressed as 'jimmy', this being a typical all-purpose vocative form, which also places him very much in Glasgow. The greatest regret concerning the situation they have found themselves in seems to be the fact that they are going to miss the football match at three o'clock. As indicated above, football is one of the most important forms of entertainment among working-class Glaswegians and very much part of the city's cultural life. The main characters here are from Glasgow and the lyrical I, in this case one of the thieves, speaks in the language of their own community. In his choice of language and the form in which it is presented, the poet here is confronting both linguistic convention concerning Standard English, the language of education and that of the Church, as well as that of the higher echelons of society. And as he did in the above-mentioned 'poster poem', he is also challenging the Literary Revival of the earlier decades and, as indicated by McClure, the different spelling forms used within Lowland Scots, which are often applied when writing in the Glasgow dialect.[11]

For someone not acquainted with the Glasgow voice, not only 'The Good Thief' but all Leonard's works—both in verse and prose—can be rather difficult to read and understand, hence another challenge readers are expected to face. Naturally, not everybody has been happy with this, especially when we go back to the late 1960s.[12] In reference to the reaction caused by Leonard's first collection of poems and his chosen form of expression, Roderick Watson observed that:

> [Leonard] created a stir by [his] fearless use of Glasgow urban speech in a phonetic spelling that catches the rhythms and nuances of actual utterance when read aloud, but which seems radically estranged on the page in its

written form. One effect of this is to make the educated English speaker 'illiterate' again as he or she struggles to decode the printed word. By these means the poem becomes a spell against complacency and a retaliatory act against what Leonard sees as the educational establishment's intolerance of local (and working-class) expression and experience. (*The Literature of Scotland*, 296)

Leonard's choice of language variety and inventive form of notation was a highly expressive way of manifesting his views and foregrounding his political agenda. Speaking out on what had been prevalent practice for near on two hundred years in Scotland's educational establishments, i.e. discrediting and eradicating all local varieties of speech forms by insisting on—with force when necessary—the use of English in the classroom, Leonard highlights the inseparable links between power and language, and how the language of certain communities can be forcefully downgraded. As Barry Wood has pointed out in his article 'Scots, Poets and the City', Leonard 'takes stock of the adequacy of the "urban dialect" as a mode of expression and explores the nature of its relationship to English, which, in its "received pronunciation" is the language of power' (346–347). An illustration of how he brings this message home is his use not of his Glaswegian speaking voice but of this very 'language of power', the language that was used in the Scottish schoolroom where corporal punishment was very often the norm. Leonard does this in a very troubling and *powerful* manner in his poem 'Four of the Belt'. Mr. Johnstone, the schoolmaster, decides that it is time for his pupil Jenkins to undergo 'some ritual humiliation' and no matter what he feels about it at present, in the future he 'will recall with pride,/ perhaps even affection,' that day when he was given 'four of the belt./ Like this. And this. And this. And this' (*Intimate Voices...*, 124). When reading the whole poem, the impact is all the stronger because Leonard here is not writing in his *mither tongue* but in the language of the cultural élite, many of whom had always been ready to degrade and depreciate those who were dependent on them. Language has always been a powerful tool and Leonard has used English here to his full advantage.

Tom Leonard's writing, including his critical work, stems 'from the conviction that the voices of many people are efficiently ignored or silenced by education and "polite" culture', to quote Roderick Watson (*The Poetry of Scotland...*, 703). Leonard is known to be generally anti-establishment and, as the above has illustrated, negatively inclined towards any dominant class, and everything that goes with it, language included. As Barry Wood pointed out, he was primarily interested in 'subverting rather than replacing English [...] and in this his purpose is quite distinct from that of the Lallans poets' (347).

This subversion and Leonard's desire to highlight the social and political problems he has always been most concerned about, is also accompanied by his deeply embedded conviction in the value of the authentic voice, the informal language as it is heard in the streets and in working-class homes. Starting with his earliest works from the late 1960s, it has been the driving force for his promotion of these forms of speech as a medium for literature. The status of Glasgow working-class diction, going hand in hand with the social position of its speakers, is all too clearly illustrated by his poems from the series 'Unrelated Incidents' or the general favourite 'right inuff' from 'Ghostie Men'(cf. *Intimate Voices* ...). In the former, it is the first three, including the poem on the six o'clock news, that in particular refer to language, intellect and inadvertently to class and power relations. The poem 'right inuff', on the other hand, sums up both the situation of the Glasgow vernacular and Leonard's attitude towards it.

The first poem of 'Unrelated Incidents' starts with the lines: 'its thi lang-/ wij a thi/ guhtr thaht hi/ said its thi/ langwij a/ thi guhtr' (*Intimate Voices...*, 86) which refer directly to the words used by Hugh MacDiarmid when he had expressed his opinion on Ian Hamilton Finlay's first use of the Glasgow vernacular in his verse (cf. Nicholson, 88). His ironic response to the great promoter of *Lallans* continues with what could be often heard concerning which language varieties should be used and when they should be used. In reference to Stanley Baxter and comedy, for example, the use of the demotic is considered fully acceptable but certainly not when it concerns science. The language of the intellect has to be English. This view, constantly repeated over the last centuries, especially after the Union of Parliaments in 1707, appears in 'Unrelated Incidents' in the form of reported speech, from someone who is about to end his life by boldly stepping into an empty lift-shaft and falling eight storeys down. Unrelated incidents indeed.

The second poem in the same series, which also contrasts language varieties and sound systems, as well as the difference between sound and object and symbol recalls the biblical Genesis where 'god said ti/ adam' that he did not care whether it is called 'an apple' or 'an aippl'. The forbidden fruit simply has to be left alone (87). Apart from the issue of pronunciation, the underlying criticism here is the reference to the fact that in Presbyterian Scotland, right from the times of the Reformation in the sixteenth century, the implemented vernacular Bible was an English translation. English was used for everything connected with religion; hence, it was commonly believed that God spoke in that language. English, not Scots, or any of its varieties, was the language of the Church of Scotland.

In reference to the same issue but also, to use one of Gerard Carruthers' terms to describe another premise of Leonard's writing, that of 'cultural snobbery', to which he reacts angrily 'by means of a stereotypically aggressive narrator' (67), let us look at the third poem from his 'Unrelated Incidents'. Here, we are indeed confronted by an aggressive BBC presenter of the six o'clock news who explains that the reason why he talks with a BBC accent is because his listeners would not want him to talk about the truth with a 'voice lik/ wanna yoo/ scruff [...]'. The speaker's emphatic and highly offensive form of address appears three times, ending with the claim that there is a right way to spell and a right way to talk, i.e. about the truth, and 'yoo scruff [...] doant no/ thi trooth/ [...] cawz/ yi canny talk/ right'. He ends his tirade with the announcement 'this is/ the six a clock/ nyooz. belt up' (88). Whether we agree with Carruthers' view that this poem 'operates as a critique of colonial power relations within the British Isles' (67) or not is a matter for debate. Undoubtedly, it can be perceived in this way, but it can also be seen as a critique of the long-standing belief—throughout the British Isles but not only—that it is solely the standard form of speech, of which BBC English was an example at the time Leonard was writing these poems, that represented everything that was 'true', 'proper', and 'correct'. The additional twist is that the 'cultural snobbery' is expressed through the means of Leonard's Glasgow voice and not the Received Pronunciation and polite manner of speech that was the BBC norm of the 1960s. Every form of speech that digressed from this norm, of course Glaswegian and its speakers included, were often associated with the lowest of the low, the 'scruff' of society. And the scruff of society could neither be trusted nor taken seriously. That is why it is a much broader power-related social issue than what may be perceived solely as the result of colonialism within the British Isles. However, what can be agreed on is Carruthers' appreciation of Leonard as a poet and his concern with linguistic and power relations:

[...] Leonard, the most successful poet in Scots of the later decades of the twentieth century, was never the 'poster-boy' of Scots language activism precisely because his work sought not to champion self-contained authenticity but to point to a wider set of *linguistic and power relations*. (160, emphasis added)

At the same time, though, even when fully acknowledging Leonard's concerns with broader linguistic issues within society as such, he invariably comes through first and foremost as a political writer from Glasgow, expressing his views and convictions through the means of his language which is a reflection of where he comes from. Through the use of contrast, symbol, intertextuality and often the absurd, appearing in many of Leonard's poems, he foregrounds what is an issue of paramount importance both to him personally as well as to many people—in and outside Glasgow—for whom their voice and the way they speak make up their space and place in the world.

If we take a closer look at the last poem introduced above, 'right inuff', apart from Leonard's somewhat varied spelling forms and lack of consistency in his chosen phonetic transcription, the final message is clear to all: 'ach well/ all livin language is sacred/ fuck thi lohta thim'. He ironically admits that 'right inuff/ ma language is disgraceful' and that just about everybody had 'tellt' him this, even the introduction to the Scottish National Dictionary[13] had 'tellt' him this (*Intimate Voices*...120). At the same time, there is no doubt at all what Leonard wants to *tell* us. For him all living languages, and this also includes the urban *patois*[14] of Glasgow, is simply sacred, and as such should be accorded both due respect and acknowledgement. He also shows that as an educated person, well versed in the ways of language and highly knowledgeable concerning such world-famous linguists as Chomsky, he still has every right to speak in *his* language, even if this language is usually associated with a totally different class of people. He is fighting convention here and the same 'cultural snobbery' discussed by Carruthers (67) and referred to above.

It was, among others, because of this pronounced negative attitude and the fact that, according to Michael Munro, '[t]he speech of the Glaswegian ha[d] been much maligned' (*The Patter*, 3) that Munro decided in 1985 to compile *The Patter*, his first guide to current Glasgow usage. In his short Introduction, he highlights that:

Glaswegian is a rich, vital, and above all a valid regional dialect which gives a true reflection of the city and its inhabitants with all their unattractive features, such as deprivation, bigotry, and pugnacity, but with all their virtues too, such as robust and irreverent humour, resilience, and abhorrence of pretension. (4)

Eleven years later, in the Introduction to *The Complete Patter* (1996), which was the third edition of this work,[15] Munro expands somewhat on this issue:

> In these books I have always supported the idea that *Glasgow language is a valid and creative dialect of Scots, not, as some would have it, a slovenly corruption of Standard English.*At times it seems that this battle has been fought and won; then a writer of the magnitude of James Kelman, an artist working at the top of his bent, of whom any national literature must be proud, can still be castigated by the ignorant for expressing himself *in the demotic language of his native city.*[16] If my work contributes to making *Glaswegian Scots* more respected then I will consider it to have been of some use. (v–vi, emphasis added)

Another poet who has in more recent years attracted a certain amount of attention, primarily due to his promotion, in poetic form, of his *mither tongue*, is Mark Thomson. His first collection of poems *Bard fae thi buildin site* came out in 2007.

Like Leonard, Thomson was born into a working-class family. He grew up in Dundee during the 1970s and 1980s on one of the many housing schemes built on the periphery of the city. When he left school he went straight into a factory job, finally ending up on a building site as a labourer, hence, the title of his first published collection. His interest in poetry and writing led him to participate in poetry slams and festivals, forming a street poetry partnership, known as Tribal Tongues, with fellow Dundonian Gary Robertson. Becoming quite a celebrity in vernacular poetry, he has taken part in a number of BBC programmes, e.g. for Radio Scotland, Radio 4, BBC 4 or BBC 2.[17] When he gave up working on building sites, he turned to teaching creative writing and poetry, also running literacy workshops, with the age range of his students varying from children to young adults. His attention has been mainly directed at young people often at risk of exclusion from society. To quote Thomson speaking about himself:

I am passionate about the Scots language and my own Dundonian dialect and use this to demonstrate to others how to find, use and be proud of their own thoughts, words and identity.[...] My work centres around what I know, my own experiences, growing up in a city in places now described as areas of deprivation. I look at School experiences where I was constantly criticized for talking in dialect as well as being left handed.[...] Subject matters of drugs and alcohol are a common theme as are Family, friends, home and Scotland. I often find myself returning to these themes, whether it's comfortable to explore or not. (*Scottish Book Trust*)

If we were to compare the two poets and their use of dialect in their writing, Leonard, in much of his later publications, especially in his critical work, essays, satires, and collages, has moved away from using his *mither tongue*, resorting to Standard English. He is not only a poet but also a scholar and a polemicist, hence, the traditional division: poetry written in a variety of Scots, Glaswegian in this case, with the majority of his other writings appearing in English.[18] Leonard is the intellectual, social background notwithstanding, his vernacular poetry being also in this vein, with his general knowledge, sometimes highly radical political views, and higher education very evident. Thomson's poetry, on the other hand, is solely in his Dundonian voice, with emphasis on everything that concerns Dundee and its people, foregrounding the language of these people which is an inseparable aspect of those people's identity. There are of course such examples where English is the norm, when his writing goes beyond the genre of poetry, as in the above quoted biographical note from the Scottish Book Trust or the short Introduction to his latest collection of poetry, *Thi 20:09* (2011),[19] but it is through his poetry, his performances, and different forms of teaching activities that he is able to touch upon what is closest to his heart. Although he is primarily concerned with the local, in *Thi 20:09*, for example, he deals with the effect some of the most famous figures of Scotland have had on the Scots and what their views of Scotland would be if they lived today. Also in his first collection from 2007, we can encounter two poems simply entitled 'Scotland (I)' and 'Scotland (II)' which, being devoted to his country of origin, go beyond his immediate locality of Dundee, at the same time stressing what he understands by 'hame'. In the former poem, we learn that '[h]ame is being Scottish/ It's thi past/ It's thi present/ It's thi here/ It's thi now' (85). He goes on to enumerate all the associations both Scots and many non-Scots have of the country, ending with: 'It's ah that, an mare,' [...] 'It's just bein Scottish/ An it's as simple as that' (87–88).

Yes, it is as simple as that, and this concerns both the understanding of Scotland and the language used by the poet to express his understanding of home, the place he belongs to. As can be easily observed, his language, manner of expression and subject matter, although consciously written in dialect for a specific reason, is in many respects quite different to Leonard's chosen mode of writing.

Leonard is a well-versed highly political writer, whose politics are sometimes overtly controversial, and who often uses his Glaswegian speaking voice quite instrumentally. What, however, appears to be the link between the younger poet and performing artist and the older highly vocal, sometimes aggressive, activist and literary figure is their imbedded concern for the same, acknowledgement of what is an essential ingredient of a person's identity, that is language. Language, or one's *mither tongue*, is in turn inextricably linked with place and space.

This concern of both poets with the *mither tongue* and the long-standing issue in Scotland of often being forced to use Standard English,[20] or at least Standard Scottish English, leads us to Thomson's 'Mind Yir Lang-Widge' which is, like Leonard's poetry, written in his own phonetic transcription. The first stanza introduces us to 'that sound/ that cums oot yir mooth, [...] when yir in thi hoose,/ whar yir tongue is/ comfae, cozy, warm an loose' (16),[21] recalling how this form of communication is not recognised by the rest of the nation who believe it is not socially acceptable and does not enjoy respect. This social attitude leads him to share with us his feeling about being stripped of his identity when forced to change his consonants and vowels, when violence is being done to his own dialect. This, in Thomson's view, is nothing short of 'scandalous', just as always 'gitin telt/ ti talk Inglish/ instead o Scottish', especially when he lives in Scotland and is proud of coming from Dundee (16). It is the conversations in their own *mither tongue* that he has with his nearest and dearest, with such folk as your 'grannie', 'aunties', 'uncles', etc.', talking about the simple things in life and sharing different points of view, that are most important to him. The tongue is 'indigenous/ so be aware that it dizzna crack or tear'. The advice Thomson leaves us with is simply: 'mind yir lang-widge' (17).

In this poem, however, in which we are also introduced to the Six o'clock news, now called BBC News at six, which has been staple viewing for all national and international news for decades, the focus is totally

different than in Leonard's poem discussed above. The television programme may be presented in the standard language but discussing the
daily news only makes sense when views are shared in 'yir tongue' and
when you do not have to 'mind yir lang-widge' (17).

In reference to the long-standing insistence by the Scottish Education
authorities that it is English that has to be taught in schools and not
Scots,[22] we are confronted with what many Scottish school children
encounter when first attending that institution and which is so clearly
illustrated in Liz Lochhead's poem 'Kidspoem/Bairnsang' (2003).
Thomson draws our attention to this in the discussed above 'Mind Yir
Lang-Widge' as well as in another poem that he originally wrote in 2003:
'Thi Language Barrier'. Here, we learn how he 'wizzna yazed ti talkin in
so-called/ proper Inglish' (56). And that it was '[o]nly when [he] sat in
thi classroom,/ did [his] tongue talk in another tune,/ it didna feel cum-
fae/ an it cheenged [his] accent, it didna flow/ an [he] couldna really git
across/ whut [he] really ment' (56). It was only in the way he knew, in
the way that had been passed down to him by his mother and his father,
outside the classroom, that he felt comfortable and could really express
his thoughts. His natural way of expression was simply in Scots.

Although he feels he has gained due respect for actually talking in his
mither tongue, his appeal, to the education authorities among others,
is for them to acknowledge the fact that for many Scots English is still a
second language and that their first language should be treated with due
respect and not as a derogatory and improper tongue. It is in his poem
'Thi Mither Tongue', dated 2002, that we encounter a certain dose of biographical detail, where Thomson tells us: 'Eh wiz boarn an bred in a toon
called Dundee,/ so wiz meh mither an father afore me' (115). They have
the habit of speaking rather fast and although some people think it is somewhat rough, we learn that he thinks quite the opposite, that 'it's fine an
dandy, it's loose an free,/ when eh talk in broad Dundee' (115). It is, as
he says, 'meh mithir tongue, it's a weh o life' (115). This *mithir tongue*, in
Thomson's case also involving his way of speaking free and loose, is talking in broad Dundee, the language of the town he is from and which is so
much part of his identity, his personal space and place, just as Glaswegian
is part and parcel of Leonard's. Their writing that has over the years
expressed their anti-establishment views concerning language and education in Scotland is aimed towards the same, acknowledgement of what is an
essential part of every individual, his/her language, no matter whether he
comes from Glasgow, Dundee or any other locality in Scotland.

NOTES

1. Cf. Gerard Carruthers' discussion on Leonard, whom he sees as 'the most successful poet in Scots of the later decades of the twentieth century [...] because his work sought not to champion self-contained authenticity but to point to a wider set of linguistic and power relations' (160). See also Matt McGuire's work *Contemporary Scottish Literature*, where he devotes a whole section to Leonard in his chapter on language (52–56).
2. Cf. His *Glasgow Beasts*, ... from 1961 (Watson, ed., 685).
3. His first poem in the Glasgow vernacular was 'Coming of the Wee Malkies' (1967).
4. It was first given this name by Professor Denis Saurat of the University of Bordeaux, whereas J. Derrick McClure described this language as a literary register 'marked by an extensive use of archaic, literary and geographically diverse words' (*Scots and Its Literature*, 3). MacDiarmid was often strongly criticised by his numerous literary opponents for making exaggerated use of, among others, Jamieson's *Etymological Dictionary of the Scottish Language*. This dictionary was first published in 1808.
5. Although in his work *Scots and Its Literature* McClure writes about Tom Leonard's interesting 'use of a phonetically-spelled representation of Glasgow *slum dialect* as a literary medium' (42, emphasis added), he also clearly points to the fact that Leonard writes in a form that is 'recognisably based on some people's actual speech' (173).
6. This will be illustrated later in the discussion on the first poem in the series 'Unrelated Incidents'.
7. A group of poets known as the 'new makars', among them Oxford scholar Douglas Young (1913–1973), met in Edinburgh in 1947 to decide on spelling rules for a modern literary Scots. However, no decision was reached then or has been reached since on this matter.
8. This text first appeared as Tom Leonard's Introduction to *Poetry in the West of Scotland from the French Revolution to the First World War* in 1990.
9. It was first published in the magazine *Scottish International* in January 1968, 'the *Glasgow University Magazine*'s printer having refused to print some of his poems because of his language' (Marsack 164). It is also interesting to note that this initially rejected poem became, in the words of McClure, 'Leonard's most famous poem' (*Language, Poetry and Nationhood*, 169).
10. For further illustration, let me quote McClure here: 'A link, hinted at by the reference to "the gemm" but not overtly mentioned, is that Parkhead, Celtic's football ground and the scene of annual tussles at which violent brawls used to occur with deadly regularity, is nicknamed "Paradise" (*today shalt thou be with me in Paradise*) – and according to an

ancient Church tradition, the death of Christ occurred at three p.m., the hour of an afternoon kick-off' (*Language, Poetry and Nationhood*, 170). We also have to keep in mind that Celtic is Glasgow's traditional Catholic football team, in constant conflict with the Protestant Rangers. The football brawls were a vivid reflection of the city's sectarian violence.

11. See, for example, Anne Donovan's *Buddha Da* (2003).

12. It is interesting to see that even in much more recent times his *Intimate Voices* was banned from Scotland's Central Region School Libraries, whereas another of his most often quoted poems, on the six o'clock news from 'Unrelated Incidents 3', is compulsory reading in the AQA English language GCSE course in England, Wales and Northern Ireland (cf. http://www.scottishpoetrylibrary.org.uk/poetry/poets/tom-leonard). Despite the fact that Scotland has a different education system than the other UK countries, it is conspicuously absent here.

13. It was in the introduction to this dictionary that William Grant, its first editor, described the dialect as being 'hopelessly corrupt' because 'of the influx of Irish and foreign migrants' (Vol. 1: xxvii). This was why it was not worth taking into consideration.

14. In his *Language, Poetry and Nationhood*, J. Derrick McClure also uses the word 'sociolect' to describe Glaswegian because of Glasgow's sudden development being 'accompanied by immigration on a massive scale, and rapid expansion of the boundaries of the city [...]' (166).

15. The second edition being *The Patter—Another Blast* (1988).

16. This comment presumably refers to the uproar caused by James Kelman receiving the Booker Prize for *How Late It Was, How Late* in 1994 and for representing the Glasgow spoken voice in phonetic transcription, together with all the characteristics of this speech form, including the abundant use of four-letter words. What Leonard was doing in his poetic oeuvre, Kelman was doing in prose, also experimenting in style and form. Their political agendas were very similar.

17. For more information on his activities in the role of 'a Scottish celebrity in vernacular poetry' see, for example, http://www.bankstreetgallery.org/4/4/Art/helen-whamond-mark-thomson.html.

18. In the already quoted *Intimate Voices* ..., which is a collection of his early poems and essays, we can come across a number of other works that have also gone against the norms of the times and are definitely thought-provoking, but have not been written in Glaswegian, e.g. 'Four Conceptual Poems' (123) or his 'Design for a commemorative stamp celebrating 1000 years of "The Language Question"' (129).

19. The collection itself, though, is in the Dundonian dialect.

20. This issue also crops up in Thomson's 'Scotland (II)': 'we still git telt it thi skail/ ti talk polite, now that's whut eh call/ "no rite"' (120).

21. Much of this poem, both in content and tone, reminds us of Liz Lochhead's "Kidspoem/Bairnsang" (2003) which touches on the same issue of children being forced to relinquish their native tongue on starting school, 'the place I'd learn to forget to say/ it wis January/ and a gey dreich day' (19). As Lochhead goes on to conclude, 'Oh saying it was one thing/ but when it came to writing it/ in black and white/ the way it had to be said/ was as if you were posh, grown-up, male, English and dead.' (20).

22. The history of this phenomenon goes back many centuries, starting with the Reformation in Scotland in the sixteenth century and the introduction of the Geneva Bible, which was an English-language translation, to the Union of the Crowns in 1603, and ending with the Union of Parliaments in 1707 and the Scottish Age of Enlightenment in the eighteenth century, during which everything that came from south of the Scottish-English border was seen as being better, more prestigious, and enjoyed the utmost respect. Scots, in turn, which never had the chance to acquire a recognized standard form, gradually disintegrated into various dialects, or varieties if we prefer, at the same time gradually losing the respect it had enjoyed in the late Middle Ages and the Renaissance.

WORKS CITED

Brown, Ian, and Colin Nicholson. 'Arcades—The 1960s and 1970s'. *The Edinburgh Companion to Twentieth-Century Scottish Literature.* Ed. Ian Brown and Alan Riach. Edinburgh: Edinburgh University Press, 2011 [2009]. 133–44. Print.

Carruthers, Gerard. *Scottish Literature.* Edinburgh: Edinburgh University Press, 2009. Print.

Donovan, Anne. *Buddha Da.* Edinburgh: Canongate, 2004. Print.

Grant, William. 'Introduction'. *Scottish National Dictionary*, Vol. 1. Ed. William Grant. Edinburgh: Scottish National Dictionary Association, 1931. Print.

Leonard, Tom, ed. *Poetry in the West of Scotland from the French Revolution to the First World War.* Edinburgh: Polygon, 1990. Print.

———. *Intimate Voices: Selected Work 1965–1983.* London: Vintage, 1995 [1984]. Print.

———. 'Literature, Language, Democracy'. *Reports from the Present: Selected Work 1982–94.* London: Jonathan Cape, 1995. 47–62. Print.

Lochhead, Liz. *The Colour of Black and White: Poems 1984–2003.* Edinburgh: Polygon, 2003. Print.

Marsack, Robyn. 'The Seven Poets Generation'. *The Edinburgh Companion to Twentieth-Century Scottish Literature.* Ed. Ian Brown and Alan Riach. Edinburgh: Edinburgh University Press, 2011 [2009]. 156–66. Print.

McClure, J. Derrick. *Scots and Its Literature*. Amsterdam and Philadelphia: John Benjamins Publishing, 1995. Print.

———. *Language, Poetry and Nationhood: Scots as a Poetic Language from 1878 to the Present*. East Lothian, Scotland: Tuckwell Press, 2000. Print.

McGuire, Matt. *Contemporary Scottish Literature*. Basingstoke and New York: Palgrave Macmillan, 2009. Print.

Mulrine, Stephen. 'The Coming of the Wee Malkies'. *Four Glasgow University Poets*. Kirkaldy: Akros Publications, 1967. 10. Print.

Munro, Michael. *The Patter: A Guide to Current Glasgow Usage*. Glasgow: Glasgow District Libraries, 1985. Print.

———. *The Patter: Another Blast*. Edinburgh: Canongate, 1988. Print.

———. *The Complete Patter*. Edinburgh: Canongate Books, 1996. Print.

Nicholson, Colin. 'Nomadic Subjects in Recent Poetry'. *The Edinburgh Companion to Contemporary Scottish Poetry*. Ed. Matt McGuire and Colin Nicholson. Edinburgh: Edinburgh University Press, 2009. 80–96. Print.

Thomson, Mark. *Bard Fae Thi Building Site*. Edinburgh: Luath Press, 2007. Print.

———. *Author Details: Biography*. 2016. Web. 16 January 2018. http://www.scottishbooktrust.com/profile-author/17137.

Watson, Roderick, ed. *The Poetry of Scotland: Gaelic, Scots and English*. Edinburgh: Edinburgh University Press, 1995. Print.

———. *The Literature of Scotland*, Vol. 2. Basingstoke and New York: Palgrave Macmillan, 2007 [1984]. Print.

Wood, Barry. 'Scots, Poets and the City'. *The History of Scottish Literature*, Vol. 4. Ed. Cairns Craig. Aberdeen: Aberdeen University Press, 1987. 337–48. Print.

WEBSITES

http://www.scottishpoetrylibrary.org.uk/poetry/poets/tom-leonard.
http://www.bankstreetgallery.org/4/4/Art/helen-whamond-mark-thomson.html.

Take the Weather with You: Robin Robertson's North-East Coast Atmospherics of Landscape and Self

Julian Wolfreys

> Here is the shipping forecast.
> Anon., UK Meteorological Office

I

An unreasonable, not to say outlandish hypothesis: poetry concerning itself with the '"natural" world'[1] is the place *par excellence* where 'modern subjectivity' finds itself, and is to be read. It is where it reads itself in reading the world it perceives as 'natural'. It, the 'I' enables its reading through reading itself as becoming embedded in that world: of it, though not wholly so, but with a difference that is realized in perception, reflection, and presentation, critical or otherwise. 'I' am embedded, touched by and touching on, the 'natural' save for the difference and diremption marked by the 'I am' that intervenes, however minimally, or with whatever critical force often countersigned today and in recent years by the term 'ecocriticism'. Perceiving the so-called natural world,

J. Wolfreys (✉)
London, UK

M. Szuba and J. Wolfreys (Eds.), *The Poetics of Space and Place in Scottish Literature*, Geocriticism and Spatial Literary Studies,
https://doi.org/10.1007/978-3-030-12645-2_14

the self cannot but help, in re-presenting that world to involve and enfold itself in that world, even as it employs the world to reflect upon itself or to employ selfhood as the medium to bear witness to 'nature', as the speaking and self-reflexive trace distinguishing itself in that place wherein there is no directly communicative self-reflexive consciousness of the order of the human. Conversely, as a coterminous effect of perception, the '"natural" world'—which was neither natural nor unnatural prior to consciousness—comes into existence. The '"natural" world' perceived, apprehended, appreciated, read and reconstructed in a language that seeks to map the most fundamental aspects of the self that attempts to grasp itself *there*, in the world, is both a vessel (constructed in consciousness) for modern subjectivity to find itself, in which it is emplaced, and also the name given that non-human unreflective exteriority awaiting its interior-thought corollary; image arrived at through constellation of traces then disseminated by the analogical linguistic construct.

'"Modern subjectivity"' is, in very general terms, characterized by a certain sense of *interiority*,[2] as Scott Marratto observes. My argument is that poetry, the poetry mediating the '"natural" world', and thus a poetry manifesting a poetics of the 'natural', is both the articulation and that place (and too a 'taking' place, through the medium of the poet's language) where 'modern subjectivity' finds its most sustained, complex and involved expression—the place between the interiority of self and the exteriority of the '"natural" world'. Marratto continues, suggesting that this subjectivity 'is reflected in the essential epistemological concern of both empiricist and rationalist philosophy, beginning in the early modern period'.[3] A question arises, however: 'if the subject encounters an external world only by means of *inner* representations of that world, how then can it be assured of possessing the kind of genuine knowledge necessary to realise the goals of an enlightened science and politics?'[4] The beginning of an answer to this question is given as follows: 'A key concept', Marratto asserts, 'in this line of questioning is "representation"'.[5] Representation, presentation, constitution or construction through poetry, and in the proximity that poetry makes available through '"modern" subjectivity', affords a realization of the intimate experience for the self of the world in which the self finds itself. Yet, in finding itself, the modern subject apperceives from the exchange with the '"natural" world' far more, I would suggest, than with any built environment, how, in the words of Edmund Husserl, '[b]etween the *perception* on the one hand, and the *depictive-symbolic* or *signitive-symbolic objectivation* on the other, there is an unbridgeable eidetic difference'.[6] Poems may well be what Tomas Tranströmer called 'meeting places'[7]; the experience of, in the meeting place, the perception of that experience is however one that is always unbridgeable, however keenly felt.

As I shall seek to explore here, Robin Robertson does not strive to close this unbridgeable difference through his poetry of the north-eastern Scottish landscape. Rather, in accepting the aporetic, sometimes anguished, often agonistic experience of self and world in intimate and proximal conjunction/disjunction, Robertson strives to map the difference through a poetics of the '"natural" world' felt through the often minimally present self as it comes to find itself through an encounter with the atmospherics of that world. For Robertson one might say, '"modern" subjectivity' is a ghost-subject, a becoming-phantom, having only the barest of traces, through which are registered the most powerful of emotional affects. Particularly apropos the apprehension of and attestation on behalf of the '"natural" world', Robertson's 'selves', the Is who appear to speak (and self is minimally implied even if it is merely implicit behind, within, the words that map or stage 'nature' in traces, surges, fragments, shifting tropes, mutable metaphors and poetic figures presenting the motions of the perceived world), are *phantasma* and *spectral*: figures become visible through the *poiesis*, the making of the visible motions and phenomena of the '"natural" world'. Thus, in Robertson's poetry, it might be said that the '"more one feels, the more one disappears, retreating into the world, within its phenomena, inside its signs.

The self becomes a *mappa mundi*, the 'meeting place' tattooed by wind and water, shades of light and dark, lines of flight and the registration of fleeting motions, which the consciousness strives to apprehend, through tropes as changeable as the weather itself. The self is the conjuration of and emerging from within atmospheric experience, whether this self is the speaker of the poem, or other human figures presented by Robertson. To take one brief example, from which to begin, with the poem, 'The Fishermen's Farewell' from *Hill of Doors*.[8] The title of the poem is, I would argue indicative of a mourning, a lament, and the register of memory itself in attesting to the human in a landscape inhabited symbiotically, in a mutual dwelling of organisms that is in turn captured in the transference and troping of language between perceptible forms and linguistically, semantically associated phenomena. The poem is not one marked by first-person selfhood. Those humans that are there are barely so; they are those titular fishermen, 'smoke-walkers' (*HD* 21), a phrase arguably suggestive both of something material and quotidian—those who work in the smokehouses preparing fish, a practice dating back to medieval times at least—and something ghostly, the trace of the human inhabiting the coastal land. Such is the haunting ephemerality of the human presence that it is observed how 'They would be rumour if they could / ... / they would be less even than rumour / to be ocean-stealers, to never throw a shadow' (*HD* 21).

Vanishing into the north-east coastal world of standing stones and turbulent waters—the fishermen are, after all, knowable chiefly through their 'farewell'—the eyes of the fishermen that construct 'long stares' are those that gaze, and are thus only known belatedly. Always already, such eyes, such stares are registered as absent, the human already transformed into elements of their land- and seascape, changed to tonal registers of atmosphere, climate, signs of animate, inhuman place: 'gone / to sea-colours: grey, foam-flecked / and black in the undertow, blue as the blue banners of the mackerel, whipping west'. And such eyes belong to 'smoke-walkers', who would be 'rumour if they could, in this frozen / landscape like a stopped sea...' (*HD* 21). These lines, these phrases and figures powerfully, yet intimately, touchingly illuminate the manner of the atmospheric entwining of the barely present self in Robertson's Scottish landscape poetics. The eyes are no longer there, they are 'gone', 'reflected' as it were, captured in passing, through the suggestive and indirect intimation, the apperception of colours, grey and black. The colours are in turn mediated, intermingled, hinted at through the alliterative impermanence of foam hinted at in the ineluctable motions of an undercurrent, this 'undertow'. Robertson's choice of word hints at the pull beneath the surface, the invisible force at work, contrary to the obvious and the visible; at the same time however the 'literal' figure is worked against, through, by the figurative significance of emotion, of what is felt beneath any superficially visible signs.

Such an undercurrent is captured in the shift and tension between the impermanence of sea-colours and the play of water—itself taken up in the transference from the movement from colours to banners to the continuous motion expressed in the gerund determined image of mackerel 'whipping westward'—and the subsequent couplet's violent halt captured in the 'frozen / landscape of a stopped sea'. In turn, the climate of the world is internalized, as 'drink storms through these men, uncompasses / them, till they're all at sea again' (*HD* 21). The abrupt arrest if the frozen landscape and stopped sea might be said to be reflexive, bearing witness to the violence of the poem's arrest of a centuries' old world transfixed in a single page, and a poem comprised of ten couplets; it is rendered the more violently in that broken, run-on shift between 'frozen' and 'landscape', redoubled through the sibilant alliteration, the solidity and stoppage themselves taken up in turn by the standing stones mentioned elsewhere. Principally though, Robertson maps the world through the impressions of water on the sensibility, and the emotional turbulence in the undercurrent that *is* the tension between ceaseless motion and the precipitate standstill; the mapping is also that of the self, generation after generation embroiled within the shifting, transforming ferocity of the '"natural" world'. The reader feels this world, this north-eastern coastal landscape/seascape primarily, in this complex encounter so typical of Robin Robertson's poetics. There is, in such a world a constant confrontation between human and inhuman, inner life and outer world, everyday history and the persistence of myth, captured finally in the closing couplet, 'where men sleep upright', become the standing stones of the landscape, yet 'in their own element, as seals' (*HD* 21). Both solid and aqueous, of the land and the water, not quite, not wholly human, suggestive of those mythical creatures the half-human shape shifting seals, the skerries, the barely human figures of 'The Fishermen's Farewell' admit to an uncanny condition of dwelling that is read as the countersignature of the commonplace. It is this doubleness of the modern self that Robertson remarks with such quiet force. The human place in the world is, as the poet has observed, made clear by the sea, in this poem and for Robertson in general. There is, for Robertson, what he describes as certainty in such implacability, such ineluctability; and, as he continues to remark of the sea, 'I can't understand how one could fail to come alive, finally, on the edge of a life-force that has everything we lack'

II

A review from *The Guardian* of Robin Robertson's *The Wrecking Light*, begins thus: 'The ceaseless throb and thrum of the natural world—which is to say the unhuman world—pulses throughout *The Wrecking Light*, Robin Robertson's fourth collection'. This world, continues the reviewer, Adam Newey, is a force 'blind to all human concerns'.[9] Were we to pause over this initial assessment, perhaps to quibble here and there about the terminology, we might not allow the full force of the following observation to resonate as it should: 'Though Robertson's work is informed by close observation of the natural world, this isn't in any sense nature writing. Even what seem at first to be straightforwardly descriptive pieces are never content with mere representation'.[10] There is to Robertson's writing both a strong sense of 'displacement and deracination' alongside, and arising out of, the 'visual richness of his descriptive writing'[11] of which much is to be read in a remark of Robertson's, cited by Newey: 'I grew up', Robertson recalls, 'with a very strong sense of place, in a landscape that seemed freighted with significance, mystery and power. Everything since has seemed a displacement, a deracination'.[12]

Robertson is talking, of course, of the Scottish landscape, not just landscape in general and particularly the north-east coast. Robertson's sense of place is of such a condition, and so significantly is that memory of place, that he confesses himself to be, in essence and in spirit, homeless and therefore haunted by loss. To speak of 'landscape' in Robertson's case is misleading, for it is, as we have already witnessed through 'The Fishermen's Farewell', a coastal world, and thus a seascape also. The remark already cited in the review from *The Guardian* comes from an interview published in the same year as Newey's review. It is worth quoting at length, in order to provide a view of lay the coastal land that informs so vitally Robertson's poetics of place:

> The countryside in which I grew up is very beautiful, with the Highlands to the west and the North Sea to the east, with the lowlands of Aberdeenshire and its barrows and circles and standing stones in between .... Seas in general—and the Scottish seas in particular—have been powerfully present in my life. I find certainty in the implacable, the ineluctable; my position as a human being in the natural world is made clear by the sea, certainly. I can't understand how one could fail to come alive, finally, on the edge of a life-force that has everything we lack: drama, beauty, mystery; a gigantic, ancient and unceasing mass of moving water, constantly changing its sound, its color, its shape....

From this confession of, or bearing witness, to the extent to which the world shapes one, and the manner of that world's interiorization as the determinate coordinates for the subject—a subject who is at once formed and informed by place but who also feels himself to be, as a consequence, homeless and possibly even 'unhomely', the poet moves to a consideration of the way in which, for him, poetry is made *in* the subject.

Poems are accretions of words and phrases and images adrift in my conscious and subconscious mind looking for partners, for a home, for completion....if the circumstances [for writing] are right I will already have the DNA.... The thrill for me is listening to the lines as they lock into the music I was after. I try to be sensitive to the weight and texture and sound of words, their sonic and semantic relationships.... I have just the one sensibility.... There are continuities of theme or subject or tone, of course, and repeated motifs.... Very few of the speakers are identifiably me. I occasionally use the first person for its immediacy.... It is very tiresome when readers identify me as the speaker in the poem and extrapolate an autobiography.... For me, writing poetry has very little to do with the intellect and therefore it is very hard to talk intelligently about the process of making poems.[13]

Poetry arrives as a response to that which calls the subject, giving a form, a response to the call of music that is, simultaneously, the manifestation of a DNA. To write poetry is to translate the unheard music and to seek to map the coordinates of the place from which music emanates. As with all maps, all guides, this is necessarily selective; a filleted sketch taken from a series of self-approximations in the form of responses to questions in an interview, here Robertson places himself in the specificities of remembered land- and seascape. There is, he admits, just 'the one sensibility', though this is not necessarily, or in any way simply, the sensibility of Robin Robertson. Though place informs the subject, and the subject in turn strives to shape a response to the musical call of place and its incorporation into the self, this is not to say that when one reads Robertson's poetry one has access to the poet.

Memory work situates the aesthetics of place before the self here. The countryside is the place in which the 'I' develops. Despite compass points and fixed locales, between which the I situates itself, memory retains 'a very strong sense of place in a landscape that seemed freighted with significance, mystery, and power', as he puts it elsewhere in the interview just cited. Of the landscape of Perthshire and the coastal areas around Aberdeen, the poet has averred elsewhere that it is a place where 'history, legend, and myth merged cohesively in the landscape' (Poetry Foundation biography). The poet's role is to unveil 'the refreshed world and through a language thick with sound and connotation and metaphor, make some sense: some new connection between what is seen and felt and what is understood'. Language in conjunction with memory 'refreshes the world', seeking to see it anew, to invent it, as if for the first time. Such invention arrives in that tension between the adult's recollection of a childhood rooted in the geographical and the resistant configurations of a pair triple-figured tropes, triangulated concatenations of forceful meanings, felt rather than understood: 'significance, mystery, and power'; 'history, legend, and myth'. Such mystery and myth, such significance just beyond the grasp of comprehension serves to displace the self of Robertson's poetic mnemotechnic.

As a result, the 'I' has an immediacy within the landscape as it looks for a home, even though that presence is precarious and not, Robertson insists that it is not to be seen as him. This is despite his earlier assertion that the landscape, the world of this particular location, with its light, its weather, the singular vividness of its terrain, is inscribed in his DNA, part of his code. I circle back around the various tropes of the subject in relation to place on the one hand and the poetry of place on the other because it is important, I feel, to understand the elusive and mutable, protean condition of Robertson's Scottish memory world. This is a world of, simultaneously, powerful continuities *and* unceasing transformation, as if one were seeking to read the terrain through watching the sky, the sea, or the motions of all that is living in the world. Thus it is that we find '"modern" subjectivity' announced in all its interiority, having an embeddedness that is preconscious, inaccessible as any self who is called or who names himself 'Robin Robertson'. Robertson's writing of the '"modern" subject' and its relation to the '"natural" world' seeks to eschew the specificities of a biographical self to reach for something much more fundamental to Being, something at once singular and yet, in that singular relation to place that which is written on the self in everyone. That place maps DNA—at least poetically, for the purposes of the conceit—suggests however how there is for the subject always an unbridgeable difference at the heart of interiority.

Admitting to the influence of Yeats, David Jones, Geoffrey Hill, and Basil Bunting, compared in a review in the *New Yorker* with Heaney or Hughes, Robin Robertson might also, equally, be compared with that much earlier 'non-nature nature' poet and witness to the unhuman world and advocate of the traces of pagan world interfering in the field of vision in the present, Thomas Hardy, or his Scottish contemporary, novelist and poet, John Burnside. Specific words 'sing' the subject as subject to, of place: unhuman, not inhuman. Decracinated rather than uncanny or diasporic. Out of a sense of uprootedness, of diasporic dislocation or isolation, the poetic subject seeks to figure a world of sense, of feeling and mnemic intimacy. For as much as Robertson's poetry details the visual density of the material world, the world he feels and invites us to see, and possibly to feel also, is one of atmospherics, of weather and shades, penumbra and seasonal transitions.

'New Gravity', the first poem of *A Painted Field*, Robertson's first collection (1997), introduces the reader to the motion of walking— treading—that precedes the subject 'through the half-light of ivy and headstone' (3). The image balances the grown and hewn through the crepuscular accommodation between the two, a liminal illumination captured mid-step and midway between that which has been shaped by human hand as the signifier of the end of human life, and that which grows from the fertile ground of the dead, without need of human help. A daughter presses acorns 'into the shadows' (3), surrounded by dead and dying leaves, so many pieces of an oak tree's 'jigsaw' (3). The world is understood as making and unmaking itself, the field of vision engaging with that ongoing process of becoming and unbecoming, as that inaugural gerund testifies. 'Shadows' in the concluding line, the darker doppelganger of the first line's 'half-light' (3), both just two from a potentially infinite series of degrees between light and dark, closes the circle, rounding life not with a sleep but death; for 'New Gravity' is a poem as brief as a life, remarking anticipated life, and remembered death, and it is this that the sensate atmospheric condition of the land-scape that is impressed on the subject. Through this quite remarkably realized registration of poetic density, the reader is afforded an encounter with 'an external world only by means of *inner* representations of that world' (Marratto 2012, 2–3).

Place abides with a material specificity in Robertson's work, and with that, the light, the weather, the weight of the intangible that makes of place the singular event when apperceived by the poet, revealed through the poet's presentation. In *Hill of Doors* (2013) the poet remembers, among other places, Tillydrone Motte (70–71) in a poem given that name as a title, an ancient earthen mound of uncertain date and human fashioning, situated in Seaton Park, Aberdeen, its north-east facing slope facing the River Dee. Whether the mound *is* a motte remains undecided, but certain for Robertson is that for 'Fifteen years in every kind of light and weather' he 'played' his 'childhood here on this highest edge / ... / amongst gorse and seabirds', the 'river-terraces below' being 'filled with cloud' (70). The childhood world is remembered as a site of spectres, ghosts, shadows, secrets and a hidden 'charmed wood' (70). A bent tree resembles 'blown smoke' (70), its solidity apprehended paradoxically as something evanescent, ephemeral. Equally transitory is the glint of 'sun skimmering in the twist of the river water', the adjacent elm trees twisted by 'the sea-wind' (70). The world of childhood is a world of the contoured, twisting landscape with meandering waterways, 'braes and weirs', proper names signing the memory's topographical projection: Walker's Haugh, Kettock's Mill, Devil's Rock, Tam's Hole, the Pot, 'the Black Neuk of the Brig o' Balgownie' (71). Despite such knowledge however, this is the epistemology of childhood, for it is only in adulthood that the subject confesses in the final stanza all that he 'didn't know'. The self remembers its other as a 'brocken spectre, / trying to cast the shadow of a man' (70). The self is barely there, doubly at a remove from physical presence, consumed within the atmosphere of place. Definition is done away with, for other truths. Even proper names prove unreliable. The 'motte' is found to be a 'Bronze Age burial cairn', while 'Tillydrone' is, it turns out *tulach draighionn*, 'the hill of thorns'. The certainties of childhood are revealed to the poet so much 'blown smoke', to recall that image of the bent hawthorn tree.

What do these two poems, one early, and one more recent share, what is sustained between them, and what might they suggest for the reading of place in the poetry of Robin Robertson? In order to proceed with this reading of Robertson's Scotland, the very precise locations of a particular part of the country—a reading that is, fundamentally, a reading of the phenomenology of place and the role of weather, season, light, atmospherics, along with those 'intangibles' and shifting ephemera of the experienced and felt world that inform our subjective perceptions, moods, recollections, and experiences, and which in turn give to the materiality of place a resonant, often haunting specificity such as the name of a nation or country cannot capture; a singularity to the event of the poet's mnemic re-encounters—it is necessary to establish or, at least trace the provisional parameters of this reading; it is necessary to map out, perhaps a little too schematically, the terrain that we must cross in order to approach the reading, accounting for the epistemological strata on which readings might situate themselves.

I have begun somewhat directly though, before withdrawing, through engaging with and opening readings of the three poems already considered, in order to place us *in* the world of Robertson's poems, in the memory of those places that the poems are, each of them individually and as a constellation of revenant *felt* worlds. In finding ourselves in such places with the poetic subject, we might come to apprehend the stakes of reading, if you will, the two commentaries announcing what is at stake in the texts, and what is at stake for a reading of the subject's memories. For—of course, there can be no doubt—this is what we read. We do not read place as such, any more than we can extrapolate from the poems 'all' of Scotland, all of what makes the place of the proper name of a country or nation. As that review cited earlier observes, Robertson's texts are no mere representations, even if they do—like so many of the poems or the prose of Thomas Hardy, or the passages figuring landscape in the novels of Virginia Woolf (in Hardy's case, sites throughout Dorset and other of the counties of his quasi-imaginary Wessex; with Woolf, the Sussex landscape for the most part)—begin *at, with* representation.

However directly representational or seemingly so, the poetics of place involves a passage between the material and immaterial. The traces, the signifiers of weather and light are merely two aspects of those modes of poetic production and presentation that cause there to be exuded 'a strange intimacy' at once 'seemingly innocuous yet enigmatic', which pushes simultaneously 'at the threshold between memory and materiality',[14] as well as making porous the space between the material and the immaterial. Were it not too fanciful, I would be tempted to suggest—at least in passing—that weather makes the memory of the world; or conversely, that memory is climatic.[15] Climate, season, light, time of day—all such attributes of the world inform the 'colouration' of the self's recollection of place, as Robertson shows, again and again. In the poetic tracing of such qualities and phenomena the Lived-Body comes back to itself as a revenant standing where it encountered and experienced place; it returns as the Body-Re-presented, as thin and insubstantial as an 'I', there and not there, here and there, in neither place exclusively and shuttling between the two, the intimacy also an irreparable rupture, a divorce as the Child-Then and the Adult-Now of 'Tillydrone Motte' illustrates. This is not to say all of Robertson's poems play explicitly on this impossible gap. But Tillydrone Motte makes explicit, reiterating the point as it does in its epistemological challenges and rewritings of pronoun, what is always implicit or inchoate in every poetic mapping and figuration of place.

What is a constant throughout Robertson's writing is the mutability of 'atmospheric conditions and...meteorological phenomena that we call weather and climate'.[16] It is the very constancy, the recurrence of weather, and those phenomena Robertson calls on in conjunction with

the figures of climate that give to the reader the sense of change, transformation. The weather is always there, and always changing. In this, his
poetry is attuned directly to registering and recalling, conjuring up the
most immediate of human experiences, the body's encounter with the
elements. The poems become a supplement to the senses, and make visible the climatic world of North-East Scotland. 'Much as the receptor
cells in the eyes of humans and other diurnal creatures have evolved to
perceive the range of frequencies of radiation from the sun—what we
term "visible light"—so too the receptor cells in the skin have evolved
to perceive the range of temperatures [and other effects] in the atmosphere'[17]; thus it is, Robertson's poetry presents a phenomenal 'skin',
a membrane through which we encounter the traces of atmospheric
Scottish conditions, as these are embedded in the mnemotechnic of the
poem, itself already a prosthesis of the subject. In Robertson's text the
observation, and implied physical experience of the weather, the light,
the time of day and year, serve to mark the manner in which memory
is affected, opening the reflecting self to strengths and vulnerabilities,
opening the self to confessional responses, with an adjunct 'strong temporal awareness'.[18] Weather in Robertson belongs to the mystical and
folkloric, mythical Scottish landscape as much as it does to the contemporary lived scene.

III

One might be tempted to suggest that the various signs of weather, or
with a deliberate strategic vagueness those manifestations of the felt
world of atmospherics, are the DNA of the perceived land- and seascapes, the apperceived singularity of place. That 'this' is 'here' and
nowhere else is undeniable. What makes a here just this, distinct from
every other here is not only mysterious or indeterminate, it is, ultimately,
undecidable. Weather does not have a nationality of course, and will not
be affected, whatever the eventual geopolitical ramifications of Brexit—
which may or may not be a done deal, and may or may not look like
anything anyone anticipated by the time anyone reads this. 'Scotland',
or more specifically the north-east coast of Scotland, will still remain to
'feel' in particular atmospheric and climatic ways, in certain sensibilities.
There are, it is almost too obvious to be worth stating, regions where
weather has, like prevailing winds, predominant patterns of recurrence
and iteration. Weather is indelibly associated with locations, regions,

cultures, shared and individual identities, and has been for thousands of years, even though anthropocene phenomena such as global warming are transforming such conditions. As long as there has been language (and probably longer), there have most likely been descriptions that abide. Adjectives accrete, tropes form like geological phenomena, becoming on the tongue and in writing tattoos, repeated rhythmic, not to say choric palimpsests and imprints attesting to the close relationship between self and world; between the self, individually and collectively and that part of the world from which one comes, which one is imprinted by, and which leaves in the self a mnemic trace as indelible as the inheritances of DNA.

Robin Robertson grasps in his poetic output the significance of this trace for the human subject and his or her memory, the auratic tenor or mood of a particular site, locale, or region being for Robertson a significant phenomenological and existential countersignature to the self. Defined as the state of the atmosphere at a particular place and time, weather—climate, atmospheric conditions, the elements—always immediately felt on the skin, apprehended through all the senses, is, for Robertson that which frames, maps, and determines the mood, the *Stimmung*[19] of the inescapably intimate and copulative self-world relation, however technologically one may be protected or removed from the 'natural' atmosphere. (Climate is never absent, there is always some atmospheric, whether that which locally rendered, a singular and yet repeatable expression of the world's atmosphere in general, in the local context of place's specificity; or whether that climatic condition is technologically produced and generated, controlled, maintained.) Robertson's poetry is very much an articulated mapping of our finding ourselves in the world, our attunement to the world; Robertson's poetry is the poetry of atmospheric attunement and phenomenological mood determined by, and mediating, the specificities of locale.

So much is Robertson involved with, informed by the weather, that even his 'versions' of the poems of Tomas Tranströmer chosen for the volume *The Deleted World*,[20] are informed by the Scottish poet's atmospheric sensibility. In a review of the volume, Sven Hakon Rossel points out that in the poet's selection for the volume of Tranströmer, Robertson 'has focused on a series of existential statements, which take their point of departure in observations of life in nature, combining sim- plicity with complexity'.[21] While the Swedish writer's concern (at least in Robertson's selection) is in rendering an 'external reality rendered with a keen sense of contrasts and duality [that] serves as a starting point for deliberations on modern man's [sic.] distance from nature and the threat of our present technological and bureaucratic world',[22] Robertson's engagement with the weather in his poetry is not freighted—at least not solely, or even primarily—with such ecocritical baggage. Robertson's atmosphere—that is to say, on the one hand, the various moods, tones, and pitch of his poetry; and on the other, the various 'moods' of the weather as this is traced in the poetry—is much more fundamental, perhaps neutral even, and certainly immediate in its staging of the experience phenomenologically of the self in its local world. This is not to say that, like his near contemporaries John Burnside and Kathleen Jamie, Robin Robertson's response to what David Borthwick calls 'contemporary alienation from place and disconnection from nature', is not marked by a concern that is 'environmental as much as cultural'.[23] It is, even though the sense of alienation' described by Borthwick is nothing new in poetry or prose, regarding the landscape and 'nature' (John Clare and Thomas Hardy are two significant writers of such cultural and environmental alienation registered in literature). My argument is that Robertson's environmental concern comes out of the indelible mark on memory, apperception, and sensibility left by lived experience in the Scottish north-east, and that his profound engagement with the landscape and its climate come before and so inform that environmental and cultural understanding.

To say that at once the landscape and weather are everywhere in Robertson's poetry is to say simultaneously something that is hyperbolically empty and blindingly obvious. Thinking the one without the other is impossible. Climate, mood, tone, pitch, phenomena of the atmospheric and the material 'worlds'[24] are all elements in a perceptual and apperceptive continuum, as in 'The Language of Birds', from *Slow Air* (2002, 6–7), and reproduced in *Sailing the Forest: Selected Poems*. Birds' beaks move as compass needles drawn and directed by the wind, this element perceived as having a compass. The 'wind's compass' (6/30) is however subject to, or part of a greater system, defined by Robertson as 'the sky's protocol' (6/30). The sky has a system, a set of rules and procedures that determine act. Thus, the beaks are not imagined as needles in a human gesture of interpretation involving simile or metaphor (at least, not obviously). Rather, in a substitution of verb for noun, Robertson reads the beaks as 'needling', an automatic, if not autonomic response, his line performing a movement, drawing the reader's attention to the estranging detail disclosed through estrangement, and from this revealing the heavens' atmospheric determination of motion. The birds do not choose the direction, they are turned towards it. So too, with the poem's minimally human presence (the subject appears in five of the twelve verses), the self is directed, drawn, to invoke once again the suggestion of a magnetic pull and response. The poem's subject first steps forward to show itself in response to the call, the 'chuckle' of a magpie, which bird is also a 'magic wand' directed away from the human presence towards the light (6/30). The subject climbs, sees hay take fire, then withdraws; having become invisible once more for three verses, 'I' returns, sight become memory, as the subject recalls the actions of crows (7/31). 'The Language of Birds' presents a world of birds who inhabit landscapes of hills, estuaries, rocks, and sea, who continue indifferent to humans, inside changes in the weather, in the light, and in the sky with its changing hues of stone and paraffin, and its shifting winds. So much are birds part of the sky-world of this poem for Robertson that they not only turn unconsciously to light and the direction of the wind, moved by an involuntary volition akin to magic hinted at by the magpie's 'magic wand of itself' (6/30), but are subsumed within that sky continuum. So much is this the case that the conventional collective nouns for rooks—parliament, clamour, building—no longer serve. Such terms are human impositions, acts of naming at odds with the poem's belief that birds will use their names, or otherwise withhold them. In the final verse, the narrator confesses to keeping an albino crow imprisoned because its name is not yet given (7/31). Instead, it is the wind, that which is of the 'sky's protocol', which defines rooks collectively as 'a blown squall' (6/30).

Thus it is that the human subject apprehends how to dwell, in the Heideggerian sense. 'I' come to speak the language of the birds determined by their environment, that which makes available their manner of dwelling, inasmuch as the birds show to dwell, 'in that they receive the sky as sky', thereby saving, preserving, as Heidegger puts it, this particular aspect of the *Geviert* ('fourfold'), that term first used by the philosopher in 1949 to signal the convergence of relationships and contiguities as these are perceived, appropriately grasped, and existed within by human beings.[25] For Robertson, the sky is what Andrew J. Mitchell calls a 'weathering medium of appearance' (2015, 116–145). Robertson understands that 'weather attends all that we do and leave undone.... All that we do is done within an environment, as our lives take place immersed in a climate. Whatever appears of the earth appears within a field of weather' (Mitchell 2015, 128). It is from this understanding that

his poetry appears. The weather exists independently of human perception but gives to human perception the *Stimmung* of interpretive, articulated reception and response. The weather is something we see, which
we record, and react to, but is 'out of our hands' (Mitchell 2015, 129).
Our words turn to the atmosphere of our world as birds' beaks needle-
or wand-turn. Robertson's poem illuminates how there is perception on
one side of the dynamic (to recall my epigraph taken from Husserl) and
symbolic representation through image or sign on the other. Perceiving
the world, apperceiving that which its weather gives me, I nonetheless
remain, however close, at a remove and marked by a difference, in the
spaces of which I can only approximate the world through images or
signs. These in turn do not close the gap, do not suture the between.
Rather, they serve, as they trace that which takes place atmospheri-
cally, to mark and maintain the gap they would bridge. The 'I' is just
one more such mark, with the privileged difference that it perceives
that which it is within. There still remains an unbridgeable eidetic difference. Robertson allows the difference to be. Indeed, it is the pared
down, often stark or violent brevity of his words, phrases, and images, his
estranging use of catachresis, which affirms the eidetic difference. For all
their apparent simplicity, Robertson's images of the atmosphere assume a
powerfully affecting vividness for the reader. Images become defamiliar-
ized through unusual conjunctions and convergences inviting new appre-
hensions and associations, which in turn give us to think differently and
to think the difference as difference.

IV

The self is barely there in Robertson; the self is a skelf to use the Scots
dialect word for a splinter (or a troublesome or annoying person). 'Skelf'
appears as the sliver of the self in the poem 'Landfall', from *The Wrecking
Light* (71). Where the self appears it is taken up in the elements, it is the
merest of fragile presences in the face of the world's forces. In 'Landfall',
the self is pulled from the waves as a skelf, a splinter from broken up
fishboxes once come from Fraserburgh, Aberdeen, Peterhead. At once
the self is both intimate, the immediacy of a name, but also distant, only
a name come from the past, being one of 'the names / of the places
I came from years ago' (71). The self as skelf is a chance appearance
subject to the whim of currents and the mutability of tides. Weather in

Robertson is more than mere memory, even though it is in the past; atmospherics, climate, the conditions of air and earth and sea: all come to pass, 'the storm passed / ...the rain finally eased'. There is a sound which the self takes 'for wind in the trees'. The self finds itself in such transitory and ephemera, only finally to catch 'sight of myself' in a 'shard / of mirror left in the frame', as the poet has it in 'The Shelter' (*Hill of Doors* 55). Elsewhere in the poem 'False Spring' (from *Slow Air*) there is a 'lift in the weather', which in turn is described as a 'clemency' that the subject 'cling[s] to like the legend / of myself' (25). Robertson's world is a world of transience, an impermanence paradoxically permanent in the constancy of change. The morning after Christmas Day is marked by 'a dripping thaw, and winter has gone from the grass' in 'Leavings' (*Swithering*, 76), while the self is nothing solid, the face 'smoke', the body 'water', tracks of the self 'made of snow', nothing more than a 'ghost-tread', merely 'stamped ellipses' of what is not (76). Here is the self as loss, as fragment or skelf, trace or ellipsis, caught up in the change of the world's seasonal shifts and climatic transformations. There is only 'foam in the sand-lap of the north-sea water' which 'fizzles out', these being 'the flecks of the last kiss / kissed away by the next wave rushing'. In the midst of all this the self barely there, if at all, remarks desire, a longing for the 'right wave', a 'special wave that toils' (like the self, one might suggest) but which (who) 'can never find a home' (Pibroch, *A Painted Field*, 19).

If, as Lévinas avers, the 'conception of the "I" [*moi*] as self-sufficient is one of the essential marks of the bourgeois spirit and its philosophy',[26] then Robin Robertson's poetic 'I' in its meagre survival offers a countersignature to that bourgeois spirit and, by extension, the thinking of the self in Western thought that leaves one at a remove from dwelling with the world authentically. While western thought privileges the illusion of presence and the present in its logocentric and metaphysical misperception, Robertson's apprehension of selfhood formed through the memory of the younger self's embodiment in place, and the memory of place dismisses any such cosy 'home'. Of and in, and with the world, the self in Robertson is, like Lear on the heath, homeless prey to the elements, at the verge, the edge of being in being so intimately embroiled. To dwell, paradoxically, one must be homeless. Nothing in the non-human world reminds us of this more immediately than climate and weather, atmosphere itself. To watch clouds moving through the sky, seeing as they pass and, in passing, change shape is to have before one the possibility of grasping impermanence, unstoppable mutability, change and disappearance. This is what Robertson seeks to grasp without fixing the self in place. As Robertson shows us, the breaking up of the self is a mode of escape into the world: 'escape is the quest for the marvellous, which is liable to break up the somnolence of our bourgeois existence'.[27] To recall Robertson's own words in the light of this remark of Lévinas': 'I can't understand how one could fail to come alive, finally, on the edge of a life-force that has everything we lack'. In this, for Robertson, there is grasped the chance of a 'possible identification between man and the nature that inspires horror in him'. Robertson's ghost-world, his mnemotechnic north-east Scotland may not create horror in any vulgar sense of the world, but it does illuminate how, immersed in such a world, finding one's self with/in the moment of the world's disclosure, there is a tremble, a shudder, a bristling or solicitation of the self, as a result of its precarious proximity. So immersed is the poetic subject in the world and so materially and memorially close does that world of Scotland's north-east coast appear (in the senses of both seeming and coming into spectral being) that the 'I' only has being in the depths of the world by being on the edge of its own disappearance.

What then, in conclusion, might Robertson's incarnation or evocation, his conjuring of the memory of a particularly sensuously apprehended world, bring about? The poet's dissolution, erasure, or breaking up of the 'I' might be read as solving a particular problem of phenomenology. David Morris states the problem thus: 'I am on a bench in the very world I am perceiving. So I would seem to be part of the depths [of the world] that I perceive'. However, in realizing this, I realize a problem. 'I perceive things in depth as here or there, near or far, in front or behind, and so on. But I do not perceive myself in this way....I am not a point within a coordinate system already fixed outside me. My body is the original 'here'.... my body appears to escape the depth orderings that apply to things around me, to belong to a different order'.[28] In reducing the self, Robertson reduces the distance between self and world. For Robertson's homeless self, the world is a more precarious and dangerous place because the self is scattered in brief upsurges, in fragments of sense and sensation, throughout the world that carries the self away, which haunts the 'I'. The self, the 'I' in Robertson is just, barely, expression. It is what Bergson describes as a 'real movement'. A thing, the body, is not being expressed. Instead, expression is the 'shifting of a state... [belonging to] an indivisible whole irreducible to a series of positions'.[29] The self is only there in the folds of the world. Scotland, the north-east coast leaves in Robertson, as a permanent haunting of the self, the incorporation of the self gathered up in the atmosphere of the world.

NOTES

1. The phrase '"natural" world' is doubly suspended so as to indicate: *on the one hand*, the material real that humans perceive, encroach on, and intervene in; *and on the other hand*, the conceptual, constellated construct, the ontological whole in the assumption of which difference is erased in the metaphysical name, 'nature', that the human mind projects as other than human or constructed by humans, yet still perceived, though nether encroached on nor intervened in, save for the most minimally invasive approach taken by walking, cycling, standing, looking, 'twitching', and so forth.
2. Scott L. Marratto, *The Intercorporeal Self: Merleau-Ponty on Subjectivity* (Albany: SUNY Press, 2012), 2.
3. Ibid., 2.
4. Ibid., 2–3.
5. Ibid., 3.
6. Edmund Husserl, *Ideen zu einer reinen Phänomenologie und phänomenologischen Philosophie. Erstes Buch: Allgemeine Einführung in die reine Phänomenologie. Jahrbuch für Philosophie und phänomenologische Forschung*, 1:1 (Halle: Max Niemeyer, 1913). Trans. by F. Kersten as *Ideas Pertaining to a Pure Phenomenology and to a Phenomenological Philosophy. First Book: General Introduction to a Pure Phenomenology* (The Hague: Kluwer, 1983), 93. This translation is modified in a footnote to Derrida's *Voice and Phenomenon: Introduction to the Problem of the Sign in Husserl's Phenomenology*. Trans. Leonard Lawlor (Evanston: Northwestern University Press, 2011), as it was in the earlier edition, *Speech and Phenomena: And Other Essays on Husserl's Theory of Signs*. Trans. David B. Allison. Preface Newton Garver (Evanston: Northwestern University Press, 1973), 60: Alison gives this as, 'between *perception* on the one hand and the *symbolic representation by means of images or signs* on the other, there exists an insurmountable eidetic difference' (60 n. 1); Lawlor's translation of Derrida's citation from the French edition of Husserl is rendered thus: 'Between *perception* on one side and *symbolic representation through image or sign* on the other, an unbridgeable eidetic difference exists' (51 n.)

7. Tomas Tranströmer, cit. Robin Robertson, 'Introduction', in *The Deleted World: Poems* by Tomas Tranströmer, versions by Robin Robertson (New York: Farrar, Straus and Giroux, 2011), ix–xiii, xiii.
8. 'The Fishermen's Farewell', *Hill of Doors* (London: Picador, 2013), 21. All further references to Robertson's poetry are given parenthetically in the body of the chapter. Where poems are reproduced in *Sailing the Forest*, I give the page references to both the original collection and the selection. Details of Robertson's volumes are as follows:
   A Painted Field (London: Picador, 1997).
   Slow Air (London: Picador, 2002).
   Swithering (London: Picador, 2006).
   The Wrecking Light (London: Picador, 2010).
   Hill of Doors (London: Picador, 2013).
   Sailing the Forest: Selected Poems (London: Picador, 2014).
9. Adam Newey, 'Review, *The Wrecking Light* by Robin Robertson', *The Guardian*, Saturday, 20 February 2010, https://www.theguardian.com/books/2010/feb/20/wrecking-light-robin-robertson-review, accessed Friday, 29 June 2018.
10. Ibid.
11. Ibid.
12. Marc Vincenz, 'A Celtic Mage's Muses', *Open Letters Monthly* (Online Magazine), January 2010, http://www.openlettersmonthly.com/interview-with-poet-robin-robertson/, accessed 6 May 2018.
13. Ibid.
14. Dylan Trigg, *The Memory of Place: A Phenomenology of the Uncanny* (Athens: Ohio University Press, 2012), xv. The phrase 'Lived-Body' used just after this quotation is Trigg's. I borrow it from the volume cited (101–167). Any further citations will be given parenthetically as *MP*.
15. I take as my inspiration for this particular idea a comment by Timothy Morton, *Dark Ecology: For a Logic of Future Coexistence* (New York: Columbia University Press, 2016), in which he observes the following: 'Like poems, wicked problems (defined by Morton as 'unique and thus *irreducible*', 'unverifiable,' *'uncertainly interminable,'* '*alogical*' [36–37]) entangle us in loops. We know that our reading of a poem is provisional and that our thoughts about what poems are influence how we read them: the same goes for global warming' (37). While I find the analogical simile to be played a little fast and loose in order to make a rhetorical *and* political point, there is an element of strategic hyperbole that I find admirable. Poems may well be all those things (though equally not every poem is) but no poem has ever caused a catastrophe on the scale of the melting of the polar ice caps, as far as I'm aware. There are numerous points of departure from Morton's thinking in my own as, rhetoric

aside, I find certain problems leading to aporia in his reasoning. While, for example, I agree that the 'ecological value of the term *Nature* is dangerously overrated,' not least in its theological and often unreflective metaphysical deployment by some eco-critics; and agree also that 'Nature isn't just a term—it's something that happened to human-built space [Morton is not the first to observe this; while "Nature" might not be just a term, it is also very much a concept, the enormity of which often gets in the way of thinking], demarcating human systems from Earth systems' (surely 'systems' is itself a problematic construct, even 'eco-systems' being anthropocentric in their perception—just because things happen and keep happening doesn't raise them to the level of a consciously designed or determined 'system') it is inaccurate to suggest that '*[t]he Anthropocene is Nature* in its toxic nightmare form' (59). Certainly the 'Anthropocene'—itself already a 'dangerously overrated' term, and concept—is responsible for the thinking of 'Nature', as it is of every other metaphysical concept. This is logocentric thought at its ubiquitous self-mystifying finest. But given we agree that this Anthropocen(tr)ic epoch (I insert the 'tr' into the term in order to illustrate the possibility that every naming of the Anthropocene is also a construction and recuperation of thought within the Anthropologocentric, a naming of an age that in its naming reflects the human back at the centre of it as presence) causes as part of its system the coming into existence of concepts mistaken not for wonders but, well, 'natural'; then Nature (sic) is always already a toxic nightmare form—after all, we, the Anthropocene, thought it up as a systemic name to impose on, and so give meaning to all that other stuff that we don't make as such through the invention and use of even the most basic modes of technology, and then coloured it in a mystifying wash of nostalgia and sentiment—that has taken for as long as there has been an Anthropocene to reveal its end game, which is to say *our* end game. Which is to say, the Anthropocene cannot be Nature in a toxic nightmare form (any more than Night is de facto the toxic nightmare form of day) because *Nature just is always this, always already this.* We are our own direction. Morton is fond of talking about humans, when not both elevated and simultaneously reduced to the 'Anthropocene' as 'we Mesopotamians' in *Dark Ecology. Nous sommes tous les autre Mésopotamiens?* Only as much as we are the other Victorians Foucault imagined; which is to say we neither are nor are not. The dangers of such 'Big Thinking', as Derrida showed of Foucault, is that it is part of the problem it seeks to criticise, and breaks down too rapidly, like a monster truck running on hybrid fuel sources. Big Thinking delights for its own hyperbolic sake in what Morton calls the '[w]ash-rinse-repeat' (58; personally, I prefer the 'bite-chew-swallow-repeat' analogy first heard in an episode from season six of *The Walking Dead*, surely the *plus non ultra* of Anthropocen(tr)ic / Nature narratives, the *Walden Pond* of the post-apocalyptic crowd) scenario. We are always, as a 'we', every epoch we have ever been. There is no beyond-the-epochal, no meta- or hyper- or post-epoch. We have not caused our own destruction, we are our own destruction.

16. Sarah Strauss and Ben Orlove, 'Up in the Air: The Anthropology of Weather and Climate', in *Weather, Climate, Culture*, ed. Sarah Strauss and Ben Orlove (Oxford: Berg, 2003), 3–17, 3.

17. Strauss and Orlove, 'Up in the Air', 3.

18. Ibid.

19. *Stimmung* is chosen in order to stress the multiple qualities of tone mood, with Martin Heidegger's use in mind. Moods for Heidegger are fundamentally existential, they arise from our relationship to the world. *Stimmung* names for Heidegger the fundamental mode of phenomeno- logical experience of the world for the human subject and, reciprocally, the manner of the world's making itself present to us. One is never not in a 'mood', a condition of felt experience, *Stimmung* is for Heidegger the manner of our being attuned to the world. We do not, nor can we, exist independently of this relationship, as Simon Critchley has argued about the ways in which we are 'always caught up in our everyday life in the world, in the throw of various moods'. Simon Critchley, 'Being and Time, Part 3: Thrown into This world', *The Guardian*, Monday, 29 June 2009, accessed Sunday, 6 May 2018.

20. Tomas Tranströmer, *The Deleted World*, trans. Robin Robertson (New York: Farrar, Straus and Giroux, 2011).

21. Sven Hakon Rossel, 'Review', *World Literature Today* 86:4 (2012): 72–73, 73.

22. Rossel, 73.

23. David Borthwick, '"The tilt from one parish / into another": Estrangement, Continuity and Connection in the Poetry of John Burnside, Kathleen Jamie, and Robin Robertson', *Scottish Literary Review* 3:2 (2011): 133–48, 135.

24. 'Worlds' are placed here in quotation marks to signal both the plurality of worlds, however over- or underlayered they are—there is no one world, there are multiple worlds—and the fact that a 'world' in this chapter sig- nifies both the locality of place and environment addressed and figured in any given poem, rather than the world in general, and also all that is in the perception of the subject *of* and *in* the poem.

25. Martin Heidegger, 'Building Dwelling Thinking', in *Poetry, Language, Thought*, trans. Albert Hofstadter (New York: HarperCollins, 1971), 141–60, 148.

In unpacking the concept of the fourfold, Graham Harman has correctly pointed out that Heidegger is notoriously vague about the meaning of the fourfold. Among the various general problems surrounding the idea of the fourfold, is the specific or 'special problem' of the term *mortals*, according to Harman. As Harman puts it, if we take the term too literally, this 'implies that human beings must be present in any case for the fourfold to exist, and this would annul or at the very least mitigate the idea of the thing existing for itself, and we 'would still basically remain within the bounds of the Kantian critical philosophy' (Graham Harman, 'Dwelling with the Fourfold', *Space and Culture* 12:3 [August 2009]: 292–302, 294–95). Yet, for the thing to be a thing, as other than the self I am, it has to be available to perception; for to name the thing 'thing' is still to give it a name. There is no way beyond the Kantian aporetic, and certainly neither Husserl nor Merleau-Ponty seem to escape this, implicitly or explicitly. The aporia in Heidegger seems to reside not in the vagueness of the fourfold and Heidegger's somewhat mystical semi-definition, but in the thinking of the thing, and the difference, as Harman suggests, in Heidegger's 'forced distinction' between objects and things (297). The problem with Graham's argument comes when he returns to criticising Heidegger for the inclusion of humans on the scene, remarking that Heidegger 'remains convinced that philosophy only has anything to tell us if some human being is on the scene' (300). While Harman seems mightily pleased with himself for his version of the fourfold as an improvement on Heidegger, which version of the fourfold now produces a 'theory of the things themselves rather than of human Dasein's access to the world' (301); and while he quite rightly questions a certain obscurantism in Heidegger's language, and in the process introduces a more dynamic model of the fourfold, it remains the case, as poets such as Robertson or philosophers such as Merleau-Ponty make available to us, that there can be no philosophy, no thinking as such, without human access, and without the give and take of the between: between self and other, subject and world. So, while '[w]ithin perception, we have the pine tree and the volcano as intentional objects that endure despite all the changes in lighting and mood and angle of observation', that 'fact' of enduring is still, and remains a perception. Robertson's language seeks to accommodate perception's intervention and interpretation with minimal 'interference', it also accords the dynamic and elemental aspects of the world-given-to-the-subject, the 'it gives', a role in shaping and articulating perception. Robertson's poetry acknowledges that we both perceive and also dwell within the atmospheric dynamic of the fourfold, so-called.

For a definitive study of the concept, see Andrew J. Mitchell, *The Fourfold: Reading the Late Heidegger* (Evanston: Northwestern

University Press, 2015), particularly Chapters 2 and 3 (71–162). Further references to this work will be given parenthetically.
26. Emmanuel Lévinas, *On Escape | De l'évasion*, int. Jacques Rolland, trans. Bettina Bergo (Stanford: Stanford University Press, 2003), 50.
27. Ibid., 53.
28. David Morris, *The Sense of Space* (Albany: State University of New York Press, 2004), 2–3.
29. Ibid., 85.

Works Cited

Borthwick, David. "'The tilt from one parish / into another": Estrangement, Continuity and Connection in the Poetry of John Burnside, Kathleen Jamie, and Robin Robertson'. *Scottish Literary Review* 3:2 (2011): 133–48.

Critchley, Simon. 'Being and Time, Part 3: Thrown into This World'. *The Guardian*, Monday, 29 June 2009.

Derrida, Jacques. *Speech and Phenomena: And Other Essays on Husserl's Theory of Signs*. Trans. David B. Allison. Preface Newton Garver. Evanston: Northwestern University Press, 1973.

———. *Voice and Phenomenon: Introduction to the Problem of the Sign in Husserl's Phenomenology*. Trans. Leonard Lawlor. Evanston: Northwestern University Press, 2011.

Harman, Graham. 'Dwelling with the Fourfold'. *Space and Culture* 12:3 (August 2009): 292–302.

Heidegger, Martin. 'Building Dwelling Thinking'. *Poetry, Language, Thought*. Trans. Albert Hofstadter. New York: HarperCollins, 1971. 141–60.

Husserl, Edmund. *Ideen zu einer reinen Phänomenologie und phänomenologischen Philosophie. Erstes Buch: Allgemeine Einführung in die reine Phänomenologie. Jahrbuch für Philosophie und phänomenologische Forschung*, 1:1. Halle: Max Niemeyer, 1913. Trans. F. Kersten. *Ideas Pertaining to a Pure Phenomenology and to a Phenomenological Philosophy. First Book: General Introduction to a Pure Phenomenology*. The Hague: Kluwer, 1983.

Lévinas, Emmanuel. *On Escape | De l'évasion*. Int. Jacques Rolland. Trans. Bettina Bergo. Stanford: Stanford University Press, 2003.

Marratto, Scott L. *The Intercorporeal Self: Merleau-Ponty on Subjectivity*. Albany: SUNY Press, 2012.

Mitchell, Andrew J. *The Fourfold: Reading the Late Heidegger*. Evanston: Northwestern University Press, 2015.

Morris, David. *The Sense of Space*. Albany: State University of New York Press, 2004.

Morton, Timothy. *Dark Ecology: For a Logic of Future Coexistence*. New York: Columbia University Press, 2016.

Newey, Adam. 'Review, *The Wrecking Light* by Robin Robertson'. *The Guardian*, Saturday, 20 February 2010.

Robertson, Robin. *A Painted Field*. London: Picador, 1997.

———. *Slow Air*. London: Picador, 2002.

———. *Swithering*. London: Picador, 2006.

———. *The Wrecking Light*. London: Picador, 2010.

———. 'Introduction'. *The Deleted World: Poems*. By Tomas Tranströmer. Versions by Robin Robertson. New York: Farrar, Straus and Giroux, 2011. ix–xiii.

———. *Hill of Doors*. London: Picador, 2013.

———. *Sailing the Forest: Selected Poems*. London: Picador, 2014.

Rossel, Sven Hakon. 'Review'. *World Literature Today* 86:4 (2012): 72–73.

Strauss, Sarah, and Ben Orlove. 'Up in the Air: The Anthropology of Weather and Climate'. *Weather, Climate, Culture*. Ed. Sarah Strauss and Ben Orlove. Oxford: Berg, 2003. 3–17.

Vincenz, Marc. 'A Celtic Mage's Muses'. *Open Letters Monthly* (Online Magazine), January 2010. http://www.openlettersmonthly.com/interview-with-poet-robin-robertson/. Accessed 6 May 2018.

PART IV

Afterword: From Word to Image

Jon Schueler (1916–1992): Intensity and Identity

Mary Ann Caws

INTRODUCTION

When I speak of nature, I speak of the sky, because the sky has become all of nature to me. But it is most particularly the brooding, storm-ridden sky over the Sound of Sleat in which I find the living images of past dreams, dreams which had emerged from memory and the swirl of paint. Here, I can see the drama of nature charged and compressed.[1]

I want to begin by singing. Looking at Jon Schueler's *Sky Song* (Fig. 1).

I see it as a proclamation against darkness and critical noise, offered upwards. "I found every passion in the sky," Schueler wrote in that very grand song of sound, *The Sound of Sleat*.[2] His own extensive autobiography, it remains the best testimony to his life and work: from his Wisconsin childhood to his postwar California training with Clyfford Still and Richard Diebenkorn and then his immersion in the East Coast art scene, intermixed with his account of impassioned living and working

M. A. Caws (✉)
Graduate School, City University of New York,
New York City, NY, USA

© The Author(s) 2019
M. Szuba and J. Wolfreys (eds.), *The Poetics of Space and Place in Scottish Literature*, Geocriticism and Spatial Literary Studies,
https://doi.org/10.1007/978-3-030-12645-2_15

Fig. 1 *Sky Song*, New York, 1985, 96 × 84 in/243.84 × 213.36 cm (o/c 1458). Jon Schueler Estate

in an old schoolhouse in Scotland, named Romasaig, in Glasnacardoch, Mallaig, by the sea, near the Isle of Skye in the Hebrides, which he used from 1970 on. His being was involved physically and, ultimately, penetrated psychologically in every way by the Sound of Sleat as the autobiography's title so perfectly suggests. Pronounced both slate and sleet, the name points to Schueler's embrace of both the hardness of the rockiness of Scotland and the harsh vagaries of the northern weather.

DYNAMICS OF STUDIO AND SKY

For the sake of locality, and for the sake of focus, I shall here concentrate on an earlier period, 1957–1958 in Mallaig Vaig, when Jon Schueler had found his first Scottish studio in a small crofting community beyond the village of Mallaig. There he painted many of his amazing visions of that nature, that sky, and that sea. In these, the sense of belonging and being is so visceral that I am impelled to offer multiple pieces of testimony to that sense and that place. I shall not call them fragments, for they are, each of them, complete in their witnessing. Witnesses to turbulence and weather, these paintings have, as Schueler's face has, a great weather within. Interior weather quite as clearly as exterior.

THE OPEN SEA

Unsurprisingly the drama and dynamism of these works achieve equal intensity in paintings like *Loch Scavaig* which draws on Schueler's experience of leaving the security of the land by going out into the sea with his friend the skipper Jim Manson. In the *Margaret Ann*, a small, wooden boat, suspended between sky and sea, he moved between land masses and peered into the sea lochs, which brought him even closer to the elemental and reawakened memories of World War II, when as a navigator he was pitted against the potential threatening force of nature (as well as the human powers of destruction). He must also have remembered Turner's journey by steamboat to Fingal's Cave on the island of Staffa and to Loch Scavaig itself on his way to Loch Coruisk.

Two of the most moving paintings of this time include in their very titles this sense of proximity—his further immersion in nature—both physical and mental: *My Garden Is the Sea* and *I Think of the Open Sea* (Fig. 2):

Both have dominant heavy red forms, with indications of water revealed through the gaps, hardly representational and certainly not topographical, but still suggesting a closing in of weather, and an exultation in nature's dominance.

Fig. 2 *I Think of the Open Sea*, Mallaig, Scotland, 1957, 72 × 60 in/182.88 × 152.4 cm (o/c 57-52). Private collection

CLOUDS AND THEIR OPENINGS

Cloud over Knoydart (Fig. 3).

This work introduces an important emphasis in Schueler's work and I would like to set his clouds in a larger artistic tradition. It seems to me that all those clouds we have loved over the centuries, by Constable and other painters and in reading David Lucas—and caring about all their theories such as Hubert Damisch's *Théorie du nuage*—serve to set the stage, quite gloriously, for the clouds we see in the works of Jon Schueler. The layered mystery of what lies beyond—through the breaks, the openings in the clouds—sets our own imaginations free and upward. To me, this suggestive layering allows for a raft of poetic possibilities and an involvement in the deepest sense of the word.

Sky songs indeed: the paintings sing in their being and forms. Such works of art never sit still, and for good reason—their dynamism provokes our own. It is our responsibility in reacting to the force of these openings of the imagination to absorb the full intensity of whatever darkness they and we encounter and then to be drawn into the light. Let me put here this amazing dark and light contrast, in his painting of *Skye* (Fig. 4).

Fig. 3 *Cloud Over Knoydart*, Mallaig, Scotland, 1957, 23.25 × 40.25 in/59.06 × 102.24 cm. (o/c 57-39). Jon Schueler Estate

Fig. 4   *Skye*, Mallaig Scotland, 1957, 42.25 × 79 in/107.32 × 200.66 cm (o/c 57-51). Private collection

Unambiguously, the work is staggeringly beautiful, in particular, the clouds in a storm and those infused by the sun, the varying colors and hues and their light and dark waverings. And here the horizon, so often implied elsewhere, begins to come into focus. Or is it the line of the land, such as that of the Sleat Peninsula as it meets with the sea? Schueler was primarily known in the 1950's as the superb colorist of raging red, of sunset yellow, of heartrending blues, of clouds and storm that take our breath away, yet the ambiguity of the line is part of his identity also.

IDENTITY AND PLACE

As we explore the intriguing question of this artist's identity from various angles, let me quote from a letter in *The Sound of Sleat* in which we already feel his extraordinary power of seeking and finding and being, as he recounts his feelings on finding Mallaig Vaig—and himself.

> Now, as regards to painting, the way it makes me feel is that there is something here that I have been searching for and that I have been thinking about, and maybe I can find out more about how it works. And it also makes me feel, more strongly than any other landscape I've ever been in, that God is creating here so fast and so powerfully and so abundantly and so magnificently that it's going to be one hell of challenge to try to create

Fig. 5   *Storm Over Skye*, Mallaig Scotland, 1958, 66 × 79 in/167.64 × 200.66 cm
(o/c 58-12). Private collection

something that will equal or (when I'm feeling particularly manic and filled
with rage at just seeing all this) outdo such a prodigal, intense, potent, and
imaginative job....[3]

Rooted in that specific time and place, as if issuing forth from that
studio, *Storm Over Skye* (Fig. 5) and *Inverness-shire* (Fig. 6), two of
the most dynamic of his paintings, seem to respond to that spirit and
impossible task. They are both anchored (if that word could possibly
be applied to such taking-off works) in that red so characteristic of his
superbly raging and manic vision, sweeping in so much else.

See how in *Storm Over Skye* (Fig. 5) the excitement has led to those
lines scratched into the paint with the tip of the brush; we have to speak
once more of the gorgeousness of Schueler's line in all its transmogrifi-
cations: forced, passionate as here or gentle, as if sometimes making the

Fig. 6 *Inverness-shire*, Mallaig Scotland, 1958, 81.75 × 72 in/207.65 × 182.88 cm (o/c 58-2). Private collection

subtlest distinctions. There is nothing gentle, about this raging painting. Look at those bursts of orange soaring up to the repeated swirls of the red and then into the red ceiling, although nothing could possibly put a ceiling on any of Schueler's paintings…They have, in their accumulated excitement, everything. The more you look, the more they have. I think the word *gift* might well apply to the way they offer life to the world.

Always there is the attention to detail amidst overpowering emotion, as again, in *Inverness-shire* (Fig. 6). The white sweeps across that red, as if in two layers, while from the middle there burst upward echoes of that white, while the differently weighted upper mass balances it all.

STRUGGLING TOWARDS EQUILIBRIUM

A word about that very balance, and the struggle to achieve it, in his life and in his painting, and the knowledge of its fragility. There hovers over all of Schueler's works the effort to balance places and sights, America and Scotland, the confines of the city and the moving expanse of water. There is the mad enthusiasm he felt about the Scottish sea and sky, and yet back in New York during the 60s, heavily involved with friends and exhibitions and cultural engagements, he tells us, "I am a city painter."[4] If nature was the motivating force, it was not because he had any desire to capture its external forms on canvas, but to harness its creative and explosive powers for the act of painting. Again, it's a question of balance: "I'm painting the dream of nature, not nature itself," he writes.[5] What seems to me clearest is Jon Schueler's identification with his work: "I had wanted to live in the middle of one of my paintings."[6]

And yes, despite the distance they imply, and, often, their great size, these paintings feel dwelled in. There is the depth of the rage, but also a kind of quiet joyousness. *Knoydart's* song (Fig. 7) is lyrical, singing with glowing colors and a gentle sunlit expansiveness, and in *Betty's View*, the gentle rhythms move across the canvas as they reveal glimpses of landforms in the distance.

CELEBRATION

We were, a few years ago, celebrating Jon Schueler on the Isle of Skye[7] where many of us spoke about his work, which has led me to reflect further on the question of his self-identity and how we readers of his texts and viewers of his work can locate him in his many varieties of painting and living experience. The greatest thing a great painter can teach is the lesson of seeing. It is often about a concentration of intensity, very much the case when we want to speak about this American painter who moved, for periods of his working life, to the coast of the Scottish Highlands—a rather unusual move. Here is Jon Schueler again reflecting on Mallaig, and we need to reflect on his reflection, believing in his vision:

Fig. 7 *Knoydart*, Mallaig Scotland, 1957, 65.25 × 48.25 in/165.74 × 122.56 cm (o/c 57-36). Private collection

Because I felt that in the work and adventure and effort and life of my seven months in Mallaig I found a moment of focus when all the contradictions and confusions of sky, image, and life were brought into a powerful focus.[8]

The extraordinary concentration—a balancing act in itself—in this northern outpost, with its lonely horizon and its awayness from all manner of things, enabled a heightened sensitivity.

I have been trying to think how such a focus, magnificent in its realization for the painter in both his visual and verbal being, is both sharable and non-sharable for the observer and reader. Do we not, in some if unspoken way, feel ourselves isolated from this vision of North-ness? I refer now to the quite extraordinary gap, if not absolute opposition, between my own Southern-ness and this other extreme.

Everything where I grew up is about heat and sun, certainly not about clouds and frost. And yet—something about the isolation of the self rings more than true. Those long saunters I made repeatedly, down the shore by the sea, unaccompanied except by the plash of the incoming waves at the highest of tides, the sand-fiddlers scurrying into their tiny holes in the damp of the receding waves at low tide, or then, back on the stretch between the beach and the mainland, the views out over the yellow-green marshes toward some distant sailboat harbored or stranded—these conveyed in my growing up days as in my remembering of them now, a kind of loneliness that nothing was ever able to assuage. That sort of loneliness has, of course, its own intensifying clarity: it could be that through your own lens you see best.

LONELINESS AND THE LINE

What is sure is that extremes touch each other, as Blaise Pascal said, and it may well be that this connection between Jon Schueler's identification with the north and my own intuition, and mental workings are not so farfetched. Inexplicable otherwise might be the fierce attachment I feel for his work and his writing. As if a feeling of otherness from others, of nearness to the natural and a deep estrangement from something were to be what linked us.

Here is Jon Schueler on this loneliness, writing in the summer of 1965, but it would seem that this emotion is already implicit in *Prussian Blue* (Fig. 8):

Fig. 8 *Prussian Blue*, Mallaig Scotland, 1958, 72 × 60 in/182.88 × 152.4 cm
(o/c 58-17). Private collection

In Scotland, I have looked each day at the lonely horizon, at that line (or is
it a line?) where the sea and the sky meet. I have tried to understand it and
tried to know how to paint it and what the painting of it might mean.

...The massive lonely line of the endless horizon over the sea has seemed to me to be the loneliest line of all. Line is poetry. Line is song. Line is about reality. ...The line, my line, could violate the very meaning and idea of that line out there in space. By destroying that which might be, I could more tell of that line, which can't be seen or understood. The lonely line of the horizon. The most lonely line.[9]

So my lines here, and wherever I have cast them, have shared that lone-liness felt in many of his paintings, in the starkness of their forms or as layers of dim color. As in *Rain* (1958), although they are not without their cloudiness and their elusiveness—if we look hard at these works, we see the line as it forms and shapes and storms about, moving evasively as one goes toward it and disappearing of its own accord as the weather and light change.

THE FULLNESS OF SOUND

In the profusion of rain and storm and calm in Jon Schueler's skies, we don't always, as spectators, need to pin down either the mood or the weather, even when we feel them subjectively. We have to trust that we will be involved in whatever it is: sunny or more frequently, stormy and cloudy, over the Sound of Sleat, for there is, in Schueler's paintings—wherever they are done or then observed, more exactly, *experienced*, for that is the more fitting verb—a discernible fullness that sweeps us in, toward his own center. Does that help us develop our own inner visualiz-ing? I would say yes to that and also to the effect and affect of Schueler's works.

Nothing about his work shuts us out, no matter our lack of painterly skill or different way of living—this is, I firmly hold, the essential of his skyscapes, landscapes, seascapes, cloudscapes, and that very inscape that Gerard Manley Hopkins sang of so quietly and enduringly. It dwells in us, as we do in these works. And they gloriously mingle.

The titles themselves are our first invitation into Schueler's works. How they came to him, through friends or his own mind, does not mat-ter. They take us into the 45 paintings from 1957–1958, into the sim-plicities and complications of the work, with their references to clouds and mist, memories of places, signs of nature, and receding and forth-coming planes, veering between abstraction and the (e)motions of weather. And then you dwell in Schueler's paintings and listen to them, even in their quiet.

Fig. 9 *The Sound of Rhum*, Mallaig, Scotland, 1957, 79 × 50 in/200.66 × 127 cm (57-44). On loan to the Scottish National Gallery of Modern Art

Jon Schueler cared about sound: New York and jazz and so much besides. Jon cared about and made music, and I can hear right through his work, various sounds in multiple senses: for example, *The Sound of Rhum* (Fig. 9) and that of another island, *Mull*, which we used to call "the fairest of them all." I want to pay homage to his music, as to his love of line, and so I am celebrating the line and the place and the soul of those paintings from Mallaig, as I best can.

I have to say, right now before going further, that some mystery must remain. There is no way that we could mistake a Schueler painting for a work of another artist, and yet—or rather, and therefore—there is a great deal not possible to speak of with what we call intelligence. Take this lovely and yet disturbing painting of the same period, *The Cruaich* (Fig. 10).

Indistinctly grounded by the bottom edge, it is troubled, if I can use that word, by that violent red patch sweeping through the painting. What, I ask myself, is that patch contributing to the rest? And then of course I wonder why we have to put everything in harmony in our mind. The harmony is in the relation of painter to the universe, and ours to his, as also to our own seeing.

Fig. 10   *The Cruaich*, Mallaig Scotland, 1958, 35.5 × 59 in/90.17 × 149.86 cm (o/c 58-6). Jon Schueler Estate

REVELATORY VISIONS

Just as the paintings of women in the 60s have a remarkable combination of intimacy and distance, so do the mountainous shapes of those from the 1950s, low-lying under the brightening clouds overhead. They speak instantly to the spirit. We can feel a brightening sky among the clouds. The shapes matter to us. We share in those storms that wreak their havoc but also their miracle on the Sound of Sleat and in the sound of Schueler's music, the sound reverberating in our own ears.

Particularly striking in this regard are *Winter Sunday* in the Ringling Museum of Art, Florida and the series of snow cloud paintings.

The passages in *The Sound of Sleat* concerning this snow cloud (and later the hovering image of the sun dog, and the vision of death), deserve their own chapters, so I shall simply use abbreviated quotations. They suggest how the looking, the rending of veils in the sky, and the observations of weather could be enlarged over the years to emerge as symbols and signs of man's relationship to nature (Fig. 11).

Here is Schueler writing from Romasaig, on November 13, 1970:

> There now have been three massive experiences I have had with the Scottish sky. The first, in March of 1958, when I had given up and, aching in my head and eyes and soul, I cycled from Mallaig Vaig to the white sands of Arisaig, where I watched the snow clouds moving toward me, implacable, from the sea. One passed over and through me, snow beating against my face. Then I turned to the south and saw the winter sun glowing in the snow cloud; strange image of light burning and dying through the shadows of a changing form.[10]

Snow Cloud and Blue Sky from the Whitney suggests what Alastair Reid calls an event—"the gradual welling up of snow clouds, a process which, in Scotland, may take the greater part of a day. On the left of the painting, the range of color is extreme, from subdued gray to intense red, and the feeling is of slow-growing rage. Opposed to it, on the right, is the simultaneous occurrence of the blue sky, serene, clear, but merging, as the eye rises, into cloud shapes, and ultimately into the charged passion of the snow clouds."[11]

Red Snow Cloud and the Sun in the Neuberger Museum (Fig. 12) is perhaps most dazzling in its incorporation of the sun.

The large yellow form of the sun radiates its glow through the red of the cloud, a gorgeous vision expanded upon during the following year in France.

Fig. 11   *The First Snow Cloud*, Mallaig Scotland, 1958, 37 × 32 in/93.98 × 81.28 cm (o/c 58-3). Jon Schueler Estate

MARKING

Now to a very different location and later time, to a passage that leaps out at us from his autobiography, insisting on the point of origin, a mark upon the canvas, and the coexistence of past and present.

Fig. 12 *Red Snow Cloud and the Sun,* Mallaig Scotland, 1958, 66 × 79 in/167.64 × 200.66 cm (58-7). Neuberger Museum

On August 7, 1962, in Stonington, Maine, Schueler writes, "Make a mark upon the canvas...I think of the Scottish sea and the Scottish sky. Right now I'm sitting in a little cottage on Deer Isle...." And as he continues, his voice reaches a yet unheard note:

> Rage red in my heart, loud voice screaming to be heard, hurt world woman wanting, and I found her for a moment in the Scottish sky. I found there, looking out across the sea, watching the weather cross the horizon and the islands of Skye and Eigg and Rhum and Muck, torturing the sky and destroying the horizon, I found there the primal scream of nature forming.[12]

I think back also to the rage of the initial paintings I invoked, *Inverness-shire* and *Storm Over Skye,* and now include *Winter Storm.* When I reflect on the times I have read this text, I see that my own memory, here a simple and readerly as well as observing memory, had absorbed its lesson: it was Scotland (coincidentally, the site of my own ancestry), and it was his past and the past of desire, and it was in the present finding of what would rule his life and emotions. It is also what explains so much of that haunting face we see in photographs of him, silhouetted against the sky, the rocks, and the sea. Schueler experienced and simultaneously conveyed his immense passions through his painting, and especially through his paintings of the Scottish sky. It was his landscape itself, all the everything he found there and then painted there, everything he loved in those islands and their inimitable view. Yes, but it has become present for us.

And for those of us, who saw our first glimpse of those grand islands of Eigg and Rhum and Muck from a boat on our way to or from Skye—where Castle Donald still remains, marking in my own memory the place my father came from—this sounds loud like some sort of scream in the memory. When I thought, so often, of Scotland as I first saw it and loved it, I thought of the clouds that hang about it so grandly, marking our horizon. And now, reading Schueler's own writing, I see some kind of primitive grand shout aloud—about what? The way the world works in its own desires and torturing greatness.

DEATH AND THE WORK

Here suddenly is what I have been wondering as I have been reading. It is not just the loneliness that is getting to me through his words, as I thought it was. I had been hearing that unforgettable song in the tones of John Jacob Niles I used to sing with my sister:

I wonder as I wander out under the sky...

And I remember how those words go back to the living that is dying, and how the sadness of that song penetrated my early days. But now, right now, I see that in the work of Schueler his rage, his shout against and within nature is not just about fury, but something richer and stronger and realer. It is about the anger at death and the determination to struggle for whatever remains. Here is what he wrote about the poem of the work, of the struggle that was for him painting:

Romasaig, 14 November 1970
   More and more I've considered that working is the point of work, and that
all else is incidental. Compared to the work in the studio, the rest of living is a
passive act. ...The residue of the struggle is the painting or the poem....
   ...It was only a week ago Sunday that I could admit death and to a fear
of death.... Ad Reinhardt is dead....Rothko is dead too, his veins slit, and
Barney Newman of a heart attack. These three with Still, were such close
friends. Within a few years, they were enemies, big men, but not speaking
to one another....
   And Jackson Pollock.... And Franz Kline is dead.... Men were bound
to one another by love for Kline.[13]

See how it all goes together, the friendship, the love, and the anger
at dying. We think of death as utter darkness, but look again now.
Something remains courageously so alive... (Fig. 13).
   See he has marked his refusal of passivity, the refusal for him of
everything that was not painting, and the struggle that was his living. Listen
again: "The residue of the struggle is the painting or the poem." That's the
real and most screamingly intense thing, that struggle to be shared.

Fig. 13 *The Sea from Mallaig Vaig*, Mallaig Scotland, 1957, 38 × 53
in/96.52 × 134.62 cm (o/c 57-54). Private collection

HIS OFFERING, OUR RESPONSIBILITY

It is clearly never a question of seeing or living only in upward flight, and yet each of these works of art triumphs, by its own power of convergence and harmony, over downturnedness and flatness. As we move through a room enlivened by Schueler's imaginings and sightings, we have a strong sense of the way the various forms move in and out from their own space to that of the beholder. They move through present and distant clouds, back and forth, and into our own space. Our space, indeed, but now it feels transformed by all this light and all this motion. Such light! In a sense, all the work feels like part of the series *The Search*, of 1981, painted in the very Edinburgh gallery in which it was to be exhibited, like some miracle courtyard inside (Fig. 14).

The search which began in the 1950s is self-reflective, seeking the myriad ways in which paint can break through space: as if, in fact, it were to be this very space, these walls on which we contemplate these paintings,

Fig. 14   Jon Schueler painting in the Talbot Rice Art Centre, University of Edinburgh, 1981 (Photo Archie Iain McLellan)

gone skyward. Similarly, "past adventures" become present ones, for all of us and not just the painter. This is an offering too, and one thing Jon Schueler learned from his onetime teacher Clyfford Still was the moral responsibility of the person painting: a duty to carry on with integrity.

Of course, what is carried on is often the ambivalent hope implied by the sun as it appears so tremendously, or tremulously, in some of the Scottish paintings of the 50s. Look at *February 22: The Day the Sun Comes Over the Cruaich* (Fig. 15)—scumblings of clouds obscure the hills, but they themselves are touched by the sun which appears in the upper right.

That's it too: these paintings, like all those of Jon Schueler, reach for a balance that sets things right, again the responsibility accepted and acted on. By all of us, as we can.

Fig. 15 *February 22: The Day the Sun Comes Over the Cruaich*, Mallaig Scotland, 1958, 41 × 58 in/104.14 × 147.32 cm (o/c 58-10). Jon Schueler Estate

Notes

1. Jon Schueler, *The Sound of Sleat: A Painter's Life*, ed. Magda Salvesen and Diane Cousineau (New York: Picador, 1999), 65.
2. Ibid., 66.
3. Ibid., 17.
4. Ibid., 124.
5. Ibid., 124.
6. Ibid., 63.
7. An Linne, Jon Schueler Centenary Symposium, Sabhal Mòr Ostaig, University of the Highlands and Islands, 2016.
8. *The Sound of Sleat*, 118.
9. Ibid., 156–57.
10. Ibid., 189.
11. *School of New York: Some Younger Artists*, ed. B. H. Friedman (New York: Grove Press, 1959), 71.
12. *The Sound of Sleat*, 131.
13. Ibid., 192–94.

Works Cited

Friedman, B. H., ed. *School of New York: Some Younger Artists*. New York: Grove Press, 1959.
Salvesen, Magda, and Diane Cousineau, eds. *The Sound of Sleat: A Painter's Life*. New York: Picador, 1999.

INDEX

CPI Antony Rowe
Eastbourne, UK
November 26, 2019